ALASTAIR SAWDAY'S

Special
places to stay

FRENCH BED & BREAKFAST

Edited by Annie Shillito

Typesetting, Conversion & Repro:......	Avonset, Bath
Maps:..	Bartholomew Mapping Service, a division of HarperCollins Publishers, Glasgow
Printing:..	Midas Book Printers, UK
Design:..	Caroline King & Springboard Design, Bristol
UK Distribution:...............................	Portfolio, Greenford, Middlesex
US Distribution:...............................	The Globe Pequot Press, Guilford, Connecticut

First published in November 2000

Alastair Sawday Publishing Co. Ltd
The Home Farm, Barrow Gurney, Bristol BS48 3RW

The Globe Pequot Press
P. O. Box 480
Guilford, Connecticut 06437
USA

Sixth edition 2000

A catalogue record for this book is available from the British Library.

ISBN 1-901970-12-4 in the UK

ISBN 0-7627-0774-7 in the US

Printed in Slovenia

JAMES/HILARY SHACKLETON·
P 876 9974

Alastair Sawday's

Special

places to stay

French Bed & Breakfast

"Be not forgetful to entertain strangers:
for thereby some have entertained angels unawares."
St Paul - Hebrews 13:1

The
Globe
Pequot
Press

Guilford
Connecticut, USA

ASP

Alastair Sawday Publishing
Bristol, UK

Contents

Contents

6

Contents

Contents

Acknowledgements

For years this hugely popular book has been researched, inspected, written, 'driven' and nurtured by Ann Cooke-Yarborough. But Ann has hung up the driving hat to be our senior advisor and chief inspector & writer, as well as continuing to be Editor of the Paris guide. So she remains deeply involved, generous with her time and knowledge. But someone has had to fill her shoes and this has been Annie Shillito.

Annie ran our travel company for many years, so came to publishing with a solid knowledge of Europe and travel - a perfect mix. She not only looks after this book but oversees all our foreign books. She has been unflappable and resourceful. She is also creating her own relationships with the owners who feature here, one which they will - I know - enjoy. Russell Wilkinson, now our web-man, was generous with his help, always patient, always good-humoured; Emma Carey then took over and has been as good-natured and efficient. In support, too, has been Jenny Purdy - marshalling a recalcitrant set of accounts. Julia Richardson has held the complex production process together and brought the book to print. Annie thus led a superb office team. She has also had the full-blooded support of a team of inspectors, all inspired amateurs of the best kind. In many ways this is their book, for it is they who inform us and help maintain the standards which we have set – and which are indefinable!

Alastair Sawday

Series Editor:	Alastair Sawday
Editor:	Annie Shillito
Editorial Assistants:	Emma Carey, Russell Wilkinson
Production Manager:	Julia Richardson
Accounts:	Sheila Clifton, Jenny Purdy, Sandra Hassell
Administration:	Kate Harris
Inspectors:	Ann Cooke-Yarborough, Douglas Arestegui, Richard & Linda Armspach, Joanna Bell-Moore, Alyson & Colin Browne, Meredith Dickinson, Sue Edrich, John Edwards, Valerie Foix, Georgina Gabriel, Michèle Goëmon, Diana Harris, Ursula Kotthaus, Carolyn McKenzie, Joanna Morris, Caroline Portway, Anna Riddle, Elizabeth Yates
Additional Writing:	Ann Cooke-Yarborough, Lindsay Butler, Jonathan Goodall, Elizabeth Yates
Symbols:	Mark Brierley
Illustrations:	Aymeric Chastenet
Title page photo:	Le Vieux Cèdre (Entry No. 59)

Introduction

How do we choose our Special Places?
It's an art!

It's certainly not a science, for each inspector is encouraged to use his or her own judgement, own taste and own prejudices. And of prejudices we could write chapters, for we are as loaded with them as anyone. We are definitely inclined to prejudge people whose letters brim with humanity and who send photos of beautiful old houses. We will prejudge those for whom 'tea and coffee-making facilities' appear to be more important than a smile. We fully confess to leaning towards the artistic and unusual rather than the formal and predictable. We are not mad about golf, but are mad about walking and biking. Our opinions on those who offer you an aperitif and then charge for it are unrepeatable. And so are our views on prominent TV sets - we avoid mentioning the wretched things.

So, we look for charm, character, authenticity, honesty, decency and a genuine welcome. Hatchet faces are avoided. We are keen on good value; however beautiful it is, we will not include a château that is overpriced. If a place is simple and unpretentious, but fantastic value, we will include it. Our owners seem to find dozens of ways of being generous.

The success of this book says it all: somehow we have caught the right mood, for we fill the book with places that we like and then cross our fingers and hope that you will too. This is a wildly eclectic collection of places: hugely entertaining, wonderfully warm and human, and often glitteringly lovely. You get so much more than you pay for.

Alastair Sawday

Introduction

What to expect

For those who are not sure what to expect in French B&Bs, just remember they are *not* hotels - in a B&B you are paying guests of owners in their homes so please don't expect hotel-like surroundings or service. Often just one or two people will be organising your room, welcoming you and cooking for you and they have the normal human limitations - although many go well beyond the norm in what they generously do for their guests. Your hosts may allow you to borrow an ice box or to picnic in their garden but they appreciate being asked first. They also like civilised diners who do not abuse their *vin à volonté* (unlimited wine with meals).

Don't count on a laundry service or your favourite type of tea being available (take your own tea-bags!). Don't imagine that your towels will be changed every day (do you, at home?), that your childrens' toys will be gathered, or that your late request for a vegetarian meal will produce anything more exciting than an omelette. What you can expect is to feel a privileged guest and to have a fascinating glimpse into a French way of life.

Although stays of more than one night are very much encouraged most hosts expect guests to be out during the day - they have their own lives to lead so they won't be on-hand all the time. If they are happy for you to be around check which parts of the house or garden you may use during the day.

Breakfasts are usually 'Continental' with home-made jams and the freshest breads, fruit and fruit juice. Occasionally eggs, cheese or meats will be offered, or you may ask; usually there will be a supplement to pay.

Non-French owners

As our aim is essentially to guide readers to meetings with French families in their homes, non-French owners have a smaller chance of being chosen. However, we include a reasonable number as many of you have written to say how good it can be to relax in your native tongue from time to time. The choice is yours.

Finding the right place for you

Do remember to interpret what you see and read. If you opt for a working farm expect cockerels to crow or tractors to set off at dawn. If you choose a "rambling château with old-fashioned bathrooms" there could be some draughty corridors and idiosyncratic plumbing. If somewhere is "deep in the countryside" study a decent map and allow time to arrive when you said you would.

Introduction

Do check on anything really important to you before confirming your booking e.g. whether the swimming pool will be ready to use at Easter, whether the bicycles available have been promised to other guests.

If you find anything we say misleading (things do change in the lifetime of a guide), or think we miss the point - if for example you were led to expect a very child-friendly, relaxed country house and were surprised by elegant white carpets and delicate ornaments at toddler-height - please let us know.

Do discuss any problems with your hosts *at the time* as they are the ones who can do something about it immediately. They would be mortified to discover afterwards that you were, for example, cold in bed, when extra blankets could easily have been provided.

Feedback

We are very grateful to readers who write to us about their B&B experiences - good and bad - and to recommend new places. They make a real contribution to this book.

- Poor reports are followed up with the owners in question: we need to see both sides but don't mention the writer's name. Really bad reports lead to incognito visits after which we may exclude a house.

- Recommendations are followed up with inspection visits where appropriate.

How to use this book

Finding the houses

The entry number, in colour on the left above the address for each entry, is the number to use when looking for places on the map pages (NB Paris flags are not positioned geographically). Each entry also has the 1/200,000 Michelin Regional Map reference as 'Michelin Map No' followed by the relevant map and fold numbers, e.g. '240-16' is Regional Map No 240, fold No 16 - this to help with the detailed pinpointing of houses.

Our maps

The General Map of France on Page 18 is divided into the same regions as the Contents and marked with the page numbers of the Detailed Maps on pages 19-37. The Detailed Maps show roughly where the B&Bs are and should be used with a large scale road map such as Michelin or Collins.

Bedrooms

In this book a 'double' means one double bed, a 'twin' means two single beds. A 'triple' or 'quadruple' may have any mix of beds for 3 or 4 people. A 'family room' will have a double bed + a number of other beds

Introduction

(sometimes sofa beds) for children. A 'suite' or 'apartment' will have two or more interconnecting rooms and one or more bathrooms. An apartment is likely to be self-contained and may have a small kitchen. A 'studio' is a bedroom with a small sitting and kitchen area. A 'duplex' is on two floors.

Extra beds and cots for children, at an extra cost, can often be provided; ask when booking.

Bathrooms

There's a wonderful variety in French homes and we've tried to make the layouts clear: bathrooms directly off the bedroom = **'with'**; not directly off the bedroom but not shared = **'private'**; shared with others = **'shared'**. Some, but not all, baths have shower attachments.

Most bathrooms are very good but if you are wary about quirky arrangements, go for the modernised places (which are probably more expensive).

Prices

Although the Euro is already running alongside the Franc it does not come fully into operation until 2002 and we decided against listing both currencies, with apologies to our 'Euro'phile readers. Please see Page 431 for a FF/Euro/$ conversion table.

The price, or price range, is for two people sharing a room and, as it's a B&B book, includes breakfast. Prices are presumed to be for 2001 but are not guaranteed so please always check. A price range may mean there are rooms at different prices or that the difference is seasonal. In France it's usual for prices to be for the room, rather than for the numbers occupying it but there will often be a reduction for single occupancy of a double room (even if it's just the cost of a breakfast).

Reductions

Most French B&Bs offer reductions for longer stays; some have attractive half-board terms, or special prices for children. Do ask when you book.

Meals - Table d'Hôtes

Don't miss the opportunity to eat honest - or even gourmet - food in an authentic family atmosphere. However, dinner *absolutely must* be booked beforehand, at least in the morning, sometimes the day before. Dinner may not be an option every day but do please turn up if you have booked it - it's distressing to prepare a meal that no-one comes to enjoy. Dinners are generally not served before 7.30pm, more usually 8 or 8.30pm, sometimes later. Very few places do lunch but occasionally picnics can be provided and this is not always mentioned in the entry.

Introduction

Dinner, including wine?

The number and type of courses you will be offered for dinner varies and we have not attempted to go into details, although price may be an indicator. When wine is included this can mean a range of things: it may mean a standard quarter-litre carafe per person; it may mean a bottomless barrel of table wine; it may mean a very decent bottle of local produce or, in some rare cases, of excellent estate wine. Whatever it is, it is usually excellent value.

Where there is no *Table d'Hôtes*, an idea of other places is given but beware, country restaurants stop taking orders at about 9pm and close one day a week.

Closed

When given in months, this means the *whole* of both months named; so Closed: November-March means closed from 1 November to 1 April.

Symbols

Symbols and their explanations are listed on the last page of the book (Page 432). Use them as a guide rather than an unequivocal statement of fact and double-check anything that is important to you.

Gîte space for ... people is to tell you what the total population staying on the property may be. Some *Gîtes* are *Gîtes d'Etape* i.e. they welcome walkers, cyclists or horse riders who are usually catered for, others are *Gîtes de Séjour* or *Gîtes Ruraux* - self-contained, holiday houses.

Directions

Apart from motorway exits, our directions take you to each house from one side only. We give cardinal directions = N-S-E-W - where appropriate and name the French roads with the letters they carry on French maps and road signs:

A = Autoroute. Toll motorways with junctions that usually have the same name/number on both sides.

N = Route Nationale. The old trunk roads that are still pretty fast, don't charge tolls, but often go through towns.

D = Route Départementale. Smaller country roads with less traffic.

Telephoning/Faxing

All telephone numbers in France have ten digits, e.g. (0)5 15 25 35 45. You should know that:

Introduction

- the initial zero (bracketed here) is for use when telephoning **from inside** France only, i.e. dial 05 15 25 35 45 from any private or public telephone;

- when dialling **from outside** France use the international access code then the country code for France - 33 - followed by the last 9 digits of the number you want, e.g. 00 33 5 15 25 35 45;

- numbers beginning (0)6 are mobile phone numbers;

- to telephone from France -

   - to Great Britain: 00 44 then the number without the initial zero,

   - to the USA, dial 00 1 then the number without the initial zero.

Télécartes phone cards (50 or 100 Frs) are widely available in France and there are plenty of 'phone boxes, even in the countryside (often they take <u>only</u> cards).

Types of properties

For a definition of château, *bastide*, *mas* see 'French words & expressions' on page 411 (where most French words used in the descriptions are also explained).

Practical Matters

Booking

It is essential to book well ahead for July and August and wise for other months. You may receive a *Contrat de Location* (Tenancy Contract) as confirmation. It must be filled in and returned, probably with a deposit, and commits both sides to the arrangement.

Remember not to telephone any later than 9 or 9.30pm at the latest and that Ireland and the UK are one hour behind the rest of Europe. Some country folk have been quite upset by enquiries coming through when they were fast asleep.

Deposits

Some owners ask for a deposit - many readers have found it virtually impossible or ridiculously expensive to do this by direct transfer, so here are two suggestions:

- Have a number of French banknotes at home (you will need some for your travels anyway) and send the appropriate amount with your confirmation by 'International Recorded' mail.

Introduction

- Send an ordinary cheque, which the owner will destroy when you
arrive (so no-one pays the charges); when you leave, they will ask you for
cash for your whole stay.

Arriving

Most owners expect you to arrive between 5 and 7pm and not during
dinner. If you come earlier, rooms may not be prepared or your hosts may
still be at work. Yet again, these are private houses and people have their
private lives to get with as well. We ask them to leave a note if they are
going to be late or have an emergency errand to run, but some are wary of
announcing 'House Empty' to the world at large. Similarly, if you are going
to be late (or early, unavoidably), please telephone and say so.

No-shows

Most owners hope you will treat them as friends too, with sensitivity,
tidiness and punctuality. It's obviously most upsetting for them to prepare
rooms, even meals and to wait up late for 'guests' who never come, never
ring, never give any further sign of life. So if you find you are not going to
take up a booking, please telephone right away.

By the way, there is a tacit agreement among a number of B&B owners that
no-show + no-call by 8, even 6pm in some cases, can be taken as a refusal
of the booking and they will re-let the room if another guest turns up.

Payment

Most French B&B owners cannot take credit cards, where they do they will
have our credit card symbol. Drawing cash is easy as virtually all ATMs in
France take Visa and Mastercard. French Franc travellers cheques should
be accepted, other currency cheques are unpopular because of commission
charges.

Taxe de séjour

This is a small tax that local councils are allowed to levy on all visitors
paying for accommodation. Some councils do, some don't. So you may find
your bill increased by 4, 5, or 9 Francs per person per day.

Children

Our symbol shows where children are welcome with no age restrictions.
They may be welcome, with restrictions (e.g. babies only, because of an
unfenced pool. Well-behaved children over 8) at other places.

Introduction

Pets

More people will now be travelling to France with their pets. Our Pets symbol tells you which houses generally welcome them but you must check whether this means the size and type of your pet and whether it will be in the house/in your room/in an outhouse. Your hosts will expect animals to be well-behaved and that you will be responsible for them at all times.

Tipping

B&B owners do not expect to be tipped (they would be taken aback). If you encounter extraordinary kindness you may feel a 'thank you' letter, Christmas card or small gift would be appropriate.

Electricity

You need a plug adaptor for the 220-volt 50-cycle AC current. Americans also need a voltage transformer (heavy and expensive) although some appliances are now made with bi-voltage capabilities.

Environment

We seek to reduce our impact on the environment where possible by:

- Planting trees to compensate for our carbon emissions (as calculated by Edinburgh University); we are officially a carbon-neutral publishing company.

- Re-using paper, recycling stationery, tins, bottles, etc.

- Encouraging staff use of bicycles (they're given free) and encouraging car-sharing.

- Celebrating the use of organic, home and locally-produced food.

- Publishing books that support, in however small a way, the rural economy and small-scale businesses.

Subscriptions

Owners pay to appear in this guide; their fee goes towards the high production costs of an all-colour book. We really do only include places and owners that we find special. It is not possible for anyone to buy their way in.

Special Places to Stay on the Internet: www.sawdays.co.uk

By the time you read this we will have roughly a thousand entries on the online database which is our web site. These are from the various titles in the *Special Places to Stay* series, so if you like the places in French Bed and Breakfast, why not browse some more?

Introduction

We flatter ourselves that the 8,000 visitors a month who come to the site have good reason to, and we think you should join them! It gives access to hundreds of places to stay across Europe and you can buy all our books direct through our window on the world wide web.

Disclaimer

We make no claims to pure objectivity in judging our Special Places to Stay. They are here because we like them. Our opinions and tastes are ours alone and this book is a statement of them; we hope you will share them.

We have done our utmost to get our facts right but apologise for any mistakes that may have crept in. Sometimes, too, prices shift, usually upwards and 'things' change. We should be grateful to be told of any errors and changes.

Finally

Do let us know how you got on in these houses - we value your feedback and recommendations enormously. There is a report form at the back of the book or email frenchbandb@sawdays.co.uk.

Happy travelling!

A short history of the company

Perhaps the best clue as to why these books have their own very particular style and 'bent' lies in Alastair's history.

After a law degree, a stint as a teacher in Voluntary Service Overseas led to a change in direction. He became a teacher (French and Spanish) and then a refugee worker, then spent several years in overseas development work before settling into environmental campaigning, and even green politics. Meanwhile, he was able to dabble - just once a year - in an old interest, taking clients on tours of special places all over Europe. This grew, eventually, into a travel company (it still exists as Alastair Sawday's Tours, operating, inter alia, walking and biking tours all over Europe).

Trying to take his clients to eat and sleep in places that were not owned by corporations and assorted bandits he found dozens of very special places in France - farms, châteaux etc - a list that grew into the first book, *French Bed and Breakfast*. It was a celebration of 'real' places to stay and the remarkable people who run them.

So, this publishing company is based on the success of that first and rather whimsical French book. It started as a mild crusade, and there it stays. For we still celebrate the unusual, the beautiful, the highly individual. We have no rules for owners; they do things their own way. We are passionate about rejecting the ugly, the cold, the banal and the indifferent. And we are still passionate about promoting the use of 'real' food. Alastair is a trustee of the Soil Association and keen to promote organic growing especially.

It is a source of huge pleasure to us that we seem to have pressed the right button: there are thousands and thousands of people who, clearly, share our views and take up our ideas. We are by no means alone in trumpeting the virtues of standing up to the monstrous uniformity of so much of our culture.

The greatest accolade we have had was in *The Bookseller* magazine, which described us as 'head and shoulders above the rest'. That meant a lot. But even more satisfying is that we are building a company in which people matter. We are delighted to hear of new friendships between those in the book and those using it and to know that there are many people - among them artists, farmers, champions of the countryside - who have been enabled to pursue their unusual lives thanks to the extra income the book brings them.

Of course we want the company to flourish, but this isn't just about money; it is about people, too.

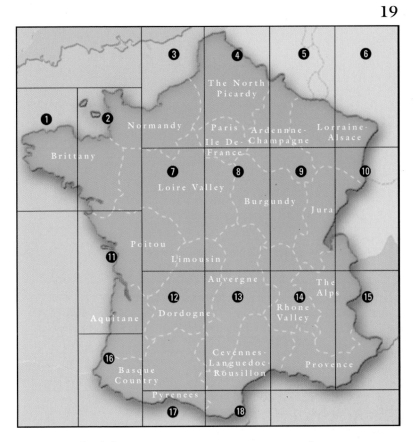

Guide to our map page numbers

20

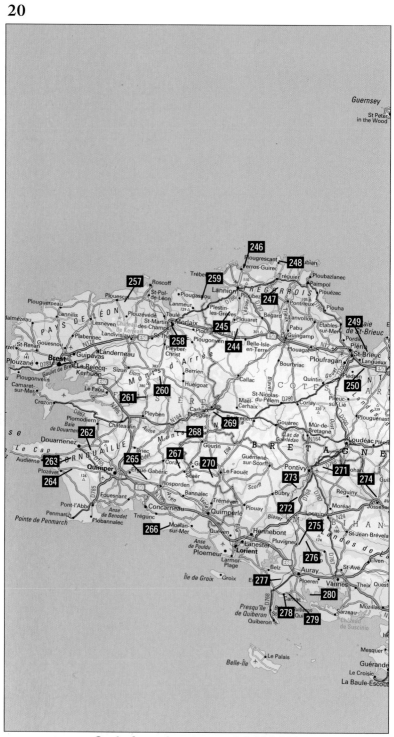

Scale for colour maps 1:1 600 000
(1cm:16km or 1 inch:25.25 miles)

Map 1

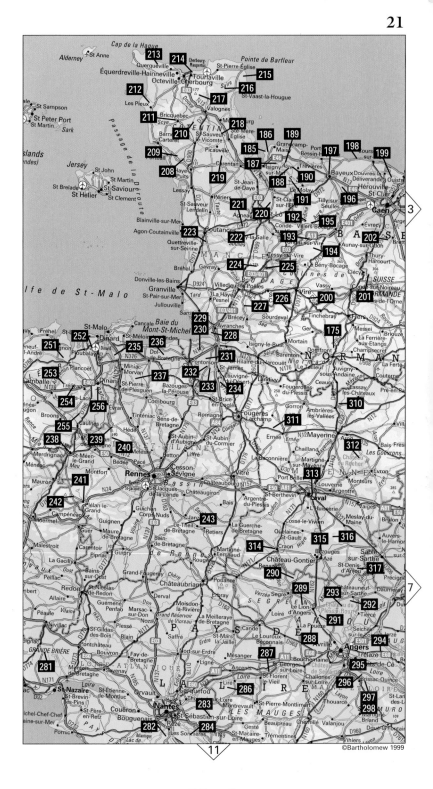

©Bartholomew 1999

Map 2

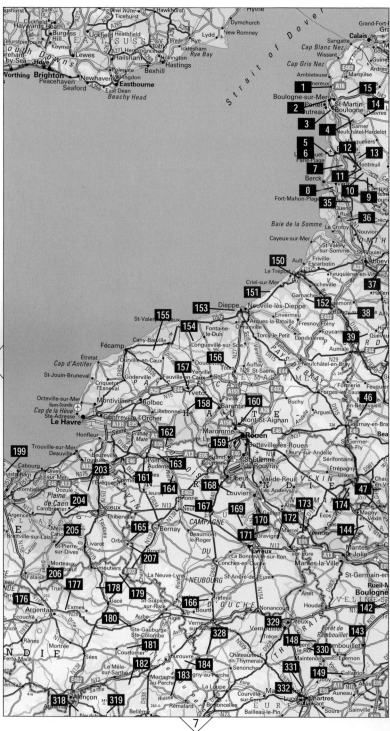

Map 3

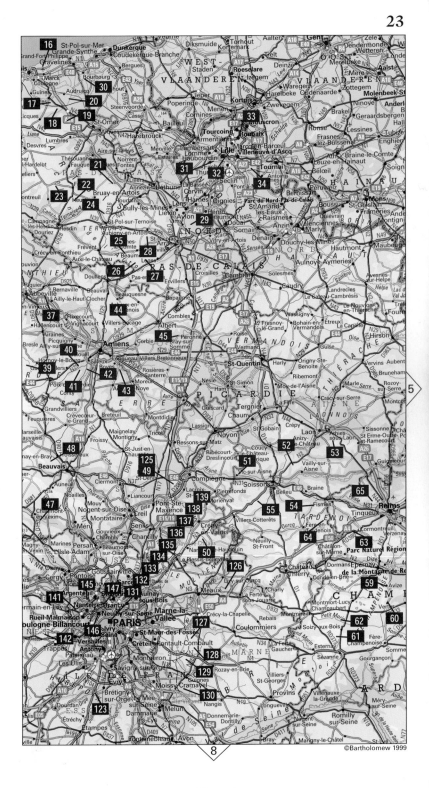

Map 4

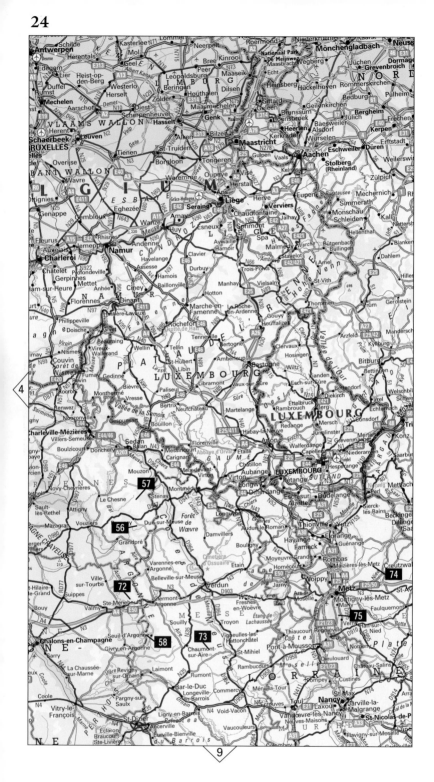

Map 5

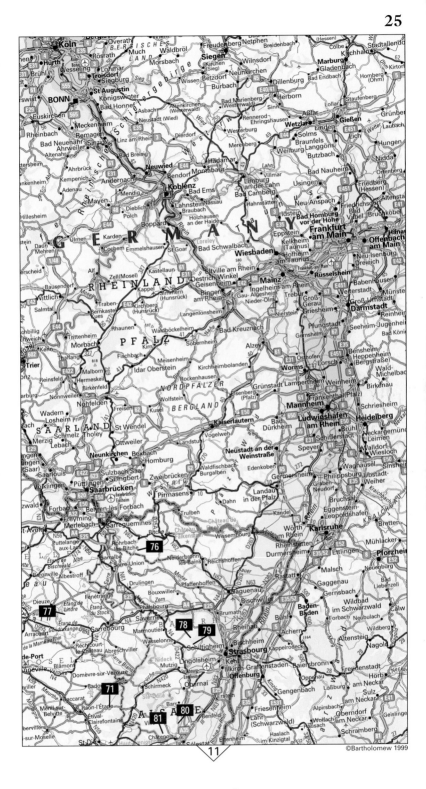

Map 6

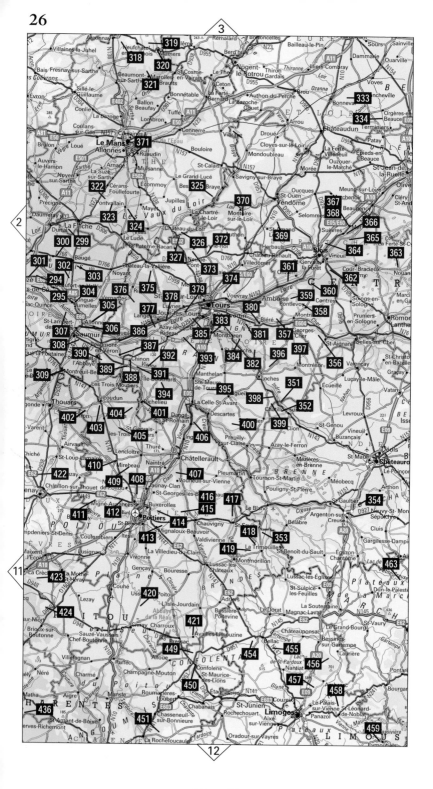

Map 7

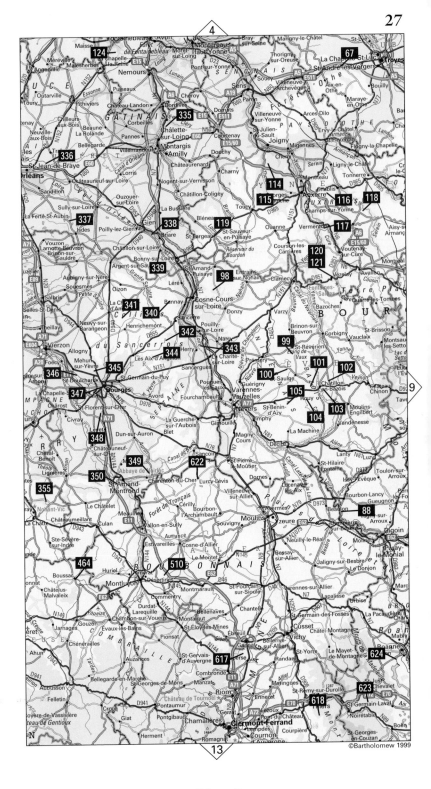

Map 8

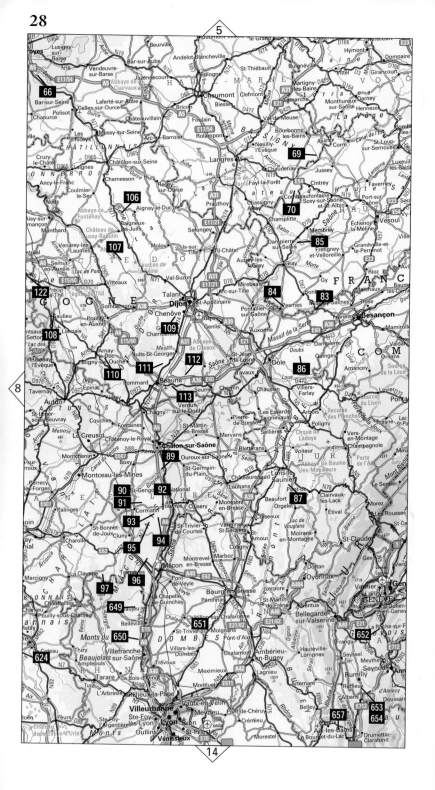

Map 9

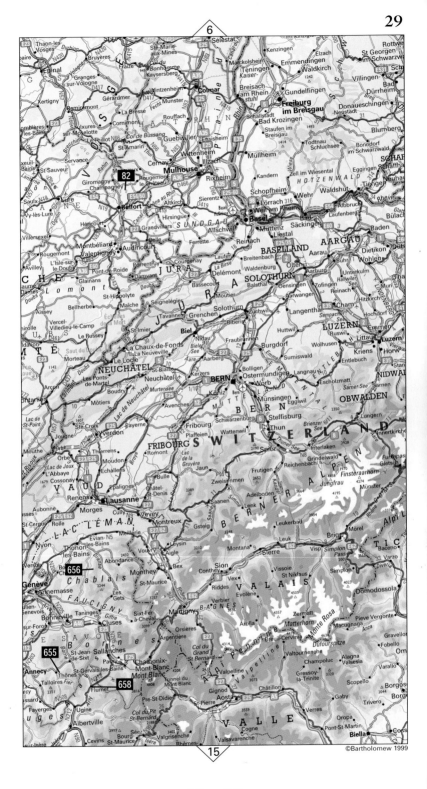

Map 10

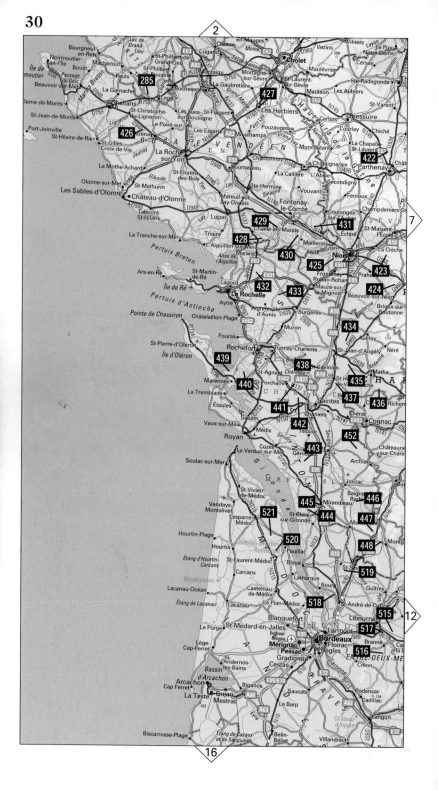

Map 11

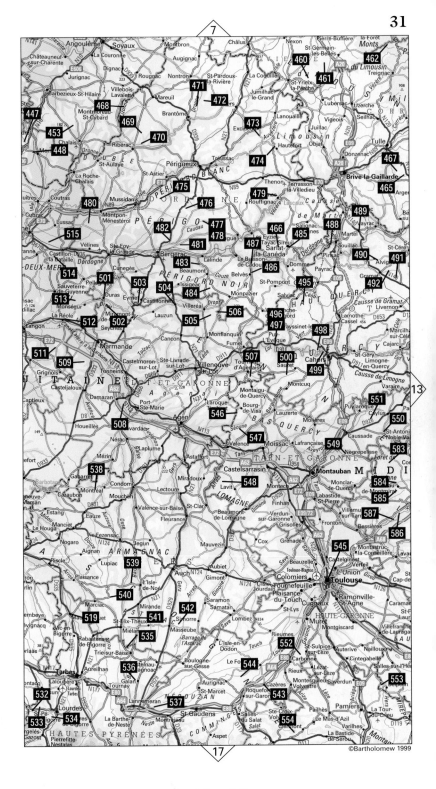

Map 12

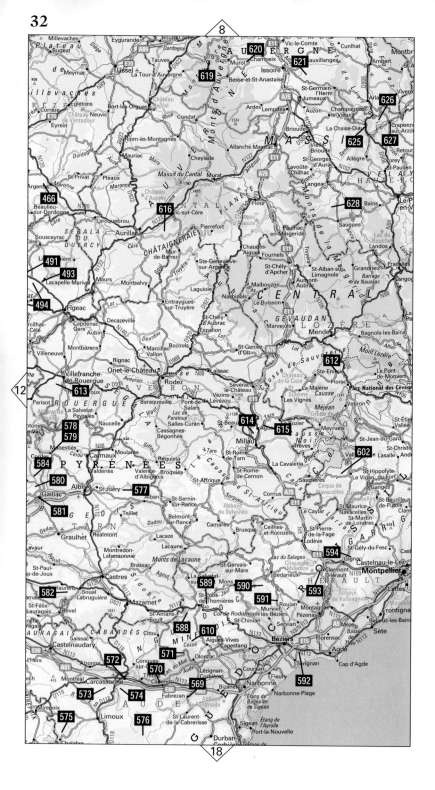

Map 13

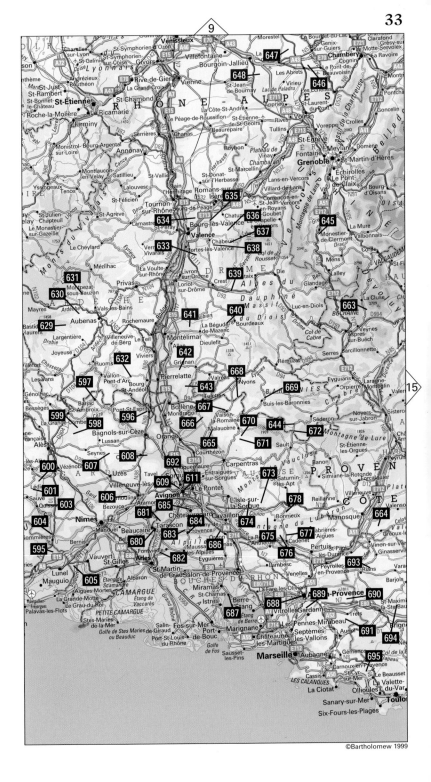

©Bartholomew 1999

Map 14

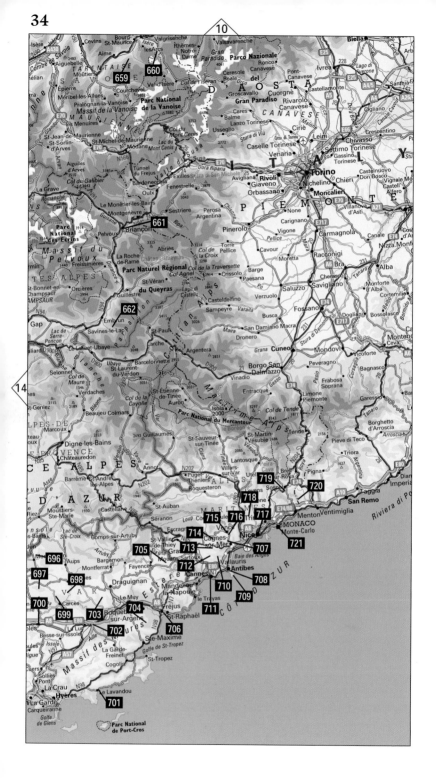

Map 15

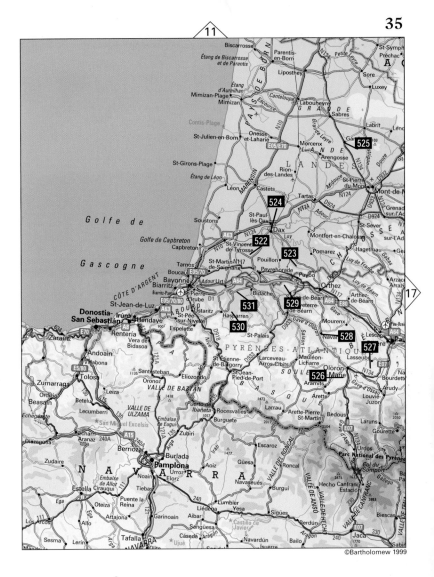

©Bartholomew 1999

Map 16

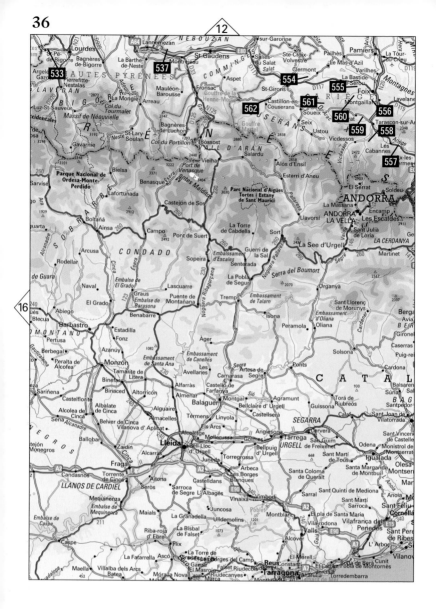

Map 17

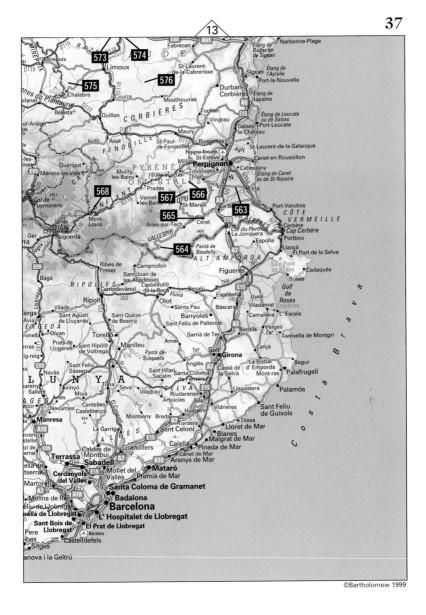

Map 18

A good base from which to explore the 'Opal Coast' made fashionable by the British in the thirties, or a perfect first or last night to your French holiday. Think *Monsieur Hulot's Holiday* and you will know the atmosphere of the town and this ravishingly exuberant house on the front. Mary has decorated it luxuriously in keeping with the period: white linen, wooden floors, carefully-chosen fabrics and furniture. She speaks excellent English and has acquired some good English habits, such as the cup of tea she may offer you in the beautiful room looking out to sea. Her huge and delicious breakfast takes place here too.

Rooms: 2 doubles, 2 twins, all with bath or shower & wc.

Price: 400-500 Frs for two; 500-600 Frs in July & August.

Meals: Wide choice locally.

Closed: Never.

From A16 exit 3 to Wimereux. In town, go to sea front. House about halfway along promenade, 100m left of Hôtel Atlantic (with your back to the sea). Michelin Map No: 236-1

Entry no: 1   Map No: 3

Mary AVOT
La Goelette
13 Digue de Mer
62930 Wimereux, Pas-de-Calais
Tel: (0)3 21 32 62 44
Fax: (0)3 21 33 77 54
e-mail: lagoelette@voila.fr
Web: www.lagoelette.com

The North – Picardy

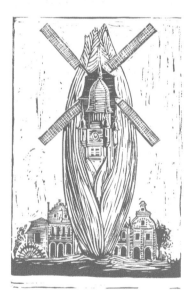

On the flat, fertile plains of Flanders, among the swathes of wheat and maize, grow windmills, belfries and the arcaded streets of lovely old Arras.

Distinctive it certainly is: well-groomed rooms and a very elegant hostess whose B&B philosophy is founded on trust and respect. She is an effervescent animal-lover whose guests have "opened the world anew to her". Heavy family furniture, a high-arched floral hall, dining space and French upright chairs for 12 in the common areas. The 'Big Bedroom' is fabulous, its bathroom almost more so; the top-floor suite is more Modern Rustic. All fascinating, capturing the flavour of one particular (and lovable) kind of France. Just 100 yards from the lovely old walled town of Boulogne.

Rooms: 1 double with bath & wc; 1 triple with shower & wc on different floor; 1 suite for 4 with shower, sharing wc.

Price: 250-350 Frs for two.

Meals: Wide choice within the ramparts, walking distance.

Closed: January.

Follow signs for 'Vieille Ville'. Rue Flahaut is off Boulevard Mariette which runs below the ramparts on the northern side of the city past the Porte des Dunes. Michelin Map No: 236-1

Entry no: 2   Map No: 3

Simone & Édouard DELABIE
26 rue Flahaut
62200 Boulogne sur Mer
Pas-de-Calais
Tel: (0)3 21 31 88 74
Web: www.sawdays.co.uk

There are only a few horses in the stables now: the main stud farm is further away. This means that your hosts have a very busy life and may be a little preoccupied, though Madame is lively and fun when relaxed. The bedrooms, in a self-contained unit which looks out onto the courtyard and surrounding wooded hills, have simple, modern décor and the breakfast/living room is also very straightforward. The garden and orchard go down to the river and this is a good family stopover.

Rooms: 2 doubles, 2 twins, all with shower & wc.

Price: 250 Frs for two.

Meals: In village.

Closed: Christmas & New Year.

Gîte space for 9 people.

From Boulogne sur Mer, D940 direction St Léonard. There, at 2nd lights, left onto small road (to Echingen, not signed); in village centre, left into tiny street immediately after sharp bend then left into first gateway. Michelin Map No: 236-2

Entry no: 3   Map No: 3

Jacqueline & Jean-Pierre
BOUSSEMAERE
Rue de l'Eglise
62360 Echinghen
Pas-de-Calais
Tel: (0)3 21 91 14 34
Fax: (0)3 21 31 15 05

Flat onto the street, the house unfolds around the courtyard, over the porch and into an unexpectedly lovely garden. It is a generous *Notaire's* house, (the shield is his symbol of office) with original mouldings, tiles and fireplaces. The big, prettily traditional French rooms have antiques, good rugs on wooden floors, modern bathrooms. There's a gloriously original attic *salon* for guests with all the furniture gathered in the centre. Breakfast includes *clafoutis* if you're lucky. The village is genuinely unspoilt, your hosts have a similar olde-worlde air to them and modernity intrudes very little in the form of traffic noise at night.

These two are fabulously alive and attentive, cultivated and communicative. Georges is an Orson-Wellesian figure, well able to talk at the same time as gentle but determined Marie... a sort of irresistible double act. The well-proportioned house is an architectural flourish, the contents tastefully modern. Guest rooms, with their own entrances, have pretty bedding, one or two antiques and good bathrooms. The only possible drawback is the Holiday Inn opposite but it's a quiet family hotel, the sea is just 10 minutes away through the trees and there's stacks to do locally. Perfect for children, raucous and great fun. And Georges paints extremely well.

Rooms: 2 doubles, 1 twin, each with bath or shower & wc.

Price: 250 Frs for two.

Meals: In Samer or choice 5km.

Closed: Never.

Rooms: 1 double, 1 twin, each with bath & wc.

Price: 350 Frs for two; under 7s free.

Meals: Wide choice within walking distance.

Closed: Mid-November-mid-March.

From Boulogne N1 S towards St Léonard & Montreuil for approx. 15km. In Samer, take road that goes down to right of church; house on left, near top of hill.
Michelin Map No: 236-12

Entry no: 4   Map No: 3

Joëlle MAUCOTEL
127 rue du Breuil
62830 Samer
Pas-de-Calais
Tel: (0)3 21 33 50 87/
      (0)3 21 87 64 19
Fax: (0)3 21 33 35 53
Web: www.sawdays.co.uk

From A16 take exit for Le Touquet, through Etaples, then follow signs for Le Touquet centre. After 4th lights, take 2nd right towards Holiday Inn. House is 2nd on right opposite telephone box.
Michelin Map No: 236-11

Entry no: 5   Map No: 3

Georges & Marie VERSMÉE
Birdy Land
Avenue du Maréchal Foch
62520 Le Touquet, Pas-de-Calais
Tel: (0)3 21 05 31 46/
      (0)3 27 46 39 41
Fax: (0)3 21 05 95 07

The tufted dunes whisper in the westerly sea breeze or the easterly road hum: walk out and join riders and walkers on the path to the beach. Guests have use of the top floor of this family villa: dark, dynamic, fun-loving Elena brings breakfast to you at the flame-covered table in the bright, light living room or in the dune-view veranda. Her décor is pretty and fun with modernistic touches (I loved the bendy wire pendulum clock), sofas round a log stove for chilly evenings and snug, very individual bedrooms (minimal storage space). Plus sand-yachting and fashionable resort life at your feet. *Entire 4 room apartment also available to rent.*

Both Madame Horel and her crêpes are Breton: the former makes forty of the latter every morning to complete her already copious and delicious breakfast. You eat in the plant-filled conservatory, built onto one end of this modern house and overlooking the garden. This garden is Madame's ruling passion and she says she is incapable of letting someone sleep in a room without fresh flowers: choose the season of your visit according to your floral preferences. Her bedrooms are full of thoughtful touches – sweets by your bed, hairdryers – to add to the pretty, feminine, décor.

Rooms: 2 doubles, 1 triple, 1 twin, plus 2 bathrooms which can be shared, or private for a supplement.

Price: From 290 Frs for two.

Meals: Guest kitchen available; restaurants in Le Touquet.

Closed: Never.

Rooms: 2 triples, 1 double, each with shower & wc.

Price: 270 Frs for two.

Meals: 3 restaurants in St Josse.

Closed: Never.

At entrance of Le Touquet follow 'Base Nautique Sud' signs. Then towards Rue de Paris; head straight towards dunes. Villa on top of hill.
Michelin Map No: 236-11

From A16 exit 25 for Rang du Fliers, through roundabout on D143 towards Le Touquet. At roundabout, right on D144E to St Josse & follow signs.
Michelin Map No: 236-12

Entry no: 6   Map No: 3

Entry no: 7   Map No: 3

Elena & Fred DESPREZ
La Crête des Dunes
Avenue Blériot
62520 Le Touquet-Paris-Plage
Pas-de-Calais
Tel: (0)3 21 05 04 98
Fax: (0)3 21 05 04 98
Web: www.bnbletouquet.com

Marie-Thérèse & Maurice HOREL
Les Buissonnets
67-70 chemin des Corps Saints
62170 St Josse
Pas-de-Calais
Tel: (0)3 21 84 12 12
Fax: (0)3 21 84 12 12
Web: www.sawdays.co.uk

Built just over two decades ago to look like a little old thatched cottage, it is a real surprise in a bit of French suburbia – so is the splendidly 1930s breakfast room. All the Terriens' own work, their décor is a mix of the cosy-twee and the dramatic. Guest quarters are in the South Wing: *Tower* has an all-white mezzanine in... the 'tower', *Jaune* has a hand-painted wardrobe, *Moderne* is amazingly all grey, black and white 1990s yuppie-style. Madame, as neat and bright as her ideas, makes sure the bathrooms are properly sparkling, all accessories just so and breakfast a feast of variety.

Rooms: 4 doubles, each with shower & wc.

Price: 290 Frs for two.

Meals: Choice within 3km.

Closed: Never.

"The best cowshed I've ever stayed in" said one of the many recommenders of this house. Others claimed they'd had their "best breakfast in France" here. And we know that the Trunnets' smiles are genuine, their delight in your company unfeigned, their converted outbuilding handsome and perfectly finished (down to mosquito nets on windows), if a touch characterless, and beds excellent (one equally smart guest room is in the main house). Monsieur is only too happy to show you the flax production process (it's fascinating), while Madame will be baking yet another superb cake for tomorrow's breakfast.

Rooms: 1 double, 3 triples, each with shower & wc.

Price: 275 Frs for two.

Meals: Choice in Montreuil, 6km.

Closed: Never.

From A16 exit 25 towards Berck; at 3rd traffic light, left & follow signs for Chambres d'Hôtes or La Chaumière.
Michelin Map No: 236-12

Entry no: 8   Map No: 3

Christian & Geneviève TERRIEN
La Chaumière
19 rue du Bihen
62180 Verton
Pas-de-Calais
Tel: (0)3 21 84 27 10
e-mail: aterrien@wanadoo.fr
Web: perso.wanadoo.fr/lachaumiere

From A16 exit Montreuil towards Hesdin on D349. In Brimeux, left at junction, pass church, house on right, signposted.
Michelin Map No: 236-12

Entry no: 9   Map No: 3

M & Mme Germain TRUNNET
Ferme du Saule
20 rue de l'Église
62170 Brimeux
Pas-de-Calais
Tel: (0)3 21 06 01 28
Fax: (0)3 21 81 40 14
Web: www.sawdays.co.uk

Perfect peace here, not even a cockerel to wake you, and a warm unaffected welcome, complete with aperitif on arrival. Your hosts have nine grown-up children so it's not surprising their 18th-century house has a real family feel. Choose between the pretty fabrics and wooden floor of the room in the main house or the convenience of a room opening off the old farmyard, now a rose garden. Breakfast can include cheese and yoghurt as well as home-made jam, baguettes and croissants collected at dawn. Excellent for a quiet stopover, but the Locquevilles love getting to know their guests properly, so do stay on if you can.

Rooms: 1 double, 1 twin, each with shower & wc.

Price: 230-270 Frs for two.

Meals: Montreuil sur Mer 2km.

Closed: December-February.

This was indeed the home farm of the nearby Carthusian monastery and Anne, who manages to run the B&B, bring up three delightful children and teach part-time, is a charming, thoughtful hostess. Her talent and taste are in the guest rooms – hard to believe they were once pigsties, now transformed into pretty, not over-large but comfortably furnished bedrooms. Breakfast, which may include crêpes, is served in the enchantingly decorated kitchen/diner. Part of the monastery is open to visitors – a pleasant after-breakfast discovery, or you can play a game of tennis on the home court (lessons available too).

Rooms: 1 double, 1 triple, each with shower & wc.

Price: 250 Frs for two; 30 Frs for use of kitchenette.

Meals: Choice in Montreuil, 4km.

Closed: Never.

From A16 exit 26 to Montreuil then D439 E towards Hesdin. Go through Beaumerie St Martin & take first right at signpost.
Michelin Map No: 236-12

Entry no: 10   Map No: 3

Jeanne-Marie & Francis
LOCQUEVILLE
L'Overgne
62170 Beaumerie St Martin
Pas-de-Calais
Tel: (0)3 21 81 81 87

From A16 exit Montreuil sur Mer onto N1 direction Le Touquet/Boulogne. At lights right to Neuville then right on D113. Pass 2 other Chambres d'Hôtes – house on left next to abbey.
Michelin Map No: 236-12

Entry no: 11   Map No: 3

Anne FOURDINIER
Ferme de la Chartreuse
62170 Neuville sous Montreuil
Pas-de-Calais
Tel: (0)3 21 81 07 31
Fax: (0)3 21 81 07 31

A modern bungalow with all the heart of traditional French country life. When your hosts handed the family farm on to the next generation, they wanted to go on doing B&B in their new house. Its big windows let in the green that wraps the land outside and it has a real family feel: photos and mementoes everywhere, in the comfortable guest rooms too, with their good, pretty bathrooms. Madame, clearly a natural at grandmothering, might even mind your baby if you want to go off to sample the bright lights of Montreuil. Friendly and impeccable, it is excellent value and an ideal stopover.

In an immaculate, walled garden whose historic dovecote sings with life, the house feels almost Gothic on a dark night in its bare, white-stoned simplicity – perfectly restored for lovers of the soberly authentic. The vaulted oak and stone dining room is a great rarity; bedrooms and bathrooms are remarkable in artistry and personality: lit candles, old mirrors, appropriate pictures, bits of bronze and brass, rich tapestry and patchwork fabrics – unusual yet utterly inviting. Madame is flexible and helpful, her mornings are full of light, space and home-made jams, her passions include rescuing animals and collecting 1900s dress-dummies.

Rooms: 1 double with bath & wc; 1 quadruple with shower & wc.

Price: 240 Frs for two.

Meals: Choice in Montreuil, 3km.

Closed: Never.

Rooms: 2 doubles, 1 suite for 4, each with bath & wc.

Price: 300 Frs for two.

Meals: Wide choice 5km.

Closed: Never.

*From A16 exit Montreuil sur Mer onto N1 towards Le Touquet/Boulogne. At lights right to Neuville then right on D113. After 200m, house on right.
Michelin Map No: 236-12*

*From Montreuil, D901 to Neuville. In Neuville, on sharp bend, D113 past La Chartreuse to Marles sur Canche. Village centre 2km further on. House on right at crossroads after tight bend – go slowly!
Michelin Map No: 236-12*

Entry no: 12   Map No: 3

Entry no: 13   Map No: 3

Hubert & Christiane FOURDINIER
30 rue de la Chartreuse
62170 Neuville sous Montreuil
Pas-de-Calais
Tel: (0)3 21 81 95 05
Fax: (0)3 21 81 95 05

Mme Dominique LEROY
Manoir Francis
62170 Marles sur Canche
Pas-de-Calais
Tel: (0)3 21 81 38 80
Fax: (0)3 21 81 38 56
Web: www.sawdays.co.uk

Marie and Guy radiate warmth and delight in their perfect rural retreat (from teaching) among the hills and pastures, a refuge for tired horses, proud cats, exotic ducks, a beautiful Beauceron dog – and you, privileged guest. The two white, raftered attic rooms are big, warm and deeply, simply attractive but mind your head as you enter the shower room! Breakfast is a spread of local produce, candlelit in the dreamy old beamed dining room or sunlit in the twittering garden. This WWF Panda house (providing information on local flora and fauna) is actually inside the *Parc Régional* – use their knowledge and discover the natural treasures therein.

Rooms: 2 doubles, each with shower & wc (curtained off).

Price: 250 Frs for two.

Meals: Barbecue available.

Closed: Never.

From Boulogne sur Mer, D341 to Desvres, then D204/215 to Menneville; in village, left at 'Chambre d'Hôtes' sign; house on right.
Michelin Map No: 236-12

Entry no: 14   Map No: 3

Marie & Guy DESALASE
Le Mont Eventé
Menneville
62240 Desvres
Pas-de-Calais
Tel: (0)3 21 91 77 65
e-mail: guydesalase@minitel.net
Web: www.sawdays.co.uk

We love it for just being itself: rambling French country simplicity, no frills, no pretensions, no pandering to modernity. Dinners can be great fun with masses of people round the table who then retire to old-furnished rooms, some grand (the best room has walls panelled with painted cupboards and courtyard views), some plainer, where sweeties and bathrobes await them – it's immaterial that the loos are down a long corridor and the dusting isn't done every single day. The chained dog does gambol part of the time with her amiable master and Madame is gently affable. Nicer than it looks in the picture, slightly scuffed and run in a comfortably relaxed way.

Rooms: 2 twins, 2 doubles, each with shower, sharing 2 wcs.

Price: 175-200 Frs for two.

Meals: 75 Frs, including wine.

Closed: Never.

From Calais A16 for Boulogne. At Marquise, D238 to Wierre Effroy; follow D234 S; left onto D233 and left to Le Breucq.
Michelin Map No: 236-2

Entry no: 15   Map No: 3

Jacques & Isabelle de MONTIGNY
Le Breucq
62142 Belle et Houllefort
Pas-de-Calais
Tel: (0)3 21 83 31 99
Fax: (0)3 21 83 31 99
Web: www.sawdays.co.uk

All is tranquil at Meldick. The long dining room windows look out onto the pond and the fields beyond – hard to imagine that two terrible wars were waged here, but one of Madame's fascinating treasures is a real collection of medals and badges from those days. She has huge energy, a beautiful 1930s house that is a delight to be in and simply loves doing B&B because she enjoys the contact so much. Rooms are colour-themed, good-sized, carefully decorated and finely furnished; the family room is enormous! You are definitely welcomed as friends into the Houzet's home.

Rooms: 2 double, 2 twin, 1 room for 4, each with bath or shower & wc.

Price: 315 Frs for two.

Meals: Good restaurant 3km.

Closed: Never.

From A16 exit 19 to Marck. There, right on D940 then immediately left to Le Fort Vert, through Marck. At Le Fort Vert, right onto D119. House 3km along on right.
Michelin Map No: 236-3

Entry no: 16   Map No: 4

Jean & Danièle HOUZET
Manoir du Meldick
2528 ave du Général de Gaulle
Le Fort Vert
62730 Marck, Pas-de-Calais
Tel: (0)3 21 85 74 34
Fax: (0)3 21 85 74 34
e-mail: jeandaniele.houzet@free.fr

The people are delightful – an open, smiling, intelligent family who 'do' wine-tastings and will sell you wine and honey. The big park is soft and appealing and lots of animals wander around; the closeness to ferry ports is seductive although the nearby main road and TGV line may disturb some people. Straightforward and simple are the key words here – no luxury (showers are behind curtains). Breakfast is in the separate guest quarters (or the family kitchen for very early starts), where basic pine furniture and slatting grace the smallish rooms, and windows look onto lawn and trees.

Rooms: 2 triples, each with shower, sharing wc; 1 quadruple with shower & wc.

Price: From 210 Frs for two.

Meals: 1km or Ardres 5km; self-catering possible.

Closed: Never.

Gîte space for 11 people.

From A26 (exit 2 on N43) towards Calais. Wolphus is on left 1km after the junction, with woods beside road. Be careful turning in!
Michelin Map No: 236-3

Entry no: 17   Map No: 4

Jean-Jacques BEHAGHEL
La Ferme de Wolphus
62890 Zouafques
Pas-de-Calais
Tel: (0)3 21 35 61 61
Fax: (0)3 21 35 61 61
e-mail: ferme.de.wolphus@wanadoo.fr
Web: www.sawdays.co.uk

A stunning house, not big but an architectural historian's delight. It is 'French traditional' with masses of original, highly perishable details intact such as stained glass, *trompe-l'œil* wall-paintings (admire the 1850s fake marble), superb green and white tiling in the kitchen and a fine, elegant dining/sitting room. The quiet rooms are traditionally-furnished too, with rich dark wardrobes and good beds. Madame is completely available for her guests and only too happy to talk and communicate her excellent local knowledge.

Rooms: 1 double with basin, shower & wc; 1 twin, 4 doubles with basin & shower or bath, sharing wc.

Price: 220-250 Frs for two.

Meals: Restaurant 6km; Ardres 10km.

Closed: Never.

In the hall, where bobble-edged curtains and squat, plush chairs fight for the retro stakes, you meet the nicest, simplest farming folk imaginable, worn and naturally gracious after a lifetime on the land. Madame laughs easily and cooks French country meals, eaten in true conviviality and praised to the skies by readers, with home-grown ingredients (even the *kir* is made with raspberry *maison*). Rooms are simply, carefully authentic with old wooden beds, marble-top chests, one superb carved wardrobe and bed, small showers, lots of light. A real French experience – catch it before it disappears into the hi-tech millennium!

Rooms: 1 double, 1 twin, each with shower & wc.

Price: 210 Frs for two.

Meals: 95 Frs, including apéritif & wine.

Closed: Never.

Gîte space for 6 people.

A26 exit 2 direction Tournehem then immediately right to Zouafques then Tournehem. There D217 to Bonningues. House on right just after entering village.
Michelin Map No: 236-3

From A26 exit 2 on N43 towards St Omer. 3km after Nordausques, right to Nortleulinghen. In village, right to church and right into Rue de la Mairie. Signposted.
Michelin Map No: 236-3

Entry no: 18   Map No: 4

Entry no: 19   Map No: 4

Mme Christiane DUPONT
Le Manoir   *Sylv*
40 Route de Licques
62890 Bonningues les Ardres
Pas-de-Calais
Tel: (0)3 21 82 69 05
Fax: (0)3 21 82 69 05
Web: www.sawdays.co.uk

M & Mme NOËL MARTIN
8 rue de la Mairie
62890 Nortleulinghen
Pas-de-Calais
Tel: (0)3 21 35 64 60
Web: www.sawdays.co.uk

She's a lovely old lady! She talks lots, in French, and otherwise relies on radio and telly for company. Hers is a piecemeal family house with comfortable old furniture and masses of photographs (17 grandchildren). Rooms are rustically attractive: well-decorated with good beds and windows onto the peace outside. Madame loves cooking her delicious country dishes for visitors and readers have praised her natural hospitality. Ask to see the exquisite vaulted stables – built for cows and carthorses, fit for thoroughbreds and prizewinners!

Rooms: 2 doubles, 1 with cot & child's bed, each with shower & wc.

Price: 210 Frs for two.

Meals: 90 Frs, including wine.

Closed: November–March.

In calm countryside with neither cockerels nor dogs to alarm your early morning, Gina's welcome is as genuine and unpretentious as her house. There are informal wine-tastings at dinner and in the outbuilding – where guests are welcome to use the cooking equipment – and *pétanque* tournaments in summer. Madame calls her guest rooms *La Verte*, *La Rose*, *La Bleue*... and there are two other cosy ones under the roof of this 200-year-old farmhouse (mind your head up there!). Your hostess cares deeply that everyone should be happy and creates a really homely atmosphere.

Rooms: 3 doubles, 2 triples, each with bath or shower & wc.

Price: 270-300 Frs for two.

Meals: 100 Frs, including aperitif, wine & coffee.

Closed: Never.

Gîte space for 16 people.

From A26, exit 2 for Tournehem, cross N43 & follow signs to Muncq Nieurlet and continue direction Ruminghem. La Motte Obin on left, approx. 1.5km after leaving Muncq Nieurlet, at signpost.
Michelin Map No: 236-3

Entry no: 20   Map No: 4

Mme Françoise BRETON
La Motte Obin
62890 Muncq Nieurlet
Pas-de-Calais
Tel: (0)3 21 82 79 63

From Calais A26, exit 4 to Thérouanne then D341 to Auchy au Bois (12km). Right at Le Vert Dragon restaurant. 1st left; 2nd house on right after church.
Michelin Map No: 236-14

Entry no: 21   Map No: 4

Gina BULOT
Les Cohettes
28 rue de Pernes
62190 Auchy au Bois, Pas-de-Calais
Tel: (0)3 21 02 09 47
Fax: (0)3 21 02 81 68
e-mail: temps-libre-evasion@wanadoo.fr
Web: www.sawdays.co.uk

The Battle of Agincourt (remember your *Henry V*?) was in 1415; this house, tower and all, was built in 1750. You imagine hearing the clanking of swords still? Open your eyes and you may indeed see medieval knights – that's just your hosts on their way to re-enact a battle: they love their local history and tales of ghosts and archers, soldiers and horses. The pretty guest rooms, called *Voyage*, *Romantique*, *Retro* and *Espace*, are in an attached wattle-and-daub house with its own dayroom and log fire. Breakfast is in a room crammed with bric-a-brac in the tower. Huge fun.

Rooms: 3 doubles, 1 triple, all with shower & wc (1 behind curtain).

Price: 300 Frs for two.

Meals: Restaurant 1km; choice 6-15km.

Closed: Never.

There is room for all here with the wide terrace and green, flowery garden rolling into pastures beyond while the veranda is a gentle, bright space to be. Rooms are generous in comforts and floral cosiness. One has a huge carved Henri III bed, a totally French heavy-framed mirror and loads of lace. The stairs up to the suite tell many tales with pictures and objects from the past. Breakfast is as generous as the décor and your hosts, who are very young grandparents, will keep you informed and entertained. Madame makes superb jams, Monsieur's passion is Arab horses.

Rooms: 1 suite for 4 with kitchen & dining room, 2 triples, all with bath or shower & wc.

Price: 270 Frs for two; 450 Frs for 4.

Meals: Light supper for late arrivals (or families with babies) 75 Frs, including wine, by arrangement. Restaurants nearby.

Closed: Never.

Gîte space for 4 people.

From St Omer D928 dir. Abbeville. At Ruisseauville left dir. Blangy-Tramecourt; at next crossroads, left dir. Tramecourt; house 100m along. Michelin Map No: 236-13

Entry no: 22   Map No: 4

Patrick & Marie-Josée FENET
La Gacogne
62310 Azincourt
Pas-de-Calais
Tel: (0)3 21 04 45 61
Fax: (0)3 21 04 45 61

From Montreuil N39 towards Hesdin. Left on D928 towards St Omer. After Hesdin Forest 2nd left on D155 to Sains lès Fressin. House is at PR5 milestone. Michelin Map No: 236-16

Entry no: 23   Map No: 4

Jo & Jacques RIEBEN
Chantelouve
35 rue Principale
62310 Sains lès Fressin
Pas-de-Calais
Tel: (0)3 21 90 60 13
Fax: (0)3 21 90 60 13
Web: www.sawdays.co.uk

A fascinating house with character, history and two dining rooms: one has a unique '1830s-Medieval' fireplace, the other is classical French with coffered ceiling, deeply carved door frames and dado, a vast Louis XIII dresser. In an outbuilding, guest rooms are simpler, each with some old furniture and a neat shower room, one with its own kitchen and garden. Madame loves telling tales of the house and its contents, has a couple of goats in the quiet garden (but weekend racetrack in the valley), will do anything she can to be of service to guests. Both your hosts work constantly on their beloved house – good folk.

Rooms: 2 doubles, 2 twins (1 on ground floor), 1 suite for 4, each with shower & wc. Kitchenette available.

Price: 240 Frs for two; under 5s free.

Meals: Choice within walking distance; self-catering possible.

Closed: Never.

From St Pol sur Ternoise, D343 NW towards Fruges. Just after entering Gauchin Verloingt, right Rue de Troisvaux then right Rue des Montifaux. House along on right. Michelin Map No: 236-14

Entry no: 24   Map No: 4

Marie-Christine & Philippe VION
Le Loubarré, 550 rue des Montifaux
62130 Gauchin Verloingt
Pas-de-Calais
Tel: (0)3 21 03 05 05
Fax: (0)3 21 41 26 76
e-mail: mcvion.loubarre@wanadoo.fr
Web: www.sawdays.co.uk

An exceptional mix of place and people. After 12 years, this dynamic family – all eight of them – have almost finished rebuilding their château, (getting covered in paint while brightening their escutcheon!), running a publishing house in Paris and leading a brilliant social life – phenomenal energy, fascinating people, natural hospitality that makes up for any residual damp. Built in 1745, the château has striking grandeur: come play lord and lady in vastly beautiful chandeliered, ancestored *salons*, enjoy an aristocratically graceful bedroom with big windows and a good bathroom and walk the rolling green parkland as if it were your own.

Rooms: 6 doubles/twins, each with bath or shower & wc.

Price: 500 Frs for two.

Meals: 2 restaurants within 4k.

Closed: Never.

From Arras, N25 towards Doullens. At L'Arbret, right on D8 to Avesnes le Comte. D75 to Grand Rullecourt (4km); château in village centre, on the square. Michelin Map No: 236-14

Entry no: 25   Map No: 4

Patrice & Chantal de SAULIEU
Château de Grand-Rullecourt
62810 Grand Rullecourt
Pas-de-Calais
Tel: (0)3 21 58 06 37
Fax: (0)1 41 27 97 30
e-mail: lsaulieu@routiers.com
Web: www.saulieu.com/chateau/

Sylvie and Emmanuel have taken over from their parents who started B&B here 10 years ago, and they are as eager to make you feel at home. The stately face has been lifted, shutters renovated, stones repointed – it looks grander than ever, surrounded by its great park and orchards (they produce delicious 'real' apples, the fruit of what is called 'Reasoned Agriculture'). Inside, it is still a warm, embracing country house with a moulded, arched, chequered hall/breakfast room and delightful rooms, most of them done with fresh pine furniture and pretty colours, a couple more traditional with sleigh beds, old fireplaces, mirrored armoires.

Rooms: 3 triples, 1 double, 1 suite for 4, all with bath or shower & wc.

Price: 290 Frs for two.

Meals: Choice 5-8km.

Closed: January.

Gîte space for 4 people.

People come to visit Arras and the military cemeteries of the Vimy Ridge but the rural simplicity of this low house, hugging its little garden behind the church, may entice you to stay longer. The very personal rooms with their air of family history are a delightful mix of modern fabrics and interesting antiques: spriggy wallpaper among the timbers, an unusual old desk in the ground-floor room, a super multi-purpose piece on the red-carpeted landing – an armchair/desk/bookcase – said to have belonged to Jules Verne..., plus well-fitted bathrooms. Madame is shyly proud of her house and serves a generous, imaginative breakfast.

Rooms: 2 doubles, 1 twin, all with bath or shower & wc.

Price: 200 Frs for two.

Meals: Basic bar/restaurant 7km.

Closed: Never.

Between Doullens & Arras. N25 direction Arras. In L'Arbret, first left to Saulty and follow signposts.
Michelin Map No: 236-24

Entry no: 26   Map No: 4

Emmanuel & Sylvie DALLE
82 rue de la Gare
62158 Saulty
Pas-de-Calais
Tel: (0)3 21 48 24 76
Fax: (0)3 21 48 18 32
Web: www.sawdays.co.uk

From Arras N25 towards Doullens. At Bac du Sud right on D66 to Gouy en Artois and Fosseux. House is near village church.
Michelin Map No: 236-15

Entry no: 27   Map No: 4

Geneviève DELACOURT
3 rue de l'Église
62810 Fosseux
Pas-de-Calais
Tel: (0)3 21 48 40 13

Madame, warmly relaxed and attentive and the pivot of her family (lots of photographs), loves interior design: beautifully-made curtains, gently-matched papers and fabrics, old-fashioned touches here (crochet, carving), modern details there in good comfortable bedrooms. Monsieur's domain, the sheltered garden going down to the little river, is splendid (swings for the children too) and the lime trees are a fitting backdrop to this imposing old manor built in soft grey stone. It originally belonged to the château next door and the drive is still flanked by a fine laurel hedge. A gentle, civilised place to stay.

Rooms: 1 family suite, 1 double, both with bath or shower & wc.

Price: 260 Frs for two.

Meals: Choice 4-7km.

Closed: Never.

This house is a fine example of northern French brick-building, as is the splendid 19th-century brewery across the road with its curious double swastika emblem. The Peugniez are lovely, gentle people whose children have grown and flown; they still farm (cereals only now, having given up beef) and enjoy good company. Their house is simple and most welcoming with a warm family feel and no pretensions. The attic-floor guest rooms have screened-off showers, old timbers and floorboards and make a good-value stopover. And don't forget that fascinating old Arras is thoroughly worth a day trip.

Rooms: 3 doubles, 1 twin, 1 quadruple, all with shower, sharing 2 wcs.

Price: 200 Frs for two.

Meals: In village or Arras 7km.

Closed: Christmas & New Year.

Gîte space for 12 people.

From Arras, N39 towards Le Touquet. After 6km under railway bridge, 1st left along D56 to Duisans. House first on left in village.
Michelin Map No: 236-15

Entry no: 28   Map No: 4

Annie & Patrick SENLIS
Le Clos Grincourt
18 rue du Château
62161 Duisans
Pas-de-Calais
Tel: (0)3 21 48 68 33
Fax: (0)3 21 48 68 33

From A1 exit 16 on N50 to Arras for 2km then left to Fampoux. In village follow Chambres d'Hôtes signs. House on right in Rue Paul Verlaine.
Michelin Map No: 236-16

Entry no: 29   Map No: 4

Dominique & Marie-Thérèse
PEUGNIEZ
17 rue Paul Verlaine
62118 Fampoux
Pas-de-Calais
Tel: (0)3 21 55 00 90
Fax: (0)3 21 55 00 90

You will get a marvellous welcome and be treated with immense care by the competent, smiling owners of this fine old house and its opulent garden. The marble-floored hall strikes you first, then the sober breakfast room, the multitudinous stuffed animals in the dining room and another stylish room with painted panelling. Bedrooms are big and most inviting and all is impeccably clean and orderly. A very good, and genteel, stop for those going to and from the ferry, just 2-3 minutes stroll from the town centre and excellent value.

Rooms: 2 doubles, each with shower & wc.

Price: 270 Frs for two.

Meals: Restaurant 100m.

Closed: Never.

In this richly interesting city where plain façades often hide unsuspected beauties, Jeannine Hulin's townhouse reflects her personality: artistic – kitchen and *salon* show masterly use of colour, and warm – she loves having guests. You breakfast at a tiled table in the bright kitchen or in the flower-filled, conservatory above the garden. Original floor tiles, stripped pine doors and masses of plants add atmosphere. The big bedroom is lovely with matching sleigh bed, wardrobe and desk, antique white linen and mirrors, and your delightful bathroom (on the floor below) has a claw-footed bath.

Rooms: 1 double with private bath & shared wc on floor below.

Price: 255 Frs for two.

Meals: Full choice in town.

Closed: Never; please telephone to book.

From Calais A16 E to exit 23b and into Bourbourg. From Place de l'Hôtel de Ville the street (Rue de l'Hôtel de Ville) is left of the town hall as you face it. Michelin Map No: 236-3

From A1 exit 20 onto D917 towards Fâches Ronchin – Lille for 4km. At traffic lights (Boulangerie Paul on corner) turn left; 1st right is Rue des Hannetons. Michelin Map No: 236-16

Entry no: 30   Map No: 4

Entry no: 31   Map No: 4

Marilou & Jacques VAN DE WALLE
25 rue des Martyrs de la Résistance
59630 Bourbourg
Nord
Tel: (0)3 28 22 21 41

Jeannine HULIN
28 rue des Hannetons
59000 Lille
Nord
Tel: (0)3 20 53 46 12
Fax: (0)3 20 53 46 12
Web: www.sawdays.co.uk

A charming hostess: her welcome more than compensates for an unremarkable modern house on a city street. And there's a lovely surprise: the picture window in the uncluttered living room gives onto a garden full of flowers where you can sit after exploring the treasures of Lille. The bedrooms are small, cosily-carpeted, pleasing and there's a little kitchen for guests. Chantal, bright, energetic and typically French, used to teach English (speaks it perfectly) then adapted her house especially to receive guests. Yves has good English too, and will dine with you – they both enjoy having an open house.

Rooms: 2 doubles, each with shower & wc; 1 twin with bath & wc.

Price: 230-260 Frs for two.

Meals: 100 Frs, including wine & coffee; self-catering possible.

Closed: Never.

From A1 exit 20/20b 'Centre Commercial'; at r'bout towards Wattignies; at T-junction right for 500m then left to Wattignies for 2km; at lights left for 'Le Village Centre' for 100m. At 'Pharmacie' right into Rue Faidherbe; house 500m on left.
Michelin Map No: 236-16

Entry no: 32   Map No: 4

Yves & Chantal LE BOT
59 rue Faidherbe
59139 Wattignies
Nord
Tel: (0)3 20 60 24 51
Web: www.sawdays.co.uk

An austere-looking northern face that conceals a houseful of riches and light, this was a Victorian textile magnate's mansion: baronial-fireplaced *grand salon*, which even big modern paintings cannot overwhelm, graceful bow-windowed dining room, little garden beyond. The delightful young owner will take you up the tall staircase to a big, airy room with coloured walls, pine furniture on polished floorboards (one has a waterbed), a light modern bathroom. Top-floor rooms have lower ceilings; there's a communal kitchen. A lovely house.

Rooms: 2 doubles, each with shower & wc; 1 double, 1 triple, each with small bath & wc on landing.

Price: 250 Frs for two.

Meals: By arrangement.

Closed: 3 weeks in August.

From A25 exit Roubaix-Tourcoing onto ring road for approx. 10km; exit Wasquehal. Right towards Croix, left at 2nd light, right at 2nd light, left and left again.
Michelin Map No: 236-16

Entry no: 33   Map No: 4

Jean-François RENART
14 rue Vauban
59100 Roubaix
Nord
Tel: (0)3 20 11 07 62
Fax: (0)3 20 11 07 62

You enter this classic French farmyard through a 17th-century archway facing the old stables (a fairly standard conversion job here) where you will find your bedroom. Rooms have been carefully colour-co-ordinated in simple cottagey style and the showers are welcomingly wide: a whole family could have fun in there. Your hosts particularly like having children (they have three of their own). Breakfast, which includes their own milk and yoghurt, wholemeal bread and waffles in winter, is a feast you can have at any time from 6am to noon. An ideal family base and really good value.

Rooms: 2 doubles, 1 twin, 1 triple, each with shower & wc.

Price: 240 Frs for two.

Meals: 80 Frs, including wine.

Closed: Never.

From A27 (Lille-Doornik) exit 'Cité Scientifique' towards Cysoing. In Sainghin, leave church on right, continue 600m, right on Rue du Cimetière, across junction into Rue Pasteur; farm 800m on right. Michelin Map No: 236-16

Entry no: 34   Map No: 4

Dominique POLLET
Ferme de la Noyelle
832 rue Pasteur
59262 Sainghin en Mélantois
Nord
Tel: (0)3 20 41 29 82
Fax: (0)3 20 79 06 99

Behind the low façade is much richness, all just so, rather like a dolls' house, down to the requisite ornaments, Madame's perfect plaything. The impression is of character and antiques with some modern bits. The big living room has pink walls, beams, marble floor and fireplace and there is an almost overwhelmingly pretty breakfast room: *objets trouvés*, plants and a Thai howdah sofa. The two first-floor rooms, one reached by an outside staircase, can communicate if you want a suite. Smart and mostly pink, they have lovely linen, good bathrooms, beams and views over church and garden. And Monsieur has lots of interesting things to tell.

Rooms: 2 double/triples, each with shower & wc.

Price: 360 Frs for two.

Meals: Choice 5km.

Closed: Never.

Gîte space for 3 people.

From A16, exit 24. From Abbeville N1 N towards Montreuil/Boulogne for 25km. In Vron left to Villers sur Authie. There right into Rue de l'Église (opposite café). At end of road, left up un-made-up, tree-lined lane; house on left. Michelin Map No: 236-12

Entry no: 35   Map No: 3

Pierre & Sabine SINGER de WAZIÈRES
La Bergerie
80120 Villers sur Authie
Somme
Tel: (0)3 22 29 21 74
Fax: (0)3 22 29 39 58

Your hosts have restored their fine brick house with respect and imagination: a lesson in that deceptively simple sobriety that turns every patch of colour, every rare object into a rich reward. Basics are white, ivory, sand; floors are pine with ethnic rugs; blue, ginger or red details shine out and great-grandfather's Flemish oil paintings are perfect finishing touches. One room is big, white and empty bar a flame-clothed table and a little round window onto ponds and the setting sun. Drink in the white-panelled, open-hearthed, brown-leather sitting room, revel in the pale, uncluttered dining room – and Claudine's good food. A glamorous, welcoming couple.

Rooms: 3 doubles, 1 suite, all with shower or bath & wc.

Price: 450-480 Frs for two.

Meals: From 135 Frs, excluding wine.

Closed: Never

Gîte space for 8 people.

From A16 exit 24 towards Boulogne through Bernay en Ponthieu then first left; through Arry; 1km beyond turn left to Le Thurel after great barn.
Michelin Map No: 236-12

Entry no: 36   Map No: 3

Claudine & Patrick VAN BREE-LECLEF
Le Thurel, Relais de Campagne
Baie de Somme Picardie
80120 Rue, Somme
Tel: (0)3 22 25 04 44
Fax: (0)3 22 25 79 69
e-mail: lethurel.relais@libertysurf.fr
Web: www.lethurel.com

Joanna is an amazing woman: founder of a tribe of 33, she is no ordinary granny. Her little old house – an 18th-century townsman's weekend house – displays a highly original sense of interior décor (daring colour combinations, strong wallpapers, highly modern bathrooms, antiques and modern pieces, crochet, plush and wickerwork) and her artistic gift with clay. It all works brilliantly and she has a great sense of fun. Her ancient garden stretches away from formal box to wild grass and the hills. Breakfast on organic jams in the conservatory among the artworks. One delicious bedroom is reached through the kitchen. In a pretty village, opposite the church.

Rooms: 1 double, 1 suite for 3, 1 suite for 5, all with shower or bath & wc.

Price: 280-320 Frs for two.

Meals: Barbecue available; choice in Abbeville.

Closed: Christmas.

From Boulogne A16, Abbeville/St Riquier exit. At first roundabout, to Vauchelles lès Quesnoy. House on main square opposite church.
Michelin Map No: 236-22

Entry no: 37   Map No: 3

Mme Joanna CRÉPELLE
Place de l'Eglise
80132 Vauchelles lès Quesnoy
Somme
Tel: (0)3 22 24 18 17
Fax: (0)3 22 24 18 17
Web: www.sawdays.co.uk

A fine-looking château, but above all a family house. Madame, mother of four lovely-mannered children and lover of things outdoor – dogs, horses, gardening – reigns with energy and a refreshingly natural attitude: what matter if a little mud walks into the hall? In pleasing contrast is the formal dining room with its fabulous patterned parquet floor, vast table, family silver and chandeliers, and excellent food. Up the brilliant ginger-clothed staircase, the comfortable rooms may seem slightly worn: they are gradually being rejuvenated. Come for lively hospitality not smart château bedrooms.

Rooms: 1 double, 1 suite for 4, each with bath or shower & wc; 2 doubles sharing bathroom.

Price: 350-400 Frs for two.

Meals: 110 Frs, including coffee.

Closed: Never.

Gîte space for 20 people.

From Abbeville, N28 direction Rouen. At St Maxent, D29 to Oisemont, then D25 dir. Sénarpont. Signposted on outskirts of Foucaucourt.
Michelin Map No: 236-22

Entry no: 38   Map No: 3

Mme Elisabeth de ROCQUIGNY
Château de Foucaucourt
Foucaucourt Hors Nesle
80140 Oisemont, Somme
Tel: (0)3 22 25 12 58
Fax: (0)3 22 25 15 58
e-mail: chateaudefoucaucourt@wanadoo.fr
Web: www.sawdays.co.uk

Monsieur, who is Dutch, grows several thousand tulips in serried ranks. He also makes honey, cider and calvados (ask to see the vaulted cellars) and keeps that supremely French animal a *trotteur* mare. Madame, a solid citizen of local stock, is Mayor of the village. They are calm, hospitable people, the first in the Somme to open their house for B&B. A very fine building with an extraordinary staircase. Bedrooms, smaller on the second floor, are comfortable and uncluttered, views are peaceful, the panelled dining room a proper setting for a fine breakfast. A good place to stay.

Rooms: 1 double with shower & wc; 3 triples, each with shower & basin, sharing wc.

Price: 230-250 Frs for two.

Meals: Barbecue & guest kitchen available.

Closed: Never.

Gîte space for 13 people.

From Abbeville, N28 direction Rouen. After 28km, left at Bouttencourt on D1015 to Sénarpont then D211 dir. Amiens. After 4.5km, left into Le Mazis; follow Chambres d'Hôtes signs.
Michelin Map No: 236-22

Entry no: 39   Map No: 3

Dorette & Aart ONDER DE LINDEN
3 rue d'Inval
80430 Le Mazis
Somme
Tel: (0)3 22 25 90 88
Fax: (0)3 22 25 76 04

The 'best' room is worth it: white all over with pools of colour in the bed hangings, soft kilim rugs, dark polished antiques, old oil paintings, gilt-framed prints. White doors lead to a gorgeous bathroom (antique basin and taps) and a tiny sitting alcove. The suite has terracotta tiles, lush Provençal and cream fabrics and a picture view of garden and hills. There's a little flask of port in each room. Madame is a painter and the peaceful charm of her garden, with bantams all about, deepens the friendly yet unintrusive atmosphere she creates. Breakfast, served in a delightful room next to Madame's studio, is a most happy affair.

Rooms: 3 doubles and 1 suite for 4, all with bath or shower & wc.

Price: 260-380 Frs for two; suite 560 Frs. (Min. 2 nights preferred; weekly terms available).

Meals: Restaurant 5km; choice 8km.

Closed: November-March.

Gîte space for 2-4 people.

From Amiens, N29 direction Poix, then left on D162 to Creuse; signposted. Michelin Map No: 236-23

Entry no: **40**   Map No: 4

Mme Monique LEMAÎTRE
26 rue Principale
80480 Creuse
Somme
Tel: (0)3 22 38 91 50
Fax: (0)3 22 38 91 50

They love horses, the place's roots go back 1000 years to the age of myths, so they call it *La Licorne*. Guests sleep in the former chapel, also a *gîte d'étape* (no B&B bookings when groups are here); there's a kitchen area, a curious free-standing fireplace shaped like an oil lamp and a massive dining table which converts for... snooker. You can light a fire, play snooker, use the kitchen, lounge in the garden. The smallish bedrooms are under the rafters (one with the loo in the room). The Richoux, eminently relaxed and likeable people, know all about local history and good hiking. Nearby are water sports, fishing and Amiens' Gothic Cathedral.

Rooms: 1 double, 1 triple, each with bath & wc.

Price: 220 Frs for two.

Meals: Self-catering or restaurants 4km.

Closed: Never.

Gîte space for 12 people.

From Amiens, N1 direction Beauvais for about 15km. Between St Sauflieu and Essertaux, right on D153 to Loeuilly; signposted. Michelin Map No: 236-33

Entry no: **41**   Map No: 4

Claudine & Bernard RICHOUX
Route de Conty
80160 Loeuilly
Somme
Tel: (0)3 22 38 15 19
Fax: (0)3 22 38 15 19
e-mail: richoux.bernard@wanadoo.fr
Web: www.sawdays.co.uk

You will be enfolded in a typically warm northern welcome by Madame, who used to be a social worker (she is at ease with all sorts and has the most infectious laugh) and Monsieur, who is a big-hearted, genuine, chatty countryman, though they don't dine with guests. Bedrooms, each with separate entrance, are decorated and furnished with panache, personality and all the necessary modernities including a kitchenette each. Bathrooms have been recently redone. Ask for the big room in the *grenier* (loft). The lush green garden at the back has wrought-iron furniture, a lily pond and hens scratching in a large pen.

Rooms: 3 triples, all with shower, wc & kitchenette.

Price: 230-270 Frs for two.

Meals: 70 Frs, excluding wine, by arrangement.

Closed: November-Easter (except by arrangement).

From Amiens N1 south to Hébécourt. Opposite church follow Chambre d'Hôtes signs to Plachy Buyon. Michelin Map No: 236-23

Entry no: 42   Map No: 4

Mme Jacqueline PILLON
L'Herbe de Grâce
Hameau de Buyon
80160 Plachy Buyon
Somme
Tel: (0)3 22 42 12 22
Fax: (0)3 22 42 04 42
Web: www.sawdays.co.uk

This house has a lovely face but the main road runs very nearby. Guest bedrooms and sitting room are in a well-converted barn that gives onto the courtyard. They are fairly blandly furnished with a mix of old and new, pleasing pine-slatted ceilings, with fresh flowers in summer and double-glazing against winter chill and road noise. If you arrive at a sensible time you may be offered a glass of home-made cider in the owners' living room at their unusual coffee table: a giant slice of fallen elm. Breakfast by the vast fireplace here is a feast and there's a very rare holly tree in the garden by the stables. Pony-and-trap rides in summer.

Rooms: 1 double, 1 twin, 1 triple, 1 suite, all with bath or shower & wc.

Price: 310 Frs for two.

Meals: Within walking distance.

Closed: Never.

Gîte space for 11 people.

From A16 Dury exit onto N1 S towards Breteuil and Paris. Arriving in Dury, left at traffic lights. House is first on right. Michelin Map No: 236-24

Entry no: 43   Map No: 4

Alain & Maryse SAGUEZ
2 rue Grimaux
80480 Dury
Somme
Tel: (0)3 22 95 29 52
Fax: (0)3 22 95 29 52

Near the WW1 battlefields, the emphasis here is on country family hospitality and Madame, smiling, uncomplicated, often clad in a white linen apron, gives guests a big welcome. It's a paradise for children, the rambling garden has stone love-seats and two ponds, the enclosed yard has swings and a playhouse and the old manor house the feel of an adventure story. The redecorated living room has smart grey and white floor tiles and stylish blue stencilling on the ceiling beams. The fresh, rustic bedrooms have marble fireplaces, square French pillows on the beds, floral 1950s country-style décor and complicated bathroom arrangements.

Rooms: 1 double, ground floor, with bath & wc; 2 doubles, 1st floor, with showers sharing wc; 1 twin, 1 double, 2nd floor, sharing bath & wc. 2 small extra rooms for children.

Price: 250 Frs for two; reservations only.

Meals: Restaurants 5-10km. Picnic possible.

Closed: December-February.

From Amiens D929 towards Albert. At Pont Noyelles, left onto D115 towards Contay; signposted in Bavelincourt. Michelin Map No: 236-24

Entry no: **44**   Map No: 4

M & Mme Noël VALENGIN
Les Aulnaies
15 Grande Rue
80260 Bavelincourt
Somme
Tel: (0)3 22 40 51 51

The whole area is a watery paradise, surrounded by the River Somme and acres of ponds. A canal flows behind the old farmhouse and guests can join the villagers fishing, boating or lazing on the edge. You can also fish in Madame's private pond. The decent-sized guest breakfast and sitting room has this view, as do the small, brightly-clothed and functional bedrooms. Here, Madame will help you prepare your day. In the evening, she serves her excellent regional specialities in her big, gable-timbered, flower-filled dining room.

Rooms: 2 doubles, 1 twin, all with shower & wc.

Price: 280 Frs for two.

Meals: 90 Frs, including coffee, by arrangement.

Closed: Never.

Gîte space for 5 people.

From A1, Péronne exit onto N29 westwards and immediately right on D146 towards Feuillères. Before village, D146E to Frise. First farm after bridge. Michelin Map No: 236-25

Entry no: **45**   Map No: 4

Annick RANDJIA-LEPINE
La Ferme de l'Écluse
80340 Frise
Somme
Tel: (0)3 22 84 59 70
Fax: (0)3 22 83 17 56
Web: www.sawdays.co.uk

The warm, enthusiastic Verhoevens live in an old farmhouse in an idyllic village of handsome old houses surrounded by rolling farmland and green woods. Cows graze in the field and apples grow in the small orchard. Furniture and décor are in various colours, textures and styles, all carefully chosen and placed. Guest rooms in the modern extension have good repro pieces too, and new mattresses. Monsieur is proud to have been a proper 'natural' farmer and Madame is every inch the chatty, friendly, elderly farmer's wife. She is also a charming hostess who loves tending her orchard and kitchen garden... and her guests.

Rooms: 2 doubles, each with shower, bath & wc.

Price: 250 Frs for two.

Meals: 3 restaurants within 2km.

Closed: Never.

From Beauvais, direction Le Tréport to Troissereux then D133 to Songeons, then D143 direction Gournay en Bray. 1st village on leaving forest is Buicourt; house near church.
Michelin Map No: 236-32

Entry no: 46   Map No: 3

Eddy & Jacqueline VERHOEVEN
3 rue de la Mare
60380 Buicourt
Oise
Tel: (0)3 44 82 31 15

In 1927 Auguste Perret, king of concrete, added a piece of design history to a pretty old house. His immense living room is squares in squares: panels, bookshelves, floor tiles, the huge table. Above is the, green and puce (so's the bathroom), Perret-panelled bedroom with a flourish of columns, super 1930s furniture, terrace and vast view. Other rooms have lovely ethnic fabrics, much light, sophisticated bathrooms. Madame loves her house and enjoys sharing its delights with you. Monsieur is mad about horses; their pasture is part of the sweeping view from the quiet garden. And the train can carry you straight from the village to Paris... and back again.

Rooms: 1 double, 2 triples, all with bath or shower & wc.

Price: 300 Frs for two.

Meals: 150 Frs, including aperitif, wine & coffee.

Closed: Never.

From Calais A16 exit 13 (Méru) W towards Chaumont en Vexin. In Loconville, left to Liancourt St Pierre; right to post office & follow left into Rue du Donjon (no through road); high gate on left.
Michelin Map No: 237-4

Entry no: 47   Map No: 3

Luc GALLOT
La Pointe
60240 Liancourt St Pierre
Oise
Tel: (0)3 44 49 32 08
Fax: (0)3 44 49 32 08

In the rose-climbed former bakery, where bread was once made for humans and potatoes cooked for pigs, guests are now made very welcome in rooms with space, simple furniture, an Indian cotton throw at each bedhead, magnificent 17th-century roof timbers and sober carpets. There are two pretty breakfast rooms where the vast bread oven, beams and character have been preserved. Your active, quiet hosts have taste and humour. Their small farmhouse rooms have been turned into a lovely open-plan space with timber framing, where you may dine with them in all simplicity and soak up the warm, natural atmosphere.

Rooms: 1 quadruple, 1 triple, 2 doubles, all with shower & wc.

Price: 240 Frs for two.

Meals: 80 Frs, including wine & coffee.

Closed: Never.

Gîte space for 13 people.

From Beauvais N31 towards Rouen. Leaving Beauvais pick up signs to Savignies. Farm in village, 50m from church.
Michelin Map No: 236-33

Entry no: 48   Map No: 4

Annick & Jean-Claude LETURQUE
La Ferme du Colombier
60650 Savignies
Oise
Tel: (0)3 44 82 18 49
Fax: (0)3 44 82 53 70
e-mail: ferme.colombier@wanadoo.fr
Web: www.sawdays.co.uk

Behind the high brick walls and imposing archway hides a secret garden with a goldfish pond, lots of interesting mementoes and your hostess – a retired chemist who loves laughter and travelling. She also loves her dogs – and contact with visitors. Your beamed, fireplaced, mellow rooms, furnished like drawing rooms with old pieces and soft fabrics, are in the original house (with kettle etc); she lives in the brilliantly-converted barn, and all is harmony and warmth among the family antiques. Drink in the atmosphere and her talk of France, the French and the rest of the world. Rest in peace, rouse to the dawn chorus, then enjoy breakfast in the sunshine.

Rooms: 1 twin with shower & basin, 1 double with bath & basin, sharing wc.

Price: 300 Frs for two.

Meals: Restaurants 4-6km.

Closed: Never; booking essential.

From A1 exit 10 direction Compiègne for 4km. By caravan yard right at small turning direction Jaux. 1st right to Varanval, up hill then down. House on right opposite château gates.

Entry no: 49   Map No: 4

Françoise GAXOTTE
La Gaxottière
60880 Jaux Varanval
Oise
Tel: (0)3 44 83 22 41
Fax: (0)3 44 83 22 41
Web: www.sawdays.co.uk

The Hamelins, intelligent, smiling farmers, have thoughtfully installed swings, slides and a tennis court in their garden; the farm, surrounded by woods and fields, has an elegant cobbled farmyard at its heart. Cleverly-renovated cottages provide delightful, clean, modern rooms with pretty fabrics and good bedding; the 'best' room has a fine pale-wood Louis XVI cane bed. In a converted vaulted barn are two huge rooms that make this place ideal for families: the games room has table football, ping-pong and a piano; the stone-walled sitting/dining room has a big log fire, comfortable chairs, an old dresser and painted jugs.

Rooms: 1double, 1 twin, 1 family suite (twin & bunks), all with bath or shower & wc.

Price: Price: 300 Frs for two.

Meals: Choice in Crépy, 9km.

Closed: January.

From A1 Senlis exit onto N324 to Crépy en Valois, then D332 direction Lévignen and Betz. 3km after Lévignen right to Macquelines. Right at T-junction; farm immediately on right.
Michelin Map No: 237-20

Entry no: **49**   Map No: 4

Philippe & Marthe HAMELIN
Ferme de Macquelines
60620 Betz
Oise
Tel: (0)3 44 87 20 21
Fax: (0)3 44 87 20 21

In this comfortable old family mansion, Madame's natural hospitality embraces all sorts; she has even installed a 'secret studio' in a medieval tower for artists to escape to while others buy *brocante* below. Rooms are mostly big, some smarter than others, all family-furnished with decent bathrooms; the stables studio is in modern pine and fresh fabrics; the fine garden runs down past the giant draughts board to the river. Fish, swim in the pool (at the higher price), play tennis, admire the occasional reception. Simple breakfasts and excellent dinners are served at separate tables, the big *salon* is very relaxing.

Rooms: 2 doubles, 3 triples, all with shower & wc.

Price: 330-390 Frs for two.

Meals: 100 Frs, excluding wine.

Closed: Never.

Gîte space for 14 people.

From Compiègne, N31 dir. Soissons; after 22km, left to Vic sur Aisne. Right after restaurant 'Le Donjon' then first right again. Right at 'Stop' then immediately left.
Michelin Map No: 236-36

Entry no: **51**   Map No: 4

Jean & Anne MARTNER
Domaine des Jeanne
02290 Vic sur Aisne
Aisne
Tel: (0)3 23 55 57 33
Fax: (0)3 23 55 57 33

If you want to sleep in a tower, try this: the vast bedroom and smaller room for children (across the hall from the main double room) have been imaginatively and attractively housed in the octagonal tower, which is one of the charms of this delicious *troubadour*-style château. Jacques' family have been here for five generations and are likely to remain, judging by the tribe of exquisitely-behaved children he and Marie-Catherine have produced! Breakfast and dinner (by arrangement) are served in summer in the enchanting orangery. It's a pleasure to see an old family home so well loved and used.

Genuine French generosity and real contact are here in the big old house, welcoming and warmly tatty with mix 'n' not-match wallpapers, posters on long corridors, funny old prints in bedrooms. The owners are great fun, energetic, and love their dinner parties in the dining room with its old family furniture, where guests of all nations communicate as the wine flows. They wouldn't dream of changing a thing for the sake of modern sanitising theories – may they prosper! The rooms are simple and good; one has a ship's shower room, another a Louis XVI bed, all look onto green pastures.

Rooms: 1 suite (double & single) with shower & wc.

Price: 300 Frs for two.

Meals: 120 Frs, including (good) wine.

Closed: Never.

Rooms: 1 suite for 4, 2 doubles, 1 twin, each with bath or shower & wc; 1 double, 1 twin with basins, sharing bathroom.

Price: 200-280 Frs for two.

Meals: 100 Frs, including wine (not Sun)

Closed: 16 October-14 March.

Gîte space for 12 people.

From A26 exit 13 towards Laon. Round Laon bypass towards Soissons onto N2 for about 15km, then left on D423 to Nanteuil la Fosse. Through Nanteuil, following signs for La Quincy; château on right outside village.
Michelin Map No: 236-37

From A26-E17, Laon/Chambry exit S on N2; 2nd left to Athies s/Laon; D516 to Bruyères M, left on D967 dir. Fismes; Chérêt signed on leaving Bruyères.
Michelin Map No: 238-38

Entry no: 52   Map No: 4

Entry no: 53   Map No: 4

Jacques & Marie-Catherine CORNU-LANGY
La Quincy
02880 Nanteuil la Fosse
Aisne
Tel: (0)3 23 54 67 76
Fax: (0)3 23 54 72 63

Mme Monique SIMONNOT
Le Clos
02860 Chérêt
Aisne
Tel: (0)3 23 24 80 64

Out in the wilds, Ressons is a big, active farm, with an unspoilt house among rolling hills and champagne vineyards. Your hosts are hard-working and good company; they also hunt. Madame, an architect, works from home, brings up three children AND nurtures her guests. The deeply-carved Henri III furniture is an admirable family heirloom; rooms are colour-co-ordinated, beds are beautiful, views are stunning, dinners cooked with home-grown produce are excellent; bring rod and permit and you can fish in the pond. Arms are open for you in this civilised household.

Rooms: 1 double, 1 twin, both with bath, sharing wc; 2 doubles & 1 twin, sharing bath & 2 wcs.

Price: 250-300 Frs for two.

Meals: 100 Frs, excl. wine (from 70 Frs).

Closed: Christmas.

Gîte space for 12 people.

From Fismes D967 towards Fère en Tardenois & Château Thierry for 4km. DON'T go to Mont St Martin. Continue 800m beyond turning; white house on left.
Michelin Map No: 237-10

Entry no: 54   Map No: 4

Valérie & Jean-Paul FERRY
Ferme de Ressons
02220 Mont St Martin
Aisne
Tel: (0)3 23 74 71 00
Fax: (0)3 23 74 28 88
Web: www.sawdays.co.uk

This exceptionally warm and intelligent couple will share their lively interest in life and people as well as their lovely and ancient family home. It rambles, you see traces of seven children, admire fine furniture in a very practical environment, delight in flights of decorative imagination. Two rooms have a private sitting space each, others are just as pretty. Madame deals with ease and energy with family and friends (that's you), concocts beautifully personal flower arrangements – her big garden is full of flowers; you may picnic there and drink in the view – she also serves seriously good breakfasts and loves having children to stay.

Rooms: 4 doubles, 2 with bath or shower & wc, 2 sharing shower & wc.

Price: 260 Frs for two.

Meals: 100 Frs, including coffee.

Closed: Never.

From Soissons, N2 direction Paris. At 4th main crossroads, D172 left direction Chaudun. About 4km on, D177 left to Léchelle. (1 hour from Paris.)
Michelin Map No: 237-9

Entry no: 55   Map No: 4

Jacques & Nicole MAURICE
Hameau de Léchelle
02200 Berzy le Sec
Aisne
Tel: (0)3 23 74 83 29
Fax: (0)3 23 74 82 47

The house is 800 years old – utterly splendid and a great place to escape from the pressures of modern hecticity. One of the three tower rooms has a Louis XV stone fireplace and a pale blue bathroom. Another huge old room has the usual fireplace, bedstead with family crest, wooden floor with rug. The *salon* has a 1567 painted ceiling, a huge Renaissance fireplace with family crest, formal chairs and sofas, desk and table. It is all very grand but your hosts are down-to-earth and charming people. Guests have admired the fantastic buildings and loved the warm welcome. *Pets by arrangement.*

Rooms: 4 doubles, each with bath or shower & wc.

Price: 480-530 Frs for two.

Meals: Choice 7-20km.

Closed: January & February.

Ardennes – Champagne

The angel of Reims smiles eternally upon the Kings of France anointed in his Cathedral and upon the incomprehending soldier slain in the battlefields.
And the ephemeral bubbles burst on.

From Reims, N46 then N47 direction Luxembourg; go through Vouziers to Buzancy, turn right onto D12 and follow signs.
Michelin Map No: 241-18

Entry no: 56   Map No: 5

Jacques & Véronique de MEIXMORON
Château de Landreville
08240 Bayonville
Ardennes
Tel: (0)3 24 30 04 39
Fax: (0)3 24 30 04 39

An honest place, not a whiff of pretension (as we are fond of saying), and authentically itself. It has only one window, whereas popular prejudice (as Dickens would have it) runs in favour of more, such frugality is an attractive rarity these days. This humble abode gives poignancy to Oscar Wilde's dictum that it is always nice to be expected and not to arrive. It is the sort of place where you wash the soap after you have taken a bath. But the owners are the main reason for its inclusion; they are rarely there.

Rooms: 1 'multifunctional' duplex with original trough bath.

Price: 50 Frs for two, no breakfast.

Meals: Self cater or little choice in village.

Closed: January-December.

Your hosts recently converted the farm stables and handed the farm over to their son but there are still cows grazing and grandchildren come and go easily. Two rooms have their own ground-floor entrance; the third is upstairs in the main house; all three are done in brave contemporary colours that set off the mix of old and new furniture perfectly: bright and pleasing with lovely linen, good mattresses, clean-cut bathrooms. Madame is fun and an excellent cook (lots of organic and farm-grown ingredients), Monsieur is a whizz on local history; both are proud of their country heritage, wonderful with children and deeply committed to 'real B&B'. Great value.

Rooms: 1 double, 1 suite for 4, 1 quadruple, each with shower & wc.

Price: 220 Frs for two.

Meals: 80 Frs, including wine & coffee.

Closed: Never.

From Calais take A26 S. After 35 km left towards Rouen then immediately right direction St Sauveur les Moutons on D425bis. Cross railway track, river and 3 fields – Can be tricky to find (follow the electricity poles).

Entry no: 57   Map No: 5

Pierre de la TERRE
La Bergerie
51206 Atelier en Champs
Marne
Tel: (0)3 55 66 77 88

*From A4, exit Ste Menehould on D982 (382 on some maps) to Givry en Argonne. There, left on D54 to Les Charmontois (9km).
Michelin Map No: 241-26*

Entry no: 58   Map No: 5

M & Mme Bernard PATIZEL
5 rue St Bernard
51330 Les Charmontois
Marne
Tel: (0)3 26 60 39 53
Fax: (0)3 26 60 39 53
e-mail: nicole.patizel@wanadoo.fr
Web: www.chez.com/patizel

So beautiful behind its sober façade: a generously hospitable marriage of old and new, French and English. Didier, house-restorer supreme, makes champagne. Imogen, warm, relaxed and informed, has done designing, book-binding, teaching... and now runs two small children and this fine *Champenoise* house. They have decorated the guest rooms to great effect: two have space, light and luxurious sitting room/bathrooms; the smaller has a richly-canopied bed, a green and pink oriental atmosphere and a superb claw-footed bath. Work continues on the ground floor, Imogen is an excellent cook, champagne is served at dinner. You'll want to stay for ever.

Rooms: 2 doubles, 1 twin, each with bathroom.

Price: 270 Frs for two.

Meals: 140 Frs, including champagne & wine, by arrangement. Must book.

Closed: 2 weeks in September.

From Calais follow motorway for Reims. At Reims follow signs to Epernay, then at Epernay for Chalons en Champagne, then for Avize. In Avize follow signs for Lycée Viticole, house is opposite Lycée. Michelin Map No: 237-23

Entry no: 59   Map No: 4

Imogen & Didier PIERSON WHITAKER
Le Vieux Cèdre
14 route d'Oger
51190 Avize, Marne
Tel: (0)3 26 57 77 04
Fax: (0)3 26 57 97 97
e-mail: champagnepiersonwhitaker@worldnet.fr

It is so quiet here that the grandfather clock inside and the doves cooing in the trees outside can seem deafening. A timeless feel wafts through the newish house from that grandfather clock, the pretty, traditionally-decorated bedrooms (*lits bateau*, Louis Philippe furniture), the piano and the old Singer sewing machine in its corner. Huguette and her husband, who runs the beef and cattle farm, are generous hosts offering traditional unpretentious farmhouse hospitality. You can opt for champagne from their son-in-law's nearby vineyard, with a meal to match the quality of the wine and the welcome.

Rooms: 2 doubles, 1 triple, each with bath or shower & wc.

Price: 250-270 Frs for two.

Meals: 105 Frs (with wine) or 150 Frs (with champagne), including aperitif & coffee.

Closed: Never.

Gite space for 14 people.

From Châlons en Champagne RD933 to Bergères (29km) then right on D9 to Vertus. Through Vertus and left; follow signs to La Madeleine for 3km. Michelin Map No: 237-23

Entry no: 60   Map No: 4

Huguette CHARAGEAT
La Madeleine
51130 Vertus
Marne
Tel: (0)3 26 52 11 29
Fax: (0)3 26 59 22 09

You will be welcomed to this impressive 17th-century farm with its two courtyards by a wonderful woman who really understands hospitality and good food: it is all simple and real. The converted stables have a living room with original mangers, log fire and kitchenette, then steep stairs up to two simply-decorated, warmly-carpeted, roof-lit rooms. The third room, in the main house, is bigger and cosier with old furniture and a view of the pond. You breakfast next to the kitchen but dine at the big old table in the family *salon* on home-produced fruit, vegetables, eggs and poultry. Fabulous walks to be had in the great Forêt du Gault nearby.

Rooms: 1 twin, 1 double, 1 triple, all with shower or bath & wc.

Price: 220 Frs for two.

Meals: 95 Frs, including wine & coffee.

Closed: Never.

Cows, chickens, ducks, guinea fowl, turkeys, donkey, sheep, goats... children love it here, and love the higgledy-piggledy buildings too; school groups come for visits. The house is full of beams, the rooms are full of swags, flowers and antique bits, and one bathroom is behind a curtain. Our readers have loved the house, the family and the food. Little English is spoken but the welcome is so exceptional, the generosity so genuine, that communication is easy. Superb outings in the area for all.

Rooms: 1 suite with shower & wc; 3 doubles, each with bath & wc (1 curtained off).

Price: 275-335 Frs for two.

Meals: 140 Frs, including wine & coffee.

Closed: Never.

From Calais A26 to St Quentin; D1 to Montmirail then D373 direction Sézanne for 7km. On leaving Le Gault left at silo; signposted.
Michelin Map No: 237-22

Entry no: 61   Map No: 4

Nicole & Guy BOUTOUR
Ferme de Désiré
51210 Le Gault Soigny
Marne
Tel: (0)3 26 81 60 09
Fax: (0)3 26 81 67 95

From Epernay, D51 towards Sézanne. At Baye, just before church, right onto D343. At Bannay turn right. Farm is before small bridge.
Michelin Map No: 237-22

Entry no: 62   Map No: 4

Muguette & Jean-Pierre CURFS
Ferme de Bannay
51270 Bannay
Marne
Tel: (0)3 26 52 80 49
Fax: (0)3 26 59 47 78
Web: www.sawdays.co.uk

The guest rooms, and the terrace where you breakfast in summer, of this old family farmhouse (rebuilt in the '20s after war destruction), look out onto the quiet courtyard: you can't hear the road, only the sound of the two running springs. So sleep till 11 if you like – that's the latest Nathalie serves freshly-squeezed fruit juice and masses of croissants. The vast bedrooms are comfortably furnished and have everything you need. Éric works at the Crédit Agricole (bank) on the other side of the road. With their three children, they are a delightful young family, and there's a pony in the field next door.

Rooms: 4 suites for 3/4, each with shower & wc.

Price: 290 Frs for two.

Meals: Restaurant in village.

Closed: Never.

These independent champagne growers delight in showing guests round vineyards and cellars (tastings included). Through the flower-filled courtyard and up a private staircase, the bright, airy attic bedroom has beams, dormers, matching handmade curtains and covers, and wicker furniture. Breakfast is served in the lovely old family house with fine jams made by Madame. She's a wonderful woman who started doing B&B for champagne buyers who did not want to leave after tasting! Guests have use of a fridge and freezer – great for picnic provisions. *Latest bookings taken at 7pm.*

Rooms: 3 doubles, all with bath or shower & wc.

Price: 250-260 Frs for two.

Meals: Choice in Fismes, 11km.

Closed: 2 weeks in August.

Gîte space for 6 people.

From Reims RD980 SW to Ville en Tardenois (20km). House in town centre opposite Crédit Agricole (bank). Michelin Map No: 237-10

Entry no: 63   Map No: 4

Nathalie & Eric LELARGE
Ferme du Grand Clos
51170 Ville en Tardenois
Marne
Tel: (0)3 26 61 83 78
Fax: (0)3 26 50 01 32

From Epernay N51 N towards Reims for 4km then left on D386 towards Fismes for 30km. At Crugny left on D23 to Brouillet. House with Ariston Fils sign on right; Gîtes de France sign. Michelin Map No: 237-10

Entry no: 64   Map No: 4

Remi & Marie ARISTON
Champagne Ariston Fils
4 & 8 Grande Rue
51170 Brouillet
Marne
Tel: (0)3 26 97 43 46
Fax: (0)3 26 97 49 34
e-mail: champagne.ariston.fils@wanadoo.fr

The Harlauts produce their own marque of champagne and, although bottles are for sale, it is for the first-class food and the atmosphere that guests return. Dinner is eaten with the family, either in the dining room, or on the terrace overlooking the garden. Your hosts love entertaining and are keen to provide good value. There are steep narrow stairs up to the warm, uncluttered guest rooms which share a loo – a minor concern as everything is as spotless as it should be. The views are great over the plains of Reims. Try the champagne cakes.

Rooms: 1 double with shower & wc; 1 double, 1 twin, each with shower & washbasin, sharing wc.

Price: 230-260 Frs for two.

Meals: 120 Frs, including wine & coffee.

Closed: January & Easter.

From A26 exit 15 Reims La Neuvillette onto N44 towards Laon for 2km. Left to St Thierry. House in village. Michelin Map No: 237-11

Entry no: 65   Map No: 4

Evelyne & Remi HARLAUT
5 rue du Paradis
51220 St Thierry
Marne
Tel: (0)3 26 03 13 75
Fax: (0)3 26 03 03 65
e-mail: contact@champagne-harlaut.fr
Web: www.champagne-harlaut.fr

The key to the local church is with Madame; do look round it. Her own house is the medieval priory with two 11th-century towers... superb. She is an extremely friendly, busy, chatty young mother, originally from Quebec and definitely French-speaking, with teenage children, a farming husband and parents-in-law 'through the wall'. Splendid rooms: the ground floor one, for example, is enormous, with a huge stone fireplace, two queen beds, wattle walls between great timbers, a wooden roof with more beams, a basic bathroom. Breakfast is superb. "Better than any five-star hotel on all counts", said one reader.

Rooms: 2 quadruples, 2 triples, 1 family room for 5, each with bath or shower & wc.

Price: 220-270 Frs for two.

Meals: Restaurant 5 mins walk.

Closed: Never.

Gîte space for 15 people.

From Troyes N71 SE for 22km. In Fouchères left onto D81 direction Poligny; house just behind church. Michelin Map No: 237-48

Entry no: 66   Map No: 9

M & Mme Gilles BERTHELIN
Le Prieuré
Place de l'Église
10260 Fouchères
Aube
Tel: (0)3 25 40 98 09
Fax: (0)3 25 40 98 09

A fish farm! 500 fishers may gather, on Sundays, to catch trout in the spring water that feeds the ponds. The secluded old mill buildings house two owner families, a fish tasting and takeaway restaurant, several guest rooms and 50 tons of live fish. Breakfast and *table d'hôtes* are shared with your enthusiastic hosts – they created this place from nothing 40 years ago – in the big beamy restaurant (groups come for speciality lunches). Bedrooms under the eaves are compact, small-windowed, simply furnished, prettily decorated in rustic or granny style, the larger annexe rooms are more modern. Great fun for children. Good English spoken.

Rooms: 4 doubles, 1 suite, each with bath & wc.

Price: 360 Frs for two.

Meals: 115 Frs, including wine & coffee.

Closed: Never.

From Paris A5 exit 19 onto N60 to Estissac. In village, right on Rue Pierre Brossolette; mill at end of lane (1km). Michelin Map No: 237-34

Entry no: 67   Map No: 8

Edouard-Jean & Chantal MESLEY
Domaine du Moulin d'Eguebaude
10190 Estissac
Aube
Tel: (0)3 25 40 42 18
Fax: (0)3 25 40 40 92
Web: www.sawdays.co.uk

An irresistible spot for recharging the batteries – for walkers, bird-watchers, fishermen (there's a river and magnificent mature parkland) and architecture buffs – the local half-timbered churches are considered one of the 100 most beautiful attractions in France. Afternoon tea is served in the elegantly panelled *salon*; later, dinner, eaten either communally or separately, awaits you – possibly with home-raised boar or home-fished carp but not with your hosts, delightful as they are: they prefer to concentrate on the cooking which is good *cuisine maison*. Bedrooms are comfortable and attractive. *Children over seven welcome.*

Rooms: 2 doubles, 2 twins, 1 suite, all with bath or shower & wc.

Price: 290-350 Frs for two.

Meals: 150 Frs, including wine & coffee.

Closed: Never.

From Troyes, D960 to Brienne, D400 towards St Dizier. At Louze, D182 to Longeville then D174 towards Boulancourt; house on left at 1st crossroads. Michelin Map No: 241-34

Entry no: 68   Map No: 5

Philippe & Christine VIEL-CAZAL
Domaine de Boulancourt
Boulancourt
52220 Montier en Der
Haute-Marne
Tel: (0)3 25 04 60 18
Fax: (0)3 25 04 60 18
Web: www.sawdays.co.uk

If your family are straining at the leash, bring them here to let off steam: there is riding (and space for 15 guest horses), pony-trapping, walking, mountain-biking, archery, orienteering and a bit of gentle ping-pong. This is a most friendly place, simple and easy, with breakfasts (home-made jams, fresh brioche, lots of coffee) available until midday. The rooms are right for the price, warmly carpeted (after the corridor upstairs with its 'artexed' walls and 'lino' floor) with good storage space. You dine well in the nearby village (the Mayoress is the chef).

Rooms: 3 doubles, 1 twin sharing shower & wc.

Price: 190 Frs for two.

Meals: Restaurant 3km.

Closed: Never.

Gîte space for 19 people.

The bedrooms are named after members of the family who lived here before the Poopes: while Evelyne and Michel were restoring it they found the family photographs which inspired the decoration of each room. They clearly adore their life as B&B owners and go to immense trouble to make you feel comfortable and at home. Breakfast is as local as you can get – yoghurt from the farm, honey from the village and Evelyne's home-made jam all feature, while dinner may include such delicacies as blue cheese tart with artichokes or flamed turkey; Michel is chief pastry-cook.

Rooms: 1 double, 1 twin each with shower, sharing wc; 1 triple, 1 suite, each with shower & wc.

Price: 220-300 Frs for two.

Meals: 75 Frs, including wine.

Closed: Never.

From Langres, N19 towards Vesoul. Left on D460 towards Bourbonne; right on D34; 3rd left to Velles. Through village to grass triangle; house on left. Michelin Map No: 241-48

Entry no: 69   Map No: 9

Alain & Christine ROUSSELOT
Les Randonnées du Précheny
52500 Velles
Haute-Marne
Tel: (0)3 25 88 85 93
Fax: (0)3 25 88 85 93

From A31 exit 7 to North Langres then N19 E direction Vesoul for 30km. Right at Chambres d'Hôtes sign to Pressigny; house just after pond on left. Michelin Map No: 241-51

Entry no: 70   Map No: 9

Evelyne & Michel POOPE
Maison Perrette
24 rue Augustin Massin
52500 Pressigny
Haute-Marne
Tel: (0)3 25 88 80 50
Fax: (0)3 25 88 80 49
Web: www.sawdays.co.uk

'Grandma's Fields' are surrounded by vast views across lakes, woods and hills. The house is like a chalet, all warm, glowing wood. Here, it's bed and breakfast PLUS afternoon tea and cake... and apparently Madame's chocolate-and-cherry is to die for. This is a quiet, bookish house (no telly), the perfect spot for a holiday of walking, swimming with the trout in the pond near the house, or reading. Go mushrooming in autumn and spring and cook your catch in Madame's kitchen where you also eat a breakfast which can be French, German or English, to taste. Supremely peaceful house, place and person.

Rooms: 2 doubles, sharing bathroom.

Price: 350 Frs for two & afternoon tea.

Meals: Use of kitchen & barbecue. Restaurants in Senones 2km.

Closed: Never.

From Strasbourg A352 W then N420 to St Blaise la Roche (45km); right on D424 14km towards Senones to La Petite Raon; right after church towards Moussey; 3rd left (after café) then left, left and left to house.
Michelin Map No: 242-27

Entry no: 71   Map No: 6

Judith LOTT
Les Champs Grandmère
Thiamont
88210 La Petite Raon
Vosges
Tel: (0)3 29 57 68 08
Fax: (0)3 29 57 68 83
e-mail: judelott@aol.com

Lorraine – Alsace

Storks still build their messy nests on the chimney stacks of breweries and biscuit factories where women once wore the giant bow as their traditional headdress.

This is an everlasting project, so chat to Monsieur as he assiduously restores the house to its former glory – more rooms and bathrooms have been redecorated, some bits are still waiting – and enjoy Madame's charming affability, the goodnight chocolates and the kettle kit for the morning. There are elegant terraces, a super garden, stylish furniture to impress you, lots of religion on view (bedside Bibles are French Catholic, not American Gideon), a genuine welcome to win you over. The house is beside a fairly busy road, so traffic noise may intrude, and some shower/loo rooms are pretty tight.

Rooms: 2 doubles, 1 twin, 1 triple, 1 suite with kitchenette & garden, all with shower & wc.

Price: 250-300 Frs for two.

Meals: Choice locally & self-catering in suite.

Closed: Never.

Gîte space for 7 people.

From A4, St Menehould exit onto N3 direction Verdun-Chalons. House is signposted in La Vignette, the hamlet before Les Islettes.
Michelin Map No: 241-22

Entry no: 72   Map No: 5

M & Mme Léopold CHRISTIAENS
Villa des Roses
La Vignette, Les Islettes
55120 Clermont en Argonne
Meuse
Tel: (0)3 26 60 81 91
Fax: (0)3 26 60 23 09
Web: www.sawdays.co.uk

There is now an 'artists' path' to explore in the nearby forest and a golf practice area laid out by Monsieur in the garden. They are very proud of their house and, although renovation may have hidden two centuries of history, it has produced very big, plush, slightly hotel-like guest rooms; the suite even has its own television and telephone... Dinner is authentic, however: a chance to sample some of the region's best dishes (terrines, *magret*, home-made pastries); Madame will join you for dessert and a chat. An excellent stopover between the ferries and Germany.

Rooms: 2 doubles, each with shower & wc; 1 suite with bath, shower & wc.

Price: 350-500 Frs for two.

Meals: 160 Frs, including wine & coffee.

Closed: Never.

From Reims A4 exit 'Voie Sacrée' on N35 towards Bar le Duc. At Chaumont sur Aire, D902 left to Longchamps sur Aire then D121 left to Thillombois. House is next to château.
Michelin Map No: 241-27

Entry no: 73   Map No: 5

Lise TANCHON
Le Clos du Pausa
Rue du Château
55260 Thillombois
Meuse
Tel: (0)3 29 75 07 85
Fax: (0)3 29 75 00 72
Web: www.sawdays.co.uk

A most interesting couple: he's a retired French architect (who's done wonders in the kitchen), she's a Polish painter (work in progress on the easel), patchworker (her bedcovers adorn your room) and dancer. They are both passionate about the environment and keen to chat over dinner. It is good news, too, for vegetarians who like a change: Alina is a 'veggie' and will rustle up a warm red *borsch* or a dish of *pierogi* (vegetable ravioli) though her talent stretches to delicious meaty things and home-made bread too. An excellent and friendly house.

Rooms: 1 twin with shower & wc.

Price: 270 Frs for two.

Meals: 100 Frs (meat or fish) or 75 Frs (vegetarian), including wine & coffee.

Closed: Never.

Clearly not the place to stay if you want to be modern: some of it was part of the 13th-century defensive ring around Metz. It is now a typical farmhouse with 110 acres of cereal fields. Brigitte relishes her role as hostess, does it with great talent and makes friends easily. She also cooks superb, largely organic, meals and keeps goats, rabbits, a donkey and dog. All the bedrooms are in another building, filled with her own paintings. There is a handsome dining room with great beams; try the local Moselle wine. A wonderful family and a friendly village.

Rooms: 1 triple, 1 double, each with bath & wc; 1 twin, 1 triple, each with shower, sharing wc.

Price: 300 Frs for two.

Meals: Restaurants 4km.

Closed: November-March.

From Metz D3 NE towards Bouzonville for about 21km, then right on D53a to Burtoncourt. House on left in main street.
Michelin Map No: 242-10

Entry no: 74   Map No: 5

Alina & Gérard CAHEN
51 rue Lorraine
57220 Burtoncourt
Moselle
Tel: (0)3 87 35 72 65
Fax: (0)3 87 35 72 65

South of Metz on A31 Féy exit 29; right at junction; do not go into Féy but straight on for Cuvry. Farm on edge of village past Mairie; signposted.
Michelin Map No: 242-13

Entry no: 75   Map No: 5

Brigitte & Jean-François MORHAIN
Ferme de Haute-Rive
57420 Cuvry
Moselle
Tel: (0)3 87 52 50 08
Fax: (0)3 87 52 60 20

This house, built in 1750, has a chequered history: once a bistro then a watermill, it was destroyed in the war. Louis's father restored the wheel. Inside, the house – deeply modernised, with lots of new wood and no particular trimmings – is a bit out of kilter with the charming exterior but it has very clean, comfortable rooms (showers curtained off from bedrooms) and a decent kitchen for guests' use. Breakfast, served in two large studio-style portraits. Madame has three children and is cheerful, hospitable and talkative.

Rooms: 1 double, 2 triples, all with shower & wc.

Price: 220 Frs for two.

Meals: Self-catering.

Closed: All year.

Family château life is here: rooms, not big (apart from the twin) or super-luxurious, have the patina of long history in their 18th and 19th-century furniture (carved armoires, *Voltaire* armchairs, pretty writing desks) and the softness of bygone days in bedhead draperies, pastel fabrics and plush. The real style is in the utterly French many-chaired *salon* and the dining room – reached through halls and hunting trophies – with its huge square table and man-sized ceramic stove. Here you may share splendid meals with your lively, intelligent hosts – Monsieur a mine of local history, Madame skilfully attentive to all. And always fresh flowers.

Rooms: 3 doubles, 3 twins, each with bath & wc.

Price: 590 Frs for two.

Meals: 200 Frs, excluding wine.

Closed: 15 October-15 April.

Gîte space for 10 people.

From A4 exit on N61 direction Sarreguemines then onto N62 to Rohrbach. There right on D35 direction Bining/Rahling. In village 1st right (after small bridge) then right again; signposted.
Michelin Map No: 242-15

Entry no: 76   **Map No:** 6

Louis & Anne BACH
2 rue du Vieux Moulin
57410 Rahling
Moselle
Tel: (0)3 87 09 86 85

From Nancy, N74 towards Sarreguemines & Château Salins. At Burthecourt crossroads, D38 to Dieuzé, then D999 south; after 5km, left on D199F and then right on D999G to the château.
Michelin Map No: 242-18

Entry no: 77   **Map No:** 6

Livier & Marie BARTHÉLÉMY
Château d'Alteville
Tarquimpol
57260 Dieuze, Moselle
Tel: (0)3 87 86 92 40
Fax: (0)3 87 86 02 05
e-mail: chateau.alteville@caramail.com
Web: www.sawdays.co.uk

The gentle-mannered, owners live in another house but are present, attentive hosts. Their pride and joy is Monsieur's woodwork: he has built these rooms in the old stables, using different timbers, fitting shower rooms ingeniously into the space available, making stairs, delicately painting the eaves. There is a quiet courtyard with garden; breakfast, with fresh juice, home-made jam and cakes, is in a room by the road. Rooms sparkle and English-speaking offspring are home after 8pm – ring then if you need to! (but not too late).

Rooms: 2 duplex, 3 double, all with shower (1 behind curtain) & wc.

Price: 250-310 Frs for two.

Meals: Strasbourg 12km. Self-catering in duplexes.

Closed: Never.

Gîte space for 11 people.

From A4 exit 48 on N63 dir. Vendenheim/Strasbourg. Right on D64 dir. Lampertheim. At Pfulgriesheim, right on D31 to Pfettisheim. In village follow main road; signed. Michelin Map No: 242-20

Marie-Célestine GASS
La Maison du Charron
15 rue Principale
67370 Pfettisheim
Bas-Rhin
Tel: (0)3 88 69 60 35
Fax: (0)3 88 69 77 96

So close to expensive but gorgeous Strasbourg, yet such good value. You are also right at the start of the *Route des Vins*, in the heart of a pretty Alsatian village. The house used to be a working farm, producing rosé as well as milk, but your hosts have now retired and enjoy having more time for their guests. Although on a fairly busy main road its bedrooms are at the back where it's usually quiet; they are simple, small, yet comfortable. Marie teaches German; Paul, the ex-farmer, serves the breakfast in the garden or in the dining room with its brown tiles and blue walls. A great place to know in Alsace.

Rooms: 3 doubles, each with shower & wc.

Price: 200-220 Frs for two.

Meals: Restaurants in village.

Closed: Never.

Gîte space for 6 people.

From A4, exit 45 onto N404/N4 towards Strasbourg for 16km. Farm is in middle of the village of Marlenheim on left, before post office. Michelin Map No: 242-19

Paul & Marie-Claire GOETZ
86 rue du Général de Gaulle
67520 Marlenheim
Bas-Rhin
Tel: (0)3 88 87 52 94

Readers have loved this place, and so do children – the house, the fun and *Le Petit Train* that tours the striking old village and the vineyards. The first Ruhlmann wine-grower built his lovely Alsatian house in 1688. Wine buffs will enjoy visiting the wine cellar and non-drinkers can taste the sweet water springing straight from the Vosges hills. The charming rooms under the sloping roof have new carpets and old family furniture; breakfast is served in a huge room full of relics: barrels, a wine press, a grape basket, a china stove. And you will meet the whole fun-loving family.

Rooms: 2 doubles, each with shower, sharing wc.

Price: 230 Frs for two, including wine-tasting.

Meals: 6 choices within walking distance.

Closed: December-March.

Young Madame Engel greets you with the warmest welcome and the finest Alsace cooking – she really loves receiving guests. The peaceful Swiss-style chalet, with breathtaking views of the mountains and forests, is just the place to enjoy both. All you need to do is take a deep breath, forget everything – and relax. The rooms are simply comfortable with signs of Monsieur's upholstering skills, geraniums cascading from every window, the views pouring in and a guest entrance. Breakfast tables are laden with goodies – try the home-made organic fruit jams and *kougelopf* (Alsace cake to the uninitiated).

Rooms: 2 doubles, 1 twin, each with shower & wc.

Price: 285-300 Frs for two.

Meals: Choice 4km.

Closed: January.

Dambach is about 8km north of Sélestat on D35. House in village centre, about equidistant between the two town gates on main road.
Michelin Map No: 242-27

Entry no: 80   Map No: 6

Jean-Charles & Laurence
RUHLMANN
34 rue Maréchal Foch
67650 Dambach la Ville, Bas-Rhin
Tel: (0)3 88 92 41 86
Fax: (0)3 88 92 61 81
e-mail: ruhlman.schutz@wanadoo.fr
Web: www.sawdays.co.uk

From Colmar, A35 and N83 towards Sélestat (exit 11) then N59 and D424 to Villé; D697 to Dieffenbach au Val. Careful: ask for exact address as 2 other Engels do B&B!
Michelin Map No: 242-27

Entry no: 81   Map No: 6

Doris ENGEL-GEIGER
Maison Fleurie
19 route de Neuve Église
Dieffenbach au Val
67220 Villé, Bas-Rhin
Tel: (0)3 88 85 60 48
Fax: (0)3 88 85 60 48
Web: www.sawdays.co.uk

Madame has adorned her home with hand-painted stencils (she'll teach you if you like). She and her artistic daughter often paint quietly together on the landing. The top-floor pine-clad sitting room is a delight, like being in a boat. Big cosy bedrooms, dinner with your hosts and possibly their daughters or son plus a few friends prove they know about conviviality... and Madame should charge extra for her conversation! "Lucky is the traveller who stops here," said the reader who led us to Le Montanjus. Nearby are golf and skiing and the *Ballons des Vosges* Regional Park.

Rooms: 1 double, 1 suite for 3, each with shower & wc.

Price: 305 Frs for two.

Meals: 110 Frs (weekdays) & 130 Frs (weekend), including wine & coffee.

Closed: Never.

Gite space for 4 people.

From A36 exit 14 Belfort Nord on N83 dir. Mulhouse. In Les Errues, left dir. Anjoutey and on to Étueffont. At r'bout right dir. Rougemont and left at first bend; house at end.
Michelin Map No: 243-10

Entry no: **82**   Map No: 10

Astride & Daniel ELBERT
Le Montanjus
8 rue de la Chapelle
90170 Etueffont
Territoire-de-Belfort
Tel: (0)3 84 54 68 63
e-mail: daniel.elbert@wanadoo.fr

In the big house of this tiny village, fine materials and craftsmanship breathe elegance and loving care. Superbly personal taste and gentle light, glowing old floors and delicate mouldings make the generous spaces utterly seductive. Roland combs the auction rooms for lovely rugs, little bronzes, old mirrors and modern paintings; Fabienne hangs thick curtains, places pretty desks, solid oak or carved walnut armoires and soft sofas in vast pale-walled bedrooms. He gardens passionately, she cooks brilliantly – remarkable hosts, interior designers of much flair, they are fun and excellent company. With super-luxury bathrooms to boot, this is value indeed.

Rooms: 1 double/quadruple & 2 suites (2nd double in each is a sofabed), each with bath or shower & wc.

Price: 350-400 Frs for two.

Meals: 130 Frs, including wine & coffee, by arrangement.

Closed: Never.

From Troyes A31 exit 6 (Langres-Sud) through Longeau, onto D67, through Gray towards Besançon. Cult is on right 21km beyond Gray. Follow signs in village.
Michelin Map No: 243-18

Entry no: **83**   Map No: 9

Mme Fabienne LEGO-DEIBER
Les Egrignes
70150 Cult
Haute-Saône
Tel: (0)3 84 31 92 06
Fax: (0)3 84 31 92 06

Once part of the 15th-century fortress of Pesmes, one of France's prettiest villages, it is vast. Guy bought only walls then built a house within them: it is his pride and joy. The staircase is grey-painted concrete with a wooden bannister; some of the rooms are magnificent, the sort you pay to visit on a wet Sunday afternoon. As the bedrooms are so huge the furniture can appear sparse, but they are colourful and stylish. There is a library plus a small *salon*, a 200m² reception room, a boat on the river and... too much to describe in this space. *Children over five welcome.*

Rooms: 4 doubles, 1 twin, 1 triple, each with bath or shower & wc.

Price: 400-450 Frs for two.

Meals: Choice 2 minutes away on foot.

Closed: Mid-October-mid-March.

From A36 exit 2 onto D475 to Pesmes (20km). House is at top of village on left.
Michelin Map No: 243-18

Entry no: **84**   Map No: 9

M & Mme Guy HOYET
La Maison Royale
70140 Pesmes
Haute-Saône
Tel: (0)3 84 31 23 23
Fax: (0)3 84 31 23 23
Web: www.sawdays.co.uk

As part of its 100m² suite, this château has one of the most extraordinary bathrooms this side of the Saône: panels hung with old engravings, a sunken bath and an Italian chandelier contribute to an atmosphere of elegant luxury it would be hard to match, even with five stars; bedroom and sitting room are just as amazing. All this and a family feel! Antiques, attention to detail, a charmingly formal hostess with an easy laugh, make this a really special place. Dinner, carefully chosen to suit guests' tastes (if you want snails, you'll have to ask) is exquisitely presented on Gien porcelain and served on the terrace in summer.

Rooms: 1 suite with bathroom.

Price: 420 Frs for two.

Meals: 100 Frs, including wine; 50 Frs light supper, both by arrangement.

Closed: September-mid-May.

From A36 exit 3 onto D67 towards Gray 35km. Entering Gray, right on D474 then fork left on D13 to Beaujeu and Motey sur Saône. There left to Mercey; signposted in village.
Michelin Map No: 242-41

Entry no: **85**   Map No: 9

Bernadette JANTET
Le Château
70130 Mercey sur Saône
Haute-Saône
Tel: (0)3 84 67 07 84

La vie de château for all? This fabulously renovated neo-classical house and its stylish owners can be unhesitatingly recommended for an authentic taste of château living. All rooms, with proper period furniture, engravings and family portraits, look out over the fine *Directoire*-style park. Guests have their own breakfast and sitting rooms. Madame, as elegant as her house, unintrusively provides for all and Monsieur, whose pride and joy is the park, is pleased to be told that 10 years of painstaking work have been worthwhile. They are most welcoming in English that is adequate but not fluent.

A room under the roof, a lovely view of orchards and meadows, a brook to sing you to sleep. Your organic-wine-grower hosts are the gentlest, most generous couple imaginable and their son runs wine-tasting sessions for them. Their fairly average home – is distinguished by that wonderful welcome, a fine, carved dresser, their delightful art gallery (Madame's embroidery, other artists' paintings) and a tempting garden at the back. Anyone may play the piano here or golf just down the road.

Rooms: 3 doubles, 1 suite, all with bath & wc.

Price: 600-700 Frs for two.

Meals: Auberge 4km.

Closed: Never.

Rooms: 1 twin, 1 suite for 4, both with shower & wc.

Price: 250 Frs for two.

Meals: 70 Frs, incl. coffee (wine 40 Frs).

Closed: Never.

From Besançon, N73 to St Vit. Then left through town and right onto D203 to Salans; château in village.
Michelin Map No: 243-18

In Lons le Saunier towards Chalon/Bourg en Bresse. After SNCF station left on D117 dir. Macournay, D41 to Vernantois. Left before church & follow signs.
Michelin Map No: 243-30

Entry no: 86   Map No: 9

Entry no: 87   Map No: 9

Béatrice & Claus OPPELT
Château de Salans
39700 Salans
Jura
Tel: (0)3 84 71 16 55
Fax: (0)3 84 79 41 54

Monique & Michel RYON
Rose Art
8 rue Lacuzon
39570 Vernantois
Jura
Tel: (0)3 84 47 17 28
Fax: (0)3 84 47 17 28

A lovely spot, with the Loire at the bottom of the garden and a fascinating host. Monsieur has retired to share his time between his house and his guests. He had an English nanny so is at home with the English language and culture and enjoys discussing his many interests – the region, its history and architecture, his print and corkscrew collections – over a meal; he's also passionate about cooking (and wine, and art...) The 18th-century, entirely 'lived-in' château has no end of family furniture and treasures, a boat for guests' use and the pilgrim's route (GR 13) passes close by. A chance to sample the pleasing lifestyle of the French provincial aristocracy.

Rooms: 2 doubles, 2 twins, 1 suite for 4, each with bath & wc.

Price: 350-500 Frs for two.

Meals: Dinner 150 Frs including table wine.

Closed: 31 December-1 April.

From Digoin D979 towards Bourbon Lancy for 25km. In St Aubin, 1st left at sign Les Lambeys; house on right.

Michelin Map No: 238-47

Entry no: 88   Map No: 8

Burgundy

St Claude makes the prince of pipes,
Canon Kir mixes his inimitable
vine-fruit nectar,
the fat snail creeps to marry parsley
and garlic,
the best wines fetch fabulous sums in the
courtyards of Beaune: *À table!*

Etienne de BUSSIERRE
Les Lambeys
71140 St Aubin sur Loire
Saône-et-Loire
Tel: (0)3 85 53 92 76

The *chambres d'hôtes* of this former abbey are in the 17th-century pigeon tower and those holes are where the original occupants roosted. It's all pleasingly eccentric and fun; ring at the wrought-iron gates for your young hosts, the easiest of people. There's a ground-floor sitting room with a twin room – ideal for children – off it and in the tower itself is that amazing bathroom with the main bedroom on a mezzanine floor above. Breakfast is a relaxed family affair a short walk through the park in the château kitchen; dinner may be in the graciously faded dining room.

Rooms: 1 quadruple with bath & wc.

Price: 360 Frs for two.

Meals: 150 Frs, including wine.

Closed: Never.

Gîte space for 5 people.

From A6 exit Chalon south, take N6 towards Varrennes le Grand; D6 towards Le Lac de Laives to La Ferté. House is through large iron gates at crossroads marked La Ferté. Press intercom.
Michelin Map No: 243-27

Entry no: 89   Map No: 9

Jacques & Virginie THENARD
Abbaye de la Ferté
71240 St Ambreuil
Saône-et-Loire
Tel: (0)3 85 44 17 96
Fax: (0)3 85 44 17 96
e-mail: thenardjacques@aol.com

A place to die for, and the owner, too, is passionate about it. He is a lovely man, bursting with ideas on further restoration; he also cultivates the vines. The bedrooms, in a renovated building near the main 15th-century château, are newly done (the bigger one is a gem, with superb beams and a vast mezzanine) and plain in the way so many are in France. You have a small veranda on which to sit and admire the view. Breakfast is in the château, which is a delightfully lived-in listed monument. Irresistible.

Rooms: 1 triple, 1 quadruple, each with bath or shower & wc.

Price: 400 Frs for two.

Meals: 5 restaurants within 5km.

Closed: Mid-November-March.

From Tournus D14 W towards Cormatin. House is on this road 2km after Martailly lès Brancion; leave Brancion and La Chapelle on your right.
Michelin Map No: 243-69

Entry no: 90   Map No: 9

Bertrand & Françoise de CHERISEY
Château de Nobles
71700 La Chapelle sous Brancion
Saône-et-Loire
Tel: (0)3 85 51 00 55

A wonderful place for children, who can watch the goats being milked in the clean, enclosed farmyard, even help if they (and the nannies) like. There are horses too. Your hard-working hosts, with two children of their own and sensitive to the needs of families, have made a large family room at the top of the old stone farmhouse. Bathrobes are provided for grown-ups, so everyone feels cared for. All six rooms are sparkling and charmingly simple. People return, not only for the relaxing experience, but also to stock up on the home-made cheeses, mouth-watering jams and local wines that are on sale and available at mealtimes.

Rooms: 2 doubles sharing shower & wc; 2 twins with shower & wc; 2 family suites with shower, wc and kitchen.

Price: 200-330 Frs for two.

Meals: Self-catering in two rooms. Nearby restaurant.

Closed: Never.

From Tournus, D14 direction Cluny. At Chapaize, D314 direction Bissy sous Uxelles. House next to church. Michelin Map No: 243-39

Entry no: 91   Map No: 9

Pascale & Dominique de LA BUSSIÈRE
La Ferme, 71460 Bissy sous Uxelles
Saône-et-Loire
Tel: (0)3 85 50 15 03
Fax: (0)3 85 50 15 03
e-mail: dominique.de-la-bussiere@wanadoo.fr
Web: www.m-fjsolutions.com/BB/

Do you long to know the secrets behind the scenes? You can discover how the theatre really works here, where farmhouse B&B is combined with a thriving theatre and art gallery. In June and July the local group of actor-winegrowers, *La Mère Folle*, founded in 1981 by Jean-Paul, perform in their converted barn. Régine, a musician, helps with productions. Busy, artistic people, they create an atmosphere of relaxed energy, take their B&B very seriously and offer good rooms with comfortable beds, modern décor of pale wood, original beams and, generously, *Grand-père's* excellent cubist paintings.

Rooms: 4 doubles, 1 twin, all with bath or shower & wc.

Price: 290 Frs for two.

Meals: Simple restaurant in village 2km, otherwise 6km.

Closed: Never.

From A6 exit Tournus onto D56 direction Lugny through Chardonnay. 3km after Chardonnay right on D463 & follow signs to Chambres d'Hôtes/Théâtre Champvent. Michelin Map No: 243-39

Entry no: 92   Map No: 9

Régine & Jean-Paul RULLIÈRE
Le Tinailler
Manoir de Champvent
71700 Chardonnay
Saône-et-Loire
Tel: (0)3 85 40 50 23
Fax: (0)3 85 40 50 18
Web: www.sawdays.co.uk

Do wander through the woods and gardens of this 13th-century château – it's beautiful and tours of the cellars and the *Route des Vins* can be arranged (Monsieur is a cellar master). One room, more 'period' with its small four-poster (and more expensive) is in the château, the rest (excellent too) are in the *maison vigneronne*, the old vine workers' cottages. Madame manages with charming efficiency, aperitifs in the cellar are part of the evening ritual and Monsieur may surprise you with an enormous bottle of cognac at dinner (regional food made with home-grown vegetables). A most welcoming place.

Rooms: 2 twins, 2 doubles/twins, 2 triples, all with bath & wc.

Price: 450-600 Frs for two.

Meals: 100 Frs, including coffee.

Closed: January.

Gîte space for 16 people.

From A6 exit at Tournus on D14 through Ozenay towards Marthailly. 600m after Corcelles left at sign Caveau.
Michelin Map No: 243-39

Entry no: 93   Map No: 9

Marie-Laurence FACHON
Maisons Vigneronnes
Château de Messey
71700 Ozenay, Saône-et-Loire
Tel: (0)3 85 51 16 11
Fax: (0)3 85 32 57 30
e-mail: bf@golfenfrance.com
Web: www.demessey.com

The storm felled the great cedar, but not entirely: it now stands magnificently and fittingly guard in the form of St Vincent, patron saint of wine-growers. Father and son run the vineyard (1996 Mâcon Gold Medal for Chardonnay), Madame makes jam and cheese and loves spending time with guests, old and young (they have six grandchildren). All four bedrooms are big, have warm carpets, clean-cut modern furniture and distinctive colour schemes – two pastel, two strong dark – as well as excellent bathrooms. A supremely comfortable, friendly, relaxing place to stay.

Rooms: 2 doubles, 1 twin, 1 triple, all with bath or shower & wc.

Price: 280 Frs for two.

Meals: Self-catering possible.

Closed: Never.

From Tournus, N6 direction Mâcon. After 10km, right on D163 to Uchizy; signposted.
Michelin Map No: 243-39

Entry no: 94   Map No: 9

Mme Annick SALLET
Domaine de l'Arfentière
Route de Chardonnay
71700 Uchizy
Saône-et-Loire
Tel: (0)3 85 40 50 46
Fax: (0)3 85 40 58 05

The view is of the 12th-century church, the house, only 17th-century..., has been renovated with superb attention to detail, a welcoming log fire in winter – and wait till you see the excellent bathrooms. Monsieur is charming, chatty, with lots of tales to tell, and totally French, right down to his cigarettes. He'll take good care of you, will share his love of this famous wine-making region and provide a feast of local produce for breakfast (on the terrace when days are long and warm) – jams, honey, bread, cheeses and pâtés – which should set you up perfectly for a heady day's visit to the vineyards.

Rooms: 2 doubles, each with shower or bath & wc.

Price: 290 Frs for two.

Meals: Excellent restaurant nearby.

Closed: Never.

From Tournus, D14 towards Cormatin. After 12km left on D163 towards Grévilly. After 200m, follow Grévilly on right. Straight on at T-junction. House 100m on left: outside village, just below church.
Michelin Map No: 243-39

Entry no: 95   Map No: 9

Claude DEPREAY
Le Pré Ménot
71700 Grévilly
Saône-et-Loire
Tel: (0)3 85 33 29 92
Fax: (0)3 85 33 02 79
Web: www.sawdays.co.uk

There's an old-world charm to the lovely stones and tumbling geraniums outside, the silk flowers, frilly lampshades and polished furniture inside. The breakfast room is cosily stuffed with bric-a-brac, bedrooms are family-simple. Madame was a florist: she arranges her rooms as if they were bouquets and is always refreshing them; she may put a paper heart on your pillow wishing you *bonne nuit*. She doesn't refuse children but may well be happier if you arrive with a little dog under your arm. She or her husband can do winery visits for non-Francophones. Ask for one of the larger rooms; the smallest feels cramped.

Rooms: 1 suite for 4, 2 doubles, all with bath or shower & wc.

Price: 250-300 Frs for two.

Meals: Good choice 3-5km.

Closed: Winter Sundays.

From N79 exit La Roche Vineuse. Turn left to Chaunay lès Macon (NOT La Roche Vineuse) for 500m, then left direction Sommeré, 1.5km. Up hill following EH signs- house at top of hill on left; bell on wall by gate with 4 big flowerpots.
Michelin Map No: 243-39

Entry no: 96   Map No: 9

Eliane HEINEN
Le Tinailler d'Aléane
Sommeré
71960 La Roche Vineuse
Saône-et-Loire
Tel: (0)3 85 37 80 68
Fax: (0)3 85 37 80 68

There's vast personality and an authentically worn feel to this old manor house. Madame, with her unorthodox sense of humour, is "quite a character" and wants visitors to see it was built by a 19th-century upstart *parvenu* (some delightfully OTT bits) and is now inhabited by artists (watercolours and weavings). Choose activity: cycling, walking, horse-riding; or gentility: contemplate mountain scenery, play the Erard baby grand or browse through the local guides and histories in the library. Super but smallish, old-decorated rooms, fine modern bathrooms. Give Madame time to come to the door – she may be deep in the garden.

Rooms: 1 double with bath, shower & wc; 1 suite for 5 with shower, wc & kitchen.

Price: 250 Frs for two.

Meals: Self-catering in suite; restaurant 5km.

Closed: Never.

Gîte space for 10 people.

From Mâcon, N79 towards Cluny. At Berzé le Châtel, N79 on towards Charolles, then D987 to Trambly. Left past church; house on left.
Michelin Map No: 239-12

Entry no: 97   Map No: 9

François & Florence GAUTHIER
Les Charrières
71520 Trambly
Saône-et-Loire
Tel: (0)3 85 50 43 17
Fax: (0)3 85 50 49 28
e-mail: gauthierflorence@minitel.net
Web: www.sawdays.co.uk

These people are genuine hosts who will easily get through any language barrier. Their engagingly cottagey 19th-century farmhouse has masses of character and space under its sweeping roof – exposed beams and old tiles are part of Monsieur's fine renovation job – and a charming, enthusiastic hostess, keen to provide her guests with authentic country hospitality. Rooms are traditionally decorated and comfortable. There is a pleasant living room with books and games. Breakfast (home-made jams) and dinner are eaten with the family; Madame is Portuguese and will make national specialities if asked – a real treat.

Rooms: 2 doubles, each with shower & wc.

Price: 300 Frs for two.

Meals: 120 Frs, including wine & coffee; children 60 Frs.

Closed: November-Easter.

From Cosne sur Loire, D114 to Cours & St Loup des Bois; veer left on D114; Chauffour is between St Loup and St Vérain; follow signs for Musée de la Machine Agricole then for Chambres d'Hôtes.
Michelin Map No: 231-27

Entry no: 98   Map No: 8

Elvire & René DUCHET
Chez Elvire
Chauffour
58200 St Loup
Nièvre
Tel: (0)3 86 26 20 22

We wished breakfast could be more than once a day – Madame Bürgi's cakes and jams are incomparable and it's all organic and home-made. Indeed, the whole atmosphere of generous, efficient hospitality and rural peace generated by your hosts and their surroundings is exceptional. Bedroom shutters open out to country views and a curved double staircase leads down to a kempt lawn where, rather endearingly, chickens may be roaming. Inside are open fires, antique beds (with antique monogrammed bedclothes!), sympathetic period decorations and an atmosphere of secluded comfort.

Rooms: 6 doubles/twins, each with bath or shower & wc.

Price: 350-420 Frs for two.

Meals: 150 Frs, including wine & coffee, by arrangement. Or in village.

Closed: Never.

Gîte space for 2 people.

From Nevers, D977 to Prémery. There, D977 bis direction Corbigny; St Révérien is 15km on; signposted. Michelin Map No: 238-22

Entry no: 99   Map No: 8

Bernadette BÜRGI & Florent de BEER
La Villa des Prés
58420 St Révérien, Nièvre
Tel: (0)3 86 29 04 57
Fax: (0)3 86 29 65 22
e-mail: contact@villa-des-pres.com
Web: www.villa-des-pres.com

New, energetic owners have made this an 'Equestrian Farm' with horses and ponies for rides or tours of several days. They also rear sheep and run courses for children on discovering country life, and themed weekends such as camping, lambing, map-making/reading. The whole place is being given a fresh look – bright paintwork and cheerful fabrics – but your hosts, who have made the break from city jobs, are keen to keep the overall farm atmosphere. Your children may romp with theirs, you can head for the national mountain bike centre (550km of marked track) or just 3km away you can immerse yourself in water sports. *Overnight farm stopover for 19.*

Rooms: 1 double & pullout beds for children, with shower & wc.

Price: 260 Frs for two.

Meals: 2 restaurants in St Saulge & 1 in Prémery.

Closed: Never.

From Prémery, D38 direction Châtillon en Bazois and St Saulge; signposted Gîte d'Étape at junction of D38 and D181 to St Martin. Michelin Map No: 238-34

Entry no: 100   Map No: 8

Laurence & Philippe KNEUSS
Basse Cour de St Martin
58330 Ste Marie
Nièvre
Tel: (0)3 86 58 35 15
Fax: (0)3 86 58 22 83
e-mail: phkneuss@club-internet.fr

Immaculately restored by the owners, the rooms sport good antique furniture and elegant décor with plenty of interesting wallpaper; the bathrooms are stupendous. Come at the right time of year and as far as your eye can see you'll be surrounded by fields of sunflowers. Your modest, friendly hosts clearly enjoy sharing their 1690s house in its 115 hectares of parkland. They are happy to suggest activities, from visiting local châteaux to lovely canalside walks and pony rides. Monsieur takes English lessons and is keen to flex his linguistic muscles with any willing volunteers – he has an impressive Burgundy accent!

Rooms: 4 doubles, each with bath or shower & wc.

Price: 280-350 Frs for two.

Meals: Self-catering possible; restaurant 5km.

Closed: Never.

If you are looking for a simple 'Deepest France' experience, then leave the nerve-jangling N7 behind for this secluded 19th-century house where basic rooms have wallpapered ceilings, orange bedcovers and bathrooms in partitioned corners. Breakfast is at the long wooden table in the family's marvellous living room, where traditional oak furniture and a log fire create a farmhouse atmosphere. Your welcoming, sociable hosts have years of experience looking after guests. Take advantage of Monsieur's keen knowledge of regional history – he is very erudite and loves his subject – and enjoy Madame's fine dahlia collection.

Rooms: 1 double, 2 twins, all with bath or shower & wc.

Price: 230-300 Frs for two.

Meals: Barbecue possible.

Closed: November-March, except by arrangement.

From Château Chinon, D978 through Châtillon en Bazois direction Nevers. 4km along (past Alluy), after service station, right on D112 towards Bernière; house on left after 1.5km. Michelin Map No: 238-35

Entry no: 101   Map No: 8

Colette & André LEJAULT
Bouteuille
58110 Alluy
Nièvre
Tel: (0)3 86 84 06 65
Fax: (0)3 86 84 03 41
Web: www.sawdays.co.uk

From Nevers, D978 towards Château Chinon. At Châtillon en Bazois, D945 towards Corbigny; left on D259 towards Mont et Marré; farm is 500m along. Michelin Map No: 238-35

Entry no: 102   Map No: 8

Paul & Nicole DELTOUR
Semelin
Mont et Marré
58110 Châtillon en Bazois
Nièvre
Tel: (0)3 86 84 13 94

Such a welcoming place! Meeting guests with a glass of something special reflects the Perreaus' *joie de vivre*: they are wonderful, fun-loving folk, their house and farm full of life, human and animal. It's a farm with a sideline in organic vegetables – Madame, who is a delight, loves her big *potager*, you'll love its fruits. You stay in the old farmhouse's big loft where the bright, finely-furnished bedrooms share a large sitting room and a sweet little breakfast room. Horses and foals in the meadow make a lovely backdrop to the terrace and swimming pool. A tremendous place for enjoying the good things in life.

Rooms: 2 twins, 2 doubles, sharing 2 showers & separate wcs; 1 double with shower & wc.

Price: 300 Frs for two.

Meals: 100 Frs, including wine, by arrangement.

Closed: Never.

Gîte space for 10 people.

From Nevers D978 towards Château Chinon. 3km before Châtillon right on D10 towards Alluy. In St Gratien left on C3 to La Marquise; 800m on right. Michelin Map No: 238-35

Entry no: 103	Map No: 8

Huguette & Noël PERREAU
La Marquise
58340 St Gratien Savigny
Nièvre
Tel: (0)3 86 50 01 02/06 77
Fax: (0)3 86 50 07 14
e-mail: h.collot@aol.fr

The garden goes down to the lake, the sun sets over it, you can borrow the owners' small boat and row on it... or fish, or canoe, or windsurf, and there's a private 'beach' that guests can use – a perfect place to unleash the children. Breakfast includes home-produced honey and *viennoiseries*. The big, bright rooms are French classic with gilt-framed mirrors, round tables in modern bathrooms and that particular type of wallpaper. The atmosphere is relaxedly family and Madame is taking English lessons, but her genuine welcome already transcends the language barrier. A super couple – she is level-headed and he loves to joke.

Rooms: 3 triples, 1 double, all with bath or shower & wc.

Price: 250-300 Frs for two.

Meals: Self-catering possible.

Closed: Never.

Gîte space for 6 people.

From Nevers, D978 to Rouy. There, D132 to Tintury, right on D112 to Fleury (signposted Fertrève) and first right after village. Drive up to lake and turn right; signposted. Michelin Map No: 238-35

Entry no: 104	Map No: 8

Michel & Marie-France GUÉNY
Fleury La Tour
58110 Tintury
Nièvre
Tel: (0)3 86 84 12 42
Fax: (0)3 86 84 12 42

Farmyard heaven. Marie-Georges is an energetic shepherdess and artist and loves to be surrounded by people and animals; there are also horses, dogs, goats, ducks and chickens. She runs 'Nature Days', stencilling, wool-dyeing and other courses in the converted stables, for both adults and children. The Ryans (he English, she French) came to this handsome old country priory to enjoy the countryside and they thrive on activity. Meals are happy, family affairs in the old farm kitchen, with fresh eggs and home-grown vegetables. The large, cosy *chambre d'hôtes* has its own entrance off the courtyard. There's camping here too.

Rooms: 1 suite for 4, with shower & wc.

Price: 260 Frs for two.

Meals: 100 Frs, including wine, by arrangement.

Closed: Never.

Gîte space for 4 people.

From Decise take N81 to Cercy la Tour, then the D26 towards St Benin d'Azy. After 5km turn right to Diennes Aubigny. Large house next to church in centre of hamlet, go through farm gates. Michelin Map No: 238-35

Entry no: **105**   Map No: 8

Douglas & Marie-Georges RYAN
La Réserve
58340 Diennes Aubigny
Nièvre
Tel: (0)3 86 50 05 29
Fax: (0) 3 86 50 05 29

The atmosphere is created by a deeply attractive mix of fine things – antiques, paintings, prints – and unstuffy informality. Soisick is good fun though you may find yourself waiting for her after the appointed hour and the cats may sneak onto the beds, but relaxed animal-lovers enjoy the contrast between this casual attitude and the formal air of the ancient turrets of her pretty château (mostly restored by her). Rooms are comfortable with a lived-in, once-elegant look. Dinner, superbly cooked by Claudine, is served in the family dining room but do make sure your booking is firm. Lovely gardens, fly-fishing, painting courses.

Rooms: 3 doubles, 1 twin and 1 triple, each with bath or shower & wc.

Price: 400 Frs for two.

Meals: 150 Frs, including wine & coffee, by arrangement.

Closed: 2 November-20 March.

From Dijon, N71 direction Châtillon sur Seine. Before St Marc sur Seine, right on D32 and D901 direction Aignay. Tarperon signposted on D901. Michelin Map No: 241-50

Entry no: **106**   Map No: 9

Soisick de CHAMPSAVIN &
Claudine RAILLARD
Manoir de Tarperon
21510 Aignay le Duc
Côte-d'Or
Tel: (0)3 80 93 83 74
Fax: (0)3 80 93 83 74
Web: www.sawdays.co.uk

Expect a genuine welcome to this modern house with its lovely views over the valley of historic Alesia where the Roman colonisers fought the 'native' Gauls. Having lived long in Africa, the Gounands came home to build and decorate (slightly garishly) this house, become Mayor of the village (Monsieur will describe it all over a *kir*) and offer spotless rooms, new mattresses and high-quality bathrooms to lovers of walking, medieval villages and wine. Choose Madame's good cooking or your own in the well-equipped, open-sided summer house that Monsieur has designed in the garden.

Rooms: 1 double, 1 twin, each with curtained shower, sharing wc.

Price: 220 Frs for two.

Meals: 80 Frs, including wine & coffee, by arrangement.

Closed: November-Easter, except by arrangement.

From Dijon, N71 direction Châtillon sur Seine. After Courceau, D6 left and follow signposts. House is on D19A near junction with D6.
Michelin Map No: 243-2

Entry no: 107   Map No: 9

Claude & Huguette GOUNAND
Villa le Clos
Route de la Villeneuve
21150 Darcey
Côte-d'Or
Tel: (0)3 80 96 23 20
Fax: (0)3 80 96 23 20
e-mail: claude.gounand@libertysurf.fr

The Ayletts fell in love with a dilapidated 15th-century presbytery (one cold tap and an outside privy), bought it on the spot and set about their high-standard restoration, using old materials. Marjorie's artistry is evident in the elegantly comfortable bedrooms, where rich colours echo the hand-painted tiles in the luxurious bathrooms. You will feast on excellent food, made with organically home-grown produce, in the attractive garden with superb Morvan views. Inside, there is an inglenook fireplace for cooler nights. Well worth making this more than just a one night stop.

Rooms: 3 doubles, 1 twin, each with bath or shower & wc.

Price: 400 Frs for two.

Meals: 130 Frs, including wine & coffee, by arrangement.

Closed: Never.

From Avallon N6 to Saulieu. In centre, left at Hôtel Côte-d'Or onto D26 to La Motte Ternant. In village, follow signs for church.
Michelin Map No: 243-13

Entry no: 108   Map No: 9

Marjorie & Brian AYLETT
Le Presbytère
La Motte Ternant
21210 Saulieu
Côte-d'Or
Tel: (0)3 80 84 34 85
Fax: (0)3 80 84 35 32
e-mail: lepresbytere@aol.com

Wine buffs will love the twisting drive through the vineyards of the *Routes des Vins* into the gravelled courtyard of this fine old *maison de vigneron*. Your courteous host knows a lot about wine and loves to practise his English. Sample an aperitif in his atmospheric stone-arched cellar, (if you're not a wine fan there are locally pressed fruit juices too). The house has a classic stone staircase and generous shuttered windows. The comfortable and homely bedrooms are reached by outside steps. The breakfast room has flagstones and ochre coloured walls; or you can eat in the well-kept willow-draped garden.

Rooms: 1 double, 1 twin, 1 family room, all with shower & wc.

Price: 310-350 Frs for two.

Meals: Excellent restaurant 300m.

Closed: Never.

Wooden beams and floors, huge old cupboards, shutters and stone fireplaces all contribute to the warm, relaxed feel of this lovely 18th-century presbytery. Claude Reny and her husband are Parisian bibliophiles and Claude is an enthusiastic gardener, supplying home-grown salads and always keen to swap horticultural hints. Breakfast, with home-made jam, is served round a large oval table in the dining room, and ageing bicycles are available for exploring. Monsieur is there in summer and speaks excellent English.

Rooms: 2 doubles, 1 twin, each with bath & wc.

Price: 400 Frs for two.

Meals: Choice within 6-7km.

Closed: December-Easter.

From Lyon N on A6 exit Nuits St Georges, then N74 towards Dijon. After approx. 13km left to Marsannay la Côte.
Michelin Map No: 243-16

Entry no: 109   Map No: 9

Jean-Charles & Brigitte VIENNET
34 rue de Mazy
21160 Marsannay la Côte
Côte-d'Or
Tel: (0)3 80 59 83 63
Fax: (0)3 80 59 83 28
e-mail: viennet.jean-charles@wanadoo.fr
Web: perso.wanadoo.fr/gite.marsannay

From Arnay le Duc N6 towards Châlons sur Saône for 1km then left onto D17 towards Beaune. In village, house near church (signpost on D17).
Michelin Map No: 243-14

Entry no: 110   Map No: 9

Mme Claude RENY
La Cure
21230 Foissy
Côte-d'Or
Tel: (0)3 80 84 22 92
Fax: (0)3 80 84 22 92

There's space and a welcome for all in this endearingly higgledy-piggledy yet simple 18th-century house in its attractive hilltop village. It has cheerful, plain rooms, all with independent entrances, that are lent an artistic flourish by Françoise's hand-decoration of some of the furniture: "neither marble nor satin, but wood and plaster, whiteness and colour" is how she defines her décor. Breakfast in the big, communal, all-in-together kitchen/diner features honey from Henri's own hives. You may meet him in the evening and hear about life as a beekeeper: he is genuinely fascinating, and Françoise clearly enjoys people.

Rooms: 1 quadruple, 1 triple, 3 doubles, 1 twin, all with shower or bath & wc.

Price: 210-230 Frs for two.

Meals: 90 Frs, including aperitif, wine & coffee, by arrangement.

Closed: December-February.

From Nuits St Georges, N74 towards Beaune. At Corgoloin, D115 to Magny lès Villers. There, take road towards Pernand Vergelesses; house almost immediately on right as you leave Magny, going uphill.
Michelin Map No: 243-16

Entry no: 111   Map No: 9

Françoise & Henri GIORGI
Maison des Abeilles
Route de Pernand-Vergelesses
21700 Magny lès Villiers
Côte-d'Or
Tel: (0)3 80 62 95 42

This is an 18th-century hunting lodge where the garden is full of flowers, the trees are centenarians and breakfast has the savour of yesteryear: yoghurt, fresh bread and home-made jam, a past one wouldn't mind revisiting regularly. Your hosts extend the warmest of genuine welcomes to the weary traveller – lots of towels, superb bed-linen, beautifully-judged colour schemes (Madame paints and knows about colour), fine furniture, a sprig of flowers, all combine to provide a soothing and reviving environment. The cottage is a deliciously independent blue hideaway with a working fireplace.

Rooms: 1 double, 1 twin, 1 cottage for 3, all with bath & wc.

Price: 470 Frs for two; cottage 620 Frs.

Meals: Wide choice 10km.

Closed: December-February.

From A31 exit 1 onto D35 E towards Seurre. After about 3km right towards Quincey, through Quincey and on to Antilly (4km). House on right.
Michelin Map No: 243-16

Entry no: 112   Map No: 9

Jean-François & Christiane BUGNET
Les Hêtres Rouges
Antilly
21700 Argilly
Côte-d'Or
Tel: (0)3 80 62 53 98
Fax: (0)3 80 62 54 85

A civilised house and family where you find space, warmth, good taste, intelligent company and a pretty terrace for breakfast – and so many musical events in summer. Madame is open and at ease – her house reflects her natural elegance. All is harmony in her renovated and not over-furnished manor with its pale colours, old tiles and rugs, modern art and big, soft-textured bedrooms (one more intimate and carpeted). The soft Burgundian light pours in through the big windows in the main rooms and the little village is quietly authentic.

Very grand and so very French! The 19th-century manor is set back from the lime-tree-shaded square. Persian carpets on parquet floors, antiques and good, firm beds grace the large, luminous rooms and bathrooms are well-fitted and finished. In winter a wood fire burns in the sitting room. Madame has taken great pains over her immaculate home; she puts you at your ease in these rather formal surroundings and enjoys talking to guests. Should she have to be out when you arrive, she'll leave a note on the door. "B&B perfection," wrote one reader, "for style, beds, hostess!" *Well-behaved children welcome.*

Rooms: 2 triples, 1 double, each with bath or shower & wc.

Price: 400 Frs for two.

Meals: Available locally.

Closed: Mid-October-April.

Rooms: 1 double/twin with shower & wc; 1 double, 1 twin sharing bath, shower & wc.

Price: 300-420 Frs for two.

Meals: 120 Frs, including wine, by arrangement; low season only.

Closed: Never.

From A6 Beaune/Chagny exit onto D973 towards Dole & Seurre for 10km. In Corberon house signposted up on left.
Michelin Map No: 243-28

Entry no: 113   Map No: 9

Chantal & Alain BALMELLE
L'Ormeraie
21250 Corberon
Côte-d'Or
Tel: (0)3 80 26 53 19
Fax: (0)3 80 26 54 01
Web: www.sawdays.co.uk

From A6, Joigny exit onto D943 towards Joigny then very shortly right onto D89 to Senan. Place de la Liberté is after church on right.
Michelin Map No: 237-45

Entry no: 114   Map No: 8

Mme Paule DEFRANCE
4 place de la Liberté
89710 Senan
Yonne
Tel: (0)3 86 91 59 89

Ring at the huge gates, enter, and this superb château is your home for the night. You will indeed be welcomed as family by this young couple, their little girl, their pedigree schnauzer dogs (Madame breeds them) and parakeets – all delightful. Downstairs, the thick-walled, vaulted dining and sitting rooms support the rest of the house, an impressive and original alternative to deep foundations. An oak staircase leads up to the charming, period-furnished bedrooms with views over roofs and woods. Meals come with home-grown veg and good wine from the Septiers' cellar.

Rooms: 2 doubles, each with shower and basin; 2 doubles; all sharing 2 bathrooms and wc in corridor.

Price: 350 Frs for two.

Meals: 200 Frs, including aperitif, wine and tisane, by arrangement.

Closed: Never.

Gîte space for 5 people.

From A6 exit Auxerre Nord on N6 dir. Auxerre for 0.5km; through Perrigny & St Georges dir. Villefargeau. At Relais de la Vallée restaurant left and left again to château at end of road. Michelin Map No: 238-10

Entry no: **115**   Map No: 8

Jacky & Marianne SEPTIER
1 allée du Château
89240 Villefargeau
Yonne
Tel: (0)3 86 41 37 38
Fax: (0)3 86 41 27 25
e-mail: marianne.septier@wanadoo.fr
Web: perso.wanadoo.fr/marianne.septier/

They really are the nicest possible people. Simplicity and attention to detail are Madame's keynotes and her harmonious quirky house – 'Gothic' windows even in the attic, 'Victorian' panelling, superb old patterned floor tiles – is the warm and friendly central theme. Up two floors, the simply-furnished bedrooms have sloping ceilings, ancient rafters and not one common wall. Breakfast by the old bread oven or outside before learning to 'grow' truffles, consulting Monsieur on the estate wine you'll take home (the cellar is below the house), or setting off for Auxerre. A child-friendly house.

Rooms: 4 doubles, 1 suite for 4, all with bath or shower & wc.

Price: 290-360 Frs for two.

Meals: Restaurant 2km; Auxerre or Chablis 10km.

Closed: Mid-December-mid-January.

From Auxerre, D965 towards Chablis; after passing under the A6 motorway bridge, 3km on, house on right. DO NOT go to Venoy. Michelin Map No: 238-11

Entry no: **116**   Map No: 8

François & Françoise CHONÉ
Domaine de Montpierreux
89290 Venoy
Yonne
Tel: (0)3 86 40 20 91
Fax: (0)3 86 40 28 00

You approach this handsome millhouse via a narrow, private bridge as it's completely surrounded by a rushing river and its own lake. Wander the beautiful grounds or settle yourself in the most inviting sitting room, complete with roaring log fire when it's cold. Leigh and Cinda, both relaxed and easy, have great plans, including the building (sinking?) of an ionic pool *in* the mill pond. There's a canoe, and balloon flights can be arranged. The big, light bedrooms are freshly decorated with good bathrooms and the mill race is generally noisier than the road...

Rooms: 2 doubles, 2 twins, 1 triple, 1 suite for 4, all with bath/shower & wc.

Price: 300-375 Frs for two.

Meals: Restaurant close by.

Closed: Never.

Gîte space for 6 people.

From Auxerre N6 towards Avallon for 22km. Just before the Vermenton village nameplate turn sharp right, double back on yourself and cross the bridge.
Michelin Map No: 238-11

Entry no: **117**   Map No: 8

Leigh WOOTTON & Cinda
TARASOFF
Le Moulinot
89270 Vermenton, Yonne
Tel: (0)3 86 81 60 42
Fax: (0)3 86 81 62 25
e-mail: lemoulinot@aol.com
Web: www.sawdays.co.uk

Young owners have brought vitality to this handsome old house with a clever conversion that lets in stacks of light – perfect for the exhibition of local artists' work: water colours, oils and sculptures. Corinne has decorated each bedroom as if it was her own, each is comfortable and colourful with co-ordinating headboards and bedspreads and good bathrooms. She loves her flower and vegetable garden too and meals are definitely worth staying in for (she also runs courses for groups interested in traditional French cooking) and you may choose from Pascal's excellent cellar of Yonne wines.

Rooms: 2 doubles, 1 twin, 1 family room for 4, each with shower or bath & wc.

Price: 325 Frs for two.

Meals: 125 Frs, including coffee.

Closed: Never.

From A6 exit Nitry, dir. Tonnerre for 7km, right at crossroads signed Chambres d'Hotes. Left to Mólay. In Arton, pass the 'lavoir' (wash house), house in front.
Michelin Map No: 238-12

Entry no: **118**   Map No: 8

Corinne & Pascal COLLIN
Le Calounier
5 rue de la Fontaine-Arton
89310 Mólay, Yonne
Tel: (0)3 86 82 67 81
Fax: (0)3 86 82 67 81
e-mail: info@lecalounier.fr
Web: www.lecalounier.fr

A real sense of evolving history here; different architectural periods joined, inside, by three major staircases and several minor ones (not for the stiff-limbed, although there is one bedroom in the stable block). Parts of the house are 14th-century; it was once fortified and the moat, largely, remains. Louis XIV's cousin declined to stay long, because, she said, of the ghost. Madame is direct and knowledgeable; her guest rooms large and old-fashioned, idiosyncratic rather than luxurious. There's a heated swimming pool tucked away in the large grounds. A very special, unpretentious place; can be tricky to find.

Rooms: 2 doubles, 1 twin, each with bath or shower & wc.

Price: 420-500 Frs for two.

Meals: Available locally.

Closed: Never.

From Mezilles on D965 towards St Fargeau for 3.5km, then take small road on right towards Dannery. Continue past several small farms to white fencing and take the tree-lined alley to manor house signed, but not obviously.
Michelin Map No: 238-9

Entry no: 119   Map No: 8

Mme COUITEAS
Dannery
89170 Saint Fargeau
Yonne
Tel: (0)3 86 74 09 01
Fax: (0)3 86 74 09 01

Cabalus was an abbey hospice built in the shadow of the Basilica of this pilgrim city. A gallery and coffee shop occupy the 12th-century vaulted room with its huge fireplace: guests have it to themselves for breakfast. Rooms are simple, authentic, with good beds. Eccentric, Swiss and slightly shuffling, M Cabalus is the perfect gentleman with a fine sense of humour, Madame is a welcoming artist. An exceptional and inimitable house.

Rooms: 1 triple, 1 double, each with shower & wc; 2 triples, 1 double, each with shower but sharing wcs.

Price: 340-450 Frs for two.

Meals: 85 Frs, including coffee.

Closed: Never.

In Vézelay centre, follow main street up to 'Basilique'. House is last on left before reaching Basilica but next-to-last door (marked).
Michelin Map No: 238-23

Entry no: 120   Map No: 8

M CABALUS
Cabalus
Rue Saint Pierre
89450 Vézelay, Yonne
Tel: (0)3 86 33 20 66
Fax: (0)3 86 33 38 03
e-mail: contact@cabalus.com
Web: www.cabalus.com

Soak up the physical and spiritual vibes from the great old stones and timbers of this house on the 'Eternal Hill', climbed by pilgrims over 500 years. A stone spiral staircase leads to the bedrooms; the double has a terrace overlooking the sublime Basilica, both are full of simple character. Madame is easy, unintrusive and a passionate rider. She serves breakfast in her dining room with its huge fireplace and readers have enjoyed the utter Frenchness of it all. Maps and advice for hikers and cyclists and a pretty little self-catering flat for longer stays.

Rooms: 1 double, 1 twin, sharing shower & wc.

Price: 290 Frs for two.

Meals: In Vézelay.

Closed: Never.

Gîte space for 4 people.

From Avallon, D957 to Vézelay. In town, go up towards Basilica (Rue St Étienne becomes Rue St Pierre). Turreted 100m from Basilica.
Michelin Map No: 238-23

Entry no: 121   Map No: 8

Monique & Bertrand GINISTY
La Tour Gaillon
Rue Saint Pierre
89450 Vézelay
Yonne
Tel: (0)3 86 33 25 74
Web: www.sawdays.co.uk

Was that Rapunzel? Climb the winding stone stair to the top of the turret, push the big oak door, choose your four-poster, wallow in the ingenious 'Gothicky' bathroom then lie and admire the brilliant hangings and 'authentic' lights: no need to let down your hair. All is as 12th-century as Madame can make it. The medieval atmosphere, called strange, stagey, fascinating by some, is completed by objects from the château's history, some as old as the Crusades. Madame is passionate about the place, most approachable and a talented cook – medieval dinners served in the candlelit baronial kitchen/dining room. A stylish and romantic retreat.

Rooms: 1 quadruple (2 four-posters) with bathroom.

Price: 550 Frs for two.

Meals: 150-360 Frs, including coffee (state your budget).

Closed: Never.

Gîte space for 4 people.

From Avallon, N6 direction Saulieu. As you enter Ste Magnance, first house on right.
Michelin Map No: 238-24

Entry no: 122   Map No: 9

Martine & Gérard COSTAILLE
Château Jaquot
2 route d'Avallon
89420 Ste Magnance
Yonne
Tel: (0)3 86 33 00 22
Web: www.sawdays.co.uk

The Art Deco style reigns supreme in this 19th-century hunting lodge that was exuberantly 'modernised' in the 1920s, from the high-windowed, fully-panelled dining room with its extraordinary dressers and unbelievably moustachioed grandfather to the fabulous bathroom fittings. The original features also include Versailles parquet floors and fine fireplaces: Tae uses her perfect sense of style and colour in decorating around and for these deeply-respected elements. Quiet spot, well-travelled hosts (especially South America), perfect for Chartres, Paris, Versailles...

Rooms: 2 suites for 5, each with bath & wc.

Price: 420 Frs for two.

Meals: Good restaurants in village.

Closed: Never.

From A10 exit 10 to toll gate, right on D27 to St Cyr sous Dourdan then continue dir. Arpajon; first house on left.
Michelin Map No: 237-28

Entry no: 123   Map No: 4

Paris

"Ye who sit at a pavement café in Paris will see the whole world go by" under the all-seeing eye of the long-aproned, world-weary waiter who loves his City of Light but will never let you know it.

Claude & Tae-Lye DABASSE
Le Logis d'Arnières
1 rue du Pont-Rué
91410 St Cyr sous Dourdan
Essonne
Tel: (0)1 64 59 14 89
Fax: (0)1 64 59 07 46
Web: www.sawdays.co.uk

Madame's delightful serenity must be fed by the natural air of real farm life that wafts in from the great wheat fields. Tractors come and go in the farmyard, the old horse grazes in the meadow, the five young children play in the sandpit, the dog dances in its pen. The Desforges have done an excellent barn conversion. You climb the steep stairs to the lofty raftered dayroom (tea-making equipment, an old dresser, a comfortable sofa) and to the simply pretty, good-sized bedrooms. They are furnished with grandmother's richly-carved, if short-bedded, Breton bridal suite, or grandfather's brass bed, old wardrobes and new mattresses.

Rooms: 3 doubles, 2 twins, all with shower & wc.

Price: 250 Frs for two.

Meals: Choice in Milly, 3km; picnic possible.

Closed: Mid-December-January.

From A6 exit Cely en Biere towards Milly La Foret. At Milly, 1st roundabout towards Etampes. At next roundabout, towards Gironville, turn right. Farm on right after 2km. Michelin Map No: 237-30

Entry no: 124   Map No: 8

Sophie & Jean-Charles DESFORGES
Ferme de la Grange Rouge
91490 Milly la Forêt
Essonne
Tel: (0)1 64 98 94 21
Fax: (0)1 64 98 99 91

What a mixture! A 13th-century farmhouse but super-luxy 1990s bathrooms; 20 minutes from high-tech CDG airport but a national hiking path (GR1) leading to forests just behind the house; a fluting Pan lording it over the manicured profusion of a prize-winning garden. Nothing is left to chance by your well-travelled, gracious and caring hostess. Royal breakfasts on rose-patterned porcelain in the peach-panelled *salon*; thirsty bathrobes in the marbled bathrooms for you to wear until changing for dinner which arrives under silver cloches. A form of perfection.

Rooms: 2 doubles/twins, 1 suite, each with bath & wc.

Price: 550-890 Frs for two.

Meals: 200-250 Frs, including aperitif & wine.

Closed: 2 weeks in February.

From A1 exit 'Soissons' on A104 towards Marne la Vallée then N2 towards Soissons 12km. Exit Othis. Through Othis on D13; at traffic light left to Beaumarchais. In village right after 1st speed bump. Michelin Map No: 237-19

Entry no: 125   Map No: 4

Françoise MONTROZIER
12 rue des Suisses
Beaumarchais
77280 Othis
Seine-et-Marne
Tel: (0)1 60 03 33 98
Fax: (0)1 60 03 56 71

A gorgeous setting where green swards flow down to barge-carrying river and your cosmopolitan hostess is perfectly in tune with her animal and plant companions. She loves people too, is quietly, intelligently attentive and wants you to enjoy her old family house, once home to the local tax collector/inn keeper. The Neo-Gothic goblin-guarded fireplace once belonged to Alexandre Dumas. Madame's lamp collection is fascinating and her rooms are unostentatiously friendly with well-loved old furniture – the big balcony suite is our favourite looking way out to the hills beyond the River Marne. Keen walkers can follow the Canal de l'Ourcq all the way to Paris.

Rooms: 1 suite for 3 with shower & wc; 1 suite for 5 with bath & wc.

Price: 280-340 Frs for two.

Meals: Two good restaurants nearby.

Closed: November-February.

From A4 exit 18 onto N3 towards Paris through St Jean then 1st right to Armentières; straight on at junction, past church. House is last but one on right in cul-de-sac.
Michelin Map No: 237-20

Entry no: 126   Map No: 4

Denise WOEHRLÉ
44 rue du Chef de Ville
77440 Armentières en Brie
Seine-et-Marne
Tel: (0)1 64 35 51 22
Fax: (0)1 64 35 42 95

The big informal garden flows into the fields: there are green corners and space for everyone, so don't worry about those new houses ahead. Space in the high beamed dayroom too, at the fabulous long table made of old oak beams. Upstairs, the five simple, white-painted, gently colour-themed rooms, each with two beds on a mezzanine, are ideal for families. An old mirror or table or desk adds character and new shower rooms are cleverly designed. Isabelle has made the two larger, temptingly independent lodges most attractive. She and Patrick, with all the time in the world for their guests, are wonderful hosts. And there's Disney, *bien sûr*!

Rooms: 1 triple, 4 quadruples, all with shower & wc.

Price: 290-390 Frs for two.

Meals: Choice in Villeneuve le Comte 4km.

Closed: Never.

Gîte space for 8 people.

On A4 take exit 13 for Villeneuve le Comte. In Villeneuve follow signs for Neufmoutiers en Brie; follow Chambres d'Hôtes signs.
Michelin Map No: 237-19

Entry no: 127   Map No: 4

Isabelle & Patrick GALPIN
Bellevue
77610 Neufmoutiers en Brie
Seine-et-Marne
Tel: (0)1 64 07 11 05
Fax: (0)1 64 07 19 27
e-mail: ipgalpin@club-internet.fr
Web: www.club-internet.fr/perso/ipgalpin

An architectural cuckoo? Miles from Normandy, an 'Anglo-Norman' face veneered onto a concrete skull conceals an unspoilt 1920s interior. Fascinating (great arched windows, red and black crested tiles), elegant ('Versailles' parquet), comfortable and beautifully furnished. The guest suite is as untouched as the blue-green panelled *salon*: stone walls, patterned parquet floor, marble fireplace and a delicious round sitting corner in the tower. Big breakfasts appear at the long dining table, your retired hosts will tell the history of grandfather's hunting lodge in good English (they still organise shoots) and their welcome is warmly French.

Rooms: 1 suite with bathroom & wc.

Price: 750 Frs for two.

Meals: Variety of restaurants nearby.

Closed: Never.

Behind the high blue doors, a pair of long, low stone buildings round a narrow courtyard, the apse of the medieval church looking benignly over the wall and a charming garden at the back. The Laurents are straightforward, gentle people (the marble bathroom is NOT their doing!) with ever a new project on the boil; they are 'junk-shop' hunters but they like to keep it uncluttered. A friendly couple with two children who adopt stray cats, keep miniature ponies and will do all they can to make your stay peaceful and fruitful, including organising walks and making vegetarian meals (by arrangement) in the heavily-beamed, 1930s-furnished guest dining room.

Rooms: 1 triple with bath & wc; 1 suite for 5/6 with shower & wc.

Price: 300 Frs for two.

Meals: 110 Frs, including wine & coffee.

Closed: Never.

Gîte space for 7 people.

From A4 exit 13 to Villeneuve le Comte; right on D96 towards Tournan; after Neufmentiers, 1st left on small road for 1.5km; white gates on left.
Michelin Map No: 237-19

From A4 exit on D231 to Villeneuve le Comte then right on D96 through Neufmoutiers to Châtres. House in village centre to left of church.
Michelin Map No: 237-31

Entry no: 128   Map No: 4

Entry no: 129   Map No: 4

Hubert et Francine CHARPENTIER
Manoir de Beaumarchais
77610 Les Chapelles Bourbon
Seine-et-Marne
Tel: (0)1 64 07 11 08
Fax: (0)1 64 07 14 48
e-mail: hubert.charpentier@wanadoo.fr
Web: www.le-manoir-de-beaumarchais.com

Dominique & Pierre LAURENT
Le Portail Bleu
2 route de Fontenay
77610 Châtres, Seine-et-Marne
Tel: (0)1 64 25 84 94
Fax: (0)1 64 25 84 94
e-mail: le portailbleu@voila.fr
Web: perso.wanadoo.fr/leportailbleu/

A generous farmyard surrounded by beautiful warm stone buildings and set in wide open fields. Cereals, beets and show-jumpers flourish – adding a definite touch of elegance to the landscape. Utter quiet and a genuine welcome from hosts and Labradors alike, out here where Monsieur's family has come hunting for 200 years (his great-grandfather was a surgeon with Napoleon's army). Family furniture (the 1900s ensemble is most intriguing) in light-filled rooms, spotless mod cons and a vast sitting room for guests with piano and billiards table. Your hosts are excellent tour advisers who can direct you to little-known treasures.

Rooms: 1 triple with shower & wc; 1 apartment for 4 with mini-kitchen, shower & wc.

Price: 290 Frs for two; apartment 550 Frs for four.

Meals: Good restaurant in walking distance, or 4-6km.

Closed: Christmas week.

From A5 exit 15 on N36 towards Meaux for 200m; SECOND right to Crisenoy after TGV bridge, through village then 1.5km to farm (marked on Michelin No 106).
Michelin Map No: 237-31

Entry no: 130   Map No: 4

Philippe & Jeanne MAUBAN
Ferme de Vert Saint-Père
77390 Crisenoy
Seine-et-Marne
Tel: (0)1 64 38 83 51
Fax: (0)1 64 38 83 52
e-mail: mauban.vert@wanadoo.fr
Web: www.sawdays.co.uk

Between the Seine and the rue de Rivoli, a quiet back street conceals this old Parisian building. Inside is a city home of charm and elegance whose owners managed to salvage some of the ancient timbers from the renovator's clean sweep and who live happily with deliriously sloping wrought-iron balustrades (decorative, not structural...). It is like a warm soft nest, antique-furnished, with lots of greenery and interesting artwork. Madame greatly enjoys her guests and is a source of good tips on Paris. Monsieur is a university professor. The compact guest quarters down the corridor are nicely private with good storage space, pretty quilts, lots of light.

Rooms: 1 twin with small bath/shower & wc.

Price: 420 Frs for two.

Meals: Both banks of the Seine beckon.

Closed: During school holidays.

Metro: Châtelet or Pont-Neuf. (Between the Louvre and Notre-Dame). Parking: Conforama car park, via Rue du Pont Neuf then Rue Boucher. Flat is on 3rd floor with a lift.

Entry no: 131   Map No: 4

Mme Mona PIERROT
75001 Paris
Full address on application
Tel: (0)1 42 36 50 65

With pleasing views of the rooftops and domes of Paris, the compact living room is attractive with its deep sofas, upright piano and Madame's collection of curiosities – well worth investigating. She likes to treat her guests 'properly' and to serve breakfast on fine linen in silver coffee pots. Bedrooms are simpler and perfectly comfortable with yet more interesting pictures. This is a trendy quarter with the colourful Rue Mouffetard and the quieter Jardin des Plantes, the home of the Natural History Museum. Madame is quiet, a little shy, and most helpful. She also has a self-contained one-room apartment to let near Place de la République.

Rooms: 1 triple with shower; 1 double sharing bathroom; both sharing wc.

Price: 290-400 Frs (ie 290-330 sharing bathroom, 350-400 with shower) for two; minimum 2 nights.

Meals: This is Paris!

Closed: Never.

 Ⓔ

Metro: Austerlitz. Parking: Rue Censier.

Entry no: 132   Map No: 4

Mme Lélia COHEN-SCALI
75005 Paris
Full address on application
Tel: (0)1 43 36 51 62
Fax: (0)1 45 87 94 16
e-mail: lelia-cs@yahoo.com
Web: www.sawdays.co.uk

The view of Notre Dame at the end of the road, buttresses flying in the setting sun, is breathtaking. In this air, the history of Paris, France, Europe gets under your skin. A few yards along, a great 17th-century doorway opens onto more ancient stones under the utterly Parisian porch. Old stone stairs bring you to a high-ceilinged, family-loved, unpretentious but ancient duplex flat where guests have a breakfast space beside the spiral staircase and a mezzanined, fireplaced room with high windows onto an unexpected green city garden – a "bowl of air" as they say, a huge privilege in Paris. Madame is polyglot, active in the city and quietly welcoming.

Rooms: 1 room for 2-4 with bath & wc.

Price: 500 Frs for two; under 5s free.

Meals: Many restaurants nearby.

Closed: Never.

Ⓔ

Metro: Maubert-Mutualité. RER/Metro: St Michel-Notre Dame. Parking: 'Lagrange' underground car park.

Entry no: 133   Map No: 4

Mme Brigitte CHATIGNOUX
75005 Paris
Full address on application
Tel: (0)1 43 25 27 20
Fax: (0)1 43 25 27 20

In a smart Left Bank street, here are intelligence, sobriety and genuine style. Madame will welcome you into her vast, serene apartment – neither modern gadgets nor over-restored antiques, just a few good pieces, space and light. Beyond the dining room, the smaller guest room gives onto the big, silent, arcaded courtyard. Your multilingual hosts have lived all over the world, Monsieur, a retired engineer, still spends his days studying or teaching. Madame is as stylish and genuine as her surroundings and enjoys, in equal parts, renovating her old mill near Chartres and the company of like-minded visitors – she is worth getting to know.

Rooms: 1 twin with bath & wc.

Price: 460 Frs for two.

Meals: Choice within 5 minutes walk; St Germain des Prés is 10 minutes away.

Closed: Never.

Metro: Solférino, Assemblée Nationale or Invalides. Parking: Invalides. Flat is on 2nd floor with a lift from street level.

Entry no: **134**   Map No: 4

Mme Elisabeth MARCHAL
75007 Paris
Full address on application
Tel: (0)1 47 05 70 21
      (0)2 37 23 38 19

The Monbrisons have huge hearts and a tiny flat. Their living room is wonderfully cluttered 1800s with anachronistic timbers, books against every available wall, paintings and objects from all over the world. Your room is quiet over the inner courtyard, its two beds snugly side by side. Cynthia is an intelligent, cosmopolitan American who plumps for Europe, homeopathy and organic food; Christian is quintessentially French and well informed on many subjects – he deals in wine, is planning to write historical books and songs, and can guide you through the secret life of night-time Paris. Street markets down below in the day. Intimate, fun and fascinating.

Rooms: 1 double/twin with bath/shower & wc.

Price: 400 Frs for two.

Meals: Occasionally, by arrangement. Varying prices.

Closed: August.

Metro: Edgar Quinet or Montparnasse. Parking: Ask owners.

Entry no: **135**   Map No: 4

Christian & Cynthia de MONBRISON
75014 Paris
Full address on application
Tel: (0)1 45 38 68 72
Fax: (0)1 45 38 68 72

On the sixth floor of a delightfully
1930s block of flats with a superb view
from its balconies across the Seine, this
is a well-proportioned apartment with
big rooms and a well-loved, lived-in
patina, furnished with old family pieces,
mementoes from distant travels. The
unfussy guest room is big too, with that
fine view, two narrow single beds,
endearingly old-fashioned tiling in the
shower, the loo just down the passage.
With the window open, you hear the
traffic, somewhat muffled by leaves in
summer. Madame, who still travels after
all these years, has plenty of time for her
guests and lends a very attentive,
gracious ear to their own travellers'
tales.

A typical little Paris flat in a proudly
moulded and bracketed 1900s building,
Montmartre is within walking distance
but not so close that you feel harassed
by charcoal-waving portraitists. The
wooden fireplace, the floorboards, the
plasterwork are original; the décor is as
young and lively as Françoise and Hervé
themselves: theatrical bits and pieces, ivy
growing all over your balcony, a dry
garden inside with grasses and nests,
gnomes and dollies. They love their
foreign guests and are happy to share
their knowledge of Paris, French food
and wine with you. You will like their
youth, their spontaneity, their sense of
fun.

Rooms: 1 twin with shower & basin,
sharing wc.

Price: 350 Frs for two.

Meals: Choice within walking distance.

Closed: End June-mid-September.

 (E)

Rooms: 1 double sharing shower & wc.

Price: 350 Frs for two.

Meals: Plenty of choice nearby.

Closed: Never.

*Metro: Mirabeau, Église d'Auteuil,
Exelmans.Bus: 72, 22, Petite
Ceinture.Parking: Rue Wilhem.*

Entry no: 136   Map No: 4

Mme BARGETON
75016 Paris
Full address on application
Tel: (0)1 42 88 87 66
Web: www.sawdays.co.uk

Metro: Guy Moquet.

Entry no: 137   Map No: 4

Françoise & Hervé
75018 Paris
Full address on application
Tel: (0)1 44 85 06 05
Fax: (0)1 44 85 06 14
e-mail: fforet@cybercable.fr
Web: www.sawdays.co.uk

Your very proper elderly hosts moved from an isolated Mediterranean villa to this colourful quarter of Paris where you hear a multitude of languages. The ninth floor (yes, there is a lift!) apartment is all white walls, modern parquet floors and fine old family furniture. There are great long views right across Paris over to the Eiffel Tower and the Great Arch of La Défense, or up the hill to the Parc de Belleville. Breakfast on the balcony or by the amazing glass-fronted wardrobe while Madame serves fresh pastries and tells you all you need to know about everything, and Monsieur twinkles shyly. *Some Spanish spoken.*

Rooms: 1 double with shower & wc.

Price: 370 Frs for two; minimum 2 nights.

Meals: Wide choice on the doorstep.

Closed: Never.

In one of the less gentrified parts of Paris, your kind, smiling, artist hosts live between two tiny gardens and a tall house. The simple guest room, with a good double bed and a new divan, modern furniture and a pretty mirror, shares a building with Sabine's studio and the next generation's ground-floor flat. Colours and fabrics are quiet and gentle, the bathroom is old-fashioned, the tea-maker very welcome. The cosy family living room, in the main house, welcomes you for breakfast (French with a healthfood bias), or take it outside under the birdsung tree. Jules makes the bread with organic flour and big, beautiful, black Janto, his guide dog, loves people.

Rooms: 1 triple with bath & wc.

Price: 350 Frs for two.

Meals: Choice within walking distance.

Closed: Never.

Metro: Belleville. Bus: 26. Parking: Ask owners.

Entry no: **138**   Map No: 4

Danièle & Bernard de LA BROSSE
75019 Paris
Full address on application
Tel: (0)1 42 41 99 59
Fax: (0)1 42 41 99 59

Metro: Jourdain or Place des Fêtes. Parking: Place des Fêtes.

Entry no: **139**   Map No: 4

Sabine & Jules AÏM
75019 Paris
Full address on application
Tel: (0)1 42 08 23 71
Fax: (0)1 42 40 56 04

As in a Brian Rix farce, guests enter by one door while others enter or leave by another, though in this case it is unlikely to be a slick, finely co-ordinated, set of movements. You are on the outskirts of Paris, pressed against a disused factory (out of sight to the left) and a road to the right, mercifully free of traffic. The paved terrace garden, from which you can watch the sun set over the roofs and pylons, has known better days, but haven't we all? Perfect for easy access to the motorway system, but do check well ahead that the house is still actually standing.

Rooms: 1 low open-plan suite with outdoor facilities.

Price: 50-75 Frs for two, by negotiation with other residents.

Meals: Several good value industrial canteens within walking distance.

Closed: Unpredictably in bad weather.

Gîte space for 99 people.

Exit Paris 'Rive Droite' until all signs of habitation have dwindled, look out for distinctive pink doors but go slowly as road potholed.

Entry no: **140**

Jacques du SHACK
Les Portails Rose
75000 Paris
Ville de Paris
Tel: (0)1 49 00 00 99
e-mail: jacques.schack@wanadoo.fr

Fifteen minutes from Paris or Versailles and only nightingales are heard. Your hosts, sophisticated lovers of art and animals, have decorated their elegant little 1830s manor with old oils, dreamy murals (Madame is the painter's agent), some fine antiques and comfortable sofas: it's a big family house with a lived-in air and happy dogs. Two comfortable guest rooms, one large, one smaller, are here. In the rose-filled garden, the hunting lodge has become a magnificent self-contained studio with complete kitchen, the old orangery has two very pretty, snug little rooms with roses peering through the windows.

Rooms: 4 doubles each with shower & wc; 1 suite with shower, wc & kitchen.

Price: 450 Frs for two.

Meals: Restaurants nearby.

Closed: Never.

From A13 exit 6 on D186 towards St. Germain en Laye 3km; D102 right 3.5km; D321 left 3km to Chatou (along river & Ave Tilleuls left); bear left Ave Clemenceau, right V. Hugo, right Garennes.
Michelin Map No: 237-17

Entry no: **141**   Map No: 4

Françoise PASQUIER
Les Impressionnistes
6 rue des Garennes
78400 Chatou, Yvelines
Tel: (0)1 30 53 20 88
Fax: (0)1 30 53 20 88
e-mail: pasquierpdsc@aol.com
Web: www.sawdays.co.uk

That modest façade hides a generous and lovely interior where Madame's very interesting paintings – she's an art teacher and definitely an artist – stand in pleasing contrast to elegant antiques and soft plush furnishings. Picture windows let the garden in and the wooded hillside rises beyond. The larger guest room with its big bathroom is superb in blue draperies and fur bedcover; the smaller one with skylight and its own bathroom across the landing is excellent value. Madame, active and communicative, sings as well as she paints and enjoys cooking refined dinners for attentive guests; she is very good company. A short drive from Paris.

Rooms: 2 doubles (1 large, 1 small), each with bath & wc.

Price: 280-380 Frs for two.

Meals: 100 Frs, including wine & coffee.

Closed: Never.

From Paris A13 onto A12 towards St Quentin en Yvelines for 6km then exit on N12 towards Dreux. Exit to Plaisir CENTRE; 1st exit off r'bout towards Plaisir Les Gâtines, 1st left for 400m; right into Domaine des Gâtines; consult roadside plan.
Michelin Map No: 237-16

Entry no: **142**   Map No: 3

Mme Hélène CASTELNAU
7 rue Gustave Courbet
Domaine des Gâtines
78370 Plaisir
Yvelines
Tel: (0)1 30 54 05 15
Fax: (0)1 30 54 05 15

From Morocco, Indonesia and reddest America, this great traveller has amassed carvings, inlays and filigrees in brass, lacquer and wood, artefacts ancient and modern, and filled his family mansion. A collector's paradise and a housemaid's hell. All is exuberance and love of life and beautiful things and the rooms are a feast of almost baroque décor. The Coca Cola room is devastatingly... Coke (a unique collection, I'm sure), the Indonesian bed overwhelmingly rich. Your host is very good company and on weekdays his delightful assistant Taïeb will take excellent care of you. There is also a loo/library and a three-legged cat, exotic fowl and stone boars.

Rooms: 5 doubles, all with shower & wc; 1 suite for 5 with bath & wc.

Price: 325-395 Frs for two.

Meals: Three restaurants in village.

Closed: Never.

From N10 north of Rambouillet take D937 then D936 towards Poigny la Forêt for 5km. Left on D107 to Poigny. Left up road by church; house is on right.
Michelin Map No: 237-28

Entry no: **143**   Map No: 3

François LE BRET
2 rue de l'Église
78125 Poigny la Forêt
Yvelines
Tel: (0)1 34 84 73 42
Fax: (0)1 34 84 74 38
e-mail: lechateaudepoigny@compuserve.com

Utterly original and fun, a marriage of abundant creativity and scholarship, Hazeville is amazing. Your host has turned his refined château-farm, dated 1400s to 1600s, into a living expression of his art: huge abstract paintings, dozens of hand-painted plates and tiles, a dazzling 'Egyptian' reception room, kitchen and loo (oh yes!) in the barn; the stables now house hi-tech artisans. Beautifully-finished guest rooms in the pigeon tower are deeply luxurious; generous breakfasts come on china hand painted by Monsieur to match the wall covering; he also knows all the secret treasures of the Vexin. *Well-behaved children over seven welcome.*

This super couple of hard-working Parisians – he a burly, bearded epicurean, she lithe and energetic, are excellent company and really enjoy having guests. The garden studio, smart blue with soft pink oriental touches, is snugly designed with kitchen, (low-ceilinged) double sleeping platform and twin beds below. Be as independent as you like (you may subtract breakfast and do your own). In the house, above the sober wooden dining room and the colourful, cosy, booklined *salon*, the delightful bedroom has an elegant caned bed and big balcony over the 1920s colonnaded porch and garden.

Rooms: 1 double, 1 twin, both with bath, shower & wc.

Price: 700 Frs for two.

Meals: Wide choice within 5-10km.

Closed: Weekdays & school term time.

Rooms: 1 dble with shower & shared wc; garden studio (for 4) with shower & wc.

Price: 380-520 Frs for two.

Meals: Dinner possible, by arrangement.

Closed: August.

From Rouen, N14 towards Paris. 20km before Pontoise, at Magny en Vexin, right onto D983 to Arthies. Left onto D81, through Enfer; château on left. Michelin Map No: 237-16

Directions on request. Train: from St Lazare to La Garenne Colombes. Michelin Map No: 237-17

Entry no: **144**   Map No: **3**

Entry no: **145**   Map No: **4**

Guy & Monique DENECK
Château d'Hazeville
95420 Wy dit Joli Village
Val-d'Oise
Tel: (0)1 34 67 06 17/
       (0)1 42 88 67 00
Fax: (0)1 34 67 17 82

Chris & Jean-Jacques BILLON
22 rue des Arts
92700 Colombes
Hauts-de-Seine
Tel: (0)1 47 60 11 92
Fax: (0)1 47 82 35 63
e-mail: cbillon@spray.fr

Cecilia, the sweetest hostess, is delighted to chat, trilingually, and longs for you to be happy here. In the garden, Jean-Claude tends many flowers, much greenery, a white cat and quantities of plastic furniture. One room: a picture window, imitation wall-panelling, washing facilities cleverly tucked in by the door; the other: bigger shower, smaller room, less light, but its own entrance; both have a mini-kitchen and dining table. Décor, lacy and knick-knacked, motley colour schemes, natural and synthetic drapes, good carpets; the breakfast room upstairs is prettily eau de nil. And so near Paris, by train. *Italian spoken.*

In a classy block of a smart Paris suburb, lives a mild woman with a powerful brush. Ruth is an artist. You may share her atmospheric personal space: her studio is part of the splendidly mix-decorated living room – worn antiques to sit on, fashionable red table for breakfast, abstracts, collages, books – and perhaps the privilege of following a work in progress. Looking onto the quiet back garden, your simply-furnished, smallish room has all the necessities: writing desk, kettle, storage, light and live art; also a snug little shower room. One bed tucks under the other, the curtain is leopard-skin voile, the painting leaps off the wall – this is different.

Rooms: 1 twin/double with shower & wc.

Price: 350 Frs for two.

Meals: This is Paris!

Closed: Never.

Metro: Port de Levallois (10 mins walk). Bus: 174, 163, 164, 93, 82. Michelin Map No: 237-17

Entry no: **146**   Map No: **4**

Ruth HIMMELFARB
53 boulevard Victor Hugo
92200 Neuilly sur Seine
Hauts-de-Seine
Tel: (0)1 46 37 37 28
Fax: (0)1 46 37 37 28

Rooms: 1 double, 1 triple, each with shower, wc & mini-kitchen.

Price: 440 Frs for two.

Meals: Self-catering or restaurants nearby.

Closed: Occasionally.

Gîte space for 6 people.

From Paris Boulevard Peripherique, exit Porte d'Asnières through Levallois, across Seine. Ask for map. Train: from St Lazare, 'Banlieue' train to Becon Les Bruyères, exit Asnières, (6 minutes). Michelin Map No: 237-17

Entry no: **147**   Map No: **4**

M & Mme BOBRIE
10 rue Denfert-Rochereau
92600 Asnières sur Seine
Hauts-de-Seine
Tel: (0)1 47 93 53 60
Fax: (0)1 47 93 53 60
e-mail: jcbobrie@infonie.fr
Web: www.sawdays.co.uk

Readers have told of hilarious evenings in approximate French and English over honest, family meals, often made with home-grown, chemical-free vegetables. The welcome is straightforward, the house unpretentious with that friendly, lived-in air, so what matter if the oilcloth is sometimes bare on the table? The Maréchals are amiable, down-to-earth farmers who lead a sociable life and love having their grandchildren around. Low-beamed bedrooms are modest but comfortable with imitation parquet floors, pastel colours and pretty bedcovers. In summer, meals can be taken under canvas in the flower-filled courtyard.

Rooms: 3 doubles, each with bath or shower & wc.

Price: 260 Frs for two.

Meals: 85 Frs, including wine.

Closed: Never.

Gîte space for 18 people.

From Dreux, N12 to Broué; D115 to Boutigny; D101 dir. Broué; La Musse is between Boutigny & Broué, 'Chambres d'Hôtes' signposted.
Michelin Map No: 231-48

Entry no: 148   Map No: 3

Serge & Jeanne-Marie MARÉCHAL
La Ferme des Tourelles
11 rue des Tourelles
La Musse
28410 Boutigny Prouais, Eure-et-Loir
Tel: (0)2 37 65 18 74/
      (0)6 08 06 29 98 (mob)
Fax: (0)2 37 65 18 74

It feels easy, fun and intelligent. Your hosts are delightful: Virginie beautifully French, Richard a gentle, Europeanised American and their two sons. Down a long wooded drive and set in a big leafy garden, the old family house has tall windows, fine proportions and the air of a properly lived-in château: elegance and deep comfortable armchairs by the marble fireplace under crystal chandeliers. The top floor has been converted into five good rooms with sound-proofing, big beds, masses of hot water, rich, bright colour schemes... and just the right amount of family memorabilia: oils, engravings, lamps, old dishes.

Rooms: 1 triple, 3 doubles, 1 twin, all with shower & wc.

Price: 350-400 Frs for two.

Meals: Available locally.

Closed: November-February.

From A11 exit Ablis on N10 towards Chartres. At Essars, right to St Symphorien, Bleury & Ecrosnes. There right and immediately left to Jonvilliers for 2.5 km. White château gates straight ahead.

Entry no: 149   Map No: 3

Virginie & Richard THOMPSON
Château de Jonvilliers
17 rue d'Épernon, Jonvilliers
28320 Eure-et-Loir, Paris-Ile-de-France
Tel: (0)2 37 31 41 26
Fax: (0)2 37 31 56 74
e-mail: information@chateaudejonvilliers.com
Web: www.chateaudejonvilliers.com

Did Queen Victoria 'stop' here once? We'll never know, but the hunting lodge (17th-century) is ideal for parties while the owners' house (19th-century over 12th-century cellars) has one huge guest room. Monsieur manages the Port and the Chamber of Commerce, Madame the house and garden, masterfully – she has lived here since she was six. Both are proud of their region, keen to share their knowledge and advise on explorations: nature, hiking, historical visits, excellent suggestions for wet days, dry days... A delightful, welcoming couple with natural generosity, elegance, taste and manners and an open-minded approach to all.

Rooms: 1 triple, 1 double, 1 apartment for 5, each with shower & wc.

Price: 290 Frs for two.

Meals: In Eu 2km, Le Tréport 4km. Self-catering in apartment.

Closed: Never.

At Eu, head for Ponts et Marais (D49). As you leave Eu, right on Route de Beaumont (2km).
Michelin Map No: 231-12

Entry no: 150   Map No: 3

Catherine & Jean-Marie DEMARQUET
Manoir de Beaumont
76260 Eu Seine-Maritime
Tel: (0)2 35 50 91 91
e-mail: cd@fnac.net
Web: www.chez.com/demarquet

Normandy

Fierce pagan Vikings sailed warlike up the Seine in their long battle-boats... and settled into the rolling pastures to milk cows for Camembert and breed Christians for the Abbeys.

A dear little village house with a tiny garden overlooking the village green, and a big garden behind. We don't have enough of these semi-rural houses, modest yet authentically themselves. There's a small bedroom with ancient and modern furniture, good linen and mattresses; and a big one with floorboards and rugs, plain walls and *toile de Jouy* soft furnishings. Its beams are painted light blue. Two rooms are in a little building by the main house. The other is in the attic, big and comfortable. It is spotlessly clean, neat and genuine – with a big welcome. *"Très cosy, disent les Anglais"*.

An area of natural and historical delights: the Forest of Eu, lapping up to the edge of the farm, is 9,300 hectares of green space to explore and the Château of Eu is where Louis Philippe and Queen Victoria begat the Entente Cordiale. But come to La Marette for the uncanny silence at night, the birdsong at dawn, and your hosts' radiant smiles at all times. They want you to enjoy the house as it was when their daughters were here: a family atmosphere, the occasional shared shower room, masses of human warmth, not an ounce of hotellishness.

Rooms: 3 doubles, each with shower & wc.

Price: 230 Frs for two.

Meals: Restaurant in village.

Closed: Never.

Rooms: 1 suite with bath & wc; 1 suite & 1 double, each with wc, sharing shower.

Price: 200-280 Frs for two.

Meals: Choice 4-12km; self-catering possible.

Closed: Never.

Gîte space for 10 people.

From Le Tréport, D925 direction Dieppe for 15km. Turn right in village of Biville sur Mer onto rue de l'Église, No. 14 faces you in the middle of a fork in the road.
Michelin Map No: 231-11

Entry no: 151   Map No: 3

Marie-Jose KLAES
14 rue de l'Église
76630 Biville sur Mer
Seine-Maritime
Tel: (0)2 35 83 14 71

From A28 exit Blangy sur Bresle towards Le Tréport to Gamaches; left at lights on D14 to Guerville; follow signs to Melleville. Just before leaving village, right onto Route de la Marette.
Michelin Map No: 231-12

Entry no: 152   Map No: 3

Etienne & Nelly GARÇONNET
La Marette
Route de la Marette
76260 Melleville
Seine-Maritime
Tel: (0)2 35 50 81 65
Fax: (0)2 35 50 81 65

If you're a golfer you will love it here as it's right next to the third green. Green is the dominant colour inside, too, thanks not least to the exotic palms. The light, modern house is definitely creature-comfortable and copes well with the transition between '80s daring and '90s pleasing. There is a television set in each room and the sitting area is really the owners' territory, but they are extremely nice people and Madame is happy to give you a relaxing yoga lesson. Bedroom comfort is plush, bordering on the professional (eg no two bedrooms have walls in common).

Rooms: 2 twins, 1 double, each with bath or shower & wc.

Price: 320-350 Frs for two.

Meals: Full choice in Dieppe.

Closed: Never.

From Dieppe, D75 ('Route du Littoral') W along coast towards Pourville. Once you reach golf course, 1st left, 3rd house on right (signposted). Michelin Map No: 231-11

Entry no: 153   Map No: 3

Alain & Danièle NOËL
24 chemin du Golf
76200 Dieppe
Seine-Maritime
Tel: (0)2 35 84 40 37
Fax: (0)2 35 84 32 51

Gloriously restored and revived, this 17th-century listed château is surrounded by formal gardens designed by a pupil of Lenôtre, with beech maze and lime tree avenues, and a rose garden containing 900 species and 2000 varieties. The Prince (Syrian father, French mother) knows every one and the special attention it requires, while the Princess makes rose-petal jelly for breakfast in the elegant dining room. She also loves to prepare authentic 18th-century dishes from old recipes she has unearthed. The panelled bedrooms are delightfully cosy with canopied beds, proper bed linen, fluffy duvets, and sweet-smelling bathrooms. Simply irresistible.

Rooms: 2 doubles, 1 twin & 2 suites, each with bath & shower & wc.

Price: 480-800 Frs for two.

Meals: 250 Frs, including aperitif, wine & coffee.

Closed: Never.

From Paris A13 direction Rouen/Le Havre; exit 25 Pont de Bretonne/Yvetot. Through Yvetot towards St Valery en Caux. 2km after Ste Colombe turn right direction Houdetot. Château 2km on left. Michelin Map No: 231-10

Entry no: 154   Map No: 3

Princesse Anne-Marie KAYALI
Château du Mesnil Geoffroy
76740 Ermenouville
Seine-Maritime
Tel: (0)2 35 57 12 77
Fax: (0)2 35 57 10 24
e-mail: chateaumesnil.geoffroy@wanadoo.fr
Web: www.siteparc.fr/chateaumesnil

Nature lovers rejoice! Start with a view from your bed of the immaculate garden where pigeons, ducks and cats scurry. Take a long shower and enjoy fluffy towels and bathrobes, then breakfast on four kinds of bread. Fishing and hiking are at your back door, tennis a few miles away; the family suite has welcome wet-weather entertainments. Return from an afternoon jaunt to read Madame's books, relax among the lovely antiques or make yourself something in the kitchen. The owner is most amicable and gracefully succeeds in caring for her teenage children while giving time to guests.

Rooms: 1 triple with bath & wc; 1 suite with bath, shower & wc.

Price: 480-530 Frs for two; babies free. Advance bookings only.

Meals: In Valmont, 1km.

Closed: Never.

Gîte space for 6 people.

From Dieppe D925 W towards Fécamp for approx. 60km then left on D17 to Valmont. In centre, left on D150 towards Ourville for 1.2km; right on Chemin du Vivier; house is 2nd entrance on right (no. 4).
Michelin Map No: 231-9

Entry no: 155   Map No: 3

Dominique CACHERA &
François GREVERIE
Le Clos du Vivier, 4-6 chemin du Vivier
76540 Valmont, Seine-Maritime
Tel: (0)2 35 29 90 95
Fax: (0)2 35 27 44 49
e-mail: dc@le-clos-du-vivier.com
Web: www.le-clos-du-vivier.com

Madame loves to talk (in French) and has a winning smile. Her house (she was born here), which stands in a classic, square, poplar-sheltered Seine-Maritime farmyard, is 300 years old; the worn old stones, bricks and flints (less worn!) bear witness to its age – so does the fine timberwork inside. Otherwise it has been fairly deeply modernised, but the long lace-clothed breakfast table before the log fire (in winter) is most welcoming. The pleasant rooms are good if unremarkable and the only sounds are the occasional lowing of the herd and the breeze blowing in the poplars.

Rooms: 1 triple with bath & wc; 1 double with shower & wc; 2 doubles sharing shower & wc.

Price: 230 Frs for two.

Meals: Auberge 1km.

Closed: Never.

Gîte space for 10 people.

From Dieppe N27 direction Rouen for 29km; right on N29 through Yerville & direction Yvetot for 4.5km; left on D20 to Motteville; right to Flamanville. In village, Rue Verte is road behind church. Farm 300m on left; signposted.
Michelin Map No: 231-22

Entry no: 156   Map No: 3

Yves & Béatrice QUEVILLY BARET
La Ferme de la Rue Verte
76970 Flamanville
Seine-Maritime
Tel: (0)2 35 96 81 27
Web: www.sawdays.co.uk

This relatively youthful château was built in 1864, you won't find a chip in a marble fireplace, the panelling and floors are perfect, and some curtains are over 100 years old. The stained-glass windows on the first-floor landing give an almost theatrical impression. Daniel has owned the place since 1983, but moved here only recently with Gisela, who is German and speaks little French or English. The grounds are informal and rambling with ancient trees, and cattle to help with the mowing.

Rooms: 1 double, 1 twin, each with shower & wc; 3 twins, sharing bath, shower & separate wc.

Price: 300-400 Frs for two.

Meals: 150 Frs, incl. wine & coffee.

Closed: November-March.

From Yvetot, D37 (2km) then D240 to Baons le Comte. Right after church direction Loumare, 800m to junction. Then right for 600m, entrance on right. Michelin Map No: 231-21

Entry no: 157   Map No: 3

Daniel MAINÇON & Gisela NUN
Château des Baons-le-Comte
76190 Yvetot
Seine-Maritime
Tel: (0)2 35 56 72 69

Madame is a blithe soul who proclaims that she's "on holiday all year" and her welcome is terrific – nothing is too much trouble. The colourful, flowerful garden, her great love, is a wonder in almost any season, a hillside oasis of tumbling vegetation in the town (the road can be noisy but it's all right at night). Her guest rooms are cosy and tempting, reflecting the history of the old house and her collecting flair. There is a dayroom for guests but breakfast is in the pretty family dining room. A very French address, full of character, excellent value and a good base for exploring the churches and villages that fill this area.

Rooms: 2 doubles, 1 triple, 1 quadruple, each with shower & wc.

Price: 280 Frs for two.

Meals: In village; self-catering possible.

Closed: Never.

Gîte space for 4 people.

From Rouen D982 towards Le Havre; under Pont de Brotonne, in to Caudebec, right onto Rue de la République (D131) towards Yvetot; No 68 is 500m on the right. Michelin Map No: 231-21

Entry no: 158   Map No: 3

Christiane VILLAMAUX
68 rue de la République
76490 Caudebec en Caux
Seine-Maritime
Tel: (0)2 35 96 10 15
Fax: (0)2 35 96 75 25
e-mail: christiane.villamaux@libertysurf.fr
Web: villamaux.ifrance.com

The stern black front door of this solid townhouse hides a light, stylish interior with views across the old town to the spires of Rouen Cathedral. Dominique, a keen and cultured Egyptologist, has a flair for refined decoration – see her paintings, coverings and country furniture. There are rugs on the wooden floor in the sitting room and French windows lead to a balcony and the garden. Nothing standard, nothing too studied, a real personal home and a lovely setting for an unhurried feast at her flower-decked breakfast table and a chance to quiz her (her English is excellent) about her latest digs in Egypt.

In an ancient street in the historic centre of lovely old Rouen, 100m from the Cathedral, stands this 17th-century family home. Monsieur enjoys sharing, in English, German or Norman and with much wry humour, the history of Rouen and the comfort of his lovely (quiet) townhouse. It is a treasure-trove of curios, with huge beams, big windows and Norman antiques. Bathrooms are crisply modern, breakfast generous and your reception cheerful. *Car park a short walk from house.*

Rooms: 1 double with bath & wc; 2 doubles, each with bath, sharing wc.

Price: 270-300 Frs for two.

Meals: 110 Frs, including wine & coffee.

Closed: October & November.

Rooms: 2 doubles, 1 twin, both with bathrooms (can be a suite with kitchen); 1 single, sharing bathroom.

Price: 300 Frs for two.

Meals: Vast choice on the spot.

Closed: Never.

Gîte space for 8 people.

On Cathedral-side embankment: at Théâtre des Arts, take Rue Jeanne d'Arc; Rue aux Ours is 2nd on right but NO parking. Leave car in Bourse or Pucelle car parks, near house, and walk. Michelin Map No: 231-23

In Rouen, follow signs to Gare SNCF. Take Rue Rochefoucault to right of station. Left into Rue des Champs des Oiseaux, across 2 sets of lights, straight over into Rue Vigné, left at fork into Rue Hénault. Black door on left. Michelin Map No: 231-23

Entry no: 159   Map No: 3

Entry no: 160   Map No: 3

Philippe & Annick AUNAY-
STANGUENNEC
45 rue aux Ours
76000 Rouen
Seine-Maritime
Tel: (0)2 35 70 99 68
Fax: (0)2 35 98 61 35
Web: www.sawdays.co.uk

Mme Dominique GOGNY
22 rue Hénault
76130 Mont Saint Aignan
Seine-Maritime
Tel: (0)2 35 70 26 95
Fax: (0)2 35 52 03 52
e-mail: chambreavecvue@online.fr
Web: chambreavecvue.online.fr

A long drive leads past carefully-tended flowerbeds up to the old *pressoir*, built during the French Revolution and now restored by this exceptional couple – he a gentle ex-sailor who can tell a tale or two, she quiet and engaging. Bedrooms were a labour of love for her – fabrics and papers carefully chosen, flowers cut and dried to match, old trunks and carved armoires chosen from family treasure stores. Breakfast on home-made cake to classical music, dine on local specialities with flowers on the table. *Children over 12 welcome.*

Rooms: 2 doubles, each with shower & wc.

Price: 280 Frs for two.

Meals: 140 Frs, including wine & coffee.

Closed: Never.

Expect to see a brightly-coloured tanker appear from behind the trees heading for the Channel, or the great annual armada sailing past – such is the magic of this site on the banks of the Seine just below Rouen. The Laurents' garden goes down to the water's edge and they offer binoculars for bird-watching, maps and books for trail-exploring – it is a Panda (WWF) house. The big house is for guests, the owners occupy a thatched cottage next door. There are beams and panelling, antiques and windows onto that stunning view, a kitchen/diner, a very comfortable sitting room and Madame has all the time in the world for you.

Rooms: 2 suites for 3, 2 quadruples, each with bath or shower & wc.

Price: 280 Frs for two.

Meals: 85 Frs, excluding wine (wine 60 Frs, cider 26 Frs); self-catering possible.

Closed: Never.

Gîte space for 14 people.

From Le Havre towards Paris & Rouen. Over Pont de Tancarville on A131 then right on D810 to Pont Audemer. D87 through St Germain Village. Continue D87 then right into Tricqueville on CV19; signposted. Michelin Map No: 231-20

From Pont Audemer D139 NE for 10km to Bourneville & continue D139 to Aizier. In village, left at Mairie towards Vieux Port; house on right. Michelin Map No: 231-21

Entry no: 161   Map No: 3

Entry no: 162   Map No: 3

Gaston & Michelle LE PLEUX
La Clé des Champs
27500 Tricqueville
Eure
Tel: (0)2 32 41 37 99
e-mail: lepleux@club-internet.fr
Web: www.sawdays.co.uk

Yves & Marie-Thérèse LAURENT
Les Sources Bleues
Le Bourg
27500 Aizier
Eure
Tel: (0)2 32 57 26 68
Fax: (0)2 32 57 42 25
Web: www.sawdays.co.uk

This enthusiastic couple now offer special breaks for food- and wine-lovers – a natural progression as they are knowledgeable and inspiring about both and have a strong following. Nicky is English, delightful and a *cordon bleu* cook, Régis French with great taste in all departments. There will be a stylish new dining room in 2001 and there's nothing nicer than waking up in one of the attractive, antique- or ethnic-furnished rooms of this superbly-renovated farmhouse (great bathrooms too). The grounds only get prettier; strutted by poultry and overseen by black-headed sheep. Come and enjoy it!

Its atmosphere is as pleasing as its looks: this is a genuinely old, Normandy farm house (apple trees abound), its lovely external timber frame enclosing a heart-warming antique clutter spread with excellent taste over bricks and beams, original tiles and carved furniture. The delicious bedrooms are subtly lit by dormer windows, softly furnished country-style, pastel-hued and comfortably bathroomed. Monsieur is a charming gentleman, full of smiles. Madame is most attentive. Both are proud of their warmly cosy house and its ravishing garden with long views of the peaceful valley.

Rooms: 2 doubles, 1 twin, 1 triple, 1 quadruple, all with bath or shower & wc.

Price: 700 Frs for two including dinner, aperitif, wine & beverages; min. 2 nights.

Meals: Dinner included.

Closed: Never.

Rooms: 2 doubles/twins, 1 suite for 4, each with bath or shower & wc.

Price: 250-270 Frs for two.

Meals: 110 Frs, including aperitif, wine & coffee.

Closed: September-April.

From A13, Le Havre exit, on D139 towards Pont Audemer. In Fourmetot, left towards Corneville. Farm 1km from turning on left.
Michelin Map No: 231-21

Entry no: 163   Map No: 3

From Paris A13 exit 26; left on D89 to 'Médine' roundabout. Straight across direction Evreux/Appeville-Annebault; left immediately after Les Marettes sign then follow Chambres d'Hôtes signs.
Michelin Map No: 231-15

Entry no: 164   Map No: 3

Régis & Nicky DUSSARTRE
L'Aufragère
La Croisée
27500 Fourmetot, Eure
Tel: (0)2 32 56 91 92
Fax: (0)2 32 57 75 34
e-mail: regis@laufragere.com
Web: www.laufragere.com

Françoise & Yves CLOSSON MAZE
Les Aubépines
Aux Chauffourniers
27290 Appeville dit Annebault
Eure
Tel: (0)2 32 56 14 25
Fax: (0)2 32 56 14 25

Madame, tall, sophisticated and immaculate, did all the wallpapering herself and is naturally relaxed and welcoming. She finds it normal that everyone sit at the same big table in the ochre and scarlet breakfast room. There is a family-friendly common room with billiards, table tennis, picnic table, refrigerator. Bedrooms are big and beautifully decorated (*merci Madame!*); *La Jaune* has superb views. No finery, a touch of faded grandeur and all-pervasive warmth characterise this splendid house of friendship.

Rooms: 2 family rooms, 1 double, 1 twin, each with bath or shower & wc.

Price: 280 Frs for two.

Meals: Choice in Orbec.

Closed: Never.

From Lisieux on N13 towards Evreux for 18km to Thiberville. Then D145 towards Orbec for 10km. Château on right about 50m after sign 'Le Grand Bus'.
Michelin Map No: 231-32

Entry no: **165**   Map No: 3

Bruno & Laurence de PRÉAUMONT
Château du Grand Bus
St Germain la Campagne
27230 Thiberville
Eure
Tel: (0)2 32 44 71 14
Fax: (0)2 32 46 45 81

Just one loo between three bedrooms but we think that is a small price to pay for being in such a remarkable old house (rebuilt from nought in the '50s!). It was an important site in the Hundred Years War. The rickety wooden bridge across the moat is a good introduction, followed by the affable old nanny goat by the door. Madame has a touch of charming eccentricity and is an excellent hostess. The service is elegant: silver teapot, fruit juice in crystal glasses at breakfast, tea in the afternoon – and the rooms are perfect.

Rooms: 2 doubles, 1 twin, each with bath or shower, sharing wc.

Price: 400 Frs for two.

Meals: 130 Frs, including wine & coffee.

Closed: January & February.

From Breteuil, D141 direction Rugles; through forest. At Bémécourt, take left turn; 300m after the traffic lights, right into Allée du Vieux Château.
Michelin Map No: 231-34

Entry no: **166**   Map No: 3

Mme Maryvonne LALLEMAND-LEGRAS
Le Vieux Château
27160 Bémécourt
Eure
Tel: (0)2 32 29 90 47

In a softly wooded environment, with pastoral meadow and lake spread before it, Hermos is a house full of quiet history and family atmosphere. Outside, a typical 16th-century marriage of brick and stone and a baronial double staircase; inside, panels, mouldings, parquet floors, flowers all over. Madame is a most welcoming hostess, full of spontaneous smiles, whose family has owned the house for 100 years. She also gardens, organises seminars (not when B&B guests are here) and cares for two children. The large panelled bedrooms have refreshing colours, good beds, old wardrobes and windows onto the gentle world outside. Elegant and peaceful.

Rooms: 1 quadruple with bath & wc; 1 triple with shower & wc.

Price: 250-350 Frs for two.

Meals: Choice 2km.

Closed: Never.

Gîte space for 20 people.

From A13, exit Maison Brulée on N138 direction Bourgthéroulde & Brionne. 8km after Bourgthéroulde left on D83 to Le Gros Theil; on entering village sharp right on D92 & follow signs for 2km. Michelin Map No: 231-22

Entry no: **167**   Map No: 3

Béatrice & Patrice NOËL-WINDSOR
Manoir d'Hermos
27800 St Eloi de Fourques
Eure
Tel: (0)2 32 35 51 32
Fax: (0)2 32 35 51 32

French in every way: old and new furnishings, tailored and natural garden, cultural references (Saint-Exupéry, author of the immortal *Petit Prince* and a friend of Madame's father's, stayed here). The sensuous garden is full of old favourites: lilac, peonies, honeysuckle, fruit trees. In the middle of the village, the house is very old (1500s), very quiet and has an atmosphere that inspires ease and rest. Madame used to be an antique dealer so breakfast is served on old silver. She sculpts and paints, and also restores statues in the 15th-century church opposite the house.

Rooms: 2 doubles, 1 triple, 1 quadruple (in cottage), each with shower & wc.

Price: 260 Frs for two.

Meals: 90 Frs, excluding wine.

Closed: Never.

Gîte space for 12 people.

From A13 exit 19 to Louviers; D313 towards Elbeuf for 11km; left on D60 to St Didier des Bois. House with white iron gate opposite church. Michelin Map No: 231-22

Entry no: **168**   Map No: 3

Mme Annick AUZOUX
1 place de l'Église
27370 St Didier des Bois
Eure
Tel: (0)2 32 50 60 93
Fax: (0)2 32 25 41 83
Web: www.sawdays.co.uk

Close to perfection... not surprising given Janine's bubbling enthusiasm and sprightly energy. She is, nevertheless, 'classic' in her dress and appearance and creates a very special breakfast with pewter service and folded napkins. She is deeply intolerant of dust and dirt, so the immensely comfortable bedrooms might even be cleaner than your own. The downstairs sitting room is vast, about 80m², the staircase is beautifully sculpted, the garden goes down to the river and you are halfway between Giverny and Rouen.

Rooms: 1 double/twin, 1 suite for 5, each with bath & wc.

Price: 250-285 Frs for two.

Meals: In village or 6km away.

Closed: Never.

Gîte space for 4 people.

A lovely, elegant address of listed château and gardens (landscaped and formal), vast woodlands for walking (and shooting, in autumn), a tennis court, an ancient fallen mulberry tree that has rebuilt itself, two suites full of canopied beds in the 18th-century château, other fine rooms in the converted dovecote. Breakfast is served in the *salle de chasse*, try the mulberry or wild plum jam – Parma ham and eggs are also a possibility. The lady of the manor's exquisite taste has weaved its magic from floor to ceiling, from Jouy print to antique wardrobe and you will feel like prince and princess here, just 30 minutes drive from Giverny.

Rooms: 2 doubles, 1 double/twin, 2 suites for 4/5, all with bath or shower & wc.

Price: 500-900 Frs for two.

Meals: Restaurant 8km.

Closed: Never.

From Evreux, D155 north. 300m after Les Faulx hamlet, right for Heudreville. House in cul-de-sac opposite church. Michelin Map No: 231-35

From A13 exit 'Louviers' on A154 towards Évreux, exit Caër/Gravigny on D155 towards Acquigny. Through Boulay Morin, 500m after village, left to Émalleville; château opposite church. Michelin Map No: 231-35

Entry no: 169   Map No: 3

Entry no: 170   Map No: 3

Mme Janine BOURGEOIS
La Ferme
4 rue de l'Ancienne Poste
27400 Heudreville sur Eure
Eure
Tel: (0)2 32 50 20 69
Fax: (0)2 32 50 20 69

Lilian THIEBLOT
Château d'Émalleville
17 rue de l'Église
27930 Émalleville, Eure
Tel: (0)2 32 34 01 87
Fax: (0)2 32 34 30 27
e-mail: chateau_emallevil@yahoo.fr
Web: www.multimania.com/chateauemallevil

The theme indoors is decidedly Latin-American as this charming Franco-Spanish couple spent more that 20 years there before renovating their 18th-century manor house between the coast of Normandy and the châteaux of the Loire. Bedrooms aren't huge but are solidly comfortable with good furniture, interesting prints and immaculate bathrooms. There's a fully 'telecommunicating' study too. Fresh breads, fruit juice and home-made jams (always a choice; from rhubarb to cherry) for breakfast at the huge Andean cedar breakfast table. A quiet, pretty garden and good conversation in English, French, Italian, Spanish or Catalan.

Rooms: 1 suite for 2, 1 family room for 4, 1 double, each with bath or shower & wc.

Price: 270-320 Frs for two.

Meals: Auberges 5km.

Closed: Never.

From A13 exit 17 for Gaillon then W towards Evreux on D316 through Autheuil, St Vigor & up hill then right for Reuilly. House on road, 200m past Mairie on right.
Michelin Map No: 231-35

Entry no: 171   Map No: 3

Jean-Pierre & Amaia TREVISANI
Clair Matin
19 rue de l'Église
27930 Reuilly, Eure
Tel: (0)2 32 34 71 47
Fax: (0)2 32 34 97 64
e-mail: clair_matin@compuserve.com

Eliane and Michel have spent the last five years restoring this lovely 19th-century farmhouse in a particularly pretty village with great care and taste. Guests stay in a self-contained part of the house, which has its own dayroom and breakfast area with lots of space to slump in front of the fire. Bedrooms are spotless with *toile de Jouy* fabrics, beamed ceilings and polished floorboards. Outside, sweeping lawns run down to a pretty stream, which meanders beneath high wooded cliffs. Eliane is passionate about her garden and loves to chat about it, pointing out the rich and the rare.

Rooms: 1 double, 1 twin, each with bath & wc.

Price: 270Frs for two.

Meals: Choice nearby.

Closed: Never.

A13 Paris-Rouen, exit 16 direction Cocherel. After 10km direction Chambray. Left in front of monument. Left after 100m direction Fontaine sous Jouy. In centre right onto Rue de l'Ancienne Forge. After 800m Rue de l'Aulnaie on right.
Michelin Map No: 231-35

Entry no: 172   Map No: 3

Eliane & Michel PHILIPPE
L'Aulnaie
29 rue de l'Aulnaie
27120 Fontaine sous Jouy, Eure
Tel: (0)2 32 36 89 05
Fax: (0)2 32 36 89 05
e-mail: emi.philippe@worldonline.fr
Web: perso.worldonline.fr/chambre-fontaine

Exquisite!... and without a whiff of pretension. The Brunets, as delightful as their house, have the lightness of touch to combine the fresh best of modern French taste with an eye for authenticity – in a brand new house. There are recycled château windows, light flooding in from both sides of this classical narrow *maison de campagne*, eye-catching stretches of pine-floored corridor, handsome rugs, a brave mix of old and modern furniture, massive comfort. Gorgeous.

Rooms: 3 twins, 2 doubles, each with bath or shower & wc.

Price: 600-800 Frs for two; reduction 2 nights or more.

Meals: In village or 5km.

Closed: December-March, except by arrangement.

Gîte space for 10 people.

From A13 exit 14 towards Vernon/Giverny. Entering Giverny left on Rue Claude Monet. After church and Hotel Baudy first left on Rue Blanche Hoshedé Monet for 1.2km; left on white arrow, immediately right on track for 800m then left to house. Michelin Map No: 231-36

Entry no: 173   Map No: 3

Didier & Marie Lorraine BRUNET
La Réserve
27620 Giverny
Eure
Tel: (0)2 32 21 99 09
Fax: (0)2 32 21 99 09
e-mail: ml.brunet@voila.fr
Web: www.giverny.org/hotels/brunet/

The clean, cool River Epte, which Monet diverted at nearby Giverny to create the ponds for his famous *Nymphéas*, runs at the bottom of the pretty garden and bestows the same quality of serenity here. The house is beautifully furnished with family antiques and Madame, a strong, intelligent and inherently elegant person, willingly shares her extensive knowledge of all things Norman (including food). Rooms are stylish and quiet; one has an Art Deco brass bed designed by *Grand-père*. The attic twin is up steep stairs and under sloping ceilings.

Rooms: 2 doubles, each with shower or bath & wc; 1 twin sharing bathroom.

Price: 300-330 Frs for two; special rate for 3 or more nights.

Meals: 130 Frs, including wine & coffee.

Closed: 16 December-14 March.

From Dieppe, D915 to Gisors. Cross Gisors then D10 towards Vernon. In Dangu, Rue du Gué is beside the river Epte. Look for house with green shutters. Michelin Map No: 237-3

Entry no: 174   Map No: 3

Nicole de SAINT PÈRE
Les Ombelles
4 rue du Gué
27720 Dangu, Eure
Tel: (0)2 32 55 04 95
Fax: (0)2 32 55 59 87
e-mail: vextour@aol.com
Web: vextour.ifrance.com

Jean and his cousin François bought La Maigraire in 1998 and have restored it taking care to keep the right feel. Built in 1870, it stands in pretty grounds and has its own fishing. Jean studied at the Louvre and worked as an interior designer and antique dealer before falling for La Maigraire. Luckily he kept a little cache of pieces which look perfectly at home here. These new and attentive hosts will make you feel very welcome: providing delicious home-made jam for breakfast and perhaps even playing the piano while you have tea in the *grand salon*.

Rooms: 1 double & 1 suite for 2/3, each with bath or shower & wc.

Price: 450-600 Frs for two; afternoon tea included.

Meals: Several good restaurants in the area.

Closed: Never.

From the D962, between Flers and Domfront, take the D260 towards Forges de Varennes & Champsecret. After 1.5km turn left into the hamlet of La Maigraire.
Michelin Map No: 231-41

Entry no: 175   Map No: 2

Jean FISCHER
Château de la Maigraire
61700 St Bômer les Forges
Orne
Tel: (0)2 33 38 09 52
Fax: (0)2 33 38 09 52
Web: www.sawdays.co.uk

In a deeply rural spot where peace is the norm not the exception, you are unhesitatingly received into a warm and lively family and it feels GOOD. Two rooms are in a converted outbuilding and have an appropriately rustic air – the upstairs room is bigger and lighter, the ground-floor room has a little private garden; both have beams, old wardrobes and mini-kitchens. The suite, ideal for families, is in the main house. Breakfast is at the family table, there are fresh flowers everywhere and your hosts have a genuine sense of country hospitality. Children are welcome to visit the Laignel's son's farm next door.

Rooms: 2 doubles, each with shower, wc & mini-kitchen; 1 suite for 4 with bath & wc.

Price: 220 Frs for two.

Meals: Restaurant 4km. Self-catering in 2 rooms.

Closed: Never.

Gîte space for 6 people.

From Argentan N158 direction Caen. After sign for Moulin sur Orne, take next left. House 800m on left; signposted. (3.5km from Argentan.)
Michelin Map No: 231-31

Entry no: 176   Map No: 3

Janine & Rémy LAIGNEL
Le Mesnil
61200 Occagnes
Orne
Tel: (0)2 33 67 11 12

You buy into fun, a real unfussy family atmosphere and a most successful mix of things English and French in this converted manor-farm with its pigeon tower and duck stream. Your hosts have sheep, dairy cows, 300 apple trees (*Normandie oblige!*) and are thoroughly integrated, as are their daughters. Their guest bedrooms in the old Camembert-making dairy are light, soberly furnished with touches of *fantaisie* and Diana's very decorative stencils. Breakfast is superb, dinner should be an occasion to linger over and remember. *Reduction for stays of more than 1 night.*

Rooms: 1 triple, 1 double, 1 twin, each with bath or shower & wc.

Price: 330 Frs for two; reduction for 2 nights or more.

Meals: 130 Frs, including aperitif, wine, coffee and home-baked bread.

Closed: December-February.

From Vimoutiers, D916 direction Argentan. Just outside Vimoutiers take left fork D16 signed Exmes then D26 signed Survie & Exmes.
Michelin Map No: 231-43

Entry no: 177   Map No: 3

Diana & Christopher
WORDSWORTH
Les Gains, Survie
61310 Exmes, Orne
Tel: (0)2 33 36 05 56
Fax: (0)2 33 35 03 65
e-mail: christopher.wordsworth@libertysurf.fr
Web: www.sawdays.co.uk

These are caring, generous, sensitive farmers who like contact and share their quiet sense of humour with each other, their guests and their children. Rooms, called *Spring, Summer, Autumn* and... *Cashmere*, have cane or brass bedsteads, plain country décor and fresh flowers. Madame spoils you at breakfast and dinner with local honey and Camembert, her own poultry and rabbit from the field across the stream. Her home-made jam repertoire includes dandelion-flower and apple. Meals are normally taken with the family – most convivial despite limited English. The sitting room, playroom and kitchen facilities are a bonus.

Rooms: 2 doubles, 1 triple, 1 quadruple, each with shower & wc.

Price: 230 Frs for two.

Meals: 90 Frs, including wine & coffee (Thursday & Saturday only).

Closed: Never.

From Argentan, N26 direction L'Aigle and Paris. Left at Silli en Gouffern. At Ste Eugénie, last farm on left.
Michelin Map No: 231-31

Entry no: 178   Map No: 3

Pierre & Ghislaine MAURICE
La Grande Ferme
Ste Eugénie
61160 Aubry en Exmes
Orne
Tel: (0)2 33 36 82 36
Fax: (0)2 33 36 99 52

They somehow keep going with the farm, although they long for a younger farmer to take over. Any takers? We are delighted to have the Bourgaults in the book for there is something quintessentially *chambre d'hôtes* about them and their house. It is unaffected, authentic, low-ceilinged and comfortable. The rooms have a very personal mix of old and new furniture... another traditional B&B touch. Madame bubbles with energy, loves children and gives you the sort of welcome that makes you glow.

Rooms: 1 double, 1 triple, each with bath or shower & wc. (Overflow room available.)

Price: 250 Frs for two.

Meals: Choice within 3km.

Closed: Never.

Inside is as angular as outside: the staircase is a monumental piece of carpentry elbowing its way up to the second floor where a panoramic window lets in the whole sky. Grandmother's toy camel stands here in its 1905 skin: the house was built by her parents in 1910 to an open, American-style plan and sliding glass partitions give generous ground-floor spaces. Guest rooms are good too, much-windowed, with soft colours, marble fireplaces and old mirrors. All spotless, it is the pride and joy of your alert, eager hostess who talks and laughs readily and manages her home and guests expertly.

Rooms: 1 twin with bath & wc; 1 suite for 4 with shower & wc.

Price: 330 Frs for two.

Meals: 145 Frs, including aperitif, wine & coffee.

Closed: December-February.

From Rouen, N138 direction Alençon, through Bernay to Monnai. There, right onto D12; after 2km, follow signs to Chambres d'Hôtes.
Michelin Map No: 231-32

Entry no: 179   Map No: 3

Gérard & Emilienne BOURGAULT
Les Roches
61470 Le Sap
Orne
Tel: (0)2 33 39 47 39
Web: www.sawdays.co.uk

From Argentan N26 E for 37km. Entrance 4km after Planches on right by small crucifix; long lime-bordered drive.
Michelin Map No: 231-44

Entry no: 180   Map No: 3

Antoine & Nathalie LE BRETHON
La Bussière
61370 Ste Gauburge-Ste Colombe
Orne
Tel: (0)2 33 34 05 23
Fax: (0)2 33 34 71 47

Utter peace among the cattle-dotted Norman pastures – one woman, her horses, dogs and cats in a low-lying farmhouse, beautifully rebuilt "from a pile of stones", where old and new mix easily and flowers rampage all around. Barbara calls it her "corner of paradise" and her delight is contagious. The lovely sloping garden is all her own work too – she appears to have endless energy. The pastel guest rooms, two upstairs, one with garden access on the ground floor, are attractive and have brand new bathrooms. Come by horse, or walk. Beautiful country and a sociable, interesting, horse-loving woman to welcome you.

Rooms: 2 twins, 1 double, each with bath or shower & wc.

Price: 250 Frs for two.

Meals: 100 Frs, including wine & coffee.

Closed: Never.

From Courtomer, past Mairie then right after last building towards Tellières. 2km from turning, left at crossroads towards Le Marnis.
Michelin Map No: 231-44

Helen and Rex will really look after you in their old Percheron farmhouse which they are doing up after moving from the Auvergne. The region is famous for its heavy horses and Rex runs a company selling horse blankets. Feel free to potter all day on their land or venture further afield and come back to a cup of tea, a friendly welcome and a delicious supper in the farmhouse kitchen. Helen may be English but you would never guess it from her cooking: it's probably more French than her neighbours'. Rooms are comfortable and fresh in cream and white.

Rooms: 1 double, 1 triple, each with bath & wc.

Price: 300 Frs for two.

Meals: 140 Frs, including wine, by arrangement.

Closed: December.

From Mortagne au Perche take D931 towards Mamers. After 8km turn right for Coulimer at small crossroads, D650. La Simondrière 800m on left, last of small group of houses.
Michelin Map No: 231-44

Entry no: **181**	Map No: 3

Barbara GOFF
Le Marnis
Tellières le Plessis
61390 Courtomer, Orne
Tel: (0)2 33 27 47 55
Fax: (0)2 33 27 29 55
e-mail: barbaragoff@minitel.net
Web: www.sawdays.co.uk

Entry no: **182**	Map No: 3

Rex & Helen BARR
La Simondrière
61360 Coulimer
Orne
Tel: (0)2 33 25 55 34
Fax: (0)2 33 25 49 01
e-mail: prima@wanadoo.fr
Web: www.sawdays.co.uk

Fascinating hosts; they are retired doctors, enjoying their passion for beautiful countryside (they have 100 acres) and its wildlife, their garden, orchard and animals, music (the music room is truly special), mellow old buildings – made comfortable without any loss of character – good food and fine wine and, of course, people. At breakfast, probably out on the terrace, there'll be fresh eggs, home-made and pesticide-free fruit, jams and yoghurt. Two bedrooms have a private stairway in the main house, one double is in a separate building, with a big upstairs bedroom and fabulous view. Go and discover this place!

Delightful people and a fascinating house. An ancestor fled to Scotland in 1789 and returned an Adam fan, hence the *trompe l'œil* marble and Wedgwood-moulded staircase. A civilised, friendly couple welcome you: she organises chamber music in their big, log-fired drawing room; he makes top-class Camembert and mows his acres on Sundays. The elegant bedrooms have antiques, books, ancestral portraits, much soft comfort and a loo in a tower. The dining room has wrap-around oak panelling inlaid with precious woods, a fine setting for breakfast. Come and belong briefly to this wonderful world. Good walks start 2km away.

Rooms: 2 doubles, 1 twin, each with shower or bath & wc.

Price: 500-600 Frs for two.

Meals: Available locally.

Closed: Never.

Rooms: 1 twin, 2 doubles, each with bath & wc.

Price: 550-650 Frs for two.

Meals: 2 good restaurants within 5 km.

Closed: Never; open by arrangement December-March.

From Verneuil-Avre D941 to La Ferté Vidame; D4 then D11 to Logny. Then D111 to Monceaux. Right after 500m at chapel, then left onto D291 towards Maison Maugis. After 2.5km right following sign for 'L'Emière'.
Michelin Map No: 231-45

From Verneuil sur Avre, N12 SW 24km to Carrefour Ste Anne. Left on D918 towards Longny au Perche for 4.5km; left on D289 towards Moulicent. House 800m on right.
Michelin Map No: 231-45

Entry no: 183 Map No: 3

Entry no: 184 Map No: 3

Edith & Jean-Louis GRANDJEAN
Domaine de l'Emière
61110 Maison Maugis
Orne
Tel: (0)2 33 73 74 19
Fax: (0)2 33 73 69 80

Jacques & Pascale de LONGCAMP
Château de la Grande Noë
61290 Moulicent
Orne
Tel: (0)2 33 73 63 30
Fax: (0)2 33 83 62 92
e-mail: grandenoe@wanadoo.fr
Web: www.sawdays.co.uk

This ancient fortress of a farm has a stupendous tithe barn and a little watchtower transformed into a delightful gîte for two. Madame's energy is boundless, she is ever redecorating, cooking (excellent Norman cuisine), improving, much supported by her farmer husband. She is proud of her family home, its flagstones worn smooth with age and its fine country antiques so suited to the sober, high-ceilinged rooms (one has a shower in a tower, another looks over the calving field). Breakfast by the massive fireplace may be candle or oil-lamp lit on dark mornings.

Rooms: 2 triples, 1 double, each with shower & wc.

Price: 280 Frs for two.

Meals: 100 Frs, including cider.

Closed: Never.

Gîte space for 6 people.

This charming fortified working farm, parts of which are 15th century, has its own private chapel, once used as a dairy and a circular pigeonnier. Rooms are big with high beamed ceilings, and there's a fine walled garden. The whole place has been carefully restored,the result is unpretentiously stylish; the atmosphere friendly and relaxed. The bedrooms have been decorated quite beautifully, each with its own theme; one navy blue and white with nautical pictures, others more traditional with antique furniture and flowery fabrics. The sea is just a short walk away.

Rooms: 1 double, 1 twin, 1 suite, 1 quadruple, all with shower & wc.

Price: 300 Frs for two.

Meals: Choice locally.

Closed: November-March.

From Bayeux N13 for 30km; exit on D514 to Osmanville and on towards Grandchamp for 5km. Left towards Géfosse Fontenay; house 800m along on left before church.
Michelin Map No: 231-15

Gérard & Isabelle LEHARIVEL
Ferme de la Rivière
14230 Géfosse Fontenay
Calvados
Tel: (0)2 31 22 64 45
Fax: (0)2 31 22 01 18
e-mail: gerard.leharivel1@fnac.net

Leave N13 at Osmanville and take D514 towards Grandcamp Maisy. After 4km turn left onto D199a towards Géfosse-Fontenay for 400m then follow yellow signs on right.
Michelin Map No: 231-15

François & Agnès LEMARIÉ
L'Hermerel
14230 Géfosse Fontenay
Calvados
Tel: (0)2 31 22 64 12
Fax: (0)2 31 22 64 12

The dining room is the centrepiece: panelling, old tiles, windows facing both ways, sun pouring in. You eat at separate tables where the views are across the moat, over the formal garden with its swings and profusion of plants, and down to the orangery. Some of the parquet floors are magnificent, as is the whole house, which is littered with woodcarvings and furniture made by Monsieur's father. The bedrooms are, of course, splendid. The US Press Corps camped here in 1944 – sensibly. *Pets by arrangement.*

Rooms: 5 doubles, all with bath & wc.

Price: 350-400 Frs for two.

Meals: Choice 6-10km.

Closed: December-March.

Madame's son bakes the most delicious bread in the 18th-century oven he has restored. He also produces cakes and *pâtisseries* of all sorts for afternoon tea. Madame is a quiet, kindly woman and has created an easy family atmosphere. Ask for *La Chambre Ancienne*, definitely the best, with its low ceiling, antique beds and planked floor; the others have less character, though they are big and have that country feel. If you have a spare moment, do take a boat ride in the bird-full *Marais* – they'll organise it for you. There is a small camping site on the farm.

Rooms: 2 twins, 1 triple, all with shower & wc.

Price: 230 Frs for two.

Meals: Ferme-auberge 3km.

Closed: Never.

From Cherbourg, N13 to Isigny. There, right on D5 towards Le Molay. Left near Vouilly church. Château on right after 500m.
Michelin Map No: 231-15

Entry no: 187   Map No: 2

Marie-José & James HAMEL
Château de Vouilly
Vouilly
14230 Isigny sur Mer
Calvados
Tel: (0)2 31 22 08 59
Fax: (0)2 31 22 90 58
Web: www.sawdays.co.uk

From Bayeux, D5 W through Le Molay Littry direction Bernesq & Briqueville. Right about 0.75km before Bernesq; Le Ruppaley on this road, signposted.
Michelin Map No: 231-16

Entry no: 188   Map No: 2

Marcelle MARIE
Le Ruppaley
14710 Bernesq
Calvados
Tel: (0)2 31 22 54 44

Go to great lengths to stay here; the solid beauty of the old fortified farmhouse, its simplicity, and the serenity of the *Marais* lapping at the edge of the lawn all make it near-perfect. Your hosts, too, are amiable and generous, happy to wait up for you if you arrive late; the rooms are comfortably simple. This is a WWF *Gîte Panda*, a place to learn all about local flora and fauna – nature guides distributed, binoculars on loan. Stretch your eyes across a luminous landscape of marshes and fields, eat well, enjoy the cider, and sleep in bliss.

Rooms: 1 double, 1 twin, 1 suite for 5, all with bath or shower & wc.

Price: 260 Frs for two.

Meals: Available locally.

Closed: October-Easter.

How old can a house be? This one is 11th-century, renovated in 1801... The brass-railed staircase and the drawing room are gracious but not grand. The dining room, with its huge fireplace and modern bar, is relaxed in its yellow and green garb. Madame uses colour well, mixing bright with soft, just as she mixes antiques with artificial flowers. These warm folk take you naturally into their family circle. The comfortable bedrooms look onto wide fields, the smaller attic room is perfect and the 'Norman' dinners have been praised to the skies.

Rooms: 1 double, 2 quadruples, all with shower or bath & wc.

Price: 260 Frs for two; 360 Frs for three; 410 Frs for four; 300 Frs for a twin.

Meals: 110 Frs, including wine & coffee.

Closed: Never.

From Bayeux, N13 to La Cambe, then D113 south. After 1km, D124 direction St Germain du Pert (1.5km). Michelin Map No: 231-16

Entry no: **189**   Map No: 2

Paulette & Hervé MARIE
Ferme de la Rivière
14230 St Germain du Pert
Calvados
Tel: (0)2 31 22 72 92
Fax: (0)2 31 22 01 63
Web: www.sawdays.co.uk

From Bayeux N13 dir. Cherbourg; through Tour en Bessin, left on D100 dir. Crouay 1km. House on right. Michelin Map No: 231-16

Entry no: **190**   Map No: 2

Catherine & Bertrand GIRARD
Le Relais de la Vignette
Route de Crouay, Tour en Bessin
14400 Bayeux, Calvados
Tel: (0)2 31 21 52 83/
          (0)6 80 45 69 95
Fax: (0)2 31 21 52 83
e-mail: relais.vignette@wanadoo.fr

You may sleep like angels; this was a monks' dormitory in the 15th century. The Abbey is right there, floodlit at night, and the whole setting is exquisitely peaceful. The house is beguiling with its stone staircase, exposed beams, old columns and big fireplace. Monsieur, a recently retired breeder of cattle and horses, is quietly contemplative while Madame, a lively grandmother, is bright and attentive – a most pleasant pair of hosts, though they don't dine with guests. It is a no-frills, and thoroughly good, place.

Rooms: 1 twin, 2 suites for 3, each with shower or bath & wc.

Price: 240 Frs for two.

Meals: 90 Frs, including wine & coffee.

Closed: Never.

Gîte space for 11 people.

From Bayeux, N13 W for 14km; D30 direction Trévières; 2nd right, 1st right, right again on D29 direction St Lô for 1km; right on D124 to Écrammeville, and follow signs (farm near church). Michelin Map No: 231-16

Entry no: 191   Map No: 2

Louis & Annick FAUVEL
Ferme de l'Abbaye
14710 Ecrammeville
Calvados
Tel: (0)2 31 22 52 32
Fax: (0)2 31 22 47 25
Web: www.sawdays.co.uk

Well off the busy road, down its own drive, this old stone house, built in 1714, is now a dairy farm. The *salon* is very French and just the place for a quiet read. There are other fine period rooms. The big bedrooms, looking out over the large pond, are light and sunny with country furniture (one has a four-poster) and not crammed in next to each other. The family is charming, hospitable and helpful but not intrusive. Special extras are comfortable garden chairs, that pond for fishing, a horse for riding, paths for walking, home-made yoghurt and cider. Some stay a week.

Rooms: 2 doubles, 1 suite, all with shower & wc.

Price: 255 Frs for two.

Meals: 120 Frs, including wine & coffee.

Closed: Never.

From Caen, A13 direction Cherbourg then exit for Carpiquet and Caumont l'Eventé. 500m before Caumont, left at Chambres d'Hôtes sign into drive. Michelin Map No: 231-28

Entry no: 192   Map No: 2

Alain & Françoise PETITON
La Suhardière
14240 Livry
Calvados
Tel: (0)2 31 77 51 02
Fax: (0)2 31 77 51 02

There is a fun-loving, relaxed atmosphere about this place: you could scarcely find easier, friendlier hosts than Joseph and Marie-Thé. There are animals and milking for children, table football and volleyball for teenagers, *pétanque* for all. Your hosts, who have quantities of local lore and advice to communicate, will join you for a farm supper at the long table in the log-fired (winter), fresh-flowered guests' dayroom. They are simple and genuine; so are their rooms (one has an ancient dresser set into the stone wall) and their welcome. This is superb value and far enough from the road not to suffer from much traffic noise.

Rooms: 4 suites for 3/4, each with bath or shower & wc, 1 with kitchen.

Price: 200 Frs for two.

Meals: 80 Frs, including wine & coffee.

Closed: Never.

From A84/E401 Caen-Rennes motorway exit 42 onto N175 direction Cahagnes for 2km, then right following Chambres d'Hôtes signs to farm. Michelin Map No: 231-28

Entry no: 193   Map No: 2

Joseph & Marie-Thé GUILBERT
Le Mesnil de Benneville
14240 Cahagnes
Calvados
Tel: (0)2 31 77 58 05
Fax: (0)2 31 77 37 84
Web: www.sawdays.co.uk

The setting is gorgeously flowered, the walks peaceful (itineraries provided) and the farm feathered, including geese for foie gras (Madame knows how and does it all herself) and spit-roasting in winter. You are warmly greeted by your youngish hosts, the atmosphere is relaxed and if the big bedrooms are unremarkable, they are clean, with their own entrance, kitchen and sitting room. But you will come above all for Madame's talented cooking and genuine hospitality. Children are welcome: there are cots, games and bikes for them.

Rooms: 2 triples (1 on ground floor), each with shower & wc.

Price: 210 Frs for two.

Meals: 80 Frs, including aperitif, cider & coffee, by arrangement.

Closed: December-February.

Gîte space for 7 people.

From Caen, direction Cherbourg then A84 direction Avranches; exit St Martin des Besaces on D53 then left onto D165 direction Brémoy; house is on right, 4km from St Martin. Michelin Map No: 231-28

Entry no: 194   Map No: 2

Jacqueline & Gilbert LALLEMAN
Carrefour des Fosses
14260 Brémoy
Calvados
Tel: (0)2 31 77 83 22
e-mail: jg_lalleman@yahoo.fr

The English owners here have built a tennis court, turned the old pool into a pretty lily pond and made a new one in a more discreet spot, redone bathrooms with beige tiles and wooden accessories, put up calico curtains... and it is still a fascinating old inn (parts are 12th-century) with medieval beams, old flagstones and fireplaces. The attic/mezzanine suite is an exciting space under the rafters. The Bamfords are relaxed hosts, providing masses of activities in this quiet village where the only sounds are the odd car and regular church chimes.

Rooms: 1 quadruple, 2 doubles, 1 suite for 4/5, 1 triple in annexe, each with bath or shower & wc.

Price: 350 Frs for two.

Meals: 120 Frs, including wine & coffee.

Closed: Never.

Gîte space for 7 people.

From Caen D9 towards Bayeux; take direction Caumont L'Éventé. From Caumont take direction Balleroy D28, go past church, house on right by Gîte de France sign.

Entry no: 195   Map No: 2

Elizabeth & Andrew BAMFORD
Le Relais
19 rue Thiers
14240 Caumont l'Eventé, Calvados
Tel: (0)2 31 78 24 48
Fax: (0)2 31 78 24 49
e-mail: lerelais19@aol.com
Web: www.sawdays.co.uk

Through the wood and across the stream to the simplest, friendliest house you could imagine. It is about a century old while the Ameys have that timeless quality of solid country dwellers and will wrap you in blue-eyed smiles. Their welcome is all unstylish comfort and warmth. Most furnishings are 'rustic', bar two superb Norman armoires, the walls are pastel, the curtains lace, the bathroom pink, the towels small. Breakfast comes with incomparably good farm milk and butter; dinners are reliably Norman; the wisteria blooms. Excellent value.

Rooms: 3 doubles, each with basin, sharing bathroom & separate wc.

Price: 200 Frs for two.

Meals: 85 Frs, including cider & coffee.

Closed: Never.

Gîte space for 10 people.

From Caen A84 towards Mt St Michel, exit 46 'Noyers Bocage'. Right on D83 towards Cheux for 1.5km then left to Tessel; signposted.
Michelin Map No: 231-29

Entry no: 196   Map No: 2

Paul & Éliane AMEY
La Londe
14250 Tessel
Calvados
Tel: (0)2 31 80 81 12
Fax: (0)2 31 80 81 12
Web: www.sawdays.co.uk

Through the great arched gate is a lovely old house, its 17th-century golden stones now proudly on view, its courtyard housing several tribes of animal and a games room; a cider-apple orchard; a fascinating military historian who takes battlefield tours – arrange yours with him – and loves sharing his passion for the dramas that took place here; a gentle lady who serves her own jams plus fresh breads and croissants for breakfast; stone stairs to big, comfortably casual guest rooms; and above all a genuine family-friendly welcome just 15 minutes walk from the Cathedral.

Rooms: 2 doubles, 2 triples, each with shower & wc.

Price: 300 Frs; 250 Frs for 2 nights or more.

Meals: Full choice Bayeux, 1km.

Closed: Never.

Gîte space for 6 people.

On Bayeux bypass, at Campanile Hotel take D572 direction St Lô. Take 2nd right and follow signs to arched gateway.
Michelin Map No: 231-17

Entry no: 197   Map No: 2

Lt-Col & Mrs CHILCOTT
Manoir Des Doyens
Saint-Loup-Hors
14400 Bayeux, Calvados
Tel: (0)2 31 22 39 09
Fax: (0)2 31 21 97 84
e-mail: chilcott@mail.cpod.fr
Web: www.sawdays.co.uk

The style is 'contemporary' rustic and your young hosts have done a great job of renovating this 18th-century wash house; preserving old stonework and beams and installing modern showers and decent beds. Mylène has brought pretty Provençal fabrics from her native Drôme, Christian is Norman and trained as a chef. Both are friendly, relaxed and keen that their guests get a good glimpse of a French way of life. There's a wide choice of local and home-made breads and jams at breakfast, a barbecue and fridge you can use, table tennis and a couple of bikes for further exploration.

Rooms: 1 double, 1 triple, each with shower & wc.

Price: 300-380 Frs for two.

Meals: Available locally.

Closed: Never; please telephone to book.

From Caen D7 towards Douvres la Delivrande for 8km, left onto D404 for 5.5km. Then D79 to Courseulles sur Mer. There D514 to Ver sur Mer. At village entrance 1st left to Ave de la Provence. 1st right, then 1st left into short cul-de-sac. House at end on right.
Michelin Map No: 231-17

Entry no: 198   Map No: 2

Christian MERIEL & Mylene GILLES
Le Mas Normand
8 impasse de la Riviere
14114 Ver sur Mer, Calvados
Tel: (0)2 31 21 97 75
Fax: (0)2 3 1 21 97 75
Web: www.sawdays.co.uk

A converted mill (no-one knows how old it is) with a delightful bridge and terrace. The guest quarters are in the separate 'Hunting Lodge' where Madame's talented decoration marries things past and designer-colourful present and you have your own dining room and kitchen. There are nuts to be gathered in the woods, beaches nearby, the stream for entertainment on the spot. Your hosts are sweet and love having families. "My kids spent hours by the shallow stream – not dangerous if they're supervised", said a reader.

Rooms: 1 double with shower & wc; 1 double, 1 twin sharing shower & wc.

Price: 290 Frs for two.

Meals: Restaurants 2-3km. Self-catering.

Closed: Never.

Gîte space for 6 people.

From Ouistreham D35 through Douvres & Tailleville. Cross D404. At r'bout entering Reviers, turn right. 2nd Chambres d'Hôtes on left.
Michelin Map No: 231-17

Entry no: 199   Map No: 2

Patricia & Jean-Michel BLANLOT
La Malposte
15 rue des Moulins
14470 Reviers
Calvados
Tel: (0)2 31 37 51 29
Fax: (0)2 31 37 51 29

With a few sheep in the background, this is a typical old farmhouse, even down to the corrugated iron roof. The guest wing is in the converted stables where the kitchen/diner has its original stone flags and the manger. The rooms are country-comfortable, nicely decorated, functional and spotless; one has a balcony onto the farm and the apple orchard (and road at the bottom) where all sorts of games await your pleasure – as does Mireille the donkey. Your elderly hostess is friendly and glad to have your company.

Rooms: 1 double, 1 triple, each with shower & wc.

Price: 240 Frs for two.

Meals: In Vire 2km. Self-catering possible.

Closed: Never.

From Vire centre, D524 direction Tinchebray & Flers; house on right after 2km; signposted.
Michelin Map No: 231-28

Entry no: 200   Map No: 2

Mme Marcelle MARIE
La Gage
14500 Roullours
Calvados
Tel: (0)2 31 68 17 40
Fax: (0)2 31 68 17 40
Web: www.sawdays.co.uk

Here is pure, down-to-earth Norman hospitality so what matter that the house lacks years? They are close to all things natural, plough their big veg patch with the cob in harness, will drive you through the secret byways of the area in a pony-drawn trap while telling local legends, take you on night-time discovery walks, share dinners made with organic produce to old forgotten regional recipes, offer good rooms where you wake to stunning views over the hushed hills of *La Suisse Normande*. Nothing gushy or corny, these are independent, strong, comforting people who genuinely care for your well-being and that of the land.

Rooms: 2 doubles, 1 twin, 1 suite, each with shower & wc.

Price: 220 Frs for two.

Meals: 80 Frs, including aperitif, cider & coffee (not Sundays).

Closed: Never.

A handsome square-set château where you can taste the "world's best cider" (so says Monsieur), admire yourself in innumerable gilt-framed mirrors, luxuriate in a Jacuzzi or bare your chest to a hydromassage shower, play the piano, watch pop-up telly, appreciate Monsieur's very dry sense of humour and Madame's superb cooking, and at last lie down in an antique, new-mattressed bed in one of the enormous bedrooms. The period ceilings, tapestries and furniture make this a real château experience; the people make it very human.

Rooms: 2 doubles, 2 suites, all with bath or shower & wc.

Price: 550 Frs for two.

Meals: 240 Frs, including aperitif, cider/wine, coffee, calvados.

Closed: Never.

*From Caen, D562 direction Flers.
About 35km on at Le Fresne, D1
direction Falaise. After 4km, house on
right; signposted.*
Michelin Map No: 231-30

Entry no: **201**   Map No: 2

Roland & Claudine LEBATARD
Arclais
14690 Pont d'Ouilly
Calvados
Tel: (0)2 31 69 81 65
Fax: (0)2 31 69 81 65

*From Caen, N158 direction Falaise. At
La Jalousie, right on D23; right on
D235 just before Bretteville sur Laize;
signposted.*
Michelin Map No: 231-30

Entry no: **202**   Map No: 2

Anne-Marie & Alain CANTEL
Château des Riffets
14680 Bretteville sur Laize
Calvados
Tel: (0)2 31 23 53 21
Fax: (0)2 31 23 75 14

You may already have stayed with Françoise and Michel: they used to run Le Moulin, which featured in our 4th edition. After a break they are ready to welcome you once again in their typically Norman home. Le Clos is smaller but you won't feel crowded in and Françoise will produce an excellent dinner for you, likely to centre around *confit de canard* and apple or plum tart, depending on the time of year. The rooms are not large but they are cheerful and look out onto a very pretty garden. The loudest sound you might hear is the odd lawnmower.

Rooms: 1 double & 1 triple, with bath or shower & wc.

Price: 380-450 Frs for two.

Meals: 120 Frs, excluding wine (60-80 Frs).

Closed: Never.

Gîte space for 2 people.

From Pont l'Évêque take D579 towards Lisieux. At Le Breuil en Auge roundabout take D264 towards Le Torquesne. 1st right after church towards Chemin des Toutains. Le Clos St Hymer is 500m further on.
Michelin Map No: 231-20

Entry no: **203**   Map No: 3

Françoise VALLE
Le Clos St Hymer
14130 Le Torquesne
Calvados
Tel: (0)2 31 61 99 15
Fax: (0)2 31 61 99 36
Web: www.sawdays.co.uk

It may look like a film set but it is genuine early 17th-century. Inside, there is an equally astounding dining room, added on by one Monsieur Swann and resplendently carved, panelled and painted. Two big rooms – *Jaune* and *Verte* – catch the morning sun but *Saumon* is even better with its heavenly sunset prospect; all are incredible value. Madame, a beautiful lady, made all the curtains and covers. She and her diplomat husband are well-travelled, polyglot, cultured – they help make a stay here as special as any in France.

Rooms: 2 doubles, 1 twin, each with bath or shower & wc.

Price: 300 Frs for two.

Meals: Restaurant 1km.

Closed: Never.

From Caen N13 E towards Lisieux for 25km. At Carrefour St Jean, D50 (virtually straight on) towards Cambremer. 5km from junction, house signposted on right.
Michelin Map No: 231-31

Entry no: **204**   Map No: 3

Christine & Arnauld GHERRAK
Manoir de Cantepie
Le Cadran
14340 Cambremer
Calvados
Tel: (0)2 31 62 87 27

The date is precisely 1462; Annick thinks the building (not all of an age) belonged to the Abbey of Saint Pierre. The old beams are particularly impressive. It is a really lovely place, in three acres of orchards overlooking the valley of the Auge. The garden is yours and there is fishing for coloured carp in the pond. Good rooms: one on the ground floor with age-old terracotta tiles, paintings, antiques and a leather armchair, the others on the first floor – all with those long green views. Madame is a charming hostess and there is lots to do nearby. She often has to be out after lunch, so prefers you to arrive in the late afternoon if possible.

Rooms: 1 double with shower & wc; 2 triples, 1 family room, all with bath or shower, sharing 3 separate wcs.

Price: 270 Frs for two; under 3s free.

Meals: Good choice nearby.

Closed: Never.

Gîte space for 12 people.

From Lisieux D511 dir. St Pierre sur Dives. Just before St Pierre D40 left dir. Livarot. After 1.5km, right to Berville; signposted.
Michelin Map No: 231-31

Entry no: 205　　　　Map No: 3

Annick DUHAMEL
Le Pressoir
Berville
14170 St Pierre sur Dives
Calvados
Tel: (0)2 31 20 51 26
Fax: (0)2 31 20 03 03
Web: www.sawdays.co.uk

Monsieur's family have owned this pretty house for 100 years, he was born here and married a local girl. They are a sweet couple, quietly and unobtrusively attentive, and you will feel well cared for. The large garden is clearly much loved and has a flowery bower with a stone table. Inside you will find some superb pieces of family furniture – country French at its best – as well as crinkly pink lights and little bits of *brocante*. Falaise was Duke William's home until he left his native Normandy to conquer other shores but this typical Falaise house is quite young, only dating from the 1600s, in a dear, quiet little Norman village.

Rooms: 1 suite for 4, 1 double/triple, both with shower & wc.

Price: 230 Frs for two.

Meals: Falaise 3km. Barbecue & picnic possible.

Closed: Never.

From Falaise D63 towards Trun for 3km. 2nd left onto D69 for 1km. At junction, cross over, go round bend; farm signposted on left.
Michelin Map No: 231-30

Entry no: 206　　　　Map No: 3

Alice & Gilbert THOMAS
Ferme la Croix
14700 Villy lez Falaise
Calvados
Tel: (0)2 31 90 19 98

You would never guess the size of 62 Rue Grande from the outside: from a small façade it stretches deep into the garden where Dorothea and Claude, a charming and elegant couple, have worked wonders with rose, wisteria and myriad colourful plants. The two quiet suites are in the old stables; the former coachman's room, now a lovely guest room, is up an extraordinary wooden spiral staircase which climbs to huge windows overlooking the light and lusciously rich garden. This polyglot home reflects its owners' polytravels as well as their passion for gardening – no wonder they illustrate their house with their garden.

Rooms: 1 apartment for 2/4, 1 double, both with shower & wc.

Price: 300 Frs for two.

Meals: Choice in Orbec.

Closed: Never.

Richard and Jay have thoroughly adopted their new country – so much so that their B&B has been classified a *Gîte Panda:* one which provides detailed information on local flora and fauna and there is an excellent 8km circular walk mapped from the house. It is a converted Norman farmhouse with big, beautifully furnished, perfectly peaceful rooms (even 7am church bells are in keeping). The Clays, modest about what they have achieved here, are kind, unassuming hosts – everyone is quickly at their ease. Breakfasts are great (home-made jams, own eggs) and children love the goats, ducks and rabbits.

Rooms: 2 doubles, both with bath or shower & wc.

Price: 210 Frs for two.

Meals: Restaurants 5km.

Closed: Never.

Gîte space for 12 people.

Orbec is 19km S of Lisieux on D519. Turn into village; house is on main street next to L'Orbecquoise restaurant. Michelin Map No: 231-32

Entry no: 207   Map No: 3

Dorothea VAILLÈRE
62 rue Grande
14290 Orbec
Calvados
Tel: (0)2 31 32 77 99
Fax: (0)2 31 32 77 99

From La Haye du Puits, D903 towards Barneville Carteret. At Bolleville, right on D127 to St Nicolas de Pierrepont; left before church; house on right after cemetery. Michelin Map No: 231-14

Entry no: 208   Map No: 2

Richard & Jay CLAY
La Ferme de l'Eglise
50250 St Nicolas de Pierrepont, Manche
Tel: (0)2 33 45 53 40
Fax: (0)2 33 45 53 40
e-mail: theclays@wanadoo.fr
Web: perso.wanadoo.fr/normandie-cottages-bed-and-breakfast

Madame is as Norman as this house, where she was born: solidly earthed and used to welcoming strangers with kindness and a strong country accent. She shares her time between family, guests and dairy cows and is extremely proud of her breakfasts. They are indeed very generous, include fresh farm eggs and are served in the wonderful family dining room amid photographs, copper pans and old beams. Less characterful, the bedrooms have country furniture, old-style wallpapers and... more photographs. A super person and remarkable value B&B.

Rooms: 2 triples, each with bath or shower & wc (1 curtained off).

Price: 200 Frs for two.

Meals: Restaurants 3km.

Closed: Never.

From Cherbourg, N13 past Valognes then right on D2 to St Sauveur le Vicomte. There, D15 towards Port Bail. Farm is on right after about 1km, before Château d'Ollonde.
Michelin Map No: 231-13

Entry no: 209   Map No: 2

Bernadette VASSELIN
La Roque de Bas
Canville la Roque
50580 Port Bail
Manche
Tel: (0)2 33 04 80 27

In attractive farmland and well placed for the attractions of Valognes, this secluded village house is run by a sweetly and peacefully hospitable elderly couple. They are very informative on local history and sights and their house, with its open fireplace, is typically French country style. The rooms, not big but comfortable, have new bedding and wallpaper and fine old family furnishings; we definitely preferred the attic room, even if the loo is down a flight of stairs. There is a kitchen specially for guests.

Rooms: 1 double with shower & wc; 1 double with shower, wc on floor below.

Price: 180 Frs for two.

Meals: Self-catering.

Closed: Never.

From Cherbourg, N13 to Valognes (slow down: signs hard to see entering Valognes). D902 towards Bricquebec. After 2km left on D87 to Yvetot Bocage. At the church, go towards Morville and take first left.
Michelin Map No: 231-14

Entry no: 210   Map No: 2

Léon & Lucienne DUBOST
Le Haut Billy
Route de Morville
50700 Yvetot Bocage, Valognes
Manche
Tel: (0)2 33 40 06 74
Web: www.sawdays.co.uk

With much laughter, talk and sincere smiles, your hosts hope to give you "the best of France, the best of England": an old Norman house with pretty fabrics, antiques from both countries, a collection of English china inside, wild French hares, kestrels and owls outside (there's a spyhole for observation). The twin is smallish, the studio room up under the eaves, big and full of light. All have good bathrooms and oodles of fluffy towels. Linda varies the daily menu, down to napkin colours and china; Ted, an expert on the Second World War, will take you round the landing beaches. Both are passionate about their house and region; their delight is catching.

Rooms: 2 doubles, each with bath & wc; 1 twin with shower & wc.

Price: 300-350 Frs for two.

Meals: 100 Frs, including wine. Picnics by arrangement.

Closed: Never.

From Cherbourg S towards Caen & Rennes then D900 to Bricquebec (via Le Pont); cont. towards Valognes, past Intermarché, left at T-junct, 1st left after 'Sapeurs Pompiers' towards Les Grosmonts; 400m on right.
Michelin Map No: 231-14

Entry no: **211**   Map No: 2

Ted & Linda MALINDINE
La Lande
Les Grosmonts
50260 Bricquebec
Manche
Tel: (0)2 33 52 24 78
Fax: (0)2 33 52 24 78
Web: www.sawdays.co.uk

This splendid group of buildings is a spectacular historical ensemble where hefty medieval walls shelter an elegant 18th-century manor from the wild sea (you can hear it one mile away). Hosts and furnishings are irreproachably French and civilisation is the keynote – books, fine china, panelling, gilt mirrors, plush chairs, engravings. Your suite has ancient floor tiles, brand new bedding, a loo in a tower. Stay a while, make your own breakfast (home-made jam and fresh eggs available) in exchange for using the very grand dining room and get to know your literary *châtelaine*.

Rooms: 1 suite for 2-4 with shower & wc.

Price: 480 Frs for two; reduction for children.

Meals: Good choice 2-15km.

Closed: Never.

Gîte space for 6 people.

From Cherbourg, D904 direction Coutances. 3km after Les Pieux, right on D62 direction Le Rozel, then right on D117 into village. House is just after you leave village; signposted.
Michelin Map No: 231-13

Entry no: **212**   Map No: 2

Josiane & Jean-Claude GRANDCHAMP
Le Château
50340 Le Rozel
Manche
Tel: (0)2 33 52 95 08
Web: www.sawdays.co.uk

Old-fashioned hospitality is the keyword here. You are just a mile from the (often) glittering sea and Michel, who makes submarines, is happy to share his passion for sailing and take you coast-hopping or out in the open sea. The shipbuilder's skill is evident in this modern house with its modern floors: the attic space has been cleverly used to make two snug rooms with showers and kitchenettes. The décor is simple, the rooms spotless and Éliane is an easy, relaxed hostess who will rise early for dawn ferry catchers. It is brilliantly quiet and ideal for beach and ferry alike.

Rooms: 2 doubles, each with shower & wc.

Price: 230 Frs for two.

Meals: 2 restaurants within 2km.

Closed: Never.

Gîte space for 5 people.

In quiet country, just 6km from the ferries (the separate room with its own outside entrance is ideal for early ferry-catchers), this old stone manor stands proudly on the Normandy coastal hiking path looking across the town and out to sea. It is spotless, not over-modernised, and furnished in very French style with lots of velvet, floral linen and marble-topped chests. Retired from farming, the sociable Guérards enjoy welcoming both their own family and guests whom they happily point towards the cliff walks and other sights worth the detour.

Rooms: Main house: 1 double, 1 twin, each with bath & wc; outside stairs to triple room with shower & wc.

Price: 250-280 Frs for two.

Meals: Cherbourg 3km.

Closed: Never.

Gîte space for 7 people.

From Cherbourg, D901 then D45 W along coast 13km to Urville Nacqueville. 1st left by Hôtel Le Beau Rivage. Up hill on D22 for 2km then 2nd left; signposted.
Michelin Map No: 231-1

Entry no: **213**   Map No: 2

Michel & Éliane THOMAS
Eudal de Bas
50460 Urville Nacqueville
Manche
Tel: (0)2 33 03 58 16
Fax: (0)2 33 03 58 16

From Cherbourg, D901 to Tourlaville & direction St Pierre Église. Right at lights direction Château des Ravalet/Hameau St Jean; up hill to 'Centre Aéré', then follow Chambres d'Hôtes signs (3km from lights).
Michelin Map No: 231-2

Entry no: **214**   Map No: 2

Mme GUÉRARD
Manoir Saint Jean
50110 Tourlaville
Manche
Tel: (0)2 33 22 00 86
Web: www.sawdays.co.uk

Great swaying pines, a wild coast and the sea have guarded this site for over 800 years (the English burnt the first castle in 1346). Lush lawns, myriad flowers and white geese soften Nature's wildness. The manor's stern stone façade hides a warm, gentle, elegant welcome in rooms with superb fireplaces, good beds, big windows to let in the light and truly personal decoration: pictures, books (breakfast is taken in the library) and antiques. Madame will enthral you with tales from Norman history and provide detailed maps for hikers.

Rooms: 1 suite for 3, 1 double, each with shower & wc.

Price: 320 Frs for two.

Meals: Auberge within walking distance.

Closed: Never.

Gîte space for 6 people.

Words are inadequate... Incredibly, your beautiful, energetic hostess is a grandmother! A farmer's wife! He now breeds racehorses, she indulges her passion for interior decoration – her spotless rooms are a festival of colours, textures, antiques, embroidered linen. You cannot fail to enjoy staying in this wonderful old building – they love having guests. The great granite fireplace is always lit for the delicious breakfast which includes local specialities. There is a richly-carved 'throne' at the head of the long table. A stupendous place, very special people.

Rooms: 2 doubles, each with shower & wc; 1 twin with bath & wc; (1 overflow room for children).

Price: 300-380 Frs for two.

Meals: Choice in Barfleur, 3km.

Closed: Never.

Gîte space for 5 people.

From Cherbourg, D901 to Barfleur. There, D1 direction St Vaast. After signpost marking the end of Barfleur, 2nd right and 1st left.
Michelin Map No: 231-3

Entry no: **215**   Map No: 2

Mme Claudette GABROY
Le Manoir
50760 Montfarville
Manche
Tel: (0)2 33 23 14 21

From Barfleur direction Quettehous, then branch right on D25 direction Valcanville. Take 2nd right; follow signs.
Michelin Map No: 231-3

Entry no: **216**   Map No: 2

Marie-France & Maurice CAILLET
La Fèvrerie
50760 Ste Geneviève
Manche
Tel: (0)2 33 54 33 53
Fax: (0)2 33 22 12 50
Web: www.sawdays.co.uk

A delightful couple live in this wonderfully ramshackle, unspoiled, even dilapidated château with their family and all the guests who come to share the hugely relaxed, some would find over-casual, atmosphere. There is a big garden to explore and variegated rooms with old-fashioned bathing spaces. The cavernous Mussolini Room has the balcony with views across the heart-shaped lawn. The Colonial Room has pith-helmets and mementoes, while the Hat Room... A very special place – not for the stuffy – and they do energetic themed weekends. There's also a great value dinner deal for guests at the local bar.

Rooms: 2 doubles & 1 twin, each with bath & wc (1 screened off); 1 quadruple, 1 triple sharing a bathroom.

Price: 240-300 Frs for two; children half price.

Meals: Choice locally.

Closed: January, February & August.

Gîte space for 15 people.

From Cherbourg, N13 direction Valognes. After 12km, right on D119 direction Ruffosses. Cross motorway bridge; follow blue & white signs.
Michelin Map No: 231-14

Entry no: 217   Map No: 2

Mark & Fiona BERRIDGE
Château Mont Epinguet
50700 Brix
Manche
Tel: (0)2 33 41 96 31
Fax: (0)2 33 41 98 77

"A real corker" enthused the inspector. "They are a delight. He has a fine dry wit and loves to chat, about everything – but especially politics. She, too, holds her own and anyone with a smattering of French would enjoy them enormously." They are farmers, and proud of it. The old manor has huge character and a small private chapel; we found the shabbiness and the haphazard décor most endearing. There is even some Art Deco furniture. Wonderful value in a natural and unsophisticated manner.

Rooms: 1 triple with bath & wc; 1 triple, 1 double sharing shower & wc.

Price: 200-220 Frs for two.

Meals: Small good-value restaurants locally.

Closed: Never.

From Cherbourg, N13 south; leave at Ste Mère l'Eglise exit. Go into Ste Mère l'Eglise & follow signs for Pont l'Abbé; house signposted on right after 3km.
Michelin Map No: 231-15

Entry no: 218   Map No: 2

Albert & Michèle BLANCHET
La Fière
Route de Pont l'Abbé
50480 Ste Mère l'Eglise
Manche
Tel: (0)2 33 41 32 66

Inside the stately 16th-century manor, up a twisty stone staircase, along a creaky corridor, is one of the finest B&B suites we know: a half-tester, carved fireplaces, a boudoir, rugs, prints and antiques, a claw-footed bath, windows onto lush gardens with ancient trees. The panelled dining room fills with light, the tiled, be-rugged guest sitting room is grand yet welcoming, your hosts are lively, cultured and fun. Belgian Yves still partly runs his family business and English Lynne can offer wonderful aromatherapy sessions.

This typical 18th-century Normandy farmhouse, its old stables and outbuildings flanking the dark-gravel courtyard, has had a thorough internal facelift since being taken over by the next generation of Buissons – he's French and works all week, she's American, perfectly bilingual and loves her new hostessing job. Rooms are pretty-papered in peach or green, beds have new mattresses, the rustic furniture is locally made with marble tops, the watercolours are done by an aunt: it is simple, fresh and most welcoming with a flower garden outside and swings for the children.

Rooms: 1 apartment (1 double, 1 twin & child's bed) with bath & wc.

Price: 630 Frs for two.

Meals: Good restaurant 3km.

Closed: October-mid-March, except by arrangement.

Rooms: 2 doubles, both with bath & wc.

Price: 190 Frs for two.

Meals: In St Lô 5km.

Closed: Never.

From Carentan D903 towards La Haye du Puits. At Baupte (5km) right on D69 to Appeville. At Appeville continue D69 towards Houtteville, take second lane on right; house on left.
Michelin Map No: 231-15

From Cherbourg, N13 and N174 to St Lô. At St Georges-Montcocq, D191 to Villiers Fossard. In village, right on C7; house is 800m on right.
Michelin Map No: 231-27

Entry no: 219   Map No: 2

Entry no: 220   Map No: 2

Yves LEJOUR & Lynne WOOSTER
Le Manoir d'Ozeville
Appeville
50500 Carentan
Manche
Tel: (0)2 33 71 55 98
Fax: (0)2 33 42 17 79
e-mail: ozeville@aol.com

Jean & Nancy BUISSON
Le Suppey
50680 Villiers Fossard
Manche
Tel: (0)2 33 57 30 23

When asked why she chose to open her farmhouse (rebuilt in 1856) to guests, the bright-eyed Madame Lepoittevin's simple reply is disarming: *"C'est la convivialité"*. You cannot fail to be won over by the warmth and friendliness of both the house and your hostess as you chat with her over a leisurely breakfast and sleep soundly in a spotless bedroom where magazines, knick-knacks, carpets and heavy old wardrobes are utterly *famille*. Dinner is not offered, but you can picnic in the garden or cook your own on the barbecue.

Rooms: 2 doubles, each with shower & wc.

Price: 210 Frs for two.

Meals: Choice 4-10km.

Closed: Never.

The Osmonds are such spontaneously welcoming, down-to-earth country folk, greeting guests with big smiles, stories and much useful local information, that people come back year after year. Madame, a delightful, humorous woman, plays the organ in the village church. Bedrooms have old family furniture (admire *grand-mère's* elaborately crocheted bedcover), really good mattresses, simple washing arrangements. It is all spotless and there is a roomy dayroom with lots of plants, and a kitchen in the old cider press.

Rooms: 1 double with shower & wc; 1 twin and 1 triple, each with shower, sharing 2 wcs.

Price: 210 Frs for two.

Meals: Restaurant 1km; choice St Lô 4km; self-catering possible.

Closed: Never.

From St Lô D972 towards Coutances, through St Gilles; house signposted on left, 4km after St Gilles, on D972.
Michelin Map No: 231-27

Entry no: 221   Map No: 2

Jean & Micheline LEPOITTEVIN
Saint-Léger
50750 Quibou
Manche
Tel: (0)2 33 57 18 41
Fax: (0)2 33 55 12 55

From St Lô D999 direction Villedieu for 3km; right on D38 direction Canisy.
House 1km along on right.
Michelin Map No: 231-27

Entry no: 222   Map No: 2

Marie-Thérèse & Roger OSMOND
La Rhétorerie
Route de Canisy
50750 St Ébremond de Bonfossé
Manche
Tel: (0)2 33 56 62 98

Monsieur breeds horses and there is riding available, but only for very experienced riders. The less horsey can enjoy an interesting visit to stables which have produced some great racers (including *La Belle Tière*). The place is a gem (note that the bedrooms are up a steep wooden staircase) and Madame cooks all the food, including her own bread and croissants. Meals are served in the beamed dining/breakfast room. The setting is charming, among hills, woods and fields; this would be a delightful place for a winter visit, too.

Rooms: 1 double, 1 twin, each with shower & wc; 1 twin for children.

Price: 200 Frs for two.

Meals: 100 Frs, including wine & coffee.

Closed: Never.

Gîte space for 5 people.

Leave Coutances on D971 S towards Granville and fork quickly left on D7 towards Gavray for 1.5km; then left on D27 to Nicorps. Through village and first right; house on left, signposted. Michelin Map No: 231-26

Entry no: 223   Map No: 2

M & Mme POSLOUX
Les Hauts Champs
La Moinerie de Haut
50200 Nicorps
Manche
Tel: (0)2 33 45 30 56
Fax: (0)2 33 07 60 21

From the new conservatory, enjoy wraparound views across the abundantly flowered garden; it's Madame's pride and joy and she'll tell you all about gardening and medicinal plants. Spy on the squirrels in the lime tree and indulge in a sinfully laden breakfast table (dare try the *Kousmine*, a muesli-type concoction to keep you energised all day). Three rooms are in a converted outbuilding, two in the enchanting main house. Beds are brass or carved wood; there are lace and pink and granny-style touches in keeping with an old farmhouse, plus some fine antiques.

Rooms: 1 twin, 3 doubles, 1 triple, all with shower & wc, 1 with kitchenette.

Price: 240-270 Frs for two; dog 35 Frs.

Meals: In village, 1.5km.

Closed: 1 week in January & Sept.

Gîte space for 2 people.

From Percy D58 direction Hambye then immed. left on D98 direction Sourdeval for 1.5km. House signed on right. Michelin Map No: 231-27

Entry no: 224   Map No: 2

Daniel & Maryclaude DUCHEMIN
Le Cottage de la Voisinière
Route de Sourdeval
50410 Percy, Manche
Tel: (0)2 33 61 18 47/
        (0)6 85 81 81 75
Fax: (0)2 33 61 43 47
Web: www.sawdays.co.uk

Miles from anywhere, apparently, but pilgrims once rested in this 12th-century farmhouse on their journey to and from the shrine at Santiago de Compostela. Today's new pilgrims can rest their weary bones at L'Orgerie during their travels in France. Their dogs greet you as you sip your *pommeau* aperitif with delightful hosts and dinner is then taken in the towering dining room with its gallery and huge fireplace. The house has a truly ancient feel but the bedrooms are snug and few will mind the loo being down the corridor. Amazing value.

These are solid, earthy, farming folk and Madame, who is a bit shy, has a lovely sunny smile. They are planning to breed rare animals such as Norman rabbit and Rouen duck and always encourage guests to visit Sourdeval on Tuesdays to see the cattle market in full swing. The rooms are unpretentiously simple with candlewick bedcovers, old floor tiles, wooden wardrobes and views across the valley. The family room has two beds on a mezzanine. Guests breakfast at one long table and are welcome to watch the milking. Really good value.

Rooms: 1 double, 1 twin (family suite), sharing shower & separate wc.

Rooms: Main house: 1 triple, 1 double sharing shower & separate wc. Cottage: family room for 5, shower & wc.

Price: 180 Frs for two.

Price: 190 Frs for two.

Meals: 70 Frs, including wine & coffee.

Meals: Choice 5km.

Closed: Never.

Closed: Never.

Gîte space for 2 people.

From Caen N175 SW towards Rennes & Villedieu. At Pont Farcy left on D52 towards Vire for 3km; house signed on right (DON'T turn to St Vigor). Michelin Map No: 231-27

From Sourdeval D977 towards Vire for 6km. Just before end of Manche sign right towards Le Val. House 2km along on right. Michelin Map No: 231-40

Entry no: 225   Map No: 2

Entry no: 226   Map No: 2

Jacques & Jacqueline GOUDE
L'Orgerie
50420 St Vigor des Monts
Manche
Tel: (0)2 31 68 85 58

Jeanne & Raymond DESDOITS
Le Val
Vengeons
50150 Sourdeval
Manche
Tel: (0)2 33 59 64 16
Fax: (0)2 33 69 36 99
Web: www.sawdays.co.uk

In her mixed-origin château – some bits 17th-century, others 18th – Madame is strong, easy-going, independent and has a fine sense of humour. She is thoroughly French and has lived in Paris, the deeply rural south-west and now Normandy with her four wonderfully-mannered children, her Dutch partner and their peaceful Labrador. She's great, the children are a delight, the grounds lush and those rolling views carry your eye for miles. Home-made cake with breakfast, refined regional cooking for dinner (vegetarian if asked for early) which may include home-grown strawberries and herbs.

Madame is the sweetest old lady, not too reserved, not gushing, just smiling and eager to please. Hers is a typical, 19th-century village house. Pleasant, country-style bedrooms have floral wallpapers and mats on polished wood floors. There's an inviting, armchaired reading corner on the landing plus a big dayroom with a fireplace. Breakfast is served here at the long 10-seater table. There are (free) tennis courts, a swimming pool and restaurants close at hand, and the proximity to Mont Saint Michel is a natural advantage. (When calling to book, better to have a French speaker to hand.)

Rooms: 2 doubles, each with bath & wc; 1 single with shower & wc.

Price: 350-430 Frs for two.

Meals: 100 Frs, excluding wine (60-100 Frs bottle).

Closed: Christmas & New Year.

Rooms: 1 double, 1 triple, sharing bath & wc; 1 twin with shower & wc.

Price: 200 Frs for two.

Meals: Gourmet auberge next door.

Closed: Never.

From Villedieu les Poêles N175 /D524 dir. Vire for 1.5km; right on D999 dir. Brecey. After Chérencé le Héron left to St Martin Bouillant, through village to sawmill & follow signs to Loges sur Brecey. House 2km along, 2nd left after wood.
Michelin Map No: 231-27

From Avranches, N175 direction Pontorson. 3km after Precey, right to Servon.
Michelin Map No: 231-38

Entry no: 227   Map No: 2

Entry no: 228   Map No: 2

Nathalie de DROUAS
Château des Boulais
Loges sur Brecey
50800 St Martin le Bouillant
Manche
Tel: (0)2 33 60 32 20
Fax: (0)2 33 60 45 20
Web: www.sawdays.co.uk

Mme Marie-Thérèse LESÉNÉCHAL
Le Bourg
6 rue du Pont Morin
50170 Servon
Manche
Tel: (0)2 33 48 92 13

Ask for the room facing Mont St Michel – it's the nicest... and that view is definitely worth the detour! You can walk to the Mount in two hours; or they have bikes for you. In the enclosed courtyard there are passion-fruit and fig trees. The Gédouins have cows and pigs; Annick makes delicious jams; Jean is Mayor – the council meets in his kitchen. Rooms are clean and compact, if short on storage space. There is a warm and kindly welcome, though, and the once-thin walls have now been properly soundproofed. Honey for breakfast, the sea only 500 yards away.

Rooms: 2 doubles, each with shower & wc.

Price: 220 Frs for two.

Meals: 80 Frs, including cider & coffee. Excellent auberge in village.

Closed: Never.

Although the 18th-century château has been renovated and modernised virtually beyond recognition, the farm buildings are genuine. Set back from the (still audible) main road, the house 'lives' on the other side: there, you discover the original pediment, facing splendid views of hills and woods. Bedrooms, freshly decorated in pink/dark green or blue/white, are simply furnished with brass or wooden beds and mirrored armoires. Breakfast is taken at the long family dining table and Madame is eager to help you plan your day. The Botanical Gardens in Avranches are superb.

Rooms: 1 double, with shower & wc; 3 doubles, each with shower, sharing wc.

Price: 200-220 Frs for two.

Meals: Locally 1.5km or Avranches 3km.

Closed: Never.

From Mt St Michel, D275 towards Pontaubault. At Montitier, D107 to Servon. There, take D113 left. House on left; signposted.
Michelin Map No: 231-38

Entry no: **229**   Map No: **2**

Annick, Jean & Valérie GÉDOUIN
Le Petit Manoir
21 rue de la Pierre du Tertre
50170 Servon
Manche
Tel: (0)2 33 60 03 44
Fax: (0)2 33 60 17 79

From Avranches, D973 direction Granville, across Pont Gilbert; 300m after shopping precinct, take 1st drive on left.
Michelin Map No: 231-38

Entry no: **230**   Map No: **2**

Eugène & Huguette TURGOT
Le Château
Marcey les Grèves
50300 Avranches
Manche
Tel: (0)2 33 58 08 65

This place is as real, unpretentious and comfortable as ever. Definitely a working farm with 800 pigs and a high-tech milking shed that attracts interest from far and wide; you can watch too. Masses of flowers sweeten the air. The young owners enjoy contact with visitors and Madame pays special attention to breakfast – her apple tart is delicious. Then you can walk directly out into the lovely countryside to see the little chapel or the local château. The guest rooms, one in the house, the other with its own entrance, are simple and good.

Rooms: 2 doubles, each with shower and wc.

Price: 180 Frs for two.

Meals: Good choice 5km.

Closed: Never.

Gîte space for 14 people.

Treat yourself and stay in this gently grand, gracious château where the Count's family have lived since it was built in 1763. He and the Countess have also lived in Paris and Chicago and theirs is an elegant, unstuffy lifestyle in which you are welcome to join. Bedrooms are beautifully furnished and decorated with personal touches: family portraits and embroidered white linen sheets. Breakfast, including home-made jams and tarts served on fine porcelain, is taken in the lovely round dining room – panelled and mirrored, with French windows to the grounds, which come complete with lake and private chapel.

Rooms: 2 doubles & 2 suites, each with bath or shower & wc.

Price: 750-900 Frs for two.

Meals: Available locally.

Closed: Never.

Gîte space for 6 people.

From Pontorson, N175 to Aucey la Plaine, then follow signs to Chambres d'Hôtes La Provostière for 3km. Farm is between Pontorson & Vessey.
Michelin Map No: 231-38

Entry no: 231   Map No: 2

Maryvonne & René FEUVRIER
La Provostière
50170 Aucey la Plaine
Manche
Tel: (0)2 33 60 33 67
Fax: (0)2 33 60 37 00

From Avranches, towards Mont St Michel, exit 34 . On N175 exit D40, Mont St Michel/Rennes , towards Rennes. After 6km onto the D40, turn left onto the D308 towards St Senier de Beuvron. Château entrance after 800m.
Michelin Map No: 231-38

Entry no: 232   Map No: 2

Regis & Nicole de ROQUEFEUIL-CAHUZAC
Château de Boucéel
50240 Vergoncey, Manche
Tel: (0)2 33 48 34 61
Fax: (0)2 33 48 16 26
e-mail: chateaudebouceel@wanadoo.fr
Web: www.chateaudebouceel.com

Very much a 'family' house, Gavards have lived here for 70 years and the children still visit at weekends. Jean-Paul and Brigitte are a friendly, interesting couple, travel a lot and talk well. He is an arbitrator and she is on the council. Meals (they are delicious) are taken in the lovely dining room with its huge fireplace. A splendid staircase leads you up to the good, snug and unfussy guest rooms. The setting of the house is glorious with a lake and a château next door and woods all around – perfect for an evening stroll. There are games galore, and it is a working farm.

Rooms: 2 doubles, 2 family rooms, all with bath or shower & wc.

Price: 230-250 Frs for two. 330 Frs for family room.

Meals: 85 Frs, including wine & coffee.

Closed: Never.

From Cherbourg A84, exit 34 direction Mt St Michel & St Malo for 600m then exit direction Mt St Michel & Rennes and onto D43 direction Rennes. At roundabout, D40 direction Rennes for 5.5km, then D308 left; signposted.
Michelin Map No: 231-38

Entry no: 233   Map No: 2

Jean-Paul & Brigitte GAVARD
La Ferme de l'Etang
Boucéel
Vergoncey
50240 St James, Manche
Tel: (0)2 33 48 34 68
Fax: (0)2 33 48 48 53
Web: www.sawdays.co.uk

It is all clean and comfortable, in solid farmhouse style. The old stable block, entirely modernised for B&B in the 1970s, has stripped wooden floors and easy furnishings, cots in the attic rooms and a kitchenette, all making it ideal for family stopovers. The Balcony Room is in a league of its own with exposed timbers, country antiques and... even a (glassed-in) balcony. Madame is very quiet, "makes a superb soufflé" and mouthwatering Norman cuisine. The poetically-named but perfectly ordinary Two Estuaries motorway now provides quick access 1km away.

Rooms: 1 triple, 1 double, 1 twin, 1 quadruple, all with bath or shower & wc.

Price: 230-250 Frs for two.

Meals: 85 Frs, including wine & coffee.

Closed: Never.

Gîte space for 6 people.

From A84 exit 32 at St James then onto D12, following signs for Super U store for 900m direction Antrain. House is on right.
Michelin Map No: 231-38

Entry no: 234   Map No: 2

François & Catherine TIFFAINE
La Gautrais
50240 St James
Manche
Tel: (0)2 33 48 31 86
Fax: (0)2 33 48 58 17
Web: www.sawdays.co.uk

The atmosphere of quiet simplicity of both house and owner are like the calm of a balmy summer's morning, but you are not cut off: modernity bustles on the village street outside the front door. Isabelle's talent seems to touch the very air that fills her old family house. There is nothing superfluous: simple carved pine furniture, an antique wrought-iron cot, dhurries on scrubbed plank floors, palest yellow or mauve walls to reflect the ocean-borne light, harmonious striped or gingham curtains. Starfish and many-splendoured pebbles keep the house sea-connected. The unspoilt seaside village is worth the trip too.

Rooms: 2 doubles, 1 twin, each with bath & wc; 2 doubles both with shower & wc (1 fully equipped for the disabled).

Price: 250-290 Frs for two.

Meals: Choice in village.

Closed: Never.

Brittany

The sea! The rocks! Fear not fisherfolk – if the lighthouse cannot save you from wrecking on the reefs, the carved calvaries will send up prayers for your souls ashore.

From St Malo, N137 towards Rennes. 6km after St Malo, right on D117 to St Suliac (3km from N137 exit to village entrance). Road leads to Grande Rue down to port; house at top on right. Michelin Map No: 230-11

Entry no: 235   Map No: 2

Isabelle ROUVRAIS
Les Mouettes
17 Grande Rue
35430 St Suliac
Ille-et-Vilaine
Tel: (0)2 99 58 30 41
Fax: (0)2 99 58 39 41

A dairy farm with a neatly-converted stone house, between St Malo and Mont St Michel, with the sea just 3km away. The comfortable rooms include two with mezzanines; the others are smaller. Marie-Madeleine is all care and attention: in winter she is up before breakfast to lay the fire in the huge hearth where you can toast bread; in summer, the garden and orchard beckon. Jean, gentle and bright-eyed, says that, although he's tied to the farm, he "travels through his guests". They both know and love their region and walks in detail. *Stays of two nights or more preferred.*

Rooms: 3 rooms for 2-4 people, all with shower or bath & wc.

Price: 250 Frs for two.

Meals: Choice in Dol de Bretagne.

Closed: Never.

From St Malo, N137 S direction Rennes for 15km; exit on N176 direction Mt St Michel for 12km. At Dol de Bretagne, D80 direction St Broladre for 3km; left on D85 direction Cherrueix; house (signed) on right before 3rd little bridge.
Michelin Map No: 230-12

Entry no: 236   Map No: 2

Jean & Marie-Madeleine GLÉMOT
La Hamelinais
35120 Cherrueix
Ille-et-Vilaine
Tel: (0)2 99 48 95 26
Fax: (0)2 99 48 89 23
Web: www.sawdays.co.uk

It is as idyllic, as bucolic as it looks; the beauty of the setting takes you by surprise and the little guesthouse is a dream. In what used to be the bakery, it is just a yard or two from the lake, where you can fish or observe all sorts of water-dwelling folk, far enough from the main house to feel secluded, snugly romantic and utterly seductive. If your need for intimacy is deep then Catherine will deliver breakfast and dinner (course by course) to your hideaway. But nicer still to join them at table; they are young and delightful and we have received nothing but praise for them.

Rooms: 1 double/quadruple in split-level room with *salon*, shower & wc. 1 double/quadruple in cottage with *salon*, shower & wc.

Price: 250-350 Frs for two.

Meals: 100 Frs, including wine & coffee.

Closed: Never.

From St Malo, N137 to St Pierre de Plesguen. On church square take D10 direction Lanhelin for 1.5km, then follow signs on right to Le Pont Ricoul Chambres d'Hôtes.
Michelin Map No: 230-25

Entry no: 237   Map No: 2

Catherine & François GROSSET
Le Pont Ricoul
35720 St Pierre de Plesguen
Ille-et-Vilaine
Tel: (0)2 99 73 92 65
Fax: (0)2 99 73 94 17
e-mail: pontricoul@aol.com
Web: www.sawdays.co.uk

All that a French townhouse should be: elegant, refined, light yet solidly comfortable, inside and out. The owners, he a photographer, she a watercolourist, have applied all their talent and taste to renovating it. The guest duplex, above Madame's studio in a separate little house, is fresh and romantic with home-sewn furnishings in restful colours (admire the curtains cleverly made from antique linen sheets). You may dine with your gentle, artistic hosts in their delicious white dining/sitting room and even take a painting course.

Rooms: Duplex for 4 with shower & wc.

Price: 270 Frs for two; duplex 430 Frs for 4.

Meals: 110 Frs, including wine.

Closed: Never.

This, the oldest house (1490s) in beautiful old Bécherel, right on the splendid Place du Vieux Marché, is as elegant inside as out with long country views at the back. Monique has talent and refined taste, speaks perfect English, loves people, books, and calligraphy and does garden and architecture tours and à la carte watercolour tuition. The bedrooms are across the patio. *Juliette* has space, a huge stone fireplace, beams, cool blue and warm ochre tones; *Joséphine* is prettily pink, checked and striped with pine furniture and garden view; both have super bathrooms.

Rooms: 1 double, 1 double/triple, each with bath or shower & wc.

Price: 300-380 Frs for two.

Meals: 120 Frs, including wine & coffee. Bicycle & picnic basket 100 Frs.

Closed: Never.

From Rennes N12 W for 36km exit St Méen le Grand. In town centre, back to Mairie, take Ave Foch between Crédit Agricole & Pharmacie. No. 39 on left.
Michelin Map No: 230-24

Entry no: 238   Map No: 2

From St Malo N137 S dir. Rennes for 43km. At Tinténiac exit, right on D20 to Bécherel. House on main square near church.
Michelin Map No: 230-25

Entry no: 239   Map No: 2

Catherine & Luc RUAN
Le Clos Constantin
39 avenue Foch
35290 St Méen le Grand
Ille-et-Vilaine
Tel: (0)2 99 09 53 09
Fax: (0)2 99 09 53 09
Web: www.sawdays.co.uk

Monique LECOURTOIS-CANET
Le Logis de la Filanderie
3 rue de la Filanderie
35190 Bécherel
Ille-et-Vilaine
Tel: (0)2 99 66 73 17
Fax: (0)2 99 66 79 07
e-mail: filanderie@aol.com

People come back to Quengo for its atmosphere, its history and the utter silence, not because it's cosy or squeaky clean. Madame, a straightforward, friendly *Bretonne*, used to manage the 9,000 egg-laying hens here. The fascinating château has a private chapel, a monumental oak staircase, marble fireplaces, 1900s wallpaper and about 30 rooms in all – too many corners for housework to reach every day; underfoot is a mosaic floor by Italian craftsmen, overhead are hand-painted beams by a 19th-century artist from Rennes who 'did' for all the local gentry. The bathroom has a claw-footed bath, bedrooms are old-fashioned too. Amazing.

Rooms: 2 doubles, 1 triple, all with basin & bidet, sharing bathroom & 3 separate wcs.

Price: 200-220 Frs for two.

Meals: Choice 4-6km.

Closed: Mid-October-March.

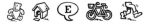

From N24 (Rennnes-Lorient) exit at Bédée on D72 to Irodouer. Arriving in Irodouer, 1st right before church; château entrance 600m along on left. Michelin Map No: 230-25

Entry no: 240   Map No: 2

Mme de LORGERIE
Château du Quengo
35850 Irodouer
Ille-et-Vilaine
Tel: (0)2 99 39 81 47

The lovely 18th-century townhouse on the church square has a delicious little 'French' garden – low walls, box hedges, a giant camellia, masses of flowers and a herb patch. Inside, there are hand-decorated beams, antiques from 25 years of dealing and from Madame's family (her grandmother lived here), plus an ocean-themed loo. A sumptuous breakfast is supplied by your lovely, leisurely hostess, she's all covered in smiles with a soft young voice. She has Breton, Creuzois, Basque and Flemish origins and spent her childhood 'commuting' between Morocco and Brittany. This makes for a powerfully interesting old lady!

Rooms: 1 double, 1 suite, each with bath & wc.

Price: 300 Frs for two; suite 450 Frs for four.

Meals: In town.

Closed: Never.

From Rennes N24 W for 27km to Plélan le Grand. House on church square: granite façade & ivy hedge. Michelin Map No: 230-39

Entry no: 241   Map No: 2

Mme Hubert de FLORIS
La Treberdière
Place de l'Église
35380 Plélan le Grand
Ille-et-Vilaine
Tel: (0)2 99 06 83 05

Just the place to visit Merlin's forest – everyone knows he was a Breton, not a Cornish, wizard and did his sorcery right here in Brocéliande... From one bedroom you can see the forest only 500m away, from another, which has a little 18th-century marble fireplace (it still works), you look out over fields. Big, bright, interesting decoration throughout thanks to Madame's good taste and new ideas in handling her lovely old house: mainly 1760s, the big manor house actually has some 15th-century bits. She serves breakfast as late as you want with real squeezed orange juice and is a most unusual, interesting companion.

Rooms: 2 doubles, 1 suite for 4, each with bath or shower & wc.

Price: 300 Frs for two.

Meals: Choice 1-5km.

Closed: Never.

Gîte space for 6 people.

From Rennes N24 for 27km. Right into Plélan le Grand; right at church on D59 towards St Malon sur Mel; 1st left: Chemin des Châteaux for 1km. House on top of small hill, entrance behind on left.
Michelin Map No: 230-38

Entry no: 242   Map No: 2

Mme Christine HERMENIER
Manoir de la Ruisselère
35380 Paimpont
Ille-et-Vilaine
Tel: (0)2 99 06 85 94

Madame wanted us to mention her passion for embroidery; there is much of it about, together with Laura Ashley fabrics, flounces, friezes and fantasy... and she is enthusing about her new *brocante* showroom where you can sit and read on an antique chair then buy it as you leave, or the table, or... They are a delightful couple but you will perhaps see less of them now they have installed a guest dining room in the converted barn. So, not always very *familiale* but thoroughly caring. Count on Beethoven, crêpes and an indoor garden for breakfast. It is in a tiny hamlet.

Rooms: 1 large suite for 5, 1 triple, both with shower & wc. 'Studio' also available.

Price: 300-350 Frs for two; lovers' night 780 Frs.

Meals: 100 Frs, excluding wine.

Closed: Never.

Gîte space for 4 people.

From Rennes, S on new road to Janzé (D163/D41). Here, right on D92 for La Couyère for approx. 6km. House is on right in La Tremblais with yellow gate; signposted. Park behind.
Michelin Map No: 230-41

Entry no: 243   Map No: 2

Claudine & Raymond GOMIS
La Raimonderie
La Tremblais
35320 La Couyère
Ille-et-Vilaine
Tel: (0)2 99 43 14 39
Fax: (0)2 99 43 14 39
Web: www.la-raimonderie.com

Enter the enclosed courtyard and you will discover the charms of this 17th-century grey stone presbytery with its blue shutters and climbing roses. Walled gardens and an orchard for picnics complete the peaceful, private mood. Rooms are interestingly furnished and have lots of personal touches, particularly the biggest which is high and stylish, the style reflected in its amazing, 50's deco, bathroom. The cosy, cottagey attic rooms have low beams and small shower rooms (not for taller people). Madame knows the area "like her pocket" and has itineraries for your deeper discovery of secret delights – plan two or three days if possible.

Rooms: 1 double and 2 twins, all with bath or shower & wc.

Price: 300 Frs for two.

Meals: 125 Frs, including wine & coffee.

Closed: Never.

Gîte space for 6 people.

From Guingamp N12 towards Morlaix, then Louargat exit. From Louargat church, D33 to Tregrom (7km). House in village centre, opposite church (blue door in wall).
Michelin Map No: 230-6

Entry no: **244**   Map No: 1

Nicole de MORCHOVEN
L'Ancien Presbytère
22420 Plouaret
Côtes-d'Armor
Tel: (0)2 96 47 94 15
Fax: (0)2 96 47 94 15
Web: www.sawdays.co.uk

A fine 15th-century manor that exudes character and history, inside and out. There are monumental fireplaces, a worn spiral staircase, ancestral portraits, fine furniture. The bedrooms have space, taste, arched doors and good bathrooms. Breakfast, a fine Breton spread, can be brought to your room if you wish. Madame planted the lovely garden some 40 years ago and still tends it; Monsieur is gracious and well-travelled. Their welcome is elegant, their conversation intelligent, their house a delight and their son breeds racehorses on the other half of the estate. *Two nights minimum stay.*

Rooms: 2 twins, each with bath & wc.

Price: 500 Frs for two.

Meals: Choice 7-10 km.

Closed: Never.

From N12 exit at Beg ar Chra/Plouaret (bet. Guingamp & Morlaix) to Plouaret. D11 direction Lannion to Kerauzern. D30 left direction St Michel en Grève & Ploumilliau, cross railway & continue for 3km; left at signpost 100m, left again, go to end.
Michelin Map No: 230-6

Entry no: **245**   Map No: 1

M & Mme Gérard de BELLEFON
Manoir de Kerguéréon
Ploubezre
22300 Lannion
Côtes-d'Armor
Tel: (0)2 96 38 91 46

Once inside this enlarged 1930s house you will understand why it is in this book: the ever-changing light of the great bay shimmers in through the vast expanse of glass whence you can watch the boats come and go, or walk to the beach (10 minutes). Guy chose the house so he could see his small boat at anchor out there (lucky guests may be taken for a sail) and Marie-Clo has enlivened the interior with her talented patchwork and embroidery. It is calm, light, bright; they are attentive hosts and breakfast is seriously good.

The estate has been in the family for 600 years and their 'latest' house (17th-19th-century) is a masterpiece of understated elegance. Ceilings are high, windows generous, guests rejoice in a granite-hearthed, tapestry-walled sitting room where old books and family portraits remind them this is "just an ordinary family house". Madame, dynamic and adorable, loves her visitors. The bedrooms vary in size and character, all are fascinating, though we preferred *La Jaune* for its panelling and lovely view. Worth every centime.

Rooms: 2 doubles, each with sitting area, sea view, shower & wc.

Price: 300 Frs for two.

Meals: Lots of choice in Perros Guirec.

Closed: Never.

Gîte space for 4 people.

Rooms: 3 doubles, 2 twins, all with bath, shower & wc.

Price: 480-580 Frs for two.

Meals: Crêperie in village; excellent restaurant nearby.

Closed: Never.

Gîte space for 10 people.

From Lannion D788 N to Perros Guirec; follow signs to Port then to 'Centre ville par la corniche'; follow round bay for approx. 1km then left at sign '3 Cléracances'. (Will fax map or collect you from railway station.) Michelin Map No: 230-6

From St Brieuc, N12 to Guingamp, then D8 direction Tréguier. At Pommerit Jaudy turn left at the lights. Michelin Map No: 230-7

Entry no: **246**   Map No: 1

Entry no: **247**   Map No: 1

Marie-Clo & Guy BIARNÈS
41 rue de la Petite Corniche
BP 24
22700 Perros Guirec, Côtes-d'Armor
Tel: (0)2 96 23 28 08
Fax: (0)2 96 23 28 23
e-mail: guy.biarnes@wanadoo.fr
Web: www.sawdays.co.uk

Comte & Comtesse de KERMEL
Château de Kermezen
22450 Pommerit Jaudy
Côtes-d'Armor
Tel: (0)2 96 91 35 75
Fax: (0)2 96 91 35 75
Web: www.sawdays.co.uk

Looking for perfect château B&B? It is here, with a couple of perfect *châtelains* to receive you. Exposed to the wild Breton elements, this fortified Bishop's seat, now a vegetable farm, has superb grounds and a luxurious interior of marble fireplaces, gilt mirrors, antiques and a classically French *salon*. Guestrooms are big and richly decorated, the tower room deliciously different, more 'rustic', with its timbers and mezzanine and the new loo fitted to the original and still functioning 14th-century drain! The twin-basined bathrooms are all quite lovely. Breakfast is a Breton feast to linger over in good company.

Rooms: 2 doubles, 1 twin, 1 triple, 2 suites for 3-4, all with private bathrooms.

Price: 600 Frs for two.

Meals: Walking distance in summer; choice 10km.

Closed: Never.

From Guingamp, D8 to Plougrescant. There, right after church (leaning spire) and right again 200m along. Michelin Map No: 230-7

Entry no: 248   Map No: 1

Vicomte & Vicomtesse de ROQUEFEUIL
Manoir de Kergrec'h
22820 Plougrescant
Côtes-d'Armor
Tel: (0)2 96 92 59 13
Fax: (0)2 96 92 51 27

There's no other like it: the sea at the bottom of the drive, an extraordinary, rather crumbly old château (Monsieur's ancestor built it in 1373!), vast and wonderful guest rooms, a lively, lovable couple of aristocratic hosts, bent on riding, hunting and entertaining you. You breakfast in the upstairs *salon*, or downstairs, through the low stone arch in the room with the boar's head and other bits of personality – such fun. Madame is applying energy and good taste to renovating some of the 30 rooms. One suite is pink, another blue and yellow. Beds are canopied, windows high, portraits ancestral, rugs cotton – atmosphere unreal.

Rooms: 2 suites, 1 double, each with bath or shower & wc.

Price: 450-750 Frs for two.

Meals: Good choice 5km.

Closed: October-April.

Gîte space for 4 people.

From St Brieuc N12 towards Lamballe exit Yffigniac-Hillion. After Yffigniac left on D80 to Hillion; D34 towards Morieux. 200m after Hillion, roadside crucifix on left by château gates. Michelin Map No: 230-9

Entry no: 249   Map No: 1

Vicomtesse Louis du FOU de KERDANIEL
Château de Bonabry
22120 Hillion
Côtes-d'Armor
Tel: (0)2 96 32 21 06
Fax: (0)2 96 32 21 06

You will have gentle piped music and Breton pancakes for breakfast in the big traditional dining room. Madame, as well as tending her immaculate garden, collects dolls and other items of folklore which peek out from nooks and corners. Great carved mirror-fronted wardrobes are standard here, beds are firm and comfortable, floors are polished wood, bathrooms are modern and the dominant colour is blue (even the radiators). You will feel well looked after in this quiet country place with genuine, direct farming folk. There is a kitchen annexe for self-catering, bikes are available and there are climbing frames for children in the front field.

Rooms: 2 doubles, 1 triple, each with bath or shower and wc.

Price: 230 Frs for two.

Meals: Choice in Yffiniac 4km; self-catering possible.

Closed: Never.

Gîte space for 25 people.

From N12 exit Yffiniac (NOT Yffiniac Gare) into village. Go 1km then left towards Plédran, through La Croix Orin; Le Grenier is down hill on left, 3.5km from Yffiniac centre.
Michelin Map No: 230-23

Entry no: 250   Map No: 1

Marie-Reine & Fernand LOQUIN
Le Grenier
22120 Yffiniac
Côtes-d'Armor
Tel: (0)2 96 72 64 55
Fax: (0)2 96 72 68 74

A long, low Breton house built on hard Breton granite, guarded by a soft Breton Spaniel and kept by a relaxed and friendly Breton woman whose family has owned it for generations (she lives in the little house). There is old wood everywhere – ceilings, wardrobes, beams, beds; there are gingham cloths, floral curtains and lace cushions. Breakfasts and evening meals (these must be requested) are cooked on a wood-fired range and served on attractive rough pottery at separate tables in the guests' dining room.

Rooms: 3 doubles, 1 twin, 1 triple, 1 double & bunks, all with bath or shower & wc.

Price: 250-275 Frs for two.

Meals: 95 Frs, including wine & coffee (not Sundays).

Closed: Never.

From Dinard, D168 to Ploubalay and D768 to Plancoët; D19 to St Lormel; left opposite school at far end of village then follow signs for 1.5km.
Michelin Map No: 230-10

Entry no: 251   Map No: 2

Évelyne LEDÉ
La Pastourelle
St Lormel
22130 Plancoët
Côtes-d'Armor
Tel: (0)2 96 84 03 77
Fax: (0)2 96 84 03 77

Your bedrooms here are in a separate building behind the main house overlooking the sheltered, flower-filled courtyard. They are spotless and stylish in that slightly stark classic French way, although there are books, plants and personal touches, antiques and the odd deco piece. Great bathrooms and a small guest sitting room. Breakfast – home-made croissants and jams – is served at individual tables in the owner's chandeliered living room. Both Edith and Jean Claude were born in Paris but have Breton roots. Edith runs the house and is friendly, chatty and elegant. Quiet countryside 4km from the coast.

Rooms: 2 doubles, 1 twin, 1 apartment for 4/5.

Price: 350 Frs for two; reduction for longer stays.

Meals: Good restaurants 4km.

Closed: 16 November-Easter.

From St Malo on D168 through Ploubalay towards St Brieuc. At first roundabout after Ploubalay D26 towards Plessix Balisson for 4km to hamlet where house is on right & signed.
Michelin Map No: 230-11

Entry no: **252**   Map No: 2

Edith & Jean-Claude REY du BOISSIEU
Le Clos Saint-Cadreuc
22650 Ploubalay, Côtes-d'Armor
Tel: (0)2 96 27 32 43
Fax: (0)2 96 27 32 43
e-mail: jc.reyduboissieu@mail.dotcom.fr
Web: www.sawdays.co.uk

This is a place for golfers – nine-hole golf course plus all the trappings (clubhouse, lessons, socialising) – with the added charm of a farm atmosphere, a cosy house and carp ponds for those with a rod. The grand 15th-century Breton *longère*, has been in the Beaupère family for four generations. Madame has a flair for decorating with velvet and florals and her rooms are very comfortable. Guests are welcome to eat *en famille*: traditional recipes and local cheeses with a choice of good wines. The old Breton bread oven is working again for the baking of bread or even, occasionally, the roasting of suckling pig.

Rooms: 2 twins, 2 doubles, all with bath or shower & wc.

Price: 290 Frs for two.

Meals: 90 Frs, excluding wine.

Closed: Never.

From Dinan, N176 direction St Brieuc. At Plélan le Petit, take D19 (right) to St Michel de Plélan. House signposted left, 1km after village.
Michelin Map No: 230-24

Entry no: **253**   Map No: 2

Odile & Henri BEAUPÈRE
La Corbinais
22980 St Michel de Plélan
Côtes-d'Armor
Tel: (0)2 96 27 64 81
Fax: (0)2 96 81 68 45
e-mail: corbinais@corbinais.com
Web: www.corbinais.com

These people turn the everyday into the remarkable: modern houses have a hard time getting into this book but this one sailed in. Clad in red cedar, open-plan to provide space for six children, its wood, metal and glass are in perfect harmony; only the best materials are used and every tiny detail has been taken care of: plain white covers on beds, Eastern-style cushions and wall hangings on plain walls, superb beds and towels, shower-pressure just right. Breakfast is *un peu brunch*, as carefully thought out as the house. Lovely people and an exquisite, serene house that seems to hug its garden to its heart.

Rooms: 1 suite for 2 with *salon*, 1 suite for 4 (2 bedrooms), each with shower & wc.

Price: 320 Frs for two.

Meals: Within walking distance.

Closed: December-March.

From Dinan N176 W towards St Brieuc for about 12km. Exit right to Plélan le Petit. Follow signs to Centre/Mairie; at Mairie right towards St Maudez then 2nd right.
Michelin Map No: 230-24

Entry no: **254**   Map No: 2

Martine & Hubert VIANNAY
Malik
Chemin de l'Étoupe
22980 Plélan le Petit
Côtes-d'Armor
Tel: (0)2 96 27 62 71/
         (0)6 09 92 35 21

Janine's love is her vegetarian cooking, Steve's is his sculpture that decorates the rambling, rose-filled garden. Our inspector loved it for its isolation, lack of pretension, and daring to be different. It is the sort of 'alternative' that we like: simple, attractive, comfortable-yet-humble... and interesting. Guests eat at separate tables, tasting, perhaps, the artichoke *aioli* or roasted cherry tomatoes. Use the living room and garden, browse through the books, make yourself coffee... your hosts are young and easy. *Advance bookings only.*

Rooms: 1 family room for 4 with shower & wc; 1 twin, 1 double, sharing bath & wc.

Price: 300-340 Frs for two; minimum 2 nights.

Meals: 100 Frs for 3-course vegetarian meal incl. wine & coffee. Packed lunch 30-40 Frs.

Closed: December-February.

Gîte space for 6 people.

From Dinan D766 S for Caulnes approx. 13km. Right on D64 to Plumaudan. Left for Caulnes for approx. 150m. 2nd right for Le Plessis. House on right after 2km.
Michelin Map No: 230-25

Entry no: **255**   Map No: 2

Janine & Steve JUDGES
Le Plessis Vegetarian Guesthouse
Le Plessis
22350 Plumaudan
Côtes-d'Armor
Tel: (0)2 96 86 00 44
Fax: (0)2 96 86 00 44
e-mail: janine.leplessis@wanadoo.fr

Still sheer delight for lovers of the utterly personal, even eccentric. In this miniature museum of a house where the stunningly-draped orange dining room leads to an elegant yellow *salon*, the infectiously vibrant Rhona will introduce you to her wiggly Chinese sofa, her husband's regimental drum, an 18th-century looking-glass (one of a remarkable collection) and other cherished household gods. A home like no other, unsurpassed hospitality, a remarkable garden (climb up to the second terrace with a book), a comfortable bed (one has a glass door onto its fine bathroom), a generous and elegant breakfast. Unforgettable.

Rooms: 2 doubles, both with bath, shower & wc.

Price: 350 Frs for two.

Meals: Wide choice close by.

Closed: November-February.

Squarely planted in its Breton soil, this is without doubt a family house open to guests not a purpose-converted undertaking. The children now run the farm and the Gralls have time for visitors. After a blissful night (warm traditional décor, excellent mattresses, neat modern bathrooms) and a bucolic awakening to birdsong in the fields, come down to Madame's home-made crêpes or *far breton* at their square Breton table beside the deeply-carved sideboard. Family antiques, family warmth, peace and unity that reassure and relax.

Rooms: 2 doubles, 1 twin, each with shower & wc.

Price: 250 Frs for two.

Meals: Restaurant 2.5km.

Closed: Never.

From Dinan central square, take Rue de Lehon, through Porte St Louis, follow road down, bear left below ramparts, straight across into Rue de Coëtquen. Michelin Map No: 230-25

From St Pol de Léon D10 W to Cléder (8km). Arriving in Cléder, take road to sea for 2km then left following signs to Ferme de Kernévez. Michelin Map No: 230-4

Entry no: 256   Map No: 2

Entry no: 257   Map No: 1

Rhona LOCKWOOD
53/55 rue de Coëtquen
22100 Dinan
Côtes-d'Armor
Tel: (0)2 96 85 23 49
Fax: (0)2 96 87 51 44
Web: www.sawdays.co.uk

François & Marceline GRALL
Kernévez
29233 Cléder
Finistère
Tel: (0)2 98 69 41 14

Built in the 1840s by well-travelled writer/merchant Corbière, whose better-known poet son Tristan was a protégé of Verlaine's, *Crow's Rock Manor* has always had these big, airy, wood-floored, lofty-ceilinged, chandeliered rooms with superb views of the generous grounds. Now admirably restored by your young and sociable hosts, it is definitely a special place with its air of old-style, refined but not overstated luxury. For a modern touch, step up to your marble bath to gaze out to hills and woods on two sides. Breakfast may include *far breton* and crêpes, strawberries and home-made jam.

Rooms: 2 twins, each with bath & wc; 1 additional twin also available.

Price: 430 Frs for two; minimum 2 nights July & August.

Meals: Bistro 1km; choice in Morlaix 3km.

Closed: Never.

From Morlaix follow right bank of river N, take SECOND right signed Ploujean (hairpin bend) for 500m. Right towards Ploujean; house 3rd on right.
Michelin Map No: 230-5

Entry no: 258   Map No: 1

Etienne & Armelle DELAISI
Manoir de Roch ar Brini
29600 Ploujean Morlaix
Finistère
Tel: (0)2 98 72 01 44
Fax: (0)2 98 88 04 49
e-mail: rochbrini@aol.com
Web: www.brittanyguesthouse.com

Above ancient Breton rocks, sea and pine trees, this modern house hides many fine old pieces, ancestral portraits and family trees. Your hosts, a great mix of French aristocracy and American academe, are cultured, polyglot, eager to share their love of Brittany. Bedrooms, cosily clothed in velvet and patchwork, decorated with unusual pictures (worth asking about) and good furniture, each have a colourful bathroom; one is on a different floor, one contains two bunk beds! (An independent wc and basin allow parents to ablute while offspring sleep.) The big, light, blue and yellow kitchen is a warm place for meals; garden and sea beckon on the doorstep.

Rooms: 1 suite, 1 double & 1 twin, each with bath & wc.

Price: 350-400 Frs.

Meals: 100-150 Frs, including aperitif, wine & coffee, by arrangement.

Closed: November-Easter.

From Morlaix towards 'Lannion par la Côte' on D64; Locquirec is 21km from Morlaix, 22km from Lannion. In village, towards 'Sables Blancs'. House on this road.
Michelin Map No: 230-6

Entry no: 259   Map No: 1

Comte & Comtesse Hubert de GERMINY
Villa Germiny
11 rue de Keraël
29241 Locquirec
Finistère
Tel: (0)2 98 67 47 11
Fax: (0)2 98 67 47 11

In a tiny, incredibly quiet hamlet on the fascinating, desolate heath of the Monts d'Arée, in the *Arée* National Park, Kreisker is a sensitive, utterly Breton conversion, all local stone, slate roofs and giant slabs of schist from the old floors. Inside there is scrubbed wood, more stone, ethnic rugs, fresh cotton and pretty china. The independent guest room has a lovely blue/grey-clothed brass bed and a fine bathroom. After the feast that is breakfast, your ears ringing with Madame's knowledgeable talk of Breton culture, go and explore this ancient land. *Children welcome if you bring a child's bed. Good-value dinner 3km – must pre-book.*

The two most memorable things here are Marie-Christine's smile as she talks about her native Brittany and the sympathetic use of wood on floor, ceilings and walls. Guest rooms are in the old cider-press – pretty, spotlessly clean, with skylight windows and handsome antiques. Breakfast, perhaps with Breton music in the background (there are Breton dresses on display too), is prepared in the dayroom and eaten at the long refectory table, with views of the garden and books all around. It is quiet and comfortable and you can be quite independent. *Dinner with Madame's daughter can be arranged!*

Rooms: 1 double with bathroom.

Price: 250 Frs for two.

Meals: Crêperies & restaurants 2.5-7km; book ahead.

Closed: Never.

Gîte space for 8 people.

Rooms: 1 double, 1 triple, each with shower & wc.

Price: 260 Frs for two.

Meals: Good crêperie in Brasparts.

Closed: Never.

From Morlaix, D785 direction Quimper. At La Croix Cassée, D42 to Botmeur. 200m after the town hall direction La Feuillée, take the first on left.
Michelin Map No: 230-19

From Morlaix D785 S towards Quimper for about 35km. 800m before Brasparts, turn right (on bend) & follow signs.
Michelin Map No: 230-19

Entry no: 260   Map No: 1

Entry no: 261   Map No: 1

Marie-Thérèse & Jean-Bernard
SOLLIEC
Kreisker
29690 Botmeur
Finistère
Tel: (0)2 98 99 63 02
Fax: (0)2 98 99 63 02
e-mail: jbsol@club-internet.fr

Marie-Christine CHAUSSY
Domaine de Rugornou Uras
Garz ar Bik
29190 Brasparts
Finistère
Tel: (0)2 98 81 47 14/
    (0)2 98 81 46 27
Fax: (0)2 98 81 47 99

This neat old farmhouse has kept watch over the bay for generations. Typically Breton, the entrance is guarded by a religious statue and, as you would expect, the *Bretonne* room has proper Breton furniture while the *Romantique* room has a canopied bed with bunches of roses. There are flowers everywhere, indoors and out, on the walls, on the balconies, in the garden, in the rustic, flagstoned dining room where you have breakfast. A peaceful house, charming hosts and just five minutes walk from the sea.

Rooms: 2 doubles (1 on ground floor), each with shower & wc.

Price: 260 Frs for two.

Meals: Choice in Douarnenez.

Closed: Never.

Gîte space for 20 people.

From Douarnenez, D7 direction Locronan. House is before village, on first road on left after sign for 'La Plage du Ris'; signposted.
Michelin Map No: 230-17

Entry no: 262   Map No: 1

Henri & Henriette GONIDEC
Lanévry
Kerlaz
29100 Douarnenez
Finistère
Tel: (0)2 98 92 19 12
Fax: (0)2 98 92 19 12

The farm is now let out so the Oliers can concentrate on their B&B. This uncomplicated couple, who have led a simple farming life, are real weather-beaten Bretons who have converted an old pighouse into three good modern rooms with restfully plain white walls, extra-wide beds, thermostatic showers (*très moderne*) and a comfortable wicker-chaired dayroom. Madame serves a Breton breakfast in her dining room; Monsieur may offer you a bunch of flowers. Their smile is a great gift. There are walks across two valleys from the house; beaches and ports are 10km away and the guest kitchen appeals to families.

Rooms: 1 double, 1 triple, 1 twin/quadruple, all with shower & wc.

Price: 260 Frs for two.

Meals: Good choice 5km; guest kitchen available.

Closed: Never.

Gîte space for 5 people.

From Douarnenez D765 direction Audierne. On entering Confort Meilars, 1st left and follow signs for 2.5km.
Michelin Map No: 230-17

Entry no: 263   Map No: 1

Anne & Jean OLIER
Kerantum
29790 Mahalon
Finistère
Tel: (0)2 98 74 51 93
Fax: (0)2 98 74 51 93

The bewitching name (of the warring knight who became first baron in 1010), the splendidness of the place, its vast, opulent rooms and magnificent grounds, seduced us utterly: a powerful experience, grand rather than intimate, but unforgettable. Built with stones from the 11th-century fortress, it is a jewel of 18th-century aristocratic architecture, inside and out. M Davy, the latest descendant, is passionate about buildings, his ancient family seat in particular, and applies all his energy and intelligence to restoring château and park, planting thousands of bulbs and bushes, and converting visitors to the same devotion. Deeply interesting and unusual.

Rooms: 4 doubles, 2 suites, each with bath or shower & wc.

Price: 650-800 Frs for two; suite 900-1300 Frs.

Meals: Choice nearby.

Closed: December-February.

Gîte space for 5 people.

From Quimper D765 W for 5km then left on D784 towards Landudec for 13km; left & follow signs.
Michelin Map No: 230-17

Entry no: 264   Map No: 1

Philippe DAVY
Domaine du Guilguiffin
29710 Landudec
Finistère
Tel: (0)2 98 91 52 11
Fax: (0)2 98 91 52 52
e-mail: chateau@guilguiffin.com
Web: www.guilguiffin.com

The view across fields and wooded hills is perfectly wonderful. Your quarters are in a converted outbuilding, separate from the owners' house, and the window in each smallish room is a double-glazed door onto the long terrace where chairs await. There is a big modern veranda room for breakfast (with crêpes or croissants), where a richly-carved Breton wardrobe takes pride of place. Modern-furnished rooms and bathrooms are identical and impeccable. Madame is efficient, full of information about Breton culture, and very purposeful. Only suitable for older children who can sleep alone.

Rooms: 4 doubles, 2 twins, all with shower & wc.

Price: 255 Frs for two.

Meals: 90 Frs (September-mid-June only); self-catering possible; restaurant 10km.

Closed: Never.

From Quimper, D765 direction Rosporden. At St Yvi left direction Kervren; at very end of lane (2.5km).
Michelin Map No: 230-33

Entry no: 265   Map No: 1

Odile LE GALL
Kervren
29140 St Yvi
Finistère
Tel: (0)2 98 94 70 34
Fax: (0)2 98 94 81 19

Madame is a darling – quiet, serene and immensely kind – and really treats her guests as friends. The long, low, granite house has been in the family for all of its 300 years, enjoying the peace of this wind-blown, bird-sung spot just five minutes walk from the sea and that gorgeous coastal path. Most of the building consists of gîtes; the *chambres d'hôtes* are squeezed into the far end – definitely small, impeccably simple, like the dining room. With charming Port Manech and some handsome beaches nearby, it is a wonderful holiday spot.

This rural haven lies between *Armor*, the land by the sea and *Argoat*, the land of woods. It is a Breton house with naturally hospitable Breton owners, Breton furniture and a huge Breton brass pot once used for mixing crêpes. They love having children to stay. Madame is welcoming and chatty (in French), Monsieur has a reassuring earthy calmness. One of the large, light, country-style rooms has been redone in sunny yellow. Copious breakfasts include those crêpes (though not mixed in the brass pot) and home-grown kiwi fruit in season.

Rooms: 2 doubles, 2 twins, all with shower & wc.

Price: 260 Frs for two.

Meals: In village, within walking distance.

Closed: Never.

Gîte space for 14 people.

Rooms: 3 doubles and 1 twin, all with shower & wc.

Price: 260 Frs for two.

Meals: Restaurant 4km.

Closed: Never.

Gîte space for 8 people.

From Pont Aven, D77 direction Port Manech; right just before the signpost Port Manech, and 1st left. Signposted Chambres d'Hôtes.
Michelin Map No: 230-33

Entry no: 266   Map No: 1

Yveline GOURLAOUEN
Kerambris
Port Manech
29920 Nevez
Finistère
Tel: (0)2 98 06 83 82
Fax: (0)2 98 06 83 82
Web: www.sawdays.co.uk

From Scaër, D50 direction Coray Briec; after 3km, left at 'Ty Ru' and follow signpost for Kerloaï.
Michelin Map No: 230-19

Entry no: 267   Map No: 1

Louis & Thérèse PENN
Kerloaï
29390 Scaër
Finistère
Tel: (0)2 98 59 42 60
Fax: (0)2 98 59 05 67

English people in a very French house. Gill, a senior member of the Quilters' Guild and much-appreciated teacher of patchwork, and Clive, a retired banker and accomplished cook of four-course dinners, are quietly friendly hosts, enjoying their year-round flowering garden, where they are constantly creating new features (pond, rockery) in the balmy Breton air. Their house (a resurrected ruin) has soft furnishings, soft cats, a fine mix of old and new. Their welcome includes good simple rooms with tea trays and informed help on what to see in the adopted country they so love.

Rooms: 1 twin, 1 family room for 5, both with shower or small bath & wc; 1 twin sharing bathroom.

Price: 240 Frs for two.

Meals: 120 Frs, including aperitif, wine & coffee.

Closed: Never.

From Morlaix, D785 towards Pleyben for 23km. Left on D764 towards Huelgoat for 7km. Right on D36 towards Châteauneuf du Faou. Laz is on the D36 after Châteauneuf; house at end of village on left. (Secure parking.) Michelin Map No: 230-19

Entry no: 268   Map No: 1

Gill & Clive THOMPSON
Les Deux Aiguilles
3 Grand'Rue
29520 Laz
Finistère
Tel: (0)2 98 26 87 23

A stupendously atmospheric place: the embracing enclosure, the ruin, the arched door through to the hugely-paved hall. And inside, more ancient stones and timbers, a generous 16th-century staircase, large and exquisitely-renovated rooms with just enough period furniture (and modern beds), soft, rich textures and excellent bathrooms. Peter and Clarissa have breathed new life into their Breton home. Relaxed and knowledgeable hosts, they organise seasonal fungus hunts and love communicating their feel for 'real' Brittany. Walk the canal path, visit the beautiful hinterland and return, perhaps, to a refined dinner with home-grown organic vegetables.

Rooms: 2 doubles, 2 twins, 1 family room for 4, all with bath or shower & wc.

Price: 260-330 Frs for two.

Meals: 120 Frs, including wine & coffee, by arrangement.

Closed: October-Easter.

From Carhaix Plouguer, take N164 southern bypass; turn off at 'Districenter' (big warehouse/shop) & continue to Prevasy; right at triangular green, straight on to house. Michelin Map No: 230-20

Entry no: 269   Map No: 1

Peter & Clarissa NOVAK
Manoir de Prevasy
29270 Carhaix
Finistère
Tel: (0)2 98 93 24 36
Fax: (0)2 98 93 24 36
Web: www.sawdays.co.uk

The setting is out of this world, the welcome just right, so what matter the youth of the house. You can boat on the lake with the wild duck walk by the babbling stream through the woods and wild rhododendron, sit on the bank under the palm tree and gaze cross the valley to the distant hills. And you can barbecue in the orchard. Hospitality comes naturally to this serene retired couple who are happy to share their truly privileged environment in a quiet hamlet. The rooms are perfectly adequate in their ubiquitous pink and blue, the atmosphere incomparable.

Rooms: 1 triple, 1 double, both with shower & wc.

Price: 230 Frs for two.

Meals: Choice 1.5km.

Closed: Never.

Deep in rural Brittany, where you feel the clock stopped 50 years ago, a forgotten peace descends, your pace slows, *la tranquillité* sets in. Peter and Pat, a warm, good-humoured couple, have converted an old farmhouse and its barns into a wonderful holiday spot, a place full of laughter and the happiness of being there. The house now sports finely-crafted (by Peter) 'Jacobean' panelling – it may be imitation but it feels deeply cosy and utterly English. The giant weekly international barbecue with guests and locals is highly appreciated, the three acres of garden give space for all (there are seven gîtes and a pool too); it is ideal for families.

Rooms: 1 twin with shower & wc; 1 2-room suite for 4 with shower & wc.

Price: 250 Frs for two.

Meals: In village or good choice 5km.

Closed: Never.

Gîte space for 35 people.

From Quimperlé D790 direction Le Faouët 9km. Left to Querien; follow signs direction Mellac. 1km after village, 1st left to Kerfaro. There left after stone house. Last house in lane. Michelin Map No: 230-34

From Pontivy D764 towards Josselin for 5km; straight on through C4 (Noyal Pontivy/St Thuriau) crossroads; 100m after crossroads, right to Pennerest. Michelin Map No: 230-22

Entry no: 270   Map No: 1

Entry no: 271   Map No: 1

Renée & Yves LE GALLIC
Kerfaro
29310 Querrien
Finistère
Tel: (0)2 98 71 30 02 / (0)6 85 17 96 43
Fax: (0)2 98 71 30 02

Peter & Pat ROBERTS
Pennerest
56920 Noyal Pontivy
Morbihan
Tel: (0)2 97 38 35 76
Fax: (0)2 97 38 23 80
e-mail: p.roberts@wanadoo.fr
Web: www.sawdays.co.uk

The situation is heavenly, cradled in a quiet hamlet 200 yards from the river in a particularly lovely corner of Brittany. The people are delightful: Martine looks after old folk and young Melissa, Philippe pots and teaches aikido, both have lots of time for their guests. The two big, superbly-converted, uncluttered attic rooms have been decorated with flair in subtle pastels and fitted with good shower rooms. Guests have their own sitting/breakfast room and kitchen. Birds sing. The cat is one of the best ever. The welcome is genuine and you may get a different kind of cake for breakfast every day. Readers' letters are full of praise.

Rooms: 2 twins, each with shower & wc.

Price: 230 Frs for two.

Meals: Wide choice in St Nicolas 3km; kitchen available for guests' use.

Closed: November-Easter, except by arrangement.

From Pontivy, D768 direction Lorient; exit for Port Arthur/St Nicolas des Eaux to St Nicolas; right immediately after bridge; follow signs Chambres d'Hôtes & Poterie for 3km.
Michelin Map No: 230-35

Entry no: 272   Map No: 1

Martine MAIGNAN &
Philippe BOIVIN
Lezerhy
56310 Bieuzy les Eaux, Morbihan
Tel: (0)2 97 27 74 59
Fax: (0)2 97 27 74 59
e-mail: boivinp@wanadoo.fr
Web: perso.wanadoo.fr/poterie-de-lezerhy/

Surrounded by meadows of wild flowers and woodland, this enchanting 18th-century farmhouse feels miles from anywhere. Bare stonework rubs shoulders with whitewashed walls, there are potted plants and dried flowers everywhere. The open-plan day room has an oak-beamed ceiling and rug-strewn floor; comfy sofas and chairs around an open fire, and a large dining area. Steep stairs lead to simply decorated bedrooms with stone walls contrasting with brightly coloured furnishings under sloping rafters. If not relaxing in the garden or strolling in fields, you can play ping-pong, badminton or croquet, go fishing or paddle a canoe.

Rooms: 2 doubles, 1 twin, each with shower & wc.

Price: 240 Frs for two.

Meals: 85 Frs, including wine & coffee.

Closed: Never.

Gîte space for 6 people.

Exit N24 dir. Baud, then D768 dir. Pontivy. At Port Arthur/St Nicolas-des-Eaux, dir. Talvern-Nenez, follow signs for Golf de Rimaison. Right opp. golf course, after 1km left and follow signs.
Michelin Map No: 230-35

Entry no: 273   Map No: 1

Marie-Thérèse VANNIER
La Baratte
Lelfaux
56310 Bieuzy les Eaux
Morbihan
Tel: (0)2 97 27 74 11

500 years of deepest Breton history sing in the stones of this fine manor farm. The pigeon-wall tells us the lord's wealth, the vastly-fireplaced *salon* where he dispensed justice shows his status. Tower and Master bedrooms are fitting names: oak floors, high beamed ceilings, stone fireplaces, big windows, pretty ground-floor bathrooms. The darker ground-floor room has a small shower room, all are big with oodles of character. Yann has expertly restored, replumbed, rewired this beautiful place, Michèle has lovingly decorated and furnished it. They are intelligent, humorous and full of enthusiasm for guests, house and garden (with discreet heated pool).

Rooms: 1 double, 1 triple, 1 quadruple, all with shower or bath & wc.

Price: 380-450 Frs for two.

Meals: Choice in Josselin 3km.

Closed: Never.

From Josselin D126 towards Guégon. Take 4th right AFTER Guégon turning. House 150m up, on left. Michelin Map No: 230-37

Entry no: 274   Map No: 1

Yann BOURDIN & Michèle ROBIC
Manoir du Val aux Houx
56120 Guégon
Morbihan
Tel: (0)2 97 22 24 32
Fax: (0)2 97 75 42 65
e-mail: yann.bourdin@wanadoo.fr

Before concentrating on the privileged few, including you, at Kerreo, Gérard used his skills as a chef for the wealthy of this world (châteaux-hotels) and the deprived (catering schools for troubled youths). The B&B is all his: Nelly works in town. He has revived the old bread oven in the lush little garden, renovated and decorated the 'cottage' with great flair and faithfulness – the rooms, named after Breton fairies, are enchanting. He is quietly welcoming and the whole family is deeply Breton, doing *Fest-Noz* with costumes, dances, bagpipes and songs, though the odd moonlight game of *boules* or darts gives a foreign flavour.

Rooms: 4 doubles, 1 twin, each with bath or shower & wc.

Price: 290-320 Frs for two.

Meals: 100 Frs, including wine/cider.

Closed: Never.

From Lorient N165 E for 20km; exit 'Landevant' onto D24 N for approx. 8km then left at sign to Chaumière de Kerreo: thatched house with fuschia-pink paintwork at hamlet crossroads. Michelin Map No: 230-36

Entry no: 275   Map No: 1

Gérard GREVÈS & Nelly LE GLEHUIR
Chaumière de Kerreo
56330 Pluvigner
Morbihan
Tel: (0)2 97 50 90 48
Fax: (0)2 97 50 90 69

The old farmyard is now impeccably clean and flower-boxed, the big beamed guest living room a lesson in French improved country style (richly-flocked wallpaper, deeply-carved repro furniture, lace cloths and masses of ornaments and mementoes). Here, Madame, an elegant and wonderfully French country lady, serves her generous breakfasts – "a little bit different every day". Within the old walls, the B&B conversion is fairly standard but each small room (the two at the front are better) has a bit of terrace, there are pleasant views all round, a pond and just a 20-minute drive to those little harbour towns, the beaches and the Belle Ile ferry.

Rooms: 5 doubles/triples, each with shower & wc.

Price: 250 Frs for two.

Meals: Good restaurants nearby. Self-catering possible.

Closed: Never.

Gîte space for 2 people.

From N24 Baud exit on D768 direction Auray for 12km. At first Pluvigner roundabout left onto D16 direction Locminé for 4km then turn right and follow signs.
Michelin Map No: 230-36

Entry no: 276   Map No: 1

Marie-Claire COLLET
Kerdavid-Duchentil
56330 Pluvigner
Morbihan
Tel: (0)2 97 56 00 59

In a beautiful setting among the fields, the standing stones of Carnac minutes away, beaches and coastal pathways close by, Kerimel is a handsome group of granite farm buildings. The bedrooms are beauties: plain walls, some panelling, pale blue covers and curtains, old stone and beams plus modern comfort. The dining room is cottage perfection: dried flowers hanging from beams over wooden table, tiled floor, vast blackened chimney, stone walls. Gentle, generous people... "We talked of flowers", wrote one guest.

Rooms: 5 doubles/twins, each with shower & wc.

Price: 300-350 Frs for two.

Meals: Good place 3km away.

Closed: Never.

From N165 exit for Quiberon/Carnac on D768 for 4km then right to Ploemel. There D105 W towards Erdeven; house signposted on right after 1.5km.
Michelin Map No: 230-35

Entry no: 277   Map No: 1

Babeth & Pierre MALHERBE
Kerimel
56400 Ploemel (Carnac)
Morbihan
Tel: (0)2 97 56 84 72
Fax: (0)2 97 56 84 72
e-mail: elisabeth.malherbe@wanadoo.fr
Web: kerimel.free.fr

The spreading creeper has softened the tautly-lifted face of the Balsans' thoroughly-renovated farmhouse, but lovers of all things clean and efficient will still delight in the order restored. The dayroom is large and light, with a lovely fire and large French windows leading onto the patio and garden. Rooms lead off a long, white passage upstairs and are extremely comfortable with proof of Monsieur's upholstering expertise. No stunning views but the sea is 500 yards away, historic towns are close and so are the mystical standing stones of Carnac. Home-made Breton cakes and jams for breakfast with genuinely friendly people.

An oyster farm, bang there on the quayside! All bedrooms have the view so close that you could dream of staying here alone with paint and brushes to soak up and capture that lovely (almost Cornish) atmosphere while drinking coffee on the balcony, smelling the sea and listening with utter contentment to the chugging of fishing boats. Madame, from northern France, was a legal advisor to businesses in England, Germany and USA – alert, efficient and chatty, she came to Brittany to help François farm oysters, and never looked back. He'll take you out there too, if you ask. Unusual and very welcoming.

Rooms: 3 doubles, 2 twins, all with shower & wc.

Price: 300-350 Frs for two.

Meals: Good choice 1km.

Closed: Never.

Rooms: 1 twin, 1 triple, 1 apartment for 3, each with shower & wc.

Price: 300-400 Frs for two.

Meals: Restaurant 500m.

Closed: Never.

Gîte space for 10 people.

From Carnac town take Avenue des Druides towards Beaumer. At crossroads left on Chemin de Beaumer. Impasse de Beaumer is 2nd on left.
Michelin Map No: 230-35

From Auray D28/D781 to Crach & La Trinité sur Mer; right at lights before bridge across to La Trinité; house 400m along on left, signed 'François Gouzer'.
Michelin Map No: 230-35

Entry no: 278   Map No: 1

Entry no: 279   Map No: 1

Marie-France & Daniel BALSAN
L'Alcyone
Impasse de Beaumer
56340 Carnac Plage
Morbihan
Tel: (0)2 97 52 78 11
Fax: (0)2 97 52 13 02

Christine & François GOUZER
Kernivilit
St Philibert
56470 La Trinité sur Mer, Morbihan
Tel: (0)2 97 55 17 78
Fax: (0)2 97 30 04 11
e-mail: fgouzer@club-internet.fr
Web: www.sawdays.co.uk

Gaze across garden and terrace at the ever-changing blue-green sea from the three attractive simply-furnished ground-floor bedrooms of this modern house of character. There are oyster beds nearby and a little beach at the end of the garden (for shallow high-tide bathing). A vast carved four-poster reigns imposingly in a first-floor bedroom that leads to an even more startling dayroom with billiard table, books all round, an oak altar, a 1950's juke box, a telescope, a child-size Louis XV armchair – all neatly arranged as if in a stately home. Madame, brisk and practical, has a style that features marked contrasts – you will warm to her.

Your graceful, cultured hosts always dine with you, creating an authentic taste of life with the French country aristocracy; dress for it, and enjoy a game of billiards afterwards. It may seem (rather endearingly) formal, with breakfast at 9am sharp and a touch of old-fashioned primness about table manners but they are good company and enjoy introducing guests to each other. Inevitably, the bedrooms are magnificent. The château has its own lake and 100 hectares of superb parkland... all within the Brière Regional Park where water and land are inextricably mingled and wildlife abounds.

Rooms: 1 double with bath; 3 doubles with basin & bidet sharing 2 showers; all sharing 6 wcs.

Price: 310-370 Frs for two.

Meals: In Larmor Baden 1.5km.

Closed: Mid-July & August.

Rooms: 2 doubles, 1 twin, all with bath or shower & wc.

Price: 500-550 Frs for two.

Meals: Candlelit dinner 250 Frs, including aperitif, wine & coffee.

Closed: Never.

Gîte space for 10 people.

From Auray D101 S to Baden; D316 S to Larmor Baden; through village N/NE to Locqueltas: small white sign on right – house 10m along on right.
Michelin Map No: 230-36

From N165, exit 15 for La Roche Bernard towards La Baule to Herbignac. Here, fork left on D47 towards St Lyphard for 4km; house on right.
Michelin Map No: 232-13

Entry no: 280   Map No: 1

Entry no: 281   Map No: 2

Mme MC HECKER
Locqueltas
56870 Larmor Baden
Morbihan
Tel: (0)2 97 57 05 85
Fax: (0)2 97 57 25 02
Web: www.sawdays.co.uk

François & Cécile de la
MONNERAYE
Château de Coët Caret
44410 Herbignac, Loire-Atlantique
Tel: (0)2 40 91 41 20
Fax: (0)2 40 91 37 46
e-mail: coetcaret@multimania.com
Web: welcome.to/coetcaret.com

Deep connections here: Le Plessis once belonged to the Roche family who crossed with William in 1066, settled in Fermoy, Ireland, then returned to France. Now very Breton, there are velvet curtains and high-back chairs in the *salon*; silver coffee pots and freshly-squeezed orange juice at breakfast; 3,000 rosebushes in the garden and bedrooms with huge character. The Belordes bought back the family seat after decades of 'alien owners'. Her father was in London with de Gaulle; she loves the English, enjoys cosmopolitan conversation (lots) and offers candlelit champagne dinners (supplement...). Expensive but special.

Rooms: 1 suite for 5, 1 double, 1 twin/quadruple, all with bath & wc.

Price: 550-900 Frs for two.

Meals: 275-350 Frs, including wine & coffee (400 Frs with champagne).

Closed: Never.

Gîte space for 4 people.

From Nantes leave A83 ringroad on D85 past airport. At T-junction at Champ de Foire left through Pont St Martin & follow signs to Le Plessis. Michelin Map No: 232-28

Entry no: 282   Map No: 2

M & Mme BELORDE
Château du Plessis-Atlantique
44860 Pont St Martin
Loire-Atlantique
Tel: (0)2 40 26 81 72
Fax: (0)2 40 32 76 67
Web: www.sawdays.co.uk

Such a pretty old coaching inn in the middle of the flat Muscadet country, with its Midi-style courtyard for turning the carriages... it was actually built just before the motor came in and the horse went out. Your ever-charming hosts have brought their fine carved armoires from their previous B&B in Normandy to add some character to the rather heavily renovated interior. Madame's dynamism and sense of fun are, of course, intact. The guest rooms, two in an annexe with kitchenette and a steep, uneven staircase, have parquet floors and good new bathrooms; fresh flowers and peace are the keynotes.

Rooms: 4 doubles, 1 twin, each with shower & wc.

Price: 260 Frs for two.

Meals: Choice 6km; self-catering in annexe.

Closed: Never.

Gîte space for 6 people.

From Nantes N249 E towards Poitiers, exit 'Vallet' towards Loroux Bottereau then Le Landreau for 5km. 600m before Le Landreau right and follow signs to La Rinière (3km). Michelin Map No: 232-29

Entry no: 283   Map No: 2

Françoise & Louis LEBARILLIER
Le Relais de La Rinière
44430 Le Landreau
Loire-Atlantique
Tel: (0)2 40 06 41 44
Fax: (0)2 51 13 10 52
e-mail: riniere@netcourrier.com
Web: www.riniere.com

The lofty dining room has massive beams, a massive table, massive old flags; the panelling took 500 hours to restore, fine period furniture gleams – Monsieur is passionate about buildings and an avid auction-goer. A feeling of Renaissance nobility extends everywhere except to the bathrooms, which are reassuringly modern. Madame seems charmingly eccentric and, under daughter Gaëlle's management, the estate produce a Muscadet from the surrounding vineyards that is served as an aperitif at about seven, before you sally forth for dinner.

Rooms: 5 doubles, all with bath or shower & wc.

Price: 470-670 Frs for two.

Meals: Wide choice within 5 minutes.

Closed: November-March, except by arrangement.

Gîte space for 10 people.

From Nantes, N249 towards Poitiers then N149 towards Le Pallet/La Haie Fouassière. 1km before Le Pallet D7 right to Monnières. In village follow signs to Gorges; château 1km on left.
Michelin Map No: 232-29

Entry no: 284   Map No: 2

Annick & Didier CALONNE
Château Plessis-Brezot
44690 Monnières
Loire-Atlantique
Tel: (0)2 40 54 63 24
Fax: (0)2 40 54 66 07
e-mail: a.calonne@online.fr
Web: www.chateauplessisbrezot.com

The typical long low 18th-century house in its vineyard setting is perfect for a quiet escape. The friendly, unobtrusive Desbrosses particularly enjoy the company of foreign visitors who may use their library and the drawing room with its deeply comfortable chairs around an imposing fireplace. Madame is an artist and potter – the strong colours are her (successful) choice, guest rooms are individually styled and dinner is served on matching blue and yellow plates. You will be taken very good care of at La Mozardière.

Rooms: 1 suite, 1 double, both with bath & wc.

Price: 315 Frs for two.

Meals: 135 Frs, including wine.

Closed: Never.

From Nantes D937 direction La Roche. At Rocheservière D753 to Legé. In village centre direction Touvois. Left just after Le Paradis restaurant. Signed Richebonne.
Michelin Map No: 232-40

Entry no: 285   Map No: 11

Christine & Gérard DESBROSSES
La Mozardière
Richebonne
44650 Legé
Loire-Atlantique
Tel: (0)2 40 04 98 51
Fax: (0)2 40 26 31 61
e-mail: lamozardiere@wanadoo.fr

An eight-metre-thick house with behind it a big barn-enclosed courtyard, two large towers and a covered terrace. The Migons couldn't be nicer and their renovation work is a great success. Bedrooms – big, north-facing, shuttered windows – are pretty, elegant, comfortable. There's a good mix of ancient and modern in the reception rooms, eg contemporary leather sofas and a suit of armour; the dining room furniture is antique and beams are painted blue and green; the games room has two billiards tables, a piano, a set of drums. Monsieur plays bass guitar so there's scope for entertaining evenings. Superb grounds with fishing pond and 'aperitif gazebo'.

Rooms: 1 twin, 4 doubles, each with bath or shower & wc.

Price: 475-525 Frs for two.

Meals: 130 Frs, including wine & coffee Wide choice of restaurants 4-10 km.

Closed: Never.

From A11 exit 20 on D923. Cross Loire to Liré on D763; right on D751 to Drain; left on D154 direction St Laurent des Autels. Entrance is 3.5 km after church.
Michelin Map No: 232-29

Entry no: 286   Map No: 2

Brigitte & Gérard MIGON
Le Mésangeau
49530 Drain
Maine-et-Loire
Tel: (0)2 40 98 21 57
Fax: (0)2 40 98 28 62
e-mail: le.mesangeau@wanadoo.fr
Web: www.sawdays.co.uk

Loire

Oh gentle living that was here – and deep, dark intrigue – when the Renaissance blossomed by the banks of France's mightiest river and kings and courtiers rode out to hunt the noble stag.

Racine was made Prior here by his uncle but was removed by the Bishop; the incident inspired *Les Plaideurs*. Rooms are in a converted priory outbuilding, each one a two-floor suite, well-but-simply furnished. The main house has a friendly family kitchen and a dining room with stacks of books and a pianola in the fireplace. The old chapel is now a garden room for breakfasts and there's a big garden with a swimming pool. Your hosts are lovely people, interesting, amusing and educated. Bernard likes to cook dinner for guests occasionally with the emphasis on simple recipes using the best quality local ingredients.

Rooms: 2 suites for 4, each with bath & 2 wcs; 1 twin with bath & wc.

Price: 400 Frs for two.

Meals: 150 Frs, including wine & coffee.

Closed: November-February.

From Angers N23 W towards Nantes for 13km. Go through St Georges, cont. for about 1.5km; left after a garage. Pass château: house is on left. Park outside and walk through gate. Michelin Map No: 232-31

Entry no: 287　　　　Map No: 2

Bernard & Geneviève GAULTIER
Prieuré de l'Epinay
49170 St Georges sur Loire
Maine-et-Loire
Tel: (0)2 41 39 14 44
Fax: (0)2 41 39 14 44
e-mail: bgaultier@compuserve.com
Web: www.sawdays.co.uk

The cheerful, cosy sitting room with its open fire immediately sets the tone – this is a charming, friendly 200-year-old farmhouse run by an extremely welcoming young couple who have twin sons and guest-loving dogs. Many readers have praised the hospitality shown to both young and old and the excellent traditional food – served in the lovely light, tiled dining room. Bedrooms, up steep stairs, are delightfully plain and simple with pale floral curtains and bedcovers and showers behind curtains, and French (small!) towels. *Please arrive after 4pm if possible – still in time for a swim!*

Rooms: 2 doubles, 2 twins, all with shower, sharing 2 separate wcs.

Price: 220-250 Frs for two (min. 2 nights July & August).

Meals: 125 Frs, including aperitif, wine & coffee.

Closed: November-mid-April.

From Angers, N162 direction Laval. At Le Lion d'Angers, D770 W towards Candé. Pass garden centre & after 1.5km left at big wooden cross; signposted. Michelin Map No: 232-19

Entry no: 288　　　　Map No: 2

M & Mme Patrick CARCAILLET
Le Petit Carqueron
49220 Le Lion d'Angers
Maine-et-Loire
Tel: (0)2 41 95 62 65

You cannot fail to warm to Madame's easy vivacity and infectious laugh. She virtually lives in her kitchen (in the house just opposite), making jams, pastries and bread in the old bread oven. This couple have lovingly preserved their typical old Segré farmhouse with its long deep roof and curious *outeau* openings (some might have put in modern dormers). The living room has great beams, a big brick fireplace, exposed stone walls and new country furniture. Rooms are deliciously rustic: crochet, terracotta, pine, sloping ceilings. The woods are full of birdlife and the cows graze peacefully under the children's window.

Rooms: 2 quadruples, 1 double, all with bath or shower & wc.

Price: 210-230 Frs for two.

Meals: Choice 2-5km; picnic in garden possible.

Closed: Never.

Gîte space for 10 people.

From Angers N162 direction Le Lion d'Angers; follow direction Rennes then D863 direction Segré for 3km. Left at Chambres d'Hôtes sign. House 1km along on left.
Michelin Map No: 232-19

Entry no: 289   Map No: 2

Jocelyne & François VIVIER
Les Travaillères
49220 Le Lion d'Angers
Maine-et-Loire
Tel: (0)2 41 61 33 56/
       (0)6 80 82 02 49

The whole family is delightful and Madame, an elegant former teacher, is a great source of local knowledge (old slate mines, model villages, river trips...). Their converted farm building, in the grounds of the Château du Teilleul, has a big, convivial, cedar-panelled sitting room. The bedroom, charmingly decorated and beamed with a sloping roof, has a clever arrangement with the bath behind a bookcase/bar and its own loo in the corridor. This is a splendid home, full of heirlooms – you feel embraced by the place the moment you walk in and the setting is totally calm (the garden has a 'real' English lawn, cut to a carpet!)

Rooms: 1 twin with bath & basin, wc down corridor.

Price: 290 Frs for two.

Meals: 120 Frs, including aperitif, wine and coffee.

Closed: Never.

From St. Sauveur D923 direction Segré. Driveway on right, 200m after village.
Michelin Map No: 232-19

Entry no: 290   Map No: 2

Marie-Alice & Michel de VITTON
Le Domaine du Teilleul
49500 St Sauveur de Flée
Maine-et-Loire
Tel: (0)2 41 61 38 84
Fax: (0)2 41 61 38 84

Cheeky red squirrels run along the stone balustrade, the wide river flows past the large, lush riverside garden: it feels like deep country but this handsome manor has urban elegance in its very stones. Panels, cornices, mouldings, subtly-muted floor tiles bring grace while traditional French furnishings add softness. In these formal surroundings Madame, energetic, relaxed and communicative, adores having guests and pampering them with luxury. Monsieur is jovial and loves fishing! Fine, plush bedrooms, three with river views, all with superb bathrooms. Walking and cycling paths now marked.

Rooms: 2 doubles, 1 twin room, each with bath/shower & wc.

Price: 380-480 Frs for two.

Meals: 150 Frs, excluding wine.

Closed: Never.

A neo-Gothic surprise with a bucolic stork-nested, deer-roamed park that runs down to the river and an interior worthy of Hollywood: the sitting room is wildly mock-medieval, the panelled drawing room was taken whole from an 18th-century château. This was once a fully self-sufficient country estate and there are the remains of a chapel, dovecote and mill (you can swim or row a boat in the river). Any proper château has a Bishop's Room, of course: you can sleep in this one; the corner room has a splendid four-poster. An elegantly warm welcome from lovely people who fill the house with friends and family and might even play bridge with you.

Rooms: 1 triple, 3 doubles, each with bath or shower & wc.

Price: 380-420 Frs for two.

Meals: 140 Frs, including wine & coffee.

Closed: November-Easter.

From Angers, N162 towards Lion d'Angers. At Grieul (20km) right on D291 to Grez Neuville. At church (1.5km), Rue de l'Écluse towards river on left.
Michelin Map No: 232-19

From Angers, N23 north. At Seiches sur Loir, D74 towards Châteauneuf sur Sarthe for 5.5km. Château on right as you leave Montreuil village.
Michelin Map No: 232-20

Jacqueline & Auguste BAHUAUD
La Croix d'Etain
2 rue de l'Ecluse
49220 Grez Neuville
Maine-et-Loire
Tel: (0)2 41 95 68 49
Fax: (0)2 41 18 02 72
Web: www.sawdays.co.uk

Jacques & Marie BAILLIOU
Château de Montreuil
49140 Montreuil sur Loir
Maine-et-Loire
Tel: (0)2 41 76 21 03
e-mail: chateau.montreuil@enjou-et-loire.com

An old farmhouse on the family estate transformed from tumbledown dereliction to rural idyll to house this charming, cultured, artistic, unpretentious couple and their four children – the place exudes age-old peace and youthful freshness. Rooms are decorated with flair and simplicity – using some strong, warm colours, sea-grass flooring and good fabrics. Wonderful meals – Regina's regional recipes are very sought after. A perfect retreat too for music, art and nature lovers – join the Tuesday choir practice at the château, take singing lessons with a sister; fish, boat, walk in the unspoilt countryside. A very special place.

Rooms: 1 twin, 1 double, 1 triple, all with bath or shower & wc.

Price: 375 Frs for two.

Meals: 150 Frs, incl. aperitif & wine.

Closed: Never.

From Angers towards Lion d'Angers. At Montreuil Juigné right on D768 towards Champigné. 500m after x-roads at La Croix de Beauvais right up drive to La Roche & Malvoisine.
Michelin Map No: 232-29

Entry no: 293   Map No: 2

Patrice & Regina de LA BASTILLE
Malvoisine
49460 Ecuillé, Maine-et-Loire
Tel: (0)2 41 93 34 44/
         (0)6 88 90 15 76
Fax: (0)2 41 93 34 44
e-mail: bastille-pr@wanadoo.fr
Web: www.malvoisine-bastille.com

What a splendid woman she is! Down-to-earth, fun-loving and decent, offering authentic farmhouse hospitality. They are both delighted to show you their exclusively grass-fed brown oxen, even sell you beef direct. You breakfast in the simple dining room which is alive with the desire to please. The attic has been converted into three good rooms and a children's room. Great old roof timbers share the space with new rustic-style beds and old armoires. It is simple and clean-cut with discreet plastic flooring, pastel walls, sparkling new shower rooms. They have two lively kids, there are toys and games and swings for yours.

Rooms: 2 triples, 1 twin, each with shower & wc.

Price: 220 Frs for two.

Meals: Choice 5km.

Closed: Never.

From Angers N23 to Seiches sur le Loir; right on D766 towards Tours for 9km; right into Jarzé on D59 towards Beaufort en Vallé. House on left 700m after Jarzé.
Michelin Map No: 232-20

Entry no: 294   Map No: 2

Véronique & Vincent PAPIAU
Le Point du Jour
49140 Jarzé
Maine-et-Loire
Tel: (0)2 41 95 46 04
Fax: (0)2 41 95 46 04

Not only a fine house, also a door onto a variety of cultural influences. Set proudly on the Loire embankment, the house has an unbeatable view of the mighty river but the road is busy (little traffic at night). Guests have a cobblestoned kitchen/diner whence the original slate stairs lead up to the house and four well-furnished double-glazed rooms (two with that view). Other, pretty rooms in the old stables in the courtyard, alongside the architecturally-correct dog kennel. Young and lively, Claudine offers a monthly cultural event: take one of her mystery tours, join a traditional Songs-of-the-Loire dinner or a story-telling cocktail party.

Rooms: 1 suite for 4, 2 triples, 2 doubles, 1 twin, all with shower & wc; 2 have kitchenettes.

Price: 330-385 Frs for two.

Meals: 140 Frs, incl. wine & coffee.

Closed: Never.

From Angers, D952 direction Saumur. House is on left-hand side of road (signposted) as you enter St Mathurin. Michelin Map No: 232-32

Entry no: 295   Map No: 2

Mme Claudine PINIER
La Bouquetterie
118 rue du Roi René
49250 St Mathurin sur Loire
Maine-et-Loire
Tel: (0)2 41 57 02 00
Fax: (0)2 41 57 31 90
e-mail: cpinier@aol.com

A nose for fine wine brought Françoise and Paul-Hervé from the world of journalism and TV in Paris to this organic wine-producing farm. A whiff of cabernet accompanies you upstairs to your loft-converted bedrooms over the old wine-press. Leading off an open kitchen-cum-sitting area, they blend frill-free contemporary design with traditional natural materials. The yellow room is large and luminous, the green room has its own outside stone stairs. Paul-Hervé loves to explain the mysteries of fine-wine-making, and you can borrow bicycles to explore the local vineyards, or relax with a book in the big tree-shaded garden.

Rooms: 1 double & 2 twins, each with bath or shower & wc.

Price: 290-390 Frs for two.

Meals: Good restaurant in Thouarcé (10km).

Closed: November-April.

From Angers towards Niort-Poitiers-Brissac. Right onto D748 towards Brissac. Right after 5km towards Homois. After 150m right towards Clabeau; continue downhill 2km & left after bridge. Michelin Map No: 232-32

Entry no: 296   Map No: 2

Françoise & Paul-Hervé VINTROU
Domaine des Charbotières
Clabeau
49320 Brissac Quincé, Maine-et-Loire
Tel: (0)2 41 91 22 87
Fax: (0)2 41 66 23 09
e-mail: contact@charbotieres.com
Web: www.charbotieres.com

The key words here are serenity, harmony, peace. The countryside may not be the most spectacular but the house is utterly tranquil in its little hamlet and Monsieur will guide beginners in the art of billiards if they wish. Madame is shy but kind, spontaneously welcoming and properly proud of her pretty, unfussy rooms where pastel colours, tiled floors and oriental rugs sit well under old rafters and stones and all is spotlessly clean. Breakfast, with home-made jams, can be in the garden on fine mornings and you can picnic there too or bicycle down to the banks of the Loire.

Rooms: 2 doubles, 1 triple, all with shower & wc.

Price: 260 Frs for two.

Meals: 110 Frs, including wine & coffee.

Closed: Never.

From Angers N761 towards Brissac & Doué. At Les Alleuds left on D90 towards Chemellier. After 3km hamlet on left.
Michelin Map No: 232-32

Entry no: 297   Map No: 2

Eliette EDON
Chambres d'Hôtes
49320 Maunit Chemellier
Maine-et-Loire
Tel: (0)2 41 45 59 50
Fax: (0)2 41 45 01 44

There is heady scent in the air and the design of this farm so pleasing – the gentle green woodwork and the stone arches soften the square symmetry of the courtyard, which has virtually no farm mess to spoil it. Yet these intelligent farmers work hard, growing fields of lupins, hollyhocks and thyme for seed. Your hosts' wing (and yours while you stay – other family members live in other wings) has been done with simple good taste; each room has a personal touch; there are landing chairs for guests to watch farmyard life go by. Martine is most likeable, young, dynamic and conscious of what B&B enthusiasts really want.

Rooms: 1 double with shower & wc; 1 double, 1 twin, both with shower, sharing 2 wcs (showers behind curtains).

Price: 250 Frs for two.

Meals: Restaurants 3-7km.

Closed: Never.

Gîte space for 18 people.

From Angers, N260 dir. Cholet, then D748 dir. Poitiers. After Brissac, D761 dir. Poitiers. House signposted on left after 2km, at end of avenue of chestnut trees.
Michelin Map No: 232-32

Entry no: 298   Map No: 2

Jean-Claude & Martine COLIBET
La Pichonnière
Charce St Ellier
49320 Brissac Quince, Maine-et-Loire
Tel: (0)2 41 91 29 37 (mealtimes)
Fax: (0)2 41 91 96 85
e-mail: gite-brissac@wanadoo.fr
Web: www.gite-brissac.com

The word could be *alternative*: it is different and great for the informal. Joyce, a thoroughly relaxed, welcoming aromatherapist, has an organic kitchen garden, cooks good veggie food, receives art, yoga and meditation workshops (lovely meditation room) and may invite guests to "come and join in". The old farm has been here for 300 years in its soft, leafy stand of poplars; beams are everywhere – take care going to bed. One room has steps down to the courtyard, the other looks over the pond, both have warm-hued furnishings in harmony with the old wood and stone. Old it feels, mature alternative it sings. Small camping site, lots of animals.

Rooms: 1 triple, 1 double, sharing bath & wc.

Price: 250 Frs for two.

Meals: Vegetarian, 75 Frs, including wine & coffee.

Closed: Never.

Gîte space for 6 people.

From Le Mans N23 to La Flèche. There D37 to Fougeré then N217 towards Baugé for 1.5km. Behind poplars on left. Michelin Map No: 232-21

Entry no: **299**   Map No: 7

Joyce RIMELL
La Besnardière
Route de Baugé
49150 Fougeré
Maine-et-Loire
Tel: (0)2 41 90 15 20

The atmosphere is artistic, relaxed, convivial. Madame's delight is to decorate her wonderful house and make sure you love it too. Monsieur is an artist. In a quiet wooded spot, the house is all dormers and balconies and Victorian extravaganza; the little tower, once dovecote and chapel, is older. Furnishings are a study in disorganised elegance, masses of antiques, *brocante* and modernities – sophisticated and fun. There are relaxation sessions, billiards, piano, and coffee-roasting on the spot; a sense of magic in the park, the odd statue peering from the vegetation, a pond fed by a reputedly miraculous spring. Good food, too.

Rooms: 1 suite for 5, 4 doubles, all with bath & wc.

Price: 340-375 Frs for two.

Meals: 130 Frs, including wine & coffee.

Closed: Never.

From A11 left on A85 towards Tours. Exit at Longué on D938 towards Baugé for 5km. Right on D62 towards Mouliherne. House 5km along on right. Michelin Map No: 232-33

Entry no: **300**   Map No: 7

Françoise & Michel TOUTAIN
Le Prieuré de Vendanger
49150 Le Guédeniau, Maine-et-Loire
Tel: (0)2 41 67 82 37/
      (0)6 12 63 03 74
Fax: (0)2 41 67 82 43
e-mail: info@vendanger.fr
Web: www.vendanger.fr

Impeccable – this conversion of farm and outbuildings is superbly done and Mireille's sense of style and attention to detail is apparent everywhere: perfectly co-ordinated colour schemes and stencilling (her own), new beds, good quality linen and nice big towels, a living area with guests' fridge and microwave, where meals are served when not outside. The garden is lovely too and *really* quiet. The Métiviers want their guests to be comfortable and relaxed; they love to chat and are fascinating about local history and the environment – but will check with you if you would prefer to eat alone. *Children under two free.*

A refreshingly young and enthusiastic family welcomes you to this 18th-century barn which has modern eyes in the back of its head – huge windows onto the garden – and is full of light inside. The old wine press (*pressoir*) has become the ping-pong and pool house. Lovingly-restored original beams, tiles and stones (Monsieur restores houses – very well) are the perfect setting for simple old armoires and bedheads. Each room has its own entrance, the suites have steep stairs up to the children's rooms, everything is in unpretentious good taste. You all eat together at the long dining table – Madame is sociable, easy-going and a good cook!

Rooms: 2 doubles with extra single bed, each with shower & wc, 1 wc separate.

Price: 280-310 Frs for two; reduction for 3 nights or more.

Meals: 100 Frs, including aperitif & wine.

Closed: 2 weeks in summer.

Gîte space for   people.

Rooms: 1 double, 1 twin, 1 triple, 2 suites, all with bath or shower & wc.

Price: 300-350 Frs for two.

Meals: 120 Frs, including wine; children 70 Frs.

Closed: Never.

From Anger N147 towards Saumur; 5km after Corné left on D61 towards Baugé. Continue 2km past dairy & agricultural co-op; take 2nd left, signposted. House 1st on right.
Michelin Map No: 232-13

From Saumur N147 N/NW 15km to Longué. After Longué right on D938 towards Baugé for 2.5km then left to Brion. House signposted in village opposite church.
Michelin Map No: 232-33

Entry no: **301**   Map No: 7

Entry no: **302**   Map No: 7

Mireille & Michel MÉTIVIER
Le Haut Pouillé
La Buissonnière
49630 Mazé
Maine-et-Loire
Tel: (0)2 41 45 13 72
Fax: (0)2 41 45 19 02
e-mail: m.metivier@wanadoo.fr

Anne & Jean-Marc LE FOULGOCQ
Le Logis du Pressoir
Villeneuve
49250 Brion, Maine-et-Loire
Tel: (0)2 41 57 27 33
Fax: (0)2 41 57 27 33
e-mail: lepressoir@wanadoo.fr
Web: www.sawdays.co.uk

Michael and Jill are fun, good talkers and good listeners and with their two lively children, their guinea pigs, cats, chickens and ponies, the whole place has a friendly family atmosphere and the old French house a rejuvenated feel. Bedrooms are big, bright and comfortable: the double, up characterfully creaky stairs, has a green 'marbled' fireplace, garden views and two deep armchairs from which to survey the scene; the quadruple, under the beamed roof and with rugged parquet floors, has those same views through low windows, a large sofa and a small shower room. Everything is clean and tidy without being oppressively so.

Rooms: 1 double with private bath & wc, 1 family room with shower & wc.

Price: 320 Frs for two.

Meals: 130 Frs, including wine & coffee.

Closed: Never.

Gîte space for 4 people.

From La Flèche, D308/D938 direction Baugé. There, follow sign for Tours & Saumur; right at traffic lights on D61 to Vieil-Baugé. Signposted after 2km. Michelin Map No: 232-21

Entry no: 303   Map No: 7

Michael & Jill COYLE
La Chalopinière
49150 Le Vieil Baugé
Maine-et-Loire
Tel: (0)2 41 89 04 38
Fax: (0)2 41 89 04 38
e-mail: rigbycoyle@aol.com

Your hosts are charming, unselfconscious aristocrats living in a Neo-Gothic folly with lots of cheerfully active children. There's a properly dark and spooky baronial hall, light, elegant reception rooms with ancestors on the walls, lots of plush and gilt. If you splurge on the 'suite' (in fact one vast room), you will have a sitting area and a library corner in an alcove. The smaller double has its shower up in a turret, its loo in another on the corridor. Both are elegantly, unfussily decorated with period French pieces and some modern fabrics. The park is huge, wild boar roam, boarlets scamper in spring. Altogether an amazing experience.

Rooms: 1 double with shower & private wc; 1 suite with bath & wc.

Price: 450-1200 Frs for two.

Meals: 250 Frs, excluding wine (Anjou 110 Frs).

Closed: Never.

From A85 exit 'Saumur' on D767 direction Le Lude. After 1km, left on D129 to Neuillé. Signposted. Michelin Map No: 232-33

Entry no: 304   Map No: 7

Monica LE PELLETIER de GLATIGNY
Château de Salvert, Salvert
49680 Neuillé, Maine-et-Loire
Tel: (0)2 41 52 55 89
Fax: (0)2 41 52 56 14
e-mail: chateau.salvert@wanadoo.fr
Web: www.saumur.cci.fr/salvert

The rambling 19th-century château stands in a 10-acre oasis of semi-wild vegetation where endangered flora and fauna take refuge. A wonderful woman greets you, a gentle artist and nature-lover with a sure and personal approach to interiors, both house and human. The suite is superb in dramatic red, white and blue (yes, it works!), the children's room deeply child-friendly. It is warm and authentic, offering timeless comfort and silence in the lush green surroundings: "magical". The woodwork has been stripped back, walls are richly clothed (all Madame's work), the furniture is old but not wealthy, the light pours in and you bask in harmony.

Rooms: 1 double, 1 triple, 1 suite for 5, all with bath or shower & wc.

Price: 350-470 Frs for two; suite 770 Frs for five.

Meals: Saumur 9km.

Closed: Never; open by arrangement in winter.

From Saumur, N147 direction Longué. At La Ronde, D767 direction Vernantes; left on D129 direction Neuillé. 1km before Neuillé take Fontaine Suzon road; signposted. Michelin Map No: 232-33

Entry no: 305   Map No: 7

Mme Monique CALOT
Château du Goupillon
49680 Neuillé
Maine-et-Loire
Tel: (0)2 41 52 51 89
Fax: (0)2 41 52 51 89

This solid old manor, between town and country, is a thoroughly French family house: the energetic Bastids have a health-food shop, four lovely children and an open, welcoming attitude. The generous reception rooms, furnished with antiques and heirlooms, are elegant but not imposing. The pleasant guest rooms are altogether simpler (two shower rooms are just curtained off) with quaint touches, such as an old stone sink and a wallpapered safe as bedside tables, while the big bosky garden is a good barrier against the road. On request, all diets can be catered for at breakfast.

Rooms: 1 suite, 1 triple, 1 double, 1 twin, all with bath or shower & wc.

Price: 250-370 Frs for two.

Meals: Wide choice in Saumur.

Closed: Never; open by arrangement in winter.

Gîte space for 5 people.

From Saumur centre N147 dir. Angers. Cross Loire & railway, straight on for 200m to Renault garage; left on Ave des Maraîchers dir. St Lambert. After 400m, right into Rue Grange Couronne; house 1st on right, signposted. Michelin Map No: 232-33

Entry no: 306   Map No: 7

Catherine & Emmanuel BASTID
La Bouère Salée, Rue Grange Couronne
49400 St Lambert des Levées, Saumur
Maine-et-Loire
Tel: (0)2 41 67 38 85/
        (0)2 41 51 12 52
Fax: (0)2 41 51 12 52
e-mail: la_bouere_salee@yahoo.fr
Web: www.sawdays.co.uk

Once the servants' quarters of the château (wealthy people who housed their servants grandly...), it is in a quiet, deep and secluded valley, right on the GR3 long-distance path and the Loire Valley walk. The bedrooms are under the high exposed roof beams, elegantly and discreetly done and with good antiques, matching wallpaper and fabrics (flowery English?), and impeccable bathrooms and loos. Breakfast is beautifully served, with linen table napkins and silver teapot; it is refined but relaxed, and you can picnic in the garden if you wish.

Rooms: 1 twin/triple, 1 suite for 4, both with shower & wc.

Price: 400 Frs for two.

Meals: Wide choice in the area.

Closed: December-Easter, except by arrangement.

Gîte space for 4 people.

From Saumur D751 W along Loire for 15km. In Gennes D69 S towards Doué la Fontaine, up hill, past church & police station. At r'bout take road past Super U; drive to house is 500m along on left.
Michelin Map No: 232-32

Entry no: 307   Map No: 7

Annick & Jean-Baptiste BOISSET
Le Haut Joreau
49350 Gennes
Maine-et-Loire
Tel: (0)2 41 38 02 58
Fax: (0)2 41 38 15 02
Web: perso.clubinternet.fr/gennes/hjoreau.htm

Sketches of Maria Callas greet you in the conservatory-like hall of this elegant unstuffy mansion, and Rossini accompanies candlelit dinner in the big-windowed dining room. Everywhere there are books, unusual objects and pictures collected by Jean-Jacques, your lively, entertaining host. The quiet, comfortable, airy bedrooms have stylish contemporary fabrics, contrasting with large 70's bathrooms. The Loire flows tantalisingly nearby, hidden by jungly woodland which threatens to engulf the tended garden round the house, and a theatrical curtain of trailing ivy conceals massive *caves*, with memories of past winemaking days.

Rooms: 2 doubles, each with bath & wc; 1 suite with bath & separate wc.

Price: 390 Frs for two; minimum 2 nights 11 November-1 March.

Meals: 200 Frs, including wine.

Closed: Never.

From Soumur D947 towards Chinon. Entrance on right 2km after the Gratien & Mayer cellars.
Michelin Map No: 232-33

Entry no: 308   Map No: 7

Didier JEHANNO
La Cour Pavée
374 route de Montsoreau
49400 Dampierre sur Loire
Maine-et-Loire
Tel: (0)2 41 67 65 88
Fax: (0)2 41 51 11 61

The house was a convent in the 1500s, a courtier's residence in the 1600s, a police station in the 1900s and is now a *chambre d'hôtes* with superb stone staircases. The *Suite Blanche* (an orange room leads to the white room) has beams, tiles, mirrors, fireplaces, carved armoires. Other rooms are big too, a little less stunning, and maintenance may be needed. But the glorious living room with its mystifying high-level door, high beamed ceiling and old built-in cupboards is worth the visit by itself. Monsieur restores antiques – his house speaks well of his trade; Madame is pleasant and efficient; restoration continues.

Rooms: 2 suites, 1 triple (with kitchenette), all with bath or shower & wc (very occasionally sharing).

Price: 350 Frs for two.

Meals: Choice in town or self-catering.

Closed: November-February.

The house is indisputably French, the owners Franco-British, the breakfast sometimes 'Scandinavian' and the squirrels on the green sward red. In this haven of quiet, Denis and Patricia will fascinate you with tales of their days as foreign correspondents. Guests enjoy good beds, their own cosy sitting room with the old bread oven, a complete kitchen and a lovely path down to the stream. After visiting villages, walking the trails, dreaming in the rolling country, return to good conversation and real hospitality.

Rooms: 2 doubles/twins, each with bath & wc.

Price: 320 Frs for two.

Meals: Auberge in village; good restaurants nearby; guest kitchen available.

Closed: 1 November-28 February.

From Saumur, D147 direction Poitiers. In Montreuil Bellay, follow signs to Les Petits Augustins la Joie Vivante; entrance to house near chapel.
Michelin Map No: 232-33

Entry no: 309   Map No: 7

Monique & Jacques GUÉZÉNEC
Demeure des Petits Augustins
Place des Augustins
49260 Montreuil Bellay
Maine-et-Loire
Tel: (0)2 41 52 33 88
Fax: (0)2 41 52 33 88

On N12 from Mayenne towards Alençon; after 5km, left on D34 towards Lassay. In Montreuil Poulay, left on D160; house is 700m along.
Michelin Map No: 231-41

Entry no: 310   Map No: 2

Denis & Patricia LEGRAS-WOOD
Le Vieux Presbytère
53640 Montreuil Poulay
Mayenne
Tel: (0)2 43 00 86 32
Fax: (0)2 43 00 81 42
e-mail: 101512.245@compuserve.com

An exceptional and engaging couple; Thérèse is vivacious and the conversation at their table is the very heart and soul of this marvellous place. At dinner, everything is home-made, from pâté to *potage* to *patisserie*... all *Normand* and attractively presented. Breakfast is a feast at which you help yourself to freshly-squeezed juice, eggs, cheese and buckets of coffee. The bedrooms are average-sized, decorated with Japanese grass paper and a few antiquey bits and bobs. Good people, and one or two sons may also be there.

Rooms: 1 triple, 1 double, 1 twin, each with shower or bath & wc.

Price: 250-270 Frs for two.

Meals: 100 Frs, including wine & coffee, by arrangement.

Closed: December-March.

Old stones, indeed, as they say in French and readers have loved the "real character of the place". It is a proudly restored 15th-century manor with staircase tower to the upstairs bedroom, bread oven and a fine dining room where breakfast is served to the chiming of the church clock. This is the Nays' old family home, well restored and really lived in. They love sharing it with guests, will teach you French, weave baskets, make music and radiate enthusiasm. A wonderful atmosphere in delectable countryside.

Rooms: 1 double, 1 triple, each with bath or shower & wc.

Price: 220-250 Frs for two.

Meals: In village or 3km.

Closed: Never.

Gîte space for 6 people.

From Fougères N12 east towards Laval for 15km where farm signposted on right.
Michelin Map No: 232-6

Entry no: 311   Map No: 2

Maurice & Thérèse TRIHAN
La Rouaudière
Mégaudais
53500 Ernée
Mayenne
Tel: (0)2 43 05 13 57
Fax: (0)2 43 05 71 15

From Laval, N157 direction Le Mans. At Soulgé sur Ouette, D20 left to Evron then D7 direction Mayenne. Signposted in Mézangers.
Michelin Map No: 232-8

Entry no: 312   Map No: 2

Léopold & Marie-Thérèse NAY
Le Cruchet
53600 Mézangers
Mayenne
Tel: (0)2 43 90 65 55
e-mail: bandb.lecruchet@wanadoo.fr

A splendid mansion and *chambres d'hôtes* on the grandest of scales in the heart of the town where the park, with its formal French box garden and romantic 'English' garden, creates a sylvan setting. Your hosts are exquisitely courteous (Monsieur speaks perfect English), the magnificently châteauesque rooms are large and light, each in individual, inimitably French, style. There's an easy mix of luxury and comfort in the cavernous bathrooms, marble fireplaces and beautiful panelling, some of it delicate blue against striking yellow curtains and bedcovers. Exceptional position, style and attention to detail.

Rooms: 3 doubles, 1 suite, all with bath & shower & wc.

Price: 550-650 Frs for two (+30 Frs for full breakfast).

Meals: Full choice in Laval.

Closed: December & January.

In Laval follow signs to Mairie then brown signs to Le Bas du Gast – opp. 'Salle Polyvalente' and 'Bibliothèque' (about 1km from Mairie). Michelin Map No: 232-7

Entry no: 313   Map No: 2

M & Mme François WILLIOT
Le Bas du Gast
6 rue de la Halle aux Toiles
53000 Laval
Mayenne
Tel: (0)2 43 49 22 79
Fax: (0)2 43 56 44 71
Web: www.sawdays.co.uk

Sprightly Monsieur le Comte is the patriarch of this very close family which extends to include guests to whom Loïk and Hélène, the younger generation, give a wonderfully relaxed welcome. This very special place has so many ways of expressing its personality: oval windows, canopied beds, sunken marble bath, children's room, lift to bathroom, ancient oaks, bread oven, ice house, pigeon house, endless reception rooms, magnificent stone staircase, pool like a 'mini-Versailles'. Teresa Berganza stayed and practised at the grand piano – she too enjoyed that gracious and natural sense of hospitality.

Rooms: 2 doubles, 1 twin, 3 singles, each with bath or shower & wc. Extra space for children.

Price: 600-900 Frs for two; 350-500 for one.

Meals: In village or picnic in park.

Closed: Mid-December-mid-January.

From Château Gontier, N171 to Craon. Château clearly signposted as you enter town. 30km south of Laval. Michelin Map No: 232-18

Entry no: 314   Map No: 2

Comte Louis de GUÉBRIANT, Loïk
& Hélène de GUÉBRIANT
Château de Craon
53400 Craon, Mayenne
Tel: (0)2 43 06 11 02
Fax: (0)2 43 06 05 18
e-mail: guebrian@club-internet.fr
Web: www.chateaudecraon.com

The easy atmosphere of genuine class reigns here beside the luminous fast-flowing river – you are welcomed by Madame's gentle intelligence and Monsieur's boundless energy. The house has been much added to since the family arrived 400 years ago but each of the objects, antiques and pictures tells a story. The 1st-floor double and big light bathroom are full of interest and comfort; the 2nd-floor suite is ideal for families with its four-poster double and choice of other rooms. The large, formal sitting room is pure 'château' while across the hall/piano room there's an elegant dining room with separate tables for breakfast.

Rooms: 1 double, 1 twin, 1 suite, each with bath & wc.

Price: 400 Frs for two; reduction 3 nights or more.

Meals: Choice in town.

Closed: Never.

In Château Gontier N162 North towards Laval. Entrance is on left 50m after last r'about as you leave town. Michelin Map No: 232-19

Entry no: 315   Map No: 2

Brigitte & François d'AMBRIÈRES
Château de Mirvault
Mirvault Azé
53200 Château Gontier, Mayenne
Tel: (0)2 43 07 10 82
Fax: (0)2 43 07 10 82
e-mail: chateau.mirvault@worldonline.fr
Web: www.sawdays.co.uk

This tremendously old, characterful farmhouse with its amazing oak staircase, is now home to the delightful young fifth generation who juggle cattle, children and guests with skill and a light, humorous touch: the iron man in the *salon*, the secret *grog flambé* recipe are reminders of ancestral traditions. In the big, soft rooms, every bed is canopied, except the single box-bed, carved and curtained to a tee. There are nooks, crannies, odd angles and crooked lines; terracotta floors, half-timbered walls, antiques – and pretty shower rooms. Ducks paddle in the enchanting pond, cows graze in the fields, apples become cider – bucolic peace.

Rooms: 2 doubles, 1 triple, 1 family room, all with shower/small bath & wc.

Price: 250-280 Frs for two.

Meals: 80 Frs, incl. aperitif & coffee.

Closed: Never.

Gîte space for 6 people.

From Laval N162 S dir. Château Gontier for 14km, then left through Villiers Charlemagne to Ruille Froid Fonds. There, left on C4 towards Bignon for 1km. Signposted. Michelin Map No: 232-19

Entry no: 316   Map No: 2

Christophe & Christine DAVENEL
Villeprouvé
53170 Ruille Froid Fonds
Mayenne
Tel: (0)2 43 07 71 62
Fax: (0)2 43 07 71 62

Hard to beat! The atmosphere is elegant yet relaxed and supremely friendly, the rooms are exquisite, the hospitality utterly natural, the noble horse and love of beautiful things inform house and hosts. In this lovely medieval village, your hosts run one of only six carriage-driving schools in France. As well as fine dinners there are superb pony-and-trap picnics – a treat not to be missed. It is peacefully off the beaten track and genuinely civilised. Our readers have been highly enthusiastic.

Rooms: 2 doubles, 1 triple, all with shower & wc.

Price: 350-395 Frs for two.

Meals: Available locally.

Closed: Never.

The whole atmosphere is deliciously relaxed and unpretentious and dinner, with masses of home-produced ingredients, is a large, gregarious affair that may last some time – wonderful for lovers of French family cooking. The guest rooms and their shower rooms, in converted outbuildings, may show signs of the passing of time... and the family cats, but you will enjoy the Langlais. They are a lively, active couple with children and a farm to run. Madame even finds time to handpaint lampshades and make 30 different types of jam! *Only well-behaved pets with watchful owners please.*

Rooms: 2 doubles, 1 twin, 1 triple, plus 1 suite in 'La Petite Maison', all with shower & wc.

Price: 270 Frs for two.

Meals: 115 Frs, including wine & coffee.

Closed: One week at Christmas.

Gîte space for 6 people.

From Sablé sur Sarthe, D309 (D27) direction Angers. On entering St Denis, 1st left at 'Renov' Cuir' sign. House is 100m along, signposted. Michelin Map No: 232-20

Entry no: 317   Map No: 2

Martine & Jacques LEFEBVRE
Le Logis Du Ray
53290 St Denis d'Anjou
Mayenne
Tel: (0)2 43 70 64 10
Fax: (0)2 43 70 65 53

From Alençon S on N138. After 4km, left onto D55, through Champfleur towards Bourg le Roi; farm signed 1km after Champfleur. Michelin Map No: 231-43

Entry no: 318   Map No: 3

Denis & Christine LANGLAIS
Garencière
72610 Champfleur
Sarthe
Tel: (0)2 33 31 75 84
Web: www.sawdays.co.uk

A house of great character and charm, it has memories of the English occupation during the 100 Years War and a turret turned into a bedroom for children – a little stone nest with exposed stone walls, old tiled floor, narrow windows and fireplace. Madame is an utterly delightful hostess, an excellent cook of regional specialities and the atmosphere of the house is one of simple, unaffected hospitality. 20-mile views across the beautiful Sarthe countryside from all rooms, space, parquet floors and period furnishings.

Rooms: 1 quadruple with bath & wc; 1 triple, 1 double with shower, sharing wc.

Price: 270-300 Frs for two.

Meals: 90 Frs, including cider & coffee.

Closed: Never.

Until a couple of years ago, Claude and Ginette had spent more than twenty years rearing chickens for the local market from this old French farmhouse, parts of which can be traced back to the 11th century. They now cook delicious meals for their guests, *poulet à l'estragon* being one of Claude's specialities. The bedrooms, which have sloping ceilings and exposed beams, are comfortable, attractively decorated and furnished. One has a fine white iron bedstead, another a tiny window at floor level. But what beats everything is the view from the dining room – the surrounding countryside is luscious.

Rooms: 3 doubles, each with shower, separate wc.

Price: 250-300 Frs for two.

Meals: 120 Frs, including wine.

Closed: Never.

Gîte space for 4 people.

From Mamers, D3 direction Le Mêle for 6km. Do not go into Aillières. Farm on left.
Michelin Map No: 231-44

Entry no: 319   Map No: 3

Marie-Rose & Moïse LORIEUX
La Locherie
Aillières
72600 Mamers
Sarthe
Tel: (0)2 43 97 76 03
Web: www.sawdays.co.uk

From Mamers D311 towards Alençon, after 7kms right on D116 towards Villaines la Carelle; enter village direction St Longis. Gîtes de France sign on left.
Michelin Map No: 231-44

Entry no: 320   Map No: 7

Claude & Ginette PELLETIER
Le Fay
72600 Villaines la Carelle
Sarthe
Tel: (0)2 43 97 73 40
e-mail: lefay@wanadoo.fr
Web: assoc.wanadoo.fr/bunia/lefay/

A jewel, in rolling parkland with sheep grazing under mature trees, horses in the paddock, swans on a bit of the moat, deer, boar... Your hosts are the nicest, easiest of aristocrats, determined to keep the ancestral home alive in a dignified manner. Bedrooms: antique furniture on parquet floors, good rugs, modern beds. Bathrooms and loos; in turrets, cupboards, alcoves. Downstairs: an elegant dining room with family silver, sitting room with log fire, family portraits, and a small book-lined library. Hunting trophies on walls, timeless tranquillity, lovely people.

Rooms: 1 suite for 3, 4 doubles, 1 twin, each with bath or shower & wc.

Price: 450-650 Frs for two.

Meals: 195 Frs including wine; 'Dîner Prestige' 320 Frs.

Closed: Never.

From Alençon N138 S towards Le Mans for approx. 14km. At La Hutte left on D310 for 10km, right on D19 through Courgains, left on D132 to Monhoudou; signposted.
Michelin Map No: 232-10

Entry no: 321   Map No: 7

Michel & Marie-Christine de
MONHOUDOU
Château de Monhoudou
72260 Monhoudou, Sarthe
Tel: (0)2 43 97 40 05
Fax: (0)2 43 33 11 58
Web: www.chateaux-
france.com/~monhoudou

Continuing the family tradition Marie and Laurent are delightful hosts. And theirs is so French a château: not overwhelming, just peaceful loveliness with a big garden set among farmland and woods. Guests who swear they never sleep beyond 7 in the morning arrive sheepishly for breakfast at 10. The sitting room, narrow and panelled, feels like the inside of an old ship and the unpretentious atmosphere is sustained by some gratifyingly untidy corners, pretty small shower rooms and much unselfconscious good taste. Dine at one big table where the wine flows and all nations commune. Ideal for families.

Rooms: 2 doubles/triples, 3 suites for 4/5, all with bath or shower & wc; 2 separate wcs.

Price: 280-320 Frs for two.

Meals: 110 Frs, including wine & coffee; on Thurs, Fri & Sun.

Closed: January.

Gîte space for 6 people.

From Le Mans, N23 dir. La Flèche. At Cérans Foulletourte, D31 to Oizé, left onto D32; signed on right.
Michelin Map No: 232-22

Entry no: 322   Map No: 7

Laurent SENECHAL &
Marie DAVID
Château de Montaupin
72330 Oizé
Sarthe
Tel: (0)2 43 87 81 70
Fax: (0)2 43 87 26 25

This creeper-clothed house is extremely and prettily flowery. Rooms have flower names that inspire the décor of floral colours, cushions, bedcovers, friezes; all sorts of chairs and side tables found in *brocante* shops then lovingly restored and painted with... flowers. Madame, determined, energetic and most hospitable, is a perfectionist. Her garden blooms as wonderfully as her house, the rich and copious breakfast is served in the old-tiled, wood-fired extension and she runs the whole show with the help of her friendly, well-behaved Alsatian.

Rooms: 1 suite (triple & single), 1 double, 1 twin, 1 quadruple, all with bath or shower & wc.

Price: 280-380 Frs for two.

Meals: Choice 3-7 km.

Closed: 1 October-1 April, except by arrangement.

From Le Mans, D147 S to Arnage (8km); left fork on D307 for 15km then right on D77 towards Mansigné for 5km; Route de Tulièvre is tiny road on left, 3km after Requeil.
Michelin Map No: 232-22

Entry no: 323   Map No: 7

Marie-Dominique BLANCHARD
La Maridaumière
Route de Tulièvre
72510 Mansigné
Sarthe
Tel: (0)2 43 46 58 52
Fax: (0)2 43 46 58 52

This is a lovely old townhouse (parts are 14th-century) with a plain façade hiding a beautifully-decorated interior, bedrooms with masses of personality, a large garden and a properly-concealed pool, all stretching back from the street. Once in the garden, you would scarcely know you're in town. The rooms, in renovated outbuildings, are pleasantly independent, while convivial meals are shared in the dining room. There is a big table with benches on the terrace, Madame is a calm feminine presence and Monsieur prides himself on his choice of Loire wines from small, unpublicised wine-growers.

Rooms: 1 double, 1 triple, 1 suite for 4/5 with small kitchen, all with shower & wc.

Price: 260-300 Frs for two.

Meals: 90 Frs, including table wine (Loire wines 50 Frs).

Closed: Never.

Gite space for 4 people.

From Arnage, then D307 to Pontvallain. House in town centre; signed.
Michelin Map No: 232-22

Entry no: 324   Map No: 7

M Guy VIEILLET
Place Jean Graffin
72510 Pontvallain
Sarthe
Tel: (0)2 43 46 36 70
Fax: (0)2 43 46 36 70

A group of low buildings in a picture of a place by a three-acre, tree-reflecting pond full of fish, frogs and ducks with a view up to a hilltop village – peace and space for all. There are games (croquet, table tennis, *pétanque*), a boat, even a sauna. Rooms are smallish, well-fitted, with separate entrances and mixed modern and old furnishings – you have a degree of independence, somewhat at the price of homeliness perhaps. Madame loves to have guests and to feed them. Monsieur twinkles and gets on with the garden. They are a charming, caring couple. Breakfast includes cheese and cold meats. Dinner is an important event, so indulge!

Rooms: 2 triples, 2 doubles, 1 twin, all with shower & wc.

Price: 270-330 Frs for two.

Meals: 90 Frs, including wine & coffee.

Closed: Mid-November-February.

From Le Mans D304 to Grand Lucé and La Chartre. Left on D305 through Pont de Braye. Left on D303 to Lavenay & follow signs (2km). Michelin Map No: 232-24

Entry no: 325   Map No: 7

Monique & Jacques DÉAGE
Le Patis du Vergas
72310 Lavenay
Sarthe
Tel: (0)2 43 35 38 18
Fax: (0)2 43 35 38 18

A fairytale cottage: mellow old stone, white shutters, green ivy, a large leafy garden, a clematis-covered well, a little wood and glimpses of the 12th-century castle round the corner (this house used to be the castle's servants' quarters). Green-eyed Michèle is modern, intelligent and interested in people; she and Michel share the hosting. The suite is three gentle Laura Ashley-inspired interconnecting bedrooms that look onto garden or endless fields. Stay a while and connect with the gentle hills, woods, streams and châteaux. Guests can be as independent as they like (separate entrance) and can take one, two or three rooms.

Rooms: 1 3-room suite for 5 with bathroom and separate wc.

Price: 260 Frs for two.

Meals: Occasionally, 80-90 Frs, including coffee.

Closed: November-March.

From Le Mans, N138 direction Tours. After Dissay/Courcillon, left onto small road on the bend & follow signs. Michelin Map No: 232-23

Entry no: 326   Map No: 7

Michèle LETANNEUX & Michel GUYON
La Châtaigneraie
72500 Dissay sous Courcillon
Sarthe
Tel: (0)2 43 79 45 30
Web: www.sawdays.co.uk

Marie-Claire is so relaxed, such good adult company, so unflappably efficient that it's hard to believe she has four children under seven! She and Martin, an ardent Anglophile, have converted this 18th-century watermill brilliantly – a labour of love, even down to the cogwheels that turn in the great kitchen where breakfast is served at the huge oak table. The double-height sitting room is full of books and videos for all to peruse. Rooms are attractive, simple, with good beds, old tiled floors, bare stone walls. The atmosphere embraces you, the country sounds of stream, cockerel and Angelus prayer bells soothe, the unsung area brims with interest.

Rooms: 2 doubles, 1 family room, each with bath or shower & wc.

Price: 270 Frs for two.

Meals: Restaurant opposite.

Closed: Never.

Anne left Citibank in Paris to move here with Jean-Pierre when their son, now 18, was born and started bed and breakfast seven years ago. The grounds are large and peaceful, with a couple of holes of golf. Inside, old oak panelling is set off by touches of aquamarine: a tablecloth in the breakfast room and a wall behind the ornate carved staircase. The bedrooms are large, elegant and truly French: two with antique sleigh beds. We really loved the children's room. No cartoon characters, just pale striped walls, white furniture and a starched cotton bedspread.

Rooms: 1 double, 1 suite for up to 4, each with bathroom & wc.

Price: 420-520 Frs for two.

Meals: Choice locally.

Closed: Never.

From Tours N138 towards Le Mans to Dissay sous Courcillon (35km). In village, left at lights; mill is just past church.
Michelin Map No: 232-23

Entry no: 327   Map No: 7

Marie-Claire BRETONNEAU
Le Moulin du Prieuré
3 rue de la Gare
72500 Dissay sous Courcillon
Sarthe
Tel: (0)2 43 44 59 79

From Verneuil sur Avre take the D941 towards La Ferte Vidame. Just before you get there take the Allee d'Arbres on the left.
Michelin Map No: 231-46

Entry no: 328   Map No: 3

Jean-Pierre & Anne JALLOT
Manoir de la Motte
28340 La Ferté Vidame
Eure-et-Loir
Tel: (0)2 37 37 51 69
Fax: (0) 2 37 37 51 56
e-mail: manoir.de.la.motte.lfv@wanadoo.fr
Web: www.sawdays.co.uk

This was the Parmentier's country cottage until Dagmar – who is German but has lived in France for many years and Roger – a retired chef, left Paris seven years ago to live here and do B&B. If you time it right, the walls are covered with roses. It looks a cosy place to stay, even from outside. Roger and Dagmar are friendly and hospitable and will probably join you for breakfast: there will be hot croissants or you could make it a huge meal, with ham, smoked salmon and cheese. One bedroom is wood-panelled, the other more typical with sloping rafters, fabrics are flowered and the varnished wooden floors floors symmetrically-rugged.

Rooms: 1 double, 1 suite for 3, each with bath & wc.

Price: 280-330 Frs for two.

Meals: 120 Frs, including wine.

Closed: February.

Jean-Marc is golf mad, Catherine is horse crazy: her mare is as understanding as a dog (together they'll take you walking or cycling) and she operates a horse-blanket laundry service; he runs golf training for all ages, all levels; their enthusiasm is infectious. In a quiet little village, behind high gates, they, their son, Labrador and Great Dane receive guests with alacrity in their big beamed kitchen and send them to sleep up the steep barn stairs in simple white-walled, Italian-tiled rooms where patches of bright colour – cushions, lampshades, towels, toothmugs – punctuate the space most effectively.

Rooms: 1 double, 2 twin, each with bath & wc.

Price: 350 Frs for two.

Meals: Restaurants in Nogent le Roi & Maintenon.

Closed: Never.

From Chartres, D939 NW towards Verneuil sur Avre. Go through Châteauneuf en Thymerais. Right onto D138 direction Blevy. On D133 follow signs to Chambres d'Hôtes.
Michelin Map No: 231-47

Entry no: **329**   Map No: 3

Roger PARMENTIER
2 route des Champarts
28170 Blévy
Eure-et-Loir
Tel: (0)2 37 48 01 21
Fax: (0)2 37 48 01 21
e-mail: parti@club-internet.fr

From Paris A13 then A12 then N12, exit Gambais towards Nogent le Roi. Entering Coulombs, left at lights towards Chandelles. Left at crossroads; house on right 1.5km along.
Michelin Map No: 231-48

Entry no: **330**   Map No: 3

Catherine & Jean-Marc SIMON
19 rue des Sablons, Chandelles
28130 Villiers le Morhier
Eure-et-Loir
Tel: (0)2 37 82 71 59
Fax: (0)2 37 82 71 59
e-mail: chandellesgolf@aol.com
Web: chandelles-golf.com

Only 15 minutes from the soaring glory of Chartres, wrapped about by fields worked single-handedly by Bruno – no typical farmer; he went to the Lycée Français in London, so conversation can be in either language. Rooms here are blissfully quiet and deeply comfortable – good linen and a satisfying mix of old-fashioned and modern. Dinner is memorable – try Nathalie's goat cheese as a starter perhaps followed by *porc avec pruneaux* – and the family eat with you, except during harvest time. Simple sitting/dining room, easy access to the garden, nice children, relaxed, refined people.

Rooms: 2 doubles, 1 twin, each with bath or shower & wc.

Price: 300-350 Frs for two.

Meals: 100 Frs, including wine & coffee. Under 12s 50 Frs.

Closed: Never.

From Chartres N154 N for Dreux. Shortly after leaving Chartres, left on D133 for Fresnay and follow signs for Chambres d'Hôtes to Levéville (or Levesville).
Michelin Map No: 231-48

Entry no: 331   Map No: 3

Nathalie & Bruno VASSEUR
Ferme du Château
Levéville
28300 Bailleau l'Évêque
Eure-et-Loir
Tel: (0)2 37 22 97 02
Fax: (0)2 37 22 97 02

Up two flights of a spiral staircase, in the attic (fear not, Monsieur will carry your bags), the bedroom feels not unlike sleeping in a church with unexpectedly comfortable beds, lots of books, and a good shower on the floor below. There are reminders of pilgrimage and religion everywhere – indeed, the little prayer room is your sitting room – but they don't intrude. So close to the great Cathedral... we are delighted to have discovered this slightly eccentric and welcoming place. Your host is a charmer and enjoys a chuckle.

Rooms: 1 twin with shower & wc.

Price: 270 Frs for two.

Meals: Choice at your doorstep.

Closed: Never.

On arriving in Chartres, follow signs for IBIS Centre and park as you reach Hotel IBIS (Place Drouaise) then walk 20m along Rue de la Porte Drouaise and on Rue Muret to No 80 (approx. 100m car to house).
Michelin Map No: 231-48

Entry no: 332   Map No: 3

Jean-Loup & Nathalie CUISINIEZ
Maison JLN
80 rue Muret
28000 Chartres
Eure-et-Loir
Tel: (0)2 37 21 98 36
Fax: (0)2 37 21 98 36

Eulogies for these people have reached us. A beautiful painted sign leads to the well-restored old house which still retains a certain quaintness. It has three cosy, white guest rooms and one very large ground-floor room, all with excellent bedding. Madame is matronly and trusting and the house has a warm family atmosphere, with old pieces of furniture. Birdsong soothes your ear and wheat fields sway before your eye as you rest in the pretty garden. Your hosts can teach you lots about the various bird species. In summer there is a children's pool. *Bookings not confirmed by 5pm on day of arrival may be re-allocated.*

An unusual kind of farmer, Michel has a rare expertise of which he is very proud: growing poppies for use in pharmaceuticals. Géraldine's lively manner and easy welcome into her delightful family relieve the dreariness of the ever-flat Beauce. The farm is set round a quiet, tidy courtyard where rabbits and hens lead their short lives, the good guest rooms are light and pleasantly if simply furnished, the bathrooms pristine. "Remarkable value. Real people. They've got it just right," said one reader, but don't expect designer décor or gourmet food at these amazing prices.

Rooms: 1 double, 1 triple, 2 quadruples, all with shower & wc (en suite or on landing).

Price: 250-270 Frs for two.

Meals: Choice 7km.

Closed: Never.

Rooms: 1 triple, 2 doubles, 1 twin, all with shower & wc.

Price: 190 Frs for two.

Meals: 60 Frs, including wine, by arrangement.

Closed: Never.

Gîte space for 5 people.

From Châteaudun, N10 direction Chartres. At Bonneval, D17 to Moriers; there, D153 to Pré St Martin; signposted. (Or A11 exit 'Thivars'.) Michelin Map No: 237-39

From A10 Allaine exit on D927 direction Châteaudun. At La Maladrerie, D39 to Loigny. Signposted opp. church. Michelin Map No: 237-39

Entry no: 333   Map No: 7

Entry no: 334   Map No: 7

Bernadette & Jean-Baptiste
VIOLETTE
Le Carcotage Beauceron,
8 rue Saint Martin
28800 Pré St Martin, Eure-et-Loir
Tel: (0)2 37 47 27 21
Fax: (0)2 37 47 38 09
e-mail: carcotage.beauceron@wanadoo.fr
Web: www.carcotage.com

Géraldine & Michel NIVET
8 rue Chanzy
28140 Loigny la Bataille
Eure-et-Loir
Tel: (0)2 37 99 70 71

There is much horsiness here: the suite is over the stables, other rooms are full of equine reminders, including Toulouse-Lautrec lithographs – a taste of real French provincial aristocratic style. You sleep in great comfort under period rafters, dine *en famille* by candlelight (outside in summer), and breakfast whenever you like – "people are on holiday", says Madame expansively. Both your hosts were members of the French National Driving team: they offer rides in their prize-winning equipage. Lots of other outdoor activities are to be found in the huge forest which surrounds the quietly elegant building.

Rooms: 2 doubles, 1 twin, 1 suite, each with bath & wc.

Price: 700 Frs for two, suite 900 Frs for four.

Meals: 200 Frs, including aperitif & wine.

Closed: Never.

From Montargis N7 towards Paris for 6km then right through forest to Paucourt. On entering village take 1st right Route de la Grotte aux Loups for 200m. House on left with ivy-covered wall.
Michelin Map No: 237-43

Entry no: 335   Map No: 8

Emmanuelle & Antoine de JESSÉ CHARLEVAL
Domaine de Bel Ebat
45200 Paucourt
Loiret
Tel: (0)2 38 98 38 47/
     (0)6 81 34 68 99
Fax: (0)2 38 85 66 43

This elegant 18th-century townhouse has retained the expansive atmosphere one associates with its wine merchant builders. They were loading their wine onto barges on the canal which flows under the windows until the 1930s. So much for the past; for the present: dine with your refined hostess in the antique-furnished, chandeliered dining room, sleep in good, very individual rooms, breakfast off ravishing Gien china with fruit from the garden, meet Lutiz the black Labrador who helps her owner welcome guests over a glass of local white wine. Madame is happy to arrange visits to wine growers.

Rooms: 1 apartment for 4, 1 triple, each with bath & wc; 1 apartment for 5 with bath & wc downstairs.

Price: 300 Frs for two.

Meals: 100 Frs, including wine.

Closed: Never.

From Orléans N60 E towards Montargis/Nevers, exit to Fay aux Loges, through Fay, cross canal, left on D709; house is 1st on left arriving in Donnery.
Michelin Map No: 237-41

Entry no: 336   Map No: 8

Nicole & Jacques SICOT
Les Charmettes
45450 Donnery
Loiret
Tel: (0)2 38 59 22 50
Fax: (0)2 38 59 26 96
e-mail: nsicot@mail.club-internet.fr

Your bubbling, smiling hostess, who left Paris for country calm, is keen on hunting and horses: hence horses and dogs outside, horns and antlers inside. Hers is a typical Sologne house in brick and stone with great beams and lovely flagstones, the talking telly in contemporary contrast. The double room is brilliantly done, small but cosy, with steeply sloping roofs – no good for the over-stretched; the suites are larger (one 60m²); all are differently furnished – this is very much a family house. Madame, genuinely eager to please, cooks only exceptionally but will happily drive you to and from the restaurant!

Rooms: 1 double, 1 suite for 4, each with bath or shower & wc.

Price: 350-500 Frs for two.

Meals: 150-200 Frs, incl. wine & coffee; 2 restaurants 1km; self-catering possible.

Closed: Never.

From Orléans N60 E to Châteauneuf sur Loire, right onto D11/D83 to Vannes. Through village; house approx. 1km further on right.
Michelin Map No: 238-6

Entry no: 337   Map No: 8

Agnès CELERIER
Domaine de Sainte-Hélène
Route d'Isdes
45510 Vannes sur Cosson, Loiret
Tel: (0)2 38 58 04 55
Fax: (0)2 38 58 28 38
e-mail: celerierloiret@netclic.fr
Web: www.sawdays.co.uk

This vast estate by the Loire even has a private hunting reserve (long-stay guests may visit it). The interior is carefully decorated and the rooms have lovely old furnishings. Breakfast is in the *salon* (games and hi-fi) or on the flowered terrace. The young hosts – he is a vet, she looks after the house, their small children and you – make it feel friendly despite the grand appearance – exotic pheasants and peacocks are a garden feature. They live in another house just nearby. Children welcome. Don't miss the canal bridge at Briare.

Rooms: 3 doubles, all with shower or bath & wc; 1 suite for 3 with bathroom & kitchen.

Price: 270-340 Frs for two; reduction 3 nights or more.

Meals: Briare or Gien 4km. Self-catering in suite.

Closed: Never.

Gîte space for 3 people.

From A6 change onto A77 dir. Nevers, exit at Briare then D952 dir. Gien. Signposted by the nurseries, between Briare and Gien.
Michelin Map No: 238-8

Entry no: 338   Map No: 8

Mme Bénédicte FRANÇOIS
Domaine de la Thiau
45250 Briare
Loiret
Tel: (0)2 38 38 20 92
Fax: (0)2 38 67 40 50
e-mail: lathiau@club-internet.fr
Web: perso.club-internet.fr/lathiau

The canal flows gently past this handsome old village house but you may hear the less gentle road in the morning. The guest rooms are rustic-furnished and very appealing – the suite in the loft in the main house with its exposed beams is particularly handsome – and there are two cosy self-contained cottages with kitchens. Your hosts are kind, well-educated and welcoming: their breakfast room is decorated with lots of pretty, personal knick-knacks. There's a barge restaurant in summer just a stroll from the house and do walk to the great 19th-century canal bridge over the Loire in Briare – a stupendous alliance of engineering and nature.

Rooms: 1 double, 1 suite for 3, each with shower & wc.

Price: 270 Frs for two.

Meals: In village.

Closed: Never.

Gîte space for 4 people.

From Châteauneuf sur Loire, D952 to Gien then towards Poilly lez Gien and on D951 to Châtillon sur Loire; signposted.
Michelin Map No: 238-8

Entry no: 339   Map No: 8

M & Mme Gilbert LEFRANC
La Giloutière
13 rue du Port
45360 Châtillon sur Loire
Loiret
Tel: (0)2 38 31 10 61

No problem with English here: Madame is married to an Englishman and her artistic daughter, who clearly inherited her talent from her mother, studied in Manchester. The guest rooms are furnished with elegance, taste and those touches of luxury which make you feel pampered. You will be greeted with a glass of Sancerre in the wonderful *salon*, whose old tiles continue into the bedrooms of this 15th-century *logis*. The whole house is full of worldwide travel memories and there's a romantic and shady walled garden where you can breakfast in traditional French fashion on brioches, croissants and garden fruits in season.

Rooms: 1 double, 1 twin, sharing shower & wc.

Price: 350 Frs for two.

Meals: Choice 10km.

Closed: October-March.

Gîte space for 4 people.

From Cosne sur Loire D55 W to Ste Gemme & on to Subligny (13km). House just beneath church in walled garden.
Michelin Map No: 238-20

Entry no: 340   Map No: 8

Agnès SINGER
La Chenevière
18260 Subligny
Cher
Tel: (0)2 48 73 89 93
Fax: (0)2 48 73 89 93
e-mail: agnes.singer@universal.fr
Web: www.sawdays.co.uk

Fantastic bedrooms! Both, which make up the 'suite' are in a pretty *dépendence*, the double on the ground floor looking onto the garden, with a green iron bed, old tiled floor and bold bedspread. The twin has the same tiled floor, beams and high wooden beds with an inviting mix of white covers and red quilts. The Count and Countess began taking guests last year and are charming and thoroughly hospitable. If you would like to eat in, you will join them for dinner in the main house. Members of the family run a vineyard in Provence, so try their wine. *Children under five free.*

Rooms: 1 suite for 2-4, with bath, shower & wc.

Price: 650 Frs for two; reduction for 3 nights or more.

Meals: From 100-150 Frs, including wine, by arrangement.

Closed: Never.

Gîte space for 6 people.

From Bourges D940 to Chapelle d'Angillon, then D12 to Ivoy le Pré. At church left onto D39 dir. Blancafort, Oizon and Château de la Verrerie. Take gate on right after 2.5km. Michelin Map No: 238-19

Entry no: 341   Map No: 8

Etienne & Marie de SAPORTA
La Verrerie
18380 Ivoy le Pré
Cher
Tel: (0)2 48 58 90 86
Fax: (0)2 48 58 92 79
e-mail: desaporta@dactyl-buro.fr
Web: www.sawdays.co.uk

Design married to old stones: the stables of this big farmhouse have been turned into brilliant guest quarters. Pale wood clothes the space with architectural features such as a double-height staircase, 14-foot wooden columns and sliding shutters. The breakfast room is a union of new wood and antique treasures; in the bedrooms, contemporary fabrics couple perfectly with lacy linen and crocheted covers. The house is full of light, the garden, where guests have a terrace, has an abundance of green and flowery things. Meals sound delicious and Madame quietly and graciously looks after you. La Reculée breathes a good air.

Rooms: 3 doubles, 2 twins, all with bath or shower & wc (2 on ground floor).

Price: 290 Frs for two.

Meals: 110 Frs, including wine & coffee.

Closed: Mid-November-mid-March.

From Sancerre, D955 direction Bourges. Take Montigny on the left and then, take D44 for 5km; signposted. Michelin Map No: 238-19

Entry no: 342   Map No: 8

Elizabeth GRESSIN
La Reculée
18250 Montigny
Cher
Tel: (0)2 48 69 59 18
Fax: (0)2 48 69 52 51
e-mail: scarroir@terre-net.fr
Web: www.sawdays.co.uk

This was the village notary's house; the tastes of the present owner show in the names she gives her rooms: *Monet, Picasso, Van Gogh*, each decorated to suit. Marie-Christine is into painting and decorating too: the panelling of the dining room/entrance hall is punctuated by stencilled flowerpots on top of columns and the whole room is a tour de painting force. Her warm welcome and her colour schemes, are worthy of the hospitable Monet: you can breakfast in the garden on fine days and she will even babysit – an extra Monet probably wouldn't have offered: Picasso possibly? The less agile should ask for *Monet* which has no mezzanine.

Rooms: 1 double, 2 quadruples, all with shower & wc.

Price: 280-320 Frs for two.

Meals: La Charité in Herry 7km. Delivery possible in summer.

Closed: Never.

From N7 exit towards Sancerre. Cross river, turn left & follow canal S to Herry. House signposted on village green.
Michelin Map No: 238-20

Entry no: **343**   Map No: 8

Marie-Christine GENOUD
10 place du Champ de Foire
18140 Herry
Cher
Tel: (0)2 48 79 59 02
Fax: (0)2 48 79 59 02
e-mail: imaghine@wanadoo.fr
Web: www.sawdays.co.uk

Reached through a big stand of poplars with mowed verges and daffodils in spring, this early 20th-century house is surrounded by 125 hectares of wheat and maize – and its quiet, leafy front garden and donkey paddock. The Proffitts are typical farmers, busy with work and children but friendly hosts. Guests lodge in a separate 'modern rustic-style' wing where bedrooms are plainly furnished, with the occasional knick-knack, and they have their own large long-tabled living room. Madame will join you here for simple meals if you wish. She is open and most helpful, especially about what to do and see.

Rooms: 1 double, 2 twins, all with shower & wc.

Price: 260 Frs for two.

Meals: 80 Frs, excl. wine & coffee (not Sun).

Closed: Never.

From Bourges, N151 dir. La Charité. At St Germain du Puy, D955 dir. Sancerre. At Les Aix d'Angillon, 2nd right dir. Ste Solange & follow Chambres d'Hôtes signs for 4km.
Michelin Map No: 238-19

Entry no: **344**   Map No: 8

Odile & Yves PROFFIT
La Chaume
18220 Rians
Cher
Tel: (0)2 48 64 41 58
Fax: (0)2 48 64 29 71
e-mail: proffityve@aol.com
Web: www.sawdays.co.uk

He's a kindly, straightforward, young grandfather, she teaches infants, they have come to this rustic haven to bring up their new family where the natural garden flows into woods and fields, deer roam and birdlife astounds. The house reflects their past: interesting bits from journeys to distant places: Indian rugs and Moroccan brasses in the pleasant ground-floor guest rooms, a collection of fossils in a vast glass cabinet in the duplex. African memorabilia and lots of old farmhouse stuff, nothing too sophisticated, and Jean will give you a light history lesson if you like. Return after contemplating Bourges to meditate in God's harmonious garden.

Rooms: 2 triples, 1 quadruple, all with shower & wc; 1 duplex for 4/5 with bath & wc.

Price: 250 Frs for two.

Meals: 80 Frs, including wine & coffee.

Closed: Never.

Here, in the heartland of unspoilt rural France, an articulate husband-and-wife team run their beef and cereals farm, taxi their children to school and dancing classes, make their own jam and still have time for their guests. Laurence is vivacious and casually elegant and runs an intelligent, welcoming house. The big, simple yet stylishly attractive bedrooms of her superior 18th-century farmhouse are of pleasing proportions – one of them in an unusual round brick-and-timber tower. Guests may use the swimming pool, set discreetly out of sight, at agreed times.

Rooms: 2 doubles, 1 twin, 1 triple, 1 quadruple, all with bath or shower & wc.

Price: 270-290 Frs for two.

Meals: In village or choice 6km.

Closed: Never.

From Bourges D944 towards Orléans. In Bourgneuf left and immediately right and follow signs 1.5km. Michelin Map No: 238-18

Entry no: **345**   Map No: **8**

Jean MALOT & Chantal CHARLON
La Grande Mouline
Bourgneuf
18110 Saint Eloy de Gy
Cher
Tel: (0)2 48 25 40 44
Fax: (0)2 48 25 40 44
Web: www.sawdays.co.uk

From Vierzon N76 towards Bourges to Mehun sur Yèvre. After town, right on D60 to Berry Bouy. Continue on D60: farm on right approx. 3km after village. Michelin Map No: 238-30

Entry no: **346**   Map No: **8**

Laurence & Géraud de LA FARGE
Domaine de l'Ermitage
18500 Berry Bouy
Cher
Tel: (0)2 48 26 87 46
Fax: (0)2 48 26 03 28

To the privilege of sleeping beneath that unsurpassed Cathedral add the company of an articulate, intelligent couple – she exudes warm serenity, he an eager interest in each visitor – and the walls of a 15th-century guesthouse to enclose you and it's a gift! In the dining room those old stones are crumbly in places where ancient timbers, niches, cupboards have been exposed in all their mixed-up glory. Bedrooms are wonderful too, if some plumbing seems only just younger than the walls, and the 'knight of the house' who beckons you upstairs is a fine touch of humour. The family live on the other side of the leafy secret garden.

Rooms: 2 suites for 3/4, each with bath & wc; 2 doubles, each with bath or shower & wc.

Price: 380-450 Frs for two.

Meals: Full choice within walking distance.

Closed: Never.

The Chambrins are quiet country folk with tanned faces, clear eyes and much gentle reality – the most honest, no-fuss, genuinely hospitable couple you could hope to meet. Special touches, such as great swathes of creeper outside and dried flowers and an old iron cot inside, give character to this simple old farmhouse set among the sunflower fields. The kitchen-cum-breakfast room, with its carved dresser, is small and intimate. The rooms are comfortable, though not huge, and there is a nice guests' sitting area on the landing with well-worn, quilt-thrown sofas, books and games.

Rooms: 1 double, 1 twin, 1 triple, all with shower & wc.

Price: 200 Frs for two.

Meals: Choice 1-6km.

Closed: Never.

Gîte space for 5 people.

In the centre of Bourges, at the foot of the cathedral. Park in yard if space permits.
Michelin Map No: 238-30

Entry no: **347**   Map No: 8

Marie-Ange BROUSTE & Nathalie LLOPIS
Les Bonnets Rouges
3 rue de la Thaumassière
18000 Bourges, Cher
Tel: (0)2 48 65 79 92
Fax: (0)2 48 69 82 05
Web: www.sawdays.co.uk

From Bourges, N144 to Levet; then D28 towards Dun sur Auron. After 2km turn right. House 300m from junction.
Michelin Map No: 238-31

Entry no: **348**   Map No: 8

Marie-Jo & Jean CHAMBRIN
Bannay
18340 St Germain des Bois
Cher
Tel: (0)2 48 25 31 03
Fax: (0)2 48 25 31 03

They are a great couple! Conversation flows effortlessly over glass and ashtray. Their 1940s manor is entirely Art Deco and has an eclectic collection of modern art. Monsieur paints and runs an antique shop. You find original art and good beds in the rooms (including an ingenious system for making twin-to-double beds), can learn how to make a properly formal French garden and breakfast whenever you want. Dine – until the small hours – in the long room with its huge collage at one end in the congenial Bohemian, fun-loving, intelligent atmosphere created by your down-to-earth hosts (both called Claude). Out of the ordinary.

Rooms: 2 doubles, 1 twin, all with bath, shower, wc.

Price: 380-450 Frs for two.

Meals: 150-200 Frs, including wine & coffee.

Closed: Never.

From St Amand Montrond, D951 towards Sancoin & Nevers. At Charenton Laugère, D953 towards Dun sur Auron; house is 300m on left. Michelin Map No: 238-31

Entry no: 349   Map No: 8

M & Mme Claude MOREAU
La Serre
18210 Charenton Laugère
Cher
Tel: (0)2 48 60 75 82
Fax: (0)2 48 60 75 82
Web: www.sawdays.co.uk

Visitors have heaped praise: "Quite the most beautiful house we've ever stayed in", "a unique experience of French hospitality and taste". In the family for over 200 years, it is indeed a beautifully proportioned house, standing in its large, shady garden. The sitting room is a cool blue/grey symphony, the dining room smart yellow/grey with a most unusual maroon and grey marble table – breakfast is in here while dinner *en famille* is in the big beamed kitchen. Each room has individual character, both elegant and comfortable, and Madame has a fine eye for detail. She is charming, dynamic, casually elegant and genuinely welcoming.

Rooms: 1 double, 2 twins, all with bath or shower & wc.

Price: 270-320 Frs for two.

Meals: 80-120 Frs, including wine.

Closed: Never.

Gîte space for 6 people.

From A71 exit 8. At roundabout take D925 W direction Lignières & Châteauroux. House signposted 500m on right. Michelin Map No: 238-31

Entry no: 350   Map No: 8

Marie-Claude DUSSERT
Domaine de la Trolière
18200 Orval
Cher
Tel: (0)2 48 96 47 45
Fax: (0)2 48 96 07 71

Like so many watermills, this place is just a delight to look at and the ground-floor double has its own door to the stream-side terrace – the soothing sound of water should drown out any overhead floorboard creaks or road noise. Pretty rooms all, with antiques and lace, a good sitting room with wonderful beam structure in the former milling area (look out for old graffiti on the stone walls) and breakfast feasts. The owners have done a sensitive restoration, are genuinely interested and caring and have a flexible approach to your needs.

Rooms: 1 double, 1 triple, 1 suite for 4, all with shower & wc.

Price: 250 Frs for two; suite 350-400 Frs for four.

Meals: 105 Frs, including kir, wine & coffee.

Closed: Never.

Your charming, talented, partly-Parisian hosts – one a window-dresser, the other a theatre hair-and-make-up artist – have created a stylish home of simple sophistication with a wonderfully relaxed atmosphere. The elegant, well-proportioned rooms have canopied beds, subtle colour schemes (*Les Mûriers* just avoids being blackberry-lurid) and good tiled bathrooms. The sitting room has white walls, good country antiques, encompassing sofas, fascinating *objets d'art* and paintings. Enjoy the lime-tree-shaded garden, its roses, lavender and wisteria and your hosts' genuine hospitality. Interesting terms for long stays.

Rooms: 1 double, 1 twin, each with shower & wc; 1 suite for 4 with bath & wc.

Price: 350 Frs for two; suite 550 Frs.

Meals: Restaurant in village.

Closed: Mid-Sept-mid-June; open winter weekends by arrangement.

From Loches N143 S towards Châteauroux for 16km. On entering Fléré, village square is on right; Moulin clearly signed at bottom of square.
Michelin Map No: 238-26

Entry no: 351   Map No: 7

Danielle AUMERCIER
Le Moulin
36700 Fléré la Rivière
Indre
Tel: (0)2 54 39 34 41
Fax: (0)2 54 39 34 93
e-mail: lemoulindeflere@wanadoo.fr

From Loches, N143 S towards Châteauroux for 16km. Go through Fléré; 1km after village, right on D13a for Cléré du Bois; signposted.
Michelin Map No: 238-26

Entry no: 352   Map No: 7

Claude RENOULT
Le Clos Vincents
36700 Fléré la Rivière
Indre
Tel: (0)2 54 39 30 98
Fax: (0)2 54 39 30 98

Don't you love those brick portholes? Set in a large park where protected species of flora and fauna thrive, it is a most striking house. Your hostess fell in love with it too and left her beloved Paris to be here, but she needs lots of people to make it hum. Relaxed and sociable, she will treat you very much as part of the family. The generous rooms have beams and old furniture, the ochre-walled hall is a homely clutter of riding gear, the dining room feels definitely lived in and the open view across parkland to the woods beyond is supremely tranquil.

Rooms: 1 double, 1 double/twin, 1 suite for 4, all with bath or shower & wc.

Price: 320 Frs for two.

Meals: 90 Frs, including wine.

Closed: November-March.

Gîte space for 4 people.

From Poitiers N151 E to Le Blanc (60km). Right before river on D10 to Bélâbre then left on D927 NE towards St Gaultier. House on right after 5km. Michelin Map No: 238-38

Entry no: 353   Map No: 7

Aude de LA JONQUIÈRE-AYMÉ
Le Grand Ajoux
36370 Chalais
Indre
Tel: (0)2 54 37 72 92
Fax: (0)2 54 37 56 60
e-mail: grandajoux@aol.com
Web: members.aol.com/grandajoux

A brave and endearing young English couple who came to farm in France, with their rabbit-eared sheep (they have two children, and cattle, too), invite you to drive 2km through the woods for a taste of rural French tranquillity with an English flavour. Their house still has some old beams and a stone fireplace. Rooms are big, pale-floored, simply-furnished, supremely peaceful: pilgrims to Compostela often stay here. Alison will take good care of you and Robin may tell you tales of shearing French sheep and settling into this other land. He can also show you where to gaze on rare orchids. Argenton, 'Venice of the Indre', is a must.

Rooms: 1 double with bath & wc; 2 doubles, 1 family room, sharing bathroom & separate wc.

Price: 280 Frs for two.

Meals: 100 Frs, including wine & coffee.

Closed: January-March.

From Châteauroux A20 exit 16 to Tendu taking 1st left into village. Pass Mairie then fork left at church towards Chavin & Pommiers. House 2km up track. Michelin Map No: 238-40

Entry no: 354   Map No: 7

Robin & Alison MITCHELL
La Chasse
36200 Tendu
Indre
Tel: (0)2 54 24 07 76

Teacher and hurdy-gurdy player involved in the summer folk festival, Solange Frenkel has converted an 18th-century *grange* (barn) into one of the friendliest *chambre d'hôtes* we know. In the remote rural area where George Sand held her salons and consorted with Chopin, it has high ceilings, huge beams, a vast fireplace in the sunken cosy living room 'pit' and pretty bedrooms with garden entrances. You can have unlimited breakfast while Lasco the Labrador waits patiently to take you walking. One reader simply wrote, "The best".

Rooms: 1 double, 1 twin, both with bath or shower & wc.

Price: 280 Frs for two.

Meals: 95 Frs, including wine, by arrangement.

Closed: Never.

From Bourges, N144 towards Montluçon. At Levet D940 towards La Châtre. At Thevet St Julien, D69 towards St Chartier. After 2km, left; after 1km, left again. Signposted. Michelin Map No: 238-41

Entry no: 355   Map No: 8

Solange FRENKEL
La Garenne
36400 Thevet St Julien
Indre
Tel: (0)2 54 30 04 51
Web: www.sawdays.co.uk

Here you are instantly one of the family, which is Hector the gentle giant hound, Persian Puss, two fine horses, a bright and friendly little girl, her congenial artist father and her relaxed linguist mother. Rooms – two in the main house, two in the garden house, where you can also study painting or French – are subtly colourful with good family furniture, vibrant bathrooms and... Jean-Lou's works on the walls. Some Aubusson tapestry cartoons too, and understated elegance in the sitting and dining rooms. A house of tradition and great originality, a joy of a garden, interesting, fun-loving hosts and a big welcoming table in the evening.

Rooms: 4 doubles, each with bath & wc.

Price: 350 Frs for two.

Meals: 150 Frs, including wine.

Closed: Never.

From Blois D956 to Contres then D675 to St Aignan. After bridge right on D17 to Mareuil sur Cher. House on left in hamlet of La Maison des Marchands (just before cat breeder sign) before main village. Michelin Map No: 238-15

Entry no: 356   Map No: 7

Martine & Jean-Lou COURSAGET
Le Moutier
13 rue de la République
41110 Mareuil sur Cher, Loir-et-Cher
Tel: (0)2 54 75 20 48
Fax: (0)2 54 75 20 48
e-mail: lemoutier.coursaget@wanadoo.fr
Web: perso.club-internet.fr/vilain/lemoutier

The 13th-century chapel is still used on the village feast day and the manor house, somewhat newer (16th-century), drips with history... which the modern décor manages to respect. The sitting and dining rooms are huge, the bedrooms are smallish and cosy. One has a large stone fireplace, stone floor, painted beams and very successful Laura Ashley fabrics. The setting is superb: high up and overlooking the Cher Valley. Fine mature trees shade the garden, and you can put your horse in the paddock. A stunning place – and you'll like your hosts. They can arrange wine tastings too.

Rooms: 1 suite, 2 doubles, each with bath or shower & wc.

Price: 400 Frs for two.

Meals: Wide range locally.

Closed: Never.

St Georges is on N76 between Chenonceau & Montrichard. In town centre, turn up hill following signs to 'La Chaise'. There, continue up Rue du Prieuré. No 8 has heavy wooden gates. Michelin Map No: 238-14

Entry no: 357   Map No: 7

Danièle DURET-THERIZOLS
Prieuré de la Chaise, 8 rue du Prieuré
41400 St Georges sur Cher
Loir-et-Cher
Tel: (0)2 54 32 59 77
Fax: (0)2 54 32 69 49
e-mail: prieuredelachaise@yahoo.fr
Web: www.prieuredelachaise.com

Sophie left theatre administration in Paris to concentrate her energy on this new project. The emphasis is on simple living and *cuisine bio* (organic cooking). Breakfast bread, from the organic bakery is made with milk and *fromage blanc* and dinner ingredients are either home-grown or from the local organic co-operative – menus are imaginative. Rooms are functional and attractive with bright bedspreads, original sketches and paintings. Sophie speaks fluent English and particularly loves talking to British guests as she's passionate about British history. She also speaks some Spanish and German.

Rooms: 3 doubles, 1 twin, each with shower & separate wc; 1 twin with shower & wc.

Price: 230-300 Frs for two.

Meals: 75 Frs, excluding wine (50-65 Frs).

Closed: November-January and occasionally.

From Blois/Tours take N152, cross the Loire at Chamont & take D114 towards Montrichard & Pontlevoy; in Pontlevoy take D764 to Sambin. Michelin Map No: 238-15

Entry no: 358   Map No: 7

Sophie GÉLINIER
Chambres d'Hôtes du Prieuré
23 rue de la Fontaine
St Urbain
41120 Sambin
Loir-et-Cher
Tel: (0)2 54 20 24 95
Fax: (0)2 54 20 24 95

People are always amazed at how quiet it is here. The drive is a half-mile pine-lined tunnel; the garden disappears into fields which disappear into woods... yet there are châteaux and wine cellars galore to be visited just down the road (even the 'big house' next door has a moat). Your dynamic, youthfully-retired hosts are eager to make your stay 'just right' in their converted 19th-century 'stables' (horses lived like kings). The big living room with its fine fireplace is a splendid space, guest rooms are big, simple and attractively furnished and the welcome is warmly genuine.

Rooms: 2 doubles, 1 twin, 2 quadruples, each with bath or shower & wc.

Price: 320 Frs for two.

Meals: 120 Frs, including aperitif, wine & coffee by arrangement.

Closed: January-March.

From Amboise D23 for 3km to Souvigny then D30 to Vallières les Grandes. In village right towards Montrichard on D27/D28. Lane 2nd left after water tower; house just after manor house. Michelin Map No: 238-14

Entry no: 359   Map No: 7

Annie & Daniel DOYER
Ferme de la Quantinière
41400 Vallières les Grandes
Loir-et-Cher
Tel: (0)2 54 20 99 53
Fax: (0)2 54 20 99 53
e-mail: fermequantiniere@minitel.net
Web: www.france-bonjour.com/la-quantiniere/

A house of endless happy discoveries. Your hostess, easy-going, chatty Marie-France, has created an oasis of sophisticated rusticity and enjoys playing shepherdess – she has some sheep and hens and loves to take children to look for fresh eggs – and working in the garden in combat gear. The house itself – open, airy and connected to the bedrooms by a glass walkway, has a soft, attractive feel (despite the marble tiles!) and a gorgeous woodsy view of the valley. There is an astonishing cylindrical shower in the centre of one of the double bedrooms – and another room sports a billiards table. A treat.

Rooms: 2 doubles, 1 suite, each with shower & wc.

Price: 380-550 Frs for two.

Meals: 2 restaurants within 3km.

Closed: November-April.

From Blois D751 13km to Candé, left after bridge towards Valaire. Pass War Memorial & grain silo. Keep right at next fork then left at sign Le Chêne Vert; house on left after small bridge Michelin Map No: 238-15

Entry no: 360   Map No: 7

Marie-France TOHIER
Le Chêne Vert
41120 Monthou sur Bièvre
Loir-et-Cher
Tel: (0)2 54 44 07 28
Fax: (0)2 54 44 07 28

What a delightful couple: welcoming, sensitive and fun! So eager to make real contact that they have taken English lessons and will 'brief' guests at length on where to go. Madame rightly calls her 18th-century farmhouse *le petit trésor caché* – it has that serendipity touch. Its shutters open onto a garden (with over 100 sorts of flower) which rambles down to the small River Cisse and water meadows; its rooms are pretty, cosy, quiet; the sitting/dining room is beamed and book-lined. Fires in winter, breakfast outside in summer – a dream of a place.

Rooms: 2 doubles, 2 twins, all with bath or shower & wc.

Price: 360 Frs for two.

Meals: Choice locally.

Closed: December-Easter.

Anita is charmingly Dutch; Didier, a French chef with cross-Channel experiences, speaks lovely English with accents as needed (Scots, London...) to colour his charming sense of humour. He will take you mushrooming, as well as cooking excellent dinners with things like home-smoked salmon, rabbit stew with... wild mushrooms, chocolate mousse. The farm has three spotlessly clean, attractively furnished bedrooms with high dormer windows overlooking fields towards the forest, and firm comfortable beds. Add a shallow swimming pool well away from the house and, if you like, cookery lessons!

Rooms: 2 suites, 2 doubles, 1 twin, each with bath or shower & wc.

Price: 295-380 Frs for two.

Meals: 125 Frs, including wine; Fri, Sat & Mon only.

Closed: Mid-December-mid-January.

Leave N152 Blois/Tours road direction Onzain opp. bridge to Chaumont. Left immediately after underpass (chemin du Roy). After 2.5km, right. Left at stop sign. House 100m on left.
Michelin Map No: 238-14

Entry no: **361**   Map No: **7**

Martine LANGLAIS
46 rue de Meuves
41150 Onzain
Loir-et-Cher
Tel: (0)2 54 20 78 82/
    (0)6 07 69 74 78
Fax: (0)2 54 20 78 82

From A10 exit Blois towards Vierzon. Join D765 to Cour Cheverny then D102 dir Contres. Lane to farm about 1.5km after Cheverny château on right; signposted.
Michelin Map No: 238-15

Entry no: **362**   Map No: **7**

Anita & Didier MERLIN
Ferme des Saules
41700 Cheverny
Loir-et-Cher
Tel: (0)2 54 79 26 95
Fax: (0)2 54 79 97 54
e-mail: merlin.cheverny@infonie.fr
Web: www.chez.com/fermedessaules

They are Irish, and delighted to be very much part of their French village. Mary, brimming with energy and optimism, teaches English to French businessmen. Patrick, soft-spoken with a lovely sense of humour, has renovated the house and now finds much enjoyment in running the B&B – you are very well looked after. Rooms, up narrow stairs under the rafters, with lots of floral patterns and pictures, are a good size, with rather small bathrooms. The garden apartment is nicely independent. You all breakfast together in the warm-hearted Crehans' cheerful dining room. Super spot for walking and bird-watching.

Rooms: 2 doubles & 1 apartment for 4/5, each with bath or shower & wc.

Price: 280 Frs for two.

Meals: Choice in village.

Closed: November-March.

From A71 exit 3 onto D923 through La Ferté Beauharnais to Neung sur Beuvron. Go through village; house on right just after turning to La Marolle.
Michelin Map No: 238-16

Entry no: 363   Map No: 7

Mary Ellen & Patrick CREHAN
Breffni Cottage
16 rue du 11 novembre
41210 Neung sur Beuvron
Loir-et-Cher
Tel: (0)2 54 83 66 56
Fax: (0)2 54 83 66 56
e-mail: breffni@wanadoo.fr

Muriel is a flower-loving perfectionist of immaculate taste and has let loose her considerable decorative flair on this miniature Italian villa where Queen Marie de Médicis used to take the waters: the fine garden still has a hot spring and the River Loire flows past behind the trees. The interior is unmistakably French in its careful colours, lush fabrics and fine details – fresh flowers too. Carved wardrobes and brass beds grace some rooms. The suite is a wonderful 1930s surprise and has a super-smart bathroom. You will be thoroughly coddled in this very elegant and stylish house.

Rooms: 1 suite, 1 quadruple, 2 doubles, 2 twins, all with bath or shower & wc.

Price: 420 Frs for two.

Meals: 200 Frs, including wine & coffee, by arrangement.

Closed: Never; open by arrangement in winter.

Macé is 3km north of Blois along N152 direction Orléans. Go into village & follow signs. House is 500m on right before church.
Michelin Map No: 238-3

Entry no: 364   Map No: 7

Muriel CABIN-SAINT-MARCEL
La Villa Médicis
Macé
41000 St Denis sur Loire
Loir-et-Cher
Tel: (0)2 54 74 46 38
Fax: (0)2 54 78 20 27

Fascinating and delightful people in a house full of style, originality and happy surprises. Madame, an art historian, talks exuberantly about everything and creates beauty with her hands. (The shimmering patchwork quilts are her work.) Monsieur has a great sense of fun too, yet their house hums with serenity. Rooms are period-themed with family pieces: the *1930s* has an old typewriter, a valve radio and an authentic, garish green bathroom; the *1900s* has a splendid carved bed. The romantic garden is a fitting mixture of French geometric and English informal and the house set back enough for the road not to be a problem.

Rooms: 1 double, 1 twin, 1 triple, 1 single, all with bath or shower & wc.

Price: 300-350 Frs for two.

Meals: 2 restaurants in village.

Closed: November-March, except by arrangement.

From A10 exit 16 & follow signs to Chambord, crossing Loire river at Mer. After bridge right on D951; house on right at end of village.
Michelin Map No: 238-3

Entry no: 365   Map No: 7

Francis & Béatrice BONNEFOY
L'Échappée Belle
120 rue Nationale
41500 St Dyé sur Loire
Loir-et-Cher
Tel: (0)2 54 81 60 01
e-mail: fbonnefoy@libertysurf.fr
Web: perso.libertysurf.fr/fbonnefoy

The white duck is a symbol of friendship and with luck you'll meet the web-footed house mascot here. Inside, a warmly sensitive atmosphere radiates from the beautiful old floor tiles, fabulous timbered ceilings, lovely family furniture. From the ground-floor bathroom you look straight onto the mill wheel (restored by Monsieur); Madame uses her innate feeling for history to advise on places to see. Both are quietly, gently caring about their guests' well-being. Bedrooms, each in a different style, are big, harmonious in fabric and colour, and look over the rambling, peaceful garden. Huge selection of teas for breakfast.

Rooms: 2 doubles, 2 triples, 1 suite, each with bath or shower & wc.

Price: 320-450 Frs for two.

Meals: Excellent choice within 7km.

Closed: Never.

From A10, exit 16 onto N152 dir Blois. 3.5km after Mer, right towards Diziers and follow Chambres d'Hôtes signs.
Michelin Map No: 238-3

Entry no: 366   Map No: 7

Marie-Françoise & André SEGUIN
Le Moulin de Choiseaux
8 rue des Choiseaux
41500 Suèvres, Loir-et-Cher
Tel: (0)2 54 87 85 01
Fax: (0)2 54 87 86 44
e-mail: choiseaux@wanadoo.fr
Web: le-village.ifrance.com/choiseaux/

Perfect for Chambord and for walks in the Sologne, this 18th-century house stands in seven acres of woodland that cut out all sight of the nuclear power station. A quiet, leafy place to rest after château-visiting exertions: one owner went through Revolution, Restoration, Napoleon, three prisons, three death sentences... and then died in his bed. Traditionally-furnished bedrooms are light, sunny, attractive: there are fine old things everywhere, including grandfather's paintings. Madame, who speaks little English, shares her time between guests and her family commitments – her welcome is appropriately formal.

Rooms: 1 double, 1 twin, 1 quadruple, all with shower & wc.

Price: 300 Frs for two.

Meals: 1 restaurant in village; choice 8km.

Closed: Never.

From Orléans, D951 direction Blois. On entering St Laurent, follow signs to Chambres d'Hôtes.
Michelin Map No: 238-4

Entry no: 367   Map No: 7

Catherine & Maurice LIBEAUT
L'Ormoie, 26 rue de l'Ormoie
St Laurent des Eaux
41220 St Laurent Nouan, Loir-et-Cher
Tel: (0)2 54 87 24 72
Fax: (0)2 54 87 24 93
e-mail: maurice.catherine.libeaut@wanadoo.fr
Web: www.sawdays.co.uk

The picture-framing workshop is where Madame is found; her jovial husband farms and will serve your breakfast. The rooms are light and simple, decorated in understated good taste and shades of off-white, grey and blue. There are beams, floors of polished parquet or tiles, billiards in the sitting room and a kitchenette for you. The garden at the back is charming, the miniature trees at the bottom screen the outbuildings. A 16th-century townhouse, but you feel you are in the countryside.

Rooms: 1 double/twin, 3 triples, 1 suite, each with bath or shower & wc.

Price: 290-400 Frs for two.

Meals: Choice in Mer.

Closed: January.

Gîte space for 6 people.

Leave N152 Orléans-Blois road in Mer and park by church. House is short walk up main shopping street; entrance in picture-framing shop on left. (Car access details on arrival.)
Michelin Map No: 238-3

Entry no: 368   Map No: 7

Joëlle & Claude MORMICHE
9 rue Dutems
41500 Mer
Loir-et-Cher
Tel: (0)2 54 81 17 36
Fax: (0)2 54 81 70 19
e-mail: mormiche@wanadoo.fr
Web: www.france-bonjour.com/mormiche/

As one reader said: "A little gem of a B&B" with its sweeping farmyard, its pond and such a welcome. You can see for miles across fields filled with larksong and cereals. It is peaceful, pretty and a place for picnics. The owners are a smiling couple who give you their time without invading your space but are delighted to show you their immaculate farm, orchard and vegetable garden if you're interested. Their rooms have gentle colours, soft materials and firm mattresses. The furniture is simple and rustic, the bedrooms and bathrooms are deeply raftered, the old farmhouse breathes through its timbers.

Rooms: 1 double with shower & wc; 2 doubles sharing bath & wc.

Price: 215-260 Frs for two.

Meals: 80 Frs, including wine (for 2+ night stay only). Restaurant 6km.

Closed: Never.

From Vendôme D957 direction Blois for 6km. Right at sign to Crucheray & Chambres d'Hôtes. House 4km from turning; signposted.
Michelin Map No: 238-2

Entry no: 369   Map No: 7

Élisabeth & Guy TONDEREAU
Les Bordes
41100 Crucheray
Loir-et-Cher
Tel: (0)2 54 77 05 43
Fax: (0)2 54 77 05 43

A very friendly, open couple, new to B&B and loving it. Grégoire has restored this fairy-tale manor house, complete with Renaissance façade, with help from Véronique when she's not working in Paris (she can fill you in on the political scene!). Access to the guest bedrooms is via the wonderful turret, draped with Indian fabrics. Ceilings are 4m-high, there are two four-poster beds, antique furniture and interesting *objets*. There's also a truly majestic guest sitting room. An amazing place to stay in the most beautiful, peaceful surroundings: you can breakfast, laze, sketch the Barbary ducks or fish in the grounds – rods are provided.

Rooms: 1 triple, 1 suite for 6, both with bath & wc.

Price: 280-300 Frs for two.

Meals: Wide choice 5km.

Closed: 30 October-1 April.

From Vendôme D917 direction Montoire. D10 direction Couture sur Loire. Continue 1.5km; take right signposted. Continue 1km, house 3rd on left (with tower).
Michelin Map No: 232-24

Entry no: 370   Map No: 7

Gregoire LUCIEN-BRUN &
Veronique DEBEAUMONT
Manoir de la Chevalinière
41800 St Martin des Bois
Loir-et-Cher
Tel: (0)2 54 72 53 94
Fax: (0)2 54 72 53 94
e-mail: gregoire@onetelnet.fr

Fabienne is a charming, sociable hostess who wants everything 'just right' for her guests. A lot of the decorative detail is hers and the pretty rooms are named after the flowers she loves and tends in her garden. Light floods in through the big windows of the dining room and there's always home-made jam and cake for breakfast. Fabienne may go with you on local walks or bike rides as she genuinely wants you to get the most out of your stay. The troglodyte village of Troo is just 4km away and it's 6km to the craft centre of Poncé, where you can watch potters and glass-blowers at work.

Rooms: 1 family suite (2 separate doubles) sharing bath & separate wc; 1 double with shower & wc.

Price: 220-250 Frs for two.

Meals: Good restaurant in Pont de Braye 2km.

Closed: November-Easter.

Gîte space for 6 people.

There are touches of fun in this simple characterful old farmhouse: a couple of parrots perch in the children's room, for example. Madame is charming, clearly delighting in her role as hostess; Monsieur quietly gets on with his gardening. Now retired, they are both active in their community, caring and unpretentious (he is Deputy Mayor). Traditionally furnished, the rooms have subtle, well-chosen colour schemes, the bathroom is new and clean. Breakfast is served in the dining room with home-made jams and crusty bread. The house backs onto the gardens of the château, is surrounded by chestnut trees and wonderfully quiet.

Rooms: 1 triple, 1 twin, 1 suite for 5, each with bath or shower & wc.

Price: 250 Frs for two.

Meals: Auberge 300m.

Closed: Never.

From Le Mans N138 to Chateau du Loir, turn left on D305 to Pont du Baye. Then continue on the D917 to Sougé sur Braye, house just before you leave the village on right.
Michelin Map No: 232-24

From Tours D29 to Beaumont la Ronce. House signposted in village.
Michelin Map No: 232-24

Entry no: 371   Map No: 7

Entry no: 372   Map No: 7

Fabienne & Alain PARTENAY
La Mulotière
10 rue du Bourg Neuf
41800 Sougé sur Braye
Loir-et-Cher
Tel: (0)6 80 33 72 55
Fax: (0)2 54 72 46 97

Michel & Andrée CAMPION
La Louisière
37360 Beaumont la Ronce
Indre-et-Loire
Tel: (0)2 47 24 42 24
Fax: (0)2 47 24 42 24

In the lesser-known and lovely Loir valley you have a little old house in the garden all to yourselves. It has a kitchen and a bathroom downstairs, two little bedrooms up a steep staircase, all recently renovated, and its own piece of flower-filled garden for intimate breakfasts. Or you can join Madame in her light and cheerful kitchen at the long check-clothed table with baskets hanging from the beams. She is friendly, cultivated and dynamic, very involved in the local music festival and tourist activities so an excellent adviser for guests, and also a great maker of jams. It's not luxurious, but elegantly homely, quiet and welcoming.

Rooms: 2 doubles in cottage, sharing bathroom.

Price: 300 Frs for two; 520 Frs for four.

Meals: 120 Frs, incl. wine & coffee.

Closed: Never.

From Tours/La Membrolle N138 towards Le Mans. At Neuillé Pont Pierre D68 to Neuvy le Roi. House on road through village; blue front door, opposite turning to Louestault.
Michelin Map No: 232-23

Entry no: 373   Map No: 7

Ghislaine & Gérard de
COUESNONGLE
20 rue Pilate
37370 Neuvy le Roi
Indre-et-Loire
Tel: (0)2 47 24 41 48
Web: www.sawdays.co.uk

High on a cliff above the Loire, it looks over the village and across the vineyards and valley to a château. Only four years old but done in *Tourangeau* style with reproduction furniture, the house is immaculate and meticulously kept: one room is in Louis XIV style, plus orangey carpet and flowery paper. There is a big dining/sitting area with tiled floor and rugs, an insert fireplace and views over the large sloping garden (under which there is a troglodyte dwelling). Mountain bikes to borrow, giant breakfasts – great value for the Loire.

Rooms: 1 suite, 3 doubles, each with bath & wc.

Price: 260-295 Frs for two.

Meals: Wide choice locally & in Tours.

Closed: Never.

From Tours A10 N towards Paris; cross River Loire then leave exit 20. Follow signs to Rochecorbon. In village left at lights then right up steep narrow lane; signposted.
Michelin Map No: 232-36

Entry no: 374   Map No: 7

Mme Jacqueline GAY
7 chemin de Bois Soleil
37210 Rochecorbon
Indre-et-Loire
Tel: (0)2 47 52 88 08
Fax: (0)2 47 52 85 90
e-mail: jacquelinegay@minitel.net
Web: www.sawdays.co.uk

A working goat-farm producing its own delicious cheese. Sleep in the pigsty (or is it the stable block?), swim in their beautiful pool then carouse over dinner in the lovely old room in the main house with its beams and large open fireplace; the meal, very much *en famille*, starts after the evening's milking. The atmosphere around the table, the unusual and lovely setting and the easy good nature of your hosts make the fairly basic rooms utterly acceptable. Bits of the house are 13th-century: it was built by a glass-maker, a very superior trade in those days, and overlooks the extraordinary ruins of a large castle.

Rooms: 2 doubles, 1 twin, 1 quadruple, each with shower & wc.

Price: 250 Frs for two.

Meals: 85 Frs, including wine & coffee.

Closed: January-February.

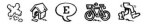

Château la Vallière is 33km NW of Tours. From Château la Vallière take D34 S direction Langeais – first right then right again, past ruined castle: house at top of track.
Michelin Map No: 232-22

Entry no: 375   Map No: 7

Gérard & Martine RIBERT
Vaujours
37330 Château la Vallière
Indre-et-Loire
Tel: (0)2 47 24 08 55
Fax: (0) 2 47 24 19 20
e-mail: rib007@aol.com

An imposing lodge set in a big 'English' garden (Madame is passionate about her flowers, both inside and out) and surrounded by forest. It has a harmonious, mellow feeling despite being built recently – but in 17th-century Angevin style with old materials from the château next door. An unusual and refreshingly natural place, it reflects the family's plan to return to country simplicity. They are gentle, caring, cultivated and creative, as proved by the delightful, carefully-designed and decorated bedrooms. There's a lovely new 'pigeon loft' room with half-timbered walls and a round window too – very enticing. *Children over 10 welcome.*

Rooms: 1 double, 2 twins, each with shower (1 behind curtain) & wc.

Price: 320-350 Frs for two.

Meals: In village.

Closed: 20 December-5 January.

From Tours, N152 direction Saumur. At St Patrice, D35 to Bourgueil. There, D749 to Gizeux then D15 to Continvoir. In village, left on D64; signposted.
Michelin Map No: 232-34

Entry no: 376   Map No: 7

Michel & Claudette BODET
La Butte de l'Épine
37340 Continvoir
Indre-et-Loire
Tel: (0)2 47 96 62 25
Fax: (0)2 47 96 07 36
Web: www.sawdays.co.uk

Such a French family house: *Oncle Vincent*'s room has two BIG single beds, one made for Vincent with matching wardrobe and chest of drawers, the other, brass-knobbed and not matching the cane chair... *Tante Angèle* did the samplers in HER room, and Madame is properly proud of her fine linen. The cottage snuggles demurely in its *Jardin Secret*, rose scent wafts, Monsieur takes you to his favourite wine growers and craftsmen. They love having guests and opening doors onto unknown Loire treasures.

A dream place! Rarely does one see so masterly a renovation and that open gallery is exceptionally rare. So is the serene and genuinely medieval atmosphere of the great square drawing room – worn flagstones, monumental fireplace, low, low doors, no curtains (not authentic), soft pink furnishings against whitewashed stone walls... and, in contrast, furniture from France, Africa, Vietnam. Magical. One bedroom has a brick-and-timber wall, a great plain wooden bed, lace covers; the other a marble washstand and a monkish mirror; the deep-tubbed, small-paned bathroom is a delight. Your hosts are excellent, cultured company. Really special – book early.

Rooms: 1 double with bath, 1 twin with shower, sharing wc. Cottage for 3.

Price: 240-260 Frs for two; cottage 300 Frs, for two.

Meals: Auberge 50m.

Closed: Never.

Rooms: 1 suite for 3/4 with bath & wc.

Price: 700 Frs for two; 1000 Frs for three or four.

Meals: Choice in Villandry.

Closed: September-April.

From Chinon, D16 to Huismes. Under arch between church and large house, 1st left: house 2nd on right.
Michelin Map No: 232-34

From Tours D7 to Savonnières. There, right across bridge then immediately left. House 3km along on right.
Michelin Map No: 232-35

Entry no: 377   Map No: 7

Entry no: 378   Map No: 7

Anne & Jean-Marc BUREAU
Le Clos de l'Ormeau
37420 Huismes
Indre-et-Loire
Tel: (0)2 47 95 41 54
Fax: (0)2 47 95 41 54

Michel & Marie-Françoise SALLES
Manoir de Foncher
37510 Villandry
Indre-et-Loire
Tel: (0)2 47 50 02 40
Fax: (0)2 47 50 09 94

Éric, a charming, energetic, artistic Anglophile with a sense of fun and a real interest in people, delights in his superb garden and the beautifully-finished details of his guest rooms. The four downstairs rooms have their own terraces, stone beams and fireplaces; upstairs, the gentle grey and white room has its own big balcony, the other is full of powerful florals; all rooms have classy bathrooms and a stylish use of colour. Hall and dining room are splendiferous, restored to 18th-century elegance: crystal chandeliers, gilt-framed mirrors, statues, and there's a cosy sitting room. The whole place is a haven of history, culture, peace – magical.

Rooms: 2 triples, 1 twin, 2 doubles, 1 suite (1 double & 1 twin), each with bath or shower & wc.

Price: 420-580 Frs for two.

Meals: In village or wide choice 2km.

Closed: February-March.

From Tours, D7 to Savonnières, then left at Hôtel Faisan on D7 towards Ballan Miré and up hill about 1km. House on left (signposted).
Michelin Map No: 232-35

Entry no: 379   Map No: 7

Éric & Christine SALMON
Prieuré des Granges
15 rue des Fontaines
37510 Savonnières, Indre-et-Loire
Tel: (0)2 47 50 09 67
Fax: (0)2 47 50 06 43
e-mail: salmon.eric@wanadoo.fr
Web: www.sawdays.com

Go from common street to stately courtyard magnolias to circular marble domed staircase and you have a *Monument Historique*, a miniature Bagatelle Palace, a bachelor's folly with a circular *salon*. The light, airy, elegant rooms, small and perfectly proportioned, are softly pink-and-grey; lean out and pick a grape from the vine-clad pergola. Monsieur was a pilot and still flys vintage aircraft. Madame was an air hostess and English teacher and is casually sophisticated and articulate about her love of fine things, places and buildings. Wonderful, and a stone's throw from Chenonceaux.

Rooms: 1 double, 1 suite for 4, each with shower & wc.

Price: 250-400 Frs for two.

Meals: Good choice within walking distance.

Closed: December-March, except by arrangement.

From Amboise D31 S to Bléré through La Croix en Touraine. Cross bridge, Rue des Déportés opposite but one-way so turn left, immediately right, 1st right, right again. Guests can be collected from private airport 5km.
Michelin Map No: 238-14

Entry no: 380   Map No: 7

Dominique GUILLEMOT
Le Belvédère
24 rue des Déportés
37150 Bléré, Indre-et-Loire
Tel: (0)2 47 30 30 25
Fax: (0)2 47 30 30 25
e-mail: guillemot@wanadoo.fr
Web: www.sawdays.co.uk

A narrow meandering track leads you through a gorgeous 'lost valley' to this light and airy house, where the lawns run down to the banks of the Cher with not a neighbour in sight. The whole place is being beautifully restored by the present owners, who moved here from Paris. Using traditional Tuffeau stone, typical of the region, they have created a magnificent dining room. The garden level bedroom has an African theme with terracotta tiling; another on the top of the house has an enormous full tester bed, which looks big enough to sleep four.

Rooms: 1 double, 2 triples, each with bath & wc.

Price: 300-400 Frs for two.

Meals: 140 Frs, including aperitif & wine.

Closed: Never.

From Tours, N76 towards Bléré. After passing the sign for Athée sur Cher, continue to Granlay. Immediately turn left towards Vallet.
Michelin Map No: 232-36

Entry no: 381   Map No: 7

Denise et Augustin CHAUDIÈRE
Le Pavillon de Vallet
4 rue de l'Acqueduc
37270 Athée sur Cher
Indre-et-Loire
Tel: (0)2 47 50 67 83
Fax: (0) 2 47 50 68 31
e-mail: pavillon.vallet@wanadoo.fr

Overlooked by a fortified farm used by Lafayette as a hunting lodge, this is an especially tranquil place which feels as old as the hills (actually the middle ages). There are ornamental geese and ducks on the lake and places to sit, read or paint in the neatly tended garden. Brightly decorated bedrooms blend well with antique furniture and lake views. The old milling machinery in the breakfast area still works – ask and Monsieur will turn it on for you – and there are relics from the days when this was a working mill, including original flour sacks from Azay. Amazing!

Rooms: 2 doubles & 2 suites, each with bath & wc.

Price: 340-380 Frs for two.

Meals: Good auberge in village 500m.

Closed: Never.

Gîte space for 6 people.

From Tours take N143 towards Loches; left onto D58 to Reignac. Then D17 towards Azay sur Indre. In village left in front of restaurant, continue & at fork take left (over two bridges). The mill is below the fortified farm on right.
Michelin Map No: 238-14

Entry no: 382   Map No: 7

Mme Danie LIGNELET
Moulin de la Follaine
37310 Azay sur Indre
Indre-et-Loire
Tel: (0)2 47 92 57 91
e-mail: moulindelafollaine@wanadoo.fr
Web: www.multimania.com/moulindefollaine

Pure magic for all *Wind in the Willows* fans! Three old mills side by side in a great sweep of the Indre, a boat for just messing about in, wooden bridges to cross from one secluded bank to another, a ship-stern view of the river from the terrace as you share a civilized dinner with your amusing, well-travelled hosts. The airy, elegant but uncluttered rooms have stunning views over the river (fear not – the sound of rushing water is limited to a gentle murmur at night), in styles to suit a Lieutenant, a Colonel and a Prior (in ascending order!).

Rooms: 2 doubles, each with shower & separate wc; 1 twin with bath & wc.

Price: 500-600 Frs for two.

Meals: 150 Frs, including aperitif, wine & coffee.

Closed: Never (by arrangement 1 November-15 March).

From Tours, N143 dir. Chateauroux for 12km. Right on D17, 500m after Esso garage. Continue 1.3km then left to Domaine de Vontes; left to Bas-Vontes. House at end of road.
Michelin Map No: 232-36

Entry no: 383   Map No: 7

Odile & Jean-Jacques DEGAIL
Les Moulins de Vontes
37320 Esvres sur Indre
Indre-et-Loire
Tel: (0)2 47 26 45 72
Fax: (0)2 47 26 45 35
e-mail: jjdegail@aol.com
Web: www.sawdays.co.uk

Once home to the 'Boher', trainer of knights for medieval jousting tournaments; things are more peaceful here now for Madame really loves flowers – her summer garden is glorious. She is relaxed and keen to make you feel at home in her pretty farmhouse (sunflowers grow in the surrounding fields). Rooms, predictably flower-themed and fresh-flower decorated, are smallish but bright and cheerful, the guests' dayroom opens onto the terrace and the family dining room is most welcoming – you might enjoy a spot of billiards practice before dinner?

Rooms: 1 double, 1 twin, 2 triples, all with bath or shower & wc.

Price: 250-270 Frs for two.

Meals: 85 Frs, including aperitif, wine & coffee.

Closed: Never.

From Tours N143 towards Loches, through Cormery and on for 10km. Left at Massy-Ferguson garage for Azay sur Indre/Chambres d'Hôtes; house 700m along, signposted.
Michelin Map No: 238-14

Entry no: 384   Map No: 7

Marie-Agnès BOUIN
La Bihourderie
37310 Azay sur Indre
Indre-et-Loire
Tel: (0)2 47 92 58 58
Fax: (0)2 47 92 22 19
Web: www.sawdays.co.uk

Philosopher Bruno and Titian-haired Nancy, an engaging couple with three young children, have turned this old family château into a delightful refuge for the world-weary traveller. The demands of children to be taken to dancing lessons, and guests requiring intellectual and physical sustenance, are met with quiet composure and good humour. Generations of sliding children have polished the banisters on the stairs leading to the large, light bedrooms, freshly decorated round splendid brass bedsteads and family memorabilia. On fine summer evenings, you can take a supper tray to picnic *à la* Glyndebourne in a favourite corner of the gardens.

Rooms: 2 doubles, 1 twin, each with bath/shower & wc.

Price: 510-550 Frs for two.

Meals: 150-180 Frs, including aperitif & wine; supper tray 100 Frs.

Closed: Never; open by arrangement.

From Tours D751 SW towards Chinon for 5km. In Ballan Miré, right at lights just before level crossing. Signposted; entrance opposite golf course.
Michelin Map No: 232-35

Entry no: 385   Map No: 7

Monsieur Bruno CLÉMENT
Château du Vau
37510 Ballan Miré
Indre-et-Loire
Tel: (0)2 47 67 84 04
Fax: (0)2 47 67 55 77
e-mail: chateauduvau@chez.com
Web: www.chez.com/chateauduvau

An elegant dressed-stone house, a well-converted stable block, the inimitable limpid light of the Loire Valley on the edge of a quiet little village – this is a protected wetland area between the Loire and Vienne rivers. The guest quarters have ancient beams, stone walls and new floors, space to sit or cook, even a little terrace. The uncluttered, sizeable rooms have the same happy mix of old and new with some fine pieces of furniture. You will be welcomed by a couple who are proud of their house and area and will direct you to less obvious places of interest. "Very clean, very friendly, very good food", say readers' letters.

Rooms: 2 triples, each with bath & wc; 1 double with shower & wc.

Price: 230-280 Frs for two.

Meals: 90 Frs, including wine & coffee (not Sunday or Monday). Self-catering possible.

Closed: Never.

From Chinon D749 towards Bourgueil for 6km. Left towards Savigny en Véron & follow signs to 'Camping'. House 1km after campsite on right.
Michelin Map No: 232-34

Entry no: 386   Map No: 7

Marie-Françoise & Michel CHAUVELIN
Cheviré
11 rue Basse
37420 Savigny en Veron
Indre-et-Loire
Tel: (0)2 47 58 42 49
Fax: (0)2 47 58 42 49

What a splendid person! What a sensitive restoration of her old farmhouse (some of it 15th-century). Intelligent, well-travelled, cultured, she took a course on food and taste awareness, started doing B&B and simply loves bringing people together over an excellent meal where all her interests are nourished. A big fire crackles in the sitting room, the old tiles and timbers glow rich and mellow, summer dinners are in the little walled courtyard, the shady garden has private corners, rooms play variations on the theme of good fabrics and furniture (the small, lower-priced room is real value). Swathes of conviviality and light envelope the place. *Gîte Panda.*

Rooms: 4 double, each with bath or shower & wc.

Price: 240-370 Frs for two.

Meals: 120 Frs, including wine & coffee.

Closed: Never.

Gîte space for 4 people.

From Chinon D749 towards Bourgueil. At roundabout in Beaumont, 3rd exit towards La Roche Honneur. Left at sign to Grézille; left again at painted sign. Michelin Map No: 232-34

Entry no: 387   Map No: 7

Antoinette DEGRÉMONT
La Balastière, Hameau de Grezille
37420 Beaumont en Veron,
Indre-et-Loire
Tel: (0)2 47 58 87 93
Fax: (0)2 47 58 82 41
e-mail: balastiere@infonie.fr
Web: perso.infonie.fr/balastiere/

Jany and Jean, back in Chinon after many years in Paris, create a thoroughly civilised atmosphere where guests bask in refined but unpretentious comfort. Their well-renovated 19th-century townhouse stands on the bank of the stately River Vienne with the little streets of medieval Chinon rising behind it up to the old castle. Both bedrooms (*Iris* and *Loriette*) overlook the water and have Jany's unmistakable personal touch. Jean sings in the local choir and his amazing CD and record collection covers two walls of his study. They are an articulate, music- and art-loving couple, and excellent hosts.

Rooms: 2 doubles, each with shower or bath & wc.

Price: 320-350 Frs for two.

meals: Good choice within walking distance.

Closed: 1 October-31 March.

Entering Chinon on D751 from Tours, drive along river past bridge and Rabelais statue. House is just after Post Office.
Michelin Map No: 232-34

Entry no: 388   Map No: 7

Jany & Jean GROSSET
84 quai Jeanne d'Arc
37500 Chinon
Indre-et-Loire
Tel: (0)2 47 98 42 78
Web: www.sawdays.co.uk

Thoroughly modern Martine has made this solid wine-grower's house sing in a subtle harmony of traditional charm and contemporary chic. Terracotta-sponged walls, creamy beams and colourful modern fabrics breathe new life into rooms with old tiled floors and stone fireplaces. Windows are flung open to let in the light, and the stresses of city-living are forgotten in cheerful, easy conversations with your hostess. There is a baby grand piano in the elegant sitting room for the musical, a pool for the energetic, and wine-tastings at the vineyard next door. A great place.

Rooms: 2 doubles, 1 suite, each with bath & wc.

Price: 480 Frs for two.

Meals: 150 Frs, including wine.

Closed: Never.

From Chinon D749 dir. Richelieu. 1km after r'about right on D115 dir. Ligré 'par le vignoble'. After 5km left to Le Rouilly. At Dozon wine warehouse left. House is 800m on left; signposted.
Michelin Map No: 232-34

Entry no: 389   Map No: 7

Martine DESCAMPS
Le Clos de Ligre
Le Rouilly
37500 Ligré
Indre-et-Loire
Tel: (0)2 47 93 95 59
Fax: (0)2 47 93 06 31
e-mail: martinedescamps@hotmail.com

In a magical garden on a steep secluded slope where troglodytes once lived (the cave with its original fireplace now contains preserves and pans), the pretty little creeper-covered old house and its renovated outbuilding (illustrated) with two excellent guest rooms, make a gentle retreat from the crowds visiting the châteaux. One room has a superbly carved Norman bridal bed (doves and sheaves for peace and prosperity), the other has a fine family armoire, both are softly furnished with good bathrooms. Madame, relaxed, cultivated and welcoming, is most knowledgeable about her beloved Loire Valley.

Rooms: 2 doubles, each with shower & wc.

Price: 270 Frs for two.

Meals: Wide choice within 5km.

Closed: November-February.

From Saumur D947 direction Chinon to Montsoreau (10km); D751 through Candes & St Germain sur Vienne. 500m after the church, at the Goujon Frétillant restaurant, right and follow signs for 1.5km.
Michelin Map No: 232-34

Entry no: 390   Map No: 7

Anne DUBARRY
7 la Vallée des Grottes
37500 St Germain sur Vienne
Indre-et-Loire
Tel: (0)2 47 95 96 45

A tree-shaded garden shields this old walnut farm-turned antique dealer's. Inside the house a cornucopia of exotica mingles well with traditional antique furniture in splendid oak-beamed, book and stone-clad rooms. The stylishly-decorated bedrooms are a good size, one bathroom is big enough to dance in, and the suite has its own large sitting room downstairs with a huge open fireplace. And if you find your antique carved bed-head irresistible, you may be able to buy it! Barbara, articulate and efficient, believes in mollycoddling her guests – there are hand-embroidered linen sheets on the beds and sumptuous breakfasts served on the best porcelain.

Rooms: 2 doubles, 1 suite for 2/4 people, each with bath & wc.

Price: 500-550 Frs for two.

Meals: Auberge in village; good choice in Chinon, 12km.

Closed: Never.

From Tours take D751 to Chinon, and then D21 to Cravant les Coteaux. Pallus is approx. 1.5km after the village on the right, with the sign 'Bernard Chauveau – Antiquaire'. Michelin Map No: 232-34

Entry no: 391   Map No: 7

Barbara CHAUVEAU
Domaine de Pallus
37500 Cravant les Côteaux
Indre-et-Loire
Tel: (0)2 47 93 08 94
Fax: (0)2 47 98 43 00
e-mail: bcpallus@clubinternet.fr

Dug into the hillside, engulfing forest behind and a wide-angle view of vines, fields and sky in front, this 'old' wine-grower's manor pretends, successfully, to have been built in the 1800s rather than the 1980s, with its venerable oak beams gnawed by generations of woodworm and stone cut by troglodyte stonemasons. The furniture in the bedrooms is equally antique – a superb carved wooden bed-head, a big puffy eiderdown, old prints. Only the pool, elegant bathrooms and guests' functional sitting and utility rooms show the owners' thoroughly contemporary concern for luxury and comfort. And there is wine to taste and buy.

Rooms: 1 suite for 3/4 in main house, 2 doubles in pool-side cabin, all with bath or shower & wc.

Price: 380-500 Frs for two.

Meals: Choice 2-9km.

Closed: Never.

Gîte space for 4 people.

From Chinon, D21 to Cravant les Côteaux. Continue towards Panzoult; house on left after 2km. Michelin Map No: 232-35

Entry no: 392   Map No: 7

Marie-Claude CHAUVEAU
Domaine de Beauséjour
37220 Panzoult
Indre-et-Loire
Tel: (0)2 47 58 64 64
Fax: (0)2 47 95 27 13
e-mail: gdc37@club-internet.fr

The house had lost most of its original features but Michelle has created a cosy atmosphere with an open fireplace and lots of antiques and ornaments. Chatty, energetic and direct, she is a keen gardener and her garden, full of hidden corners, is a riot of foliage and flowers, with plenty of shade in summer. Rooms are immaculate and stylish, here some blue stripey wallpaper and old prints, there a brass bed and white table lamps. The Indre valley is charming and Saché has strong artistic vibes: Balzac lived and wrote here; Alexander Calder lived and sculpted here. *Children over 12 welcome.*

Rooms: 2 triples, 1 double, 1 suite for 4, each with shower & wc.

Price: 400 Frs for two; minimum 2 nights.

Meals: Wide choice 10 minutes drive.

Closed: Mid-November–mid-March.

The lovely cross-shaped symmetry envelopes you, glazed fanlights on each arm of the cross look through onto trees, the welcome is open-armed. Christian, a lively, amusing, naturally hospitable host, teaches yoga, used to deal in Asian objects – the eclectic furnishings tell fascinating tales – and opens his house to walkers, yoga students (big light dojo on the top floor) and gentle therapy groups as well as B&B guests (there are other bedrooms). Expect lots of laughter and good imaginative cooking. A house of surprises and delights where you feel utterly at home, it is warm, human, harmonious and unforgettable. Doug the dog's great too.

Rooms: 2 twins, 2 doubles, each with shower & wc; 7 others with showers & sharing wcs.

Price: 250-330 Frs for two.

Meals: 130 Frs, including wine & coffee.

Closed: Never.

From Azay le Rideau D84 E towards Artannes. Hamlet of Sablonnière is 6km along; house clearly marked on left in centre of hamlet.
Michelin Map No: 232-35

From Chinon cross River Vienne & take D749 then D760 to Ile Bouchard. After entering town, 2nd right and follow signs.
Michelin Map No: 232-35

Entry no: 393   Map No: 7

Entry no: 394   Map No: 7

Mme Michelle PILLER
Les Tilleuls
16 rue de la Sablonnière
37190 Saché
Indre-et-Loire
Tel: (0)2 47 26 81 45
Fax: (0)2 47 26 84 00

Christian VAURIE
La Commanderie
16 rue de la Commanderie
37220 Brizay, Indre-et-Loire
Tel: (0)2 47 58 63 13
Fax: (0)2 47 58 55 81
e-mail: info@lacommanderie.com
Web: www.lacommanderie.com

Extremely pleasant, welcoming hosts – Joseph looks after the farm, Anne-Marie takes care of guests and cooks wonderful, generous family meals with vegetables from the garden. Bedrooms are large, light, old-tiled, well-bathroomed. Four are in the farmhouse (including the easy-access suite) and two in the restored outbuilding: the twin and a fine family room (on two levels) in the old hayloft. A calm, homely atmosphere is cultivated by these educated farmers who have the gift of working hard yet apparently having time to chat. Breakfast includes goat's cheese and apple juice from the village.

Rooms: 1 double, 1 twin, 2 triples, 1 suite, 1 family room, all with bath or shower & wc.

Price: 270-300 Frs for two.

Meals: 120 Frs, including wine & coffee.

Closed: Christmas.

From A10, Ste Maure de Touraine exit on D760, then D59 towards Ligueil. Go through Sepmes. Farm is on left as you leave village; signposted.
Michelin Map No: 232-35

Entry no: 395   Map No: 7

Anne-Marie & Joseph VERGNAUD
La Ferme les Berthiers
37800 Sepmes
Indre-et-Loire
Tel: (0)2 47 65 50 61
e-mail: lesberthiers@libertysurf.fr

The Miévilles (he English, she French) came to the Loire Valley from Paris looking for a better quality of life. They once lived in Spain too so they speak at least three languages and are interested in the cultural differences between countries. They have turned this lovely watermill into a colourful and cosy home full of flowers and scatter cushions, keeping much of the original machinery in the mill room where you have breakfast. The garden around the millpond with its own little island is gorgeous, with plenty of shade for those hot summer days and public footpaths close by.

Rooms: 2 doubles & 2 triples, each with bath & wc.

Price: 350-370 Frs for two.

Meals: Available locally.

Closed: Mid-November-February.

From Blois or Vierzon towards Montrichard; take D764 towards Genillé-Loches. From Le Liege towards Genillé. Before Genillé turn right on D10 towards St Quentin sur Indrois. Mill on left.
Michelin Map No: 238-14

Entry no: 396   Map No: 7

Josette & Clive MIEVILLE
Le Moulin de la Roche
37460 Genillé
Indre-et-Loire
Tel: (0)2 47 59 56 58
Fax: (0)2 47 59 59 62
e-mail: clive.mieville@wanadoo.fr
Web: www.moulin-de-la-roche.com

Watermills make wonderful houses and your charming hosts have recently converted theirs, near the magnificent château of Montrésor, in stylish and simple good taste: beige carpets, attractive lined curtains, co-ordinated colour schemes. A plain wooden staircase leads up to the coconut-matted landing, good linen, good towels. The atmosphere is welcoming, very warm, with lots of original features... and quiet flows the water beneath the glass panel in the dining room. Madame is as educated as she is travelled and her family has been in the château for 200 years – there is a sense of timeless peace here, off the beaten track.

Rooms: 1 double, 1 twin, 2 triples, all with bath or shower & wc.

Price: 290-340 Frs for two; under 4s free.

Meals: Choice within 5km.

Closed: Never.

Sue's welcome has been much praised, as has Andrew's cooking, the setting, the décor, the fun. Their deliciously watery home, a carefully restored mill on an island, is all ups and downs, nooks and crannies, big rooms and small, character and variety with skilful use of Sue's stencils and sponging. Plus a restful shady garden, private waterside spot and the added temptation of about 1,000 paperbacks – and a brilliant blue and yellow macaw! Check the latest news as there's the possibility of a swimming pool for summer 2001. *Not really suitable for young children.*

Rooms: 3 doubles, 1 triple, 2 twins, all with bath or shower & wc.

Price: 300-380 Frs for two.

Meals: 160 Frs, including aperitif, wine & coffee.

Closed: December & January.

From Loches D760 to Montrésor. In village, left direction Chemillé. Mill is on left; signposted.
Michelin Map No: 238-14

Entry no: 397　　　　　　Map No: 7

Sophie & Alain WILLEMS de
LADERSOUS
Le Moulin de Montrésor
37460 Montrésor
Indre-et-Loire
Tel: (0)2 47 92 68 20
Fax: (0)2 47 92 74 61
Web: www.sawdays.co.uk

From Loches, N143 direction Châteauroux; pass Perusson then left at sign to St Jean-St Germain; house is last over the bridge on the left.
Michelin Map No: 238-14

Entry no: 398　　　　　　Map No: 7

Andrew PAGE & Sue HUTTON
Le Moulin
St Jean St Germain
37600 Loches, Indre-et-Loire
Tel: (0)2 47 94 70 12
Fax: (0)2 47 94 77 98
e-mail: millstjean@aol.com
Web: www.sawdays.co.uk

An easygoing, happy family – children, dogs, cats – that will sweep you inside with real warmth. Malvina is charming and very creative – though always busy, she always has time for her guests. Bedrooms, in the converted stables, have low beams, sloping ceilings, lots of light. The floors are parquet, the walls creamy-limed, the beams scrubbed, the furniture attractively simple, and there is a small kitchen for you. In the sitting/dining room, more beams, a fireplace and a heavy oak table invite relaxation. There is a fenced-in pool behind the barn and a nine hole 'ecological' (deep-rooting grass needing minimum watering) golf course is planned.

Rooms: 2 twins, 2 triples (can be connecting), all with shower & wc.

Price: 370-480 Frs for two.

Meals: 150 Frs, including wine & coffee, by arrangement.

Closed: Never.

Gîte space for 14 people.

From Loches N143 S towards Châteauroux. After Perrusson right onto D41 to Verneuil (approx. 2km). Left in village; signposted. Michelin Map No: 238-26

Entry no: 399   Map No: 7

Malvina & Olivier MASSELOT
La Capitainerie
37600 Verneuil sur Indre
Indre-et-Loire
Tel: (0)2 47 94 88 15
Fax: (0)2 47 94 70 75
e-mail: captain@creaweb.fr
Web: www.sawdays.co.uk

The Dallais Restaurant opposite has a Michelin star! People come to this tiny village and stay in this unassuming B&B, just for that special dinner (there's a more modest eating house in the village too). But there is more: Natacha, a busy, bubbly, intelligent young mother, is sweetly attentive; her quiet, affable husband is grounded here in his family goat-cheese business (almost 200 goats 3km away – guests can visit). Le Grand Pressigny, 10km away, has a superb museum of prehistory. The fairly basic bedrooms (French cheap 'n' cheerful) are in a separate wing with a good dayroom and real disabled facilities in one room.

Rooms: 4 doubles, each with shower & wc.

Price: 250 Frs for two.

Meals: Two restaurants in village, one starred, one simple 'family'.

Closed: Never.

From Châtellerault D725 through La Roche Posay & Preuilly sur Claise. 1km after Preuilly left on D50/D41 to Le Petit Pressigny. House in centre opp. Restaurant Dallais. Michelin Map No: 232-48

Entry no: 400   Map No: 7

Bernard & Natacha LIMOUZIN
La Pressignoise
37350 Le Petit Pressigny
Indre-et-Loire
Tel: (0)2 47 91 06 06
e-mail: natacha.limouzin@wanadoo.fr

Unusual, historic Richelieu, France's first grid-based new town built from scratch in the 1600s, was almighty Cardinal Richelieu's creation. The Lawrences have set up their English-language and music schools in a long 17th-century townhouse with studios on the street side and a beamed entrance through to a sunny courtyard garden (hibiscus and banana trees) and the main house. The big rooms are softly decorated, beds are canopied with attractive fabrics chosen with flair and imagination, and have good lighting. Tim and Marion are welcoming, considerate hosts and provide bountiful breakfasts.

Rooms: 2 doubles, 1 quadruple, all with bath or shower & wc.

Price: 290-370 Frs for two.

Meals: Wide choice within 200m; picnic and barbecue possible.

Closed: Never.

A10 motorway, Richelieu exit. After entering Richelieu, take 2nd left. House 300m down on right.
Michelin Map No: 232-46

Entry no: 401   Map No: 7

Marion & Tim LAWRENCE
L'Escale
30 rue de la Galère
37120 Richelieu
Indre-et-Loire
Tel: (0)2 47 58 25 55

GREETINGS & FORMS OF ADDRESS

We drop far more easily into first-name terms than the French. This reluctance on their part is not a sign of coldness, it's simply an Old National Habit, to be respected, we feel, like any other tribal ritual. So it's advisable to wait for the signal from them as to when you have achieved more intimate status.

The French do not say 'Bonjour Monsieur Dupont' or 'Bonjour Madame Jones' – this is considered rather familiar. They just say 'Bonjour Monsieur' or 'Bonjour Madame' – which makes it easy to be lazy about remembering people's names.

This picture-book chateau in a large park is an old family seat with period pieces, family portraits and trees – your hosts have provided more twigs for those trees in the form of 11 grandchildren. Madame has a sprightly elegance and will greet you like a long-lost friend in intelligent if slightly impeded French; Monsieur is a genial, English-speaking field sportsman. Rooms and washing arrangements are also rather eccentric but have a timeless charm – showers in cupboards, a somewhat quirky use of antiques. Your hosts will gladly discuss visits to Loire châteaux, Futuroscope and other fascinations.

Rooms: 1 triple, 1 double, each with shower; 1 single with basin; 1 bathroom, 2 wcs for all (1 on another floor).

Price: 240 Frs for two.

Meals: 100 Frs, including wine & coffee.

Closed: Never.

From Loudun, D759 direction Thouars. After 7km, left on D19 to Arçay, 1km along; château on right behind big gates as you enter village (no signs). Michelin Map No: 232-45

Entry no: 402   Map No: 7

Hilaire & Sabine LEROUX de LENS
Château du Puy d'Arçay
86200 Arçay
Vienne
Tel: (0)5 49 98 29 11

Poitou-Atlantic

That golden liquid is distilled near ancient wetlands where flat-bottoms already carried marksmen and waterfowl rose when the Catholic Royalists put their hearts into bitter battles against the Revolution.

Come and experience the daily life of farmers in a small hilltop village with a fine 12th-century church. After 20-odd years of B&B, your hosts still enjoy their guests enormously. He, a jovial retired farmer (their son now runs the farm), knows his local lore; she smiles quietly and gets on with her cooking in the big homely kitchen – they are the salt of the earth. Up the superb, old, solid oak staircase, bedrooms are clean and bright with good beds, curtained-off showers and separate loos. A warm and generous welcome is guaranteed plus masses of things to do and see.

Rooms: 3 doubles, 1 with extra bed for child, each with shower & wc.

Price: 220 Frs for two.

Meals: 80 Frs, including wine & coffee.

Closed: Never.

From Loudon, follow signs for Thouars then take D60 towards Moncontour. At Mouterre Silly, find the church; house is 50m along towards Silly, signposted 'Chambres d'Hôtes'.
Michelin Map No: 232-45

Entry no: **403**   Map No: 7

Agnès & Henri BRÉMAUD
Le Bourg
86200 Mouterre Silly
Vienne
Tel: (0)5 49 98 09 72
Fax: (0)5 49 98 09 72
Web: www.sawdays.co.uk

It really is a lovely old farmhouse, built in the late 15th century, proudly set at the end of its drive. The Picards, five generations of whom have lived here, are quiet, welcoming, if busy, cereal farmers who will treat you as part of the family. Overlooking the chestnut-treed garden are the generous bedrooms where good furnishings include handsome wardrobes and firm new mattresses. Sunlight streams into the huge sitting room with its well-matched beams, white walls and terracotta-tiled floor. Breakfast is in the yellow dining room or on the leafy terrace and there are now simple cooking facilities for guests.

Rooms: 2 doubles, 1 twin, each with shower & wc.

Price: 280 Frs for two; children 60 Frs.

Meals: In village or Richelieu; self-catering possible.

Closed: Never.

Gîte space for 6 people.

From Richelieu, D7 direction Loudun. After 4km, right onto a drive with lime trees on both sides.
Michelin Map No: 232-46

Entry no: **404**   Map No: 7

Jean & Marie-Christine PICARD
Le Bois Goulu
86200 Pouant
Vienne
Tel: (0)5 49 22 52 05

The fortified farmhouse is set in highly roamable parkland – both of which are recovering from the storms of last winter. Guestrooms, in the converted stables, are small, a little faded and furnished with high old beds and family pieces. The conversion was almost all Pierre-Claude's own work. He regales guests with family history over candlelit dinners in the vast family kitchen while Chantal cooks to her own excellent recipes. Come for the food and entertainment – no matter if you roll from the shower straight into bed. Superb value and well-placed for ancient Fontevraud and modern Futuroscope.

Rooms: 3 doubles, 1 triple, 1 quadruple, all with shower & wc.

Price: 205 Frs for two.

Meals: 115 Frs, including wine & coffee. Also good, simple restaurant in village.

Closed: Never.

Gîte space for 10 people.

From Saumur, D947 to Candes, then D147 to Loudun. There, D14 to Monts sur Guesnes, left at post office; signed. Michelin Map No: 232-46

Entry no: 405   Map No: 7

Pierre-Claude & Chantal
FOUQUENET
Domaine de Bourg-Ville
86420 Monts sur Guesnes, Vienne
Tel: (0)5 49 22 81 58
Fax: (0)5 49 22 89 89
e-mail: pierre-claude@wanadoo.fr
Web: www.bourgville.com

You will be mollycoddled by these delightful people. One bedroom (full wheelchair access) is in a converted woodshed, with beams, pretty curtains, blue and yellow tiled floor and view over the large, rambling garden with its frog pond (hence *Grenouillère*). Two rooms are upstairs in a separate house across the courtyard where Madame's mother, a charming lady, lives. Pleasant, comfortable rooms, and the buildings are most attractive. Meals can be served on the shaded terrace and you can mess about in the small rowing boat.

Rooms: 2 triples, 3 doubles, each with bath or shower & wc.

Price: 220-290 Frs for two.

Meals: 100 Frs, including wine & coffee, by arrangement.

Closed: Never.

From Tours N10 S towards Châtellerault for 55km. In Dangé St Romain, right at 3rd traffic lights, cross river, keep left on little square. House 200m along on left; signposted. Michelin Map No: 232-47

Entry no: 406   Map No: 7

Annie & Noël BRAGUIER
La Grenouillère
17 rue de la Grenouillère
86220 Dangé St Romain
Vienne
Tel: (0)5 49 86 48 68
Fax: (0)5 49 86 46 56

This is a charming young couple. They have young children, are frank, sociable and very good company, spending time with guests after dinner when the family demands allow. They have converted a fine big barn into guest quarters – older than the main house, it has been very well done, muted colour schemes in the largish rooms harmonising with ethnic rugs. The superb cobbled terrace that runs the full length of the building invites you to sit on balmy even'ngs gazing across the wide landscaf e, listening to the music of the wind in the poplars. With a nature reserve on the doorstep this is a little-known corner waiting to be discovered.

Rooms: 2 triples, 2 doubles, all with bath & wc.

Price: 280-300 Frs for two.

Meals: 95 Frs, including wine.

Closed: Never.

Gîte space for 15 people.

From Châtellerault D749 to Vouneuil sur Vienne. Left in church square & follow Chambres d'Hôtes signs. Last house on right in small hamlet of Chabonne.
Michelin Map No: 232-47

Entry no: 407   Map No: 7

Florence & Antoine PENOT
Chabonne
86210 Vouneuil sur Vienne
Vienne
Tel: (0)5 49 85 28 25
Fax: (0)5 49 85 22 75
Web: www.sawdays.co.uk

So close to the lovely, lively old city of Poitiers and even closer to the high-tech Futuroscope, yet only the ping-pong of the little white ball or the splish-splosh of swimmers disturbs the hush of the tiny village. Madame, vivacious and dynamic, is delighted to welcome you to sleep in her simple, pretty rooms in the converted outbuilding, and to breakfast so copiously in courtyard or dining room that children are given doggy bags. The two rooms sharing cooking facilities have good, traditional French furnishings. The duplex, with its two smallish rooms, is more 'rustic' with an intriguing window layout. All are excellent value.

Rooms: 1 double, 1 triple, 1 duplex for 4/5, all with bath or shower & wc.

Price: 270-290 Frs for two.

Meals: Choice 3km; self-catering, excluding duplex.

Closed: Never.

Gîte space for 9 people.

From A10 exit 28 onto D18 W direction Avanton for about 2km. Signposted in hamlet of Martigny.
Michelin Map No: 232-46

Entry no: 408   Map No: 7

Annie & Didier ARRONDEAU
La Ferme du Château de Martigny
86170 Avanton
Vienne
Tel: (0)5 49 51 04 57
Fax: (0)5 49 51 04 57
e-mail: annie.arrondeau@libertysurf.fr
Web: www.sawdays.co.uk

The château, begun in the 1400s, 'finished' in the 1700s, has a properly aged face. From the dramatic dark-panelled, orange-walled hall up the superbly bannistered staircase, through a great carved screen, you reach the *salon* gallery that runs majestically the length of the house. Here you may sit, read, write, dream of benevolent ghosts. Off the gallery, the bedrooms are loaded with personality. Madame's hand-painted tiles adorn a shower, her laughter accompanies your breakfast. Monsieur tends his trees and knows all there is to do in the area. A great couple in a genuine family château.

Rooms: 1 suite, 2 twins, all with bath or shower & wc. Extra children's room.

Price: 400-450 Frs for two.

Meals: Auberge nearby; choice 10km.

Closed: Never.

Gîte space for 4 people.

From A10 Futuroscope exit take D62 to *Quatre Vents r'bout, D757 to Vendeuvre; left on D15 to Chéneché & Thurageau. Labarom 800m on right after leaving Chéneché.*
Michelin Map No: 232-46

Entry no: 409 Map No: 7

Eric & Henriette LE GALLAIS
Château de Labarom
86380 Chéneché
Vienne
Tel: (0)5 49 51 24 22/
       (0)6 83 57 68 14
Fax: (0)5 49 51 47 38
e-mail: chateau.de.labarom@wanadoo.fr

An utterly delightful couple who just cannot do enough for you. Monsieur, who once resuscitated cars for a living, now takes much more pleasure in reviving tired travellers. Their house is on the old ramparts and the pretty garden looks directly out over the boulevard below, where you would expect there to be a moat (quiet enough at night). The two rooms are neat, with good beds and old armoires. One has surprising big-flower wallpaper, the smaller is plain blue; both have space and the shower room has been prettily retiled. Breakfast in high-backed chairs at the long table in the converted stables beneath the old hay rack.

Rooms: 2 twins, each with shower or bath & wc.

Price: 230 Frs for two.

Meals: Restaurants in village.

Closed: Never.

From Châtellerault D725 towards *Parthenay for 30km. In Mirebeau, left immed. after traffic lights next to Gendarmerie; No 19 about 50m on right.*
Michelin Map No: 232-46

Entry no: 410 Map No: 7

Jacques & Annette JEANNIN
19 rue Jacquard
86110 Mirebeau
Vienne
Tel: (0)5 49 50 54 06
Fax: (0)5 49 50 54 06

Vivaldi would have delighted in this fine 18th-century coaching inn, attractively converted by Monsieur Flambeau and his vivacious English wife. The rooms are named after the seasons, *Summer* has a brass four-poster, *Winter* a white canopied bed, *Four Seasons* looks almost English with its old-style pine furniture and pretty children's bed/playroom leading to the peach-pink, Laura Ashley-draped double. All bathrooms are beautifully tiled to match the bedrooms. On the main square of a quiet village, it has a charming courtyard and a large garden planted with mature trees – an oasis of peace and greenery. *Baby-sitting available.*

Rooms: 1 suite for 4, 1 quadruple, 3 doubles, each with bath or shower & wc.

Price: 260 Frs for two.

Meals: 115 Frs, including wine & coffee.

Closed: Mid-November-February.

From Poitiers N149 W towards Nantes for 14km. At Vouillé left on D62 to Latillé. House is the largest in main village square. (Poitiers-Latillé 24km.) Michelin Map No: 233-7

Entry no: 411   Map No: 7

Yvonne FLAMBEAU
La Demeure de Latillé
1 place Robert Gerbier
86190 Latillé, Vienne
Tel: (0)5 49 51 54 74
Fax: (0)5 49 51 56 32
e-mail: latille@chez.com
Web: www.chez.com/latille

Friends and family gather round the old table in the big flagstoned kitchen of this crag-perched château to chat over the jam-making. In the sunny breakfast room hunting trophies and family portraits preside – including a mob-capped great-grandmother. The comfortable bedrooms are freshly-decorated and have old family furniture, every object telling a tale. 15th-century castles weren't designed for en suite toilets, but chamber pots are provided in case you can't face the stairs! Your charming un-snobbishly aristocratic hosts will regale you with stories of monks and brigands and are hugely knowledgeable about local Romanesque art.

Rooms: 1 double/twin, 1 double, 1 suite, each with shower or bath & wc.

Price: 350 Frs for two; reduction for 3 nights or more.

Meals: Restaurants 3km.

Closed: Never.

Gîte space for 4 people.

From A10 at Poitiers Nord, N149 direction Nantes for 12km. Turning for Masseuil is left at bottom of hill. Michelin Map No: 233-8

Entry no: 412   Map No: 7

Alain & Claude GAIL
Château de Masseuil
86190 Quinçay
Vienne
Tel: (0)5 49 60 42 15
Fax: (0)5 49 60 70 15
Web: www.sawdays.co.uk

Sophisticated, simple luxury is the keynote of this ravishing 17th-century château where each bedroom is named after the marble used in its bathroom. Michel, a retired lawyer, has not lost his professional gift of the gab and Monique is an inspired interior designer. You may eat locally-grown and often home-reared food (foie gras) by candlelight, sleep in a four-poster under a magnificent beamed ceiling and breakfast hugely next morning in the garden; this is the perfect spot for a honeymoon, first or second or – who says you can't have a honeymoon every year?

Rooms: 2 doubles, 1 twin, each with bath & wc.

Price: 520-720 Frs for two.

Meals: 150 Frs, including wine.

Closed: Never.

From Poitiers N147 towards Limoges; first left towards Savigny l'Évescault then first right on D89 for 5km. First right on entering village.
Michelin Map No: 233-9

Entry no: 413   Map No: 7

Monique & Michel TABAU
Château de la Touche
86800 Savigny l'Évescault
Vienne
Tel: (0)5 49 01 10 38
Fax: (0)5 49 56 47 82
e-mail: mtabau@net-up.com
Web: www.sawdays.co.uk

The guest quarters, in the generous château outbuildings, are decorated with a wonderful flair for fabrics and colours – mats and tablecloth match crockery, bathrooms match bedrooms. It's smart yet utterly welcoming, as befits a converted bakery. The largest room, finely renovated with exposed beams, stones and thick white curtains, holds the old bread oven. Your hosts are well-travelled, sociable people who will happily chat (Monsieur in perfect English) in the pleasant sitting area about all the things in the cultural treasure-chest that is the Poitou.

Rooms: 2 rooms for 3/4, 2 doubles, 2 twins, all with bath, shower & wc.

Price: 350-430 Frs for two.

Meals: Restaurants 2-8km; self-catering possible.

Closed: Never.

From A10 exit 29, take Rocade Est (ring road) towards Limoges & Châteauroux for 5km, exit left on D3 towards Montamisé for 3km, then right on D18 for 2.5km. Château on right.
Michelin Map No: 233-8

Entry no: 414   Map No: 7

Daniel & Agnès VAUCAMP
Château de Vaumoret
Rue du Breuil Mingot
86000 Poitiers
Vienne
Tel: (0)5 49 61 32 11
Fax: (0)5 49 01 04 54

It is SO French, this former orangery in the fine château park – not stilted, just natural. The stone-flagged *salon* has a fine jumble of 10 French chairs, bits of ancient furniture, pictures, ornaments and lamps. The dining room has traditional elegance. Every object tells a story, there are statues here and there, indoors and out; bedrooms are large, bursting with character; bathrooms too. The family is lively and fun with many interests: Monsieur's are history and his family, Madame's are art and life – they combine unselfconscious class with flashes of southern non-conformism. And this is a dog-friendly house.

Rooms: 2 doubles, 1 twin, 1 suite, all with bathrooms (1 on separate floor).

Price: 400 Frs for two; reduction for children.

Meals: 60 Frs, including wine & coffee.

Closed: Never.

From A10, Poitiers Nord exit, N10 direction Limoges. After 7km, left to Bignoux; follow signs to Bois Dousset. Michelin Map No: 233-9

Entry no: **415**   Map No: **7**

Vicomte & Vicomtesse Hilaire de
VILLOUTREYS de BRIGNAC
Logis du Château du Bois Dousset
86800 Lavoux
Vienne
Tel: (0)5 49 44 20 26
Fax: (0)5 49 44 20 26
Web: www.sawdays.co.uk

This kind, hospitable, interesting couple live in the converted château stables and the whole estate is still shared by Madame's family (her brother does B&B in the orangery). She is discreetly warm; Monsieur is a true bibliophile and vastly erudite, with a living room full of books, pictures, treasures and a sense of history. The rooms are soft and comfortable with old furniture and pale walls. The one in the house has an old raised stone fireplace occupied, surprisingly, by a spinning wheel. The cottage has its own little garden and an amusing three-hole alcove for hens' nests. Natural elegance and traditional comfort combined.

Rooms: Main house: 1 twin with shower & wc. Cottage: 1 quadruple with small bath/shower & wc.

Price: 330-350 Frs for two.

Meals: 140 Frs, including wine & coffee.

Closed: Never.

From A10 Poitiers Nord, exit on N10 direction Limoges for 7km. Left to Bignoux & follow signs to Bois Dousset/Les Godiers. Michelin Map No: 233-9

Entry no: **416**   Map No: **7**

M & Mme Philippe RABANY
Les Godiers
86800 Lavoux
Vienne
Tel: (0)5 49 61 05 18
Fax: (0)5 49 61 05 18

A bee farm! The humble bee reigns royal here where several honeys and other bee products are made – the small shop is a hive of activity. Vivacious Charline welcomes you with a genuine smile and, while Jacky actually does the bee-tending, is excellent at explaining (in French) the ancient complicity between man and insect, over breakfast in the separate guest building. Two of the bedrooms are in the converted pigsty; downstairs has ivy-framed windows, upstairs has big skylights, colourful décor and plenty of space. The third room is behind the main house – smallish and cosy with its own tiny garden. Great for children too.

Rooms: 2 doubles, 1 twin, each with bath or shower & wc.

Price: 240 Frs for two.

Meals: Restaurant in St Savin. Barbecue available.

Closed: Mid-October-mid-February.

The GR48 footpath goes past the house – this is a great place for walkers. Your delightful hosts, much involved in local life, are a friendly family with three children. Deby's brother (the sheep farmer) and parents (antique-dealers) also live on the estate. Guests are in the main family house which is comfortable and attractive, with interesting and original antiques, prints and good fabrics in the bedrooms. The sitting room is cosy, the dining room elegant. A wonderful place for nature lovers. One reader simply said "Outstanding".

Rooms: 2 doubles, 2 twins, all with bath or shower & wc.

Price: 420 Frs for two.

Meals: 95 Frs, including wine & coffee.

Closed: Never.

Gîte space for 8 people.

From Chauvigny, N151 direction St Savin. 2km before St Savin, left to Siouvre; signposted.
Michelin Map No: 233-10

Entry no: 417   Map No: 7

Charline & Jacky BARBARIN
Siouvre
36310 St Savin
Vienne
Tel: (0)5 49 48 10 19
Fax: (0)5 49 48 46 89
e-mail: charline.barbarin@wanadoo.fr
Web: perso.wanadoo.fr/hebergementmiel/

From Chauvigny, D54 to Montmorillon then D727 direction La Trimouille. House is 10km on right .
Michelin Map No: 233-11

Entry no: 418   Map No: 7

Richard & Deby EARLS
La Boulinière
Journet
86290 La Trimouille, Vienne
Tel: (0)5 49 91 55 88
Fax: (0)5 49 91 72 82
e-mail: jr-earls@interpc.fr
Web: www.interpc.fr/jr-earls/bbweb.htm

These are true farming folk (their son now 'does' the goats) with their roots in village life: they sing in the choir, act with the drama group, Madame shows her embroidery, Monsieur has been elected Mayor. And they love sharing their simple, stylish house with intelligent, cultured, like-minded guests. The suite is in the converted coach house, its kitchen in the old bread oven. All rooms, with their good fabrics and Madame's exquisite samplers, blend harmoniously with the garden and woodlands (golden orioles, hoopoes, wild orchids...). You may visit the goats, watch cheese being made, fish in their big lake.

Rooms: 2 doubles, 1 suite for 4/5 with kitchen/diner, each with bath or shower & wc. Extra room for children.

Price: 280 Frs for two.

Meals: 100 Frs, including wine. Self-catering in annexe.

Closed: Never.

From Poitiers N147 SE to Lussac les Châteaux then D727 E for 21km. Left on D121 to Journet. In village, N towards Haims; house 1km on left. Michelin Map No: 233-10

Entry no: 419   Map No: 7

Jacques & Chantal COCHIN
Le Haut Peu
86290 Journet
Vienne
Tel: (0)5 49 91 62 02
Fax: (0)5 49 91 59 71

A genial twinkly man, Jean-Louis used to farm but now confines himself to vegetables and chickens, and a role in numerous local events, while Genevieve is a keen artist. Their home is a traditional Poitevin farmhouse, rendered a sunny shade of orange, with a corridor running the width of the house and rooms opening off either side. You come to it from the back, up a long tree-lined drive, so will be surprised to find it is in fact in the middle of the village. Rooms are freshly decorated, furniture is suitably old: the canopy over one bed was made for Madame's great-grandmother's wedding.

Rooms: 1 twin with shower & separate wc; 1 quadruple with shower & wc.

Price: 240-250 Frs for two.

Meals: 65-85 Frs, including wine.

Closed: Never.

Exit A10 at Poitier Sud, dir. Angouleme on N10 to Vivonne, and 2nd exit Champagne St Hilaire Sommières du Clain. Turn right towards Civray. Champniers is 8km on the left. Follow Chambres d'Hotes signs. Michelin Map No: 233-19

Entry no: 420   Map No: 7

Genevieve & Jean-Louis FAZILLEAU
Le Bourg
86400 Champniers
Vienne
Tel: (0)5 49 87 19 04
Fax: (0)5 49 87 96 94
e-mail: jeanlouis.fazilleau@free.fr

Working the land has real meaning to the Salvaudons. They are educated, intelligent farmers – he energetic and down-to-earth, she gentle and smiling – committed to the natural way ("there's more to the Vienne than the Futuroscope"), who like swapping travellers' tales and sharing simple, lasting values. Their sheep farm lies in unspoilt, rolling, stream-run country where fishing competitions are held. All the farm produce is organic: don't miss the chance to try Madame's Limousin specialities – lamb, chicken cooked in honey, vegetable pies – round the family table.

The picture tells it all – moat, keep, drawbridge, dreams. Up two spiral stone flights is "the biggest bedroom in France" – solid granite windowsills, a giant fireplace, a canopied bed and the shower snug in the former *garde-robe* (water closet). Breakfast under the five-metre guardroom vault, your feet on the original 14th-century flagstones. The old stones are exposed, the furniture sober and the fires always laid, just like olden times. Indeed, the whole place is brilliantly authentic, the magnificent gardens glow from loving care and Pippa is eager and attentive – flowers, bubbly, fishing in the moat, all on the house!

Rooms: 1 triple, 1 double, each with shower and basin, but sharing wc.

Price: 190 Frs for two.

Meals: 80 Frs, including wine & coffee.

Closed: Never.

Gîte space for 6 people.

Rooms: 2 doubles, each with shower & wc.

Price: 650-750 Frs for two.

Meals: Restaurant 4km; choice 9km.

Closed: Never.

From Poitiers, D741 to Civray. There, D148 east and D34 to Availles. There, D100 direction Mauprévoir. After 3km, signed.
Michelin Map No: 233-20

From A10 exit 29 on N147 then N149 W to Parthenay. Round Parthenay northbound, continue on N149 towards Bressuire; 7km N of Parthenay, right at sign for château.
Michelin Map No: 232-44

Entry no: 421   Map No: 7

Entry no: 422   Map No: 7

Pierre & Line SALVAUDON
Les Ecots
86460 Availles Limousine
Vienne
Tel: (0)5 49 48 59 17
Fax: (0)5 49 48 59 17

Nicholas & Philippa FREELAND
Château de Tennessus
79350 Amailloux
Deux-Sèvres
Tel: (0)5 49 95 50 60
Fax: (0)5 49 95 50 62
e-mail: tennessus@csi.com
Web: www.tennessus.com

History and Nature meet here: this used to be a Protestant area, in the days of religious strife, and the nearby *Marais Poitevin*, a common hiding place for both sides, is worth a visit. Your hosts make a delightful partnership – she teaches, he cooks – and pops in and out of the kitchen to chat while cooking dinner, so the atmosphere is very relaxed. Much of the food is home-produced. One room for four is in the main house, the others, in an attached building, have their own corner kitchens. Excellent value in an easy and attractive house in wooded grounds on the edge of the village.

Rooms: 2 suites for 4 & 1 triple, each with shower, bath & wc

Price: 250 Frs for two.

Meals: 90 Frs, including wine & coffee; self-catering possible.

Closed: Never.

From A10 exit 32 on D7 towards Mougon for 1km. Left on D5 towards La Mothe St Héray for 7km, right for Prailles. Sign on left on entering village; continue up & turn right to house. Michelin Map No: 233-6

Entry no: 423   Map No: 7

Michel & Marie-Claude DUVALLON
Le Colombier des Rivières
79370 Prailles
Deux-Sèvres
Tel: (0)5 49 32 84 43

The family snapped the house up after the Revolution, the only time it has changed hands since the 15th century. Come not for the rooms but for the idyllic setting. It is all slightly shambolic and aristocratically faded in a way that quite won us over: utterly 'family', they serve splendid dinners, enjoy the conversation around the table and may suggest a game of bridge as well. Children love the enormous park and the boat. Monsieur uses a limpid and charming French; Madame smokes *Gauloises* and speaks with a husky voice – a most likeable pair.

Rooms: 1 triple, 2 doubles, 1 twin, each with bath or shower & wc; 2 doubles sharing shower & wc.

Price: 400 Frs for two.

Meals: 125 Frs, including wine & coffee.

Closed: Never.

From A10 exit 'Poitiers Sud' on N10 towards Angoulême for 3km; right on N11 towards Niort for 14km. From Lusignan D950 to Melle then towards Brioux for 3km; right on D301 to St Romans. House in village, near church. Michelin Map No: 233-17

Entry no: 424   Map No: 11

François RABANY & Odile de NOÜEL
Le Logis
79500 Saint Romans lès Melle
Deux-Sèvres
Tel: (0)5 49 27 04 15
Fax: (0)5 49 29 18 37
Web: www.sawdays.co.uk

This riverside setting is idyllic, with its views out to the Sèvre Niortaise, and very quiet in the evenings when the trippers have gone. There's a small boat and Monsieur, who is most knowledgeable about the utterly fascinating *Marais* area, will escort guests on boat trips (at reasonable rates). Madame is justifiably proud of this pretty single-storey house where she was born and which has a charming old-world atmosphere, rooms crammed with a lifetime's collection of objects, solid repro furniture and is good value in a touristy area. Families welcome, preferably without toddlers (unfenced water).

Rooms: 1 double, 1 triple, each with shower & wc.

Price: 260-290 Frs for two.

Meals: Restaurants within walking distance.

Closed: Never.

From Coulon centre, D23 towards Irleau. At end of village, immediately left along bank of River Sèvre which is Rue Élise Lucas.
Michelin Map No: 233-5

Entry no: 425   Map No: 11

Ginette & Michel CHOLLET
68 rue Élise Lucas
79510 Coulon
Deux-Sèvres
Tel: (0)5 49 35 91 55/42 59
Web: www.sawdays.co.uk

Most aptly named: the Pikes have two sets of identical twin sons! It is a simple, old-fashioned, pleasantly-renovated 1900s farmhouse with a large garden where children play and adults barbecue; then climb the outside stairs to the two quiet, comfortable rooms that are much appreciated after days at the seaside. Your lively, welcoming hosts came from farming in England and are thoroughly integrated here. They enjoy having guests – Ian manages the farm while Janty helps with lambing and eggs (pheasant) – , will tell you what there is to be discovered in this area that they love and take you to see the sheep if you're interested.

Rooms: 1 double with bath, shower & wc; 1 twin with shower & wc.

Price: 240 Frs for two.

Meals: Good restaurant 3km.

Closed: October-April.

From La Roche sur Yon D948 NW 25km through Aizenay; at Bel Air hamlet left on D94 towards Commequiers for about 1km (signs to La Fraternité); turn left, house on right.
Michelin Map No: 232-40

Entry no: 426   Map No: 11

Janty & Ian PIKE
La Fraternité
Maché
85190 Aizenay
Vendée
Tel: (0)2 51 55 42 58
Fax: (0)2 51 60 16 01
Web: www.chez.com/lafraternite/

Traditional Gallic civilization and charm in Thomas Hardy look-alike country. Gaze over the rolling hills, hedgerows and placid-cow-grazed fields of this unspoilt and undeservedly ignored corner of France as you linger over a gastronomic breakfast on the terrace. Or, laze in the spotless, comfortable, harmoniously decorated, traditionally tiled and beamed rooms of this old Vendéenne farmhouse. Your hosts are cultured, hard-working, nature-respecting farmers, who care passionately about preserving the quality of life. And just down the road is the stupendous Château du Puy du Fou, with its not-to-be-missed summer spectacular.

Rooms: 1 twin, 1 triple, 1 suite for 4, each with shower & separate wc.

Price: 250-300 Frs for two.

Meals: Kitchen available, restaurant 5km.

Closed: Never.

From Les Herbiers take D755 towards Pouzauges; left onto D11 towards Le Puy du Fou. First left off this road. Signed 'Garderie pour Chiens'. Michelin Map No: 232-42

Entry no: 427   Map No: 11

Jeanine & Bernard RETAILLEAU
La Mtairie du Bourg
85500 Les Herbiers
Vendée
Tel: (0)2 51 67 23 97

A fisherman's paradise, this charming traditional house beside the River Vendée on the edge of the village is owned by the delightful and welcoming Riberts. They completely renovated it six years ago and the big, light, airy rooms with their stripped doors and traditional furniture are full of fresh flowers from the secluded walled garden. You have the freedom of *salon* and library and eat excellent breakfast (cooked if requested) and dinner in the family room or in a larger dining room, depending how many you are. Lots to do in the area; they have plans for canoes on the river. Remarkable people, remarkable value.

Rooms: 5 triples, all with bath or shower & wc.

Price: 280 Frs for two.

Meals: 100 Frs, including wine & coffee.

Closed: 16 November-31 January.

From Fontenay le Comte, D938ter for 13km then right on D25. Le Gué de Velluire is 4.5km on. At end of village, turn left; beside river. Michelin Map No: 233-4

Entry no: 428   Map No: 11

Christiane & Michel RIBERT
Le Logis
5 rue de la Rivière
85770 Le Gué de Velluire
Vendée
Tel: (0)2 51 52 59 10
Fax: (0)2 51 52 57 21

At the very end of the lane, just yards from the river, Massigny is a secret corner of marshy Vendée. The rooms are as handsome as you'll find: Jean-Claude used to teach cabinet-making and his delight in wood is evident. Add beds made for deep sleep, unfussy fabrics, papers and painted beams for aesthetic satisfaction, a guest sitting room with two carved armoires and a lovely copper tub for plants, and all you need is to sit a while with these friendly, open people and share their wide-ranging conversation. Remarkable value in a memorable and unsung spot.

Rooms: 2 doubles, each with shower & wc.

Price: 280 Frs for two.

Meals: Choice 3-10 km.

Closed: Never.

A dream... a fine house with its own boat to drift you deep into the *Marais*, or *Venise Verte* (as they call it here – oddly) and its own fishing spot. The old *maison de maître*, in the village, has a glorious walled garden with over 70 varieties of iris. Monsieur is a doctor; Liliane, bright and enthusiastic, is a local guide. The bedrooms: parquet floors, photos of the *Marais*, regional furniture, in one a four-poster with views of the water. Downstairs: books, a chess table, more parquet. Rabelais lived in the Abbey, a stone's throw away. All rather poetic and very special.

Rooms: 3 doubles, 1 triple, 1 twin, all with bath or shower & wc.

Price: 350-380 Frs for two.

Meals: In village.

Closed: Never.

From A83 exit at Fontenay le Comte on D938ter and go SW towards La Rochelle for 6km, then right at small sign for Massigny.
Michelin Map No: 233-4

Entry no: 429   Map No: 11

Marie-Françoise & Jean-Claude
NEAU
Massigny
85770 Velluire
Vendée
Tel: (0)2 51 52 30 32
Fax: (0)2 51 52 30 32
Web: www.sawdays.co.uk

From Fontenay le Comte N148 towards Niort for 9km then right on D15 to Maillezais. There, follow signs for L'Abbaye. House on left, signposted.
Michelin Map No: 233-4

Entry no: 430   Map No: 11

Mme Liliane BONNET
69 rue de l'Abbaye
85420 Maillezais
Vendée
Tel: (0)2 51 87 23 00
Fax: (0)2 51 00 72 44

A solidly reliable address, this 18th-century village house is just yards from the beautiful cloisters of the Royal Abbey where Eleanor of Aquitaine was born and her mother buried. The rooms are well converted, simply and with subdued rustic good taste (one is very big), and look over the walled garden. The dining room is in the old stable block and there is a small sitting room in the former wash-house where Christine will make up a fire if it's cold. She and her parents, who live in the main house, are most welcoming.

Rooms: 2 triples, 1 double, 1 twin, each with shower & wc.

Price: 270-290 Frs for two.

Meals: Available locally.

Closed: November-March.

An interesting young couple and great Anglophiles. Madame knows about nutrition and serves generous breakfasts with home-made organic jams, cheeses, yoghurts and cereals, all on local earthenware. Monsieur teaches engineering in nearby La Rochelle, where they'll point you towards the lesser-known things to see. The old farmhouse, lovingly restored and decorated by themselves, is simple, pristine, with big, comfortable rooms overlooking a pretty garden where you're welcome to picnic (there is a useful guest kitchen too). The Prous love children of any age – there's some baby kit, table tennis and country peace Good value. *No pets in rooms.*

Rooms: 1 family room for 4 or 1 double, with bath, shower & wc; 1 triple with shower & wc.

Price: 270-310 Frs for two.

Meals: Occasionally by arrangement; 120 Frs, including wine. Restaurants within 10 minutes drive.

Closed: Never.

From Niort N148 NW towards Fontenay le Comte for 20km. After Oulmes right to Nieul sur l'Autize; follow signs to Abbey; house just before it on left.
Michelin Map No: 233-5

From La Rochelle N11 E for 11km; north on D112 to Longèves; in village, right at 'Alimentation', first left, past Mairie; house 700m on left.
Michelin Map No: 233-4

Entry no: **431**   Map No: 11

Entry no: **432**   Map No: 11

Christine CHASTAIN-POUPIN
Le Rosier Sauvage
1 rue de l'Abbaye
85240 Nieul sur l'Autize
Vendée
Tel: (0)2 51 52 49 39
Fax: (0)2 51 52 49 46

Marie-Christine PROU
43 rue du Marais
17230 Longèves
Charente-Maritime
Tel: (0)5 46 37 11 15
e-mail: prou@eigsi.fr
Web: www.sawdays.co.uk

They are a lively young family who all enjoy having guests; parents cook together (lots of organic ingredients) while three children entertain young visitors – an excellent team. Theirs is a lovingly-restored old house where old and modern each have their place. Antique armoires and big new beds, a collection of old scales and full disabled facilities (in the slightly more modern-décor cottage), lots of treasures and a tennis court. The air is full of warm smiles, harmony breathes from the old walls and woodwork. They have thought of everything to make you comfortable and families are positively welcome.

Rooms: 1 triple, 1 suite for 6, 1 cottage for 5, each with bath or shower & wc.

Price: 350 Frs for two.

Meals: 120 Frs, including wine & coffee.

Closed: Never.

From Surgères Gendarmerie & fire station, take D115 NW towards Marans & Puyravault & follow signs for 5km.
Michelin Map No: 233-3

Entry no: **433**   Map No: 11

Brigitte & Patrick FRANÇOIS
Le Clos de la Garenne
9 rue de la Garenne
17700 Puyravault, Charente-Maritime
Tel: (0)5 46 35 47 71
Fax: (0)5 46 35 47 91
E-mail: BPAML.francois@wanadoo.fr
Web: perso.wanadoo.fr/la-garenne/

This old farmhouse – built in 1600, renovated in 1720 – stands in a garden of mature trees that goes right down to the River Boutonne for peaceful walks and shallow swimming. Guests have a big dayroom with comfortable chairs, games and a full-size French billiards table. The clean, fresh bedrooms have good beds and large armoires. Indeed, the whole place has a totally French country feel to it: you might be staying with your favourite granny. There are good bike trails to spin off on and fabulous Romanesque churches to visit in the area.

Rooms: 1 double/twin with shower & wc; 1 suite for 4 with bath & wc.

Price: 270 Frs for two.

Meals: 95 Frs, including aperitif, wine & coffee.

Closed: Never.

From the Gendarmerie in St Jean d'Angély, D127 direction Dampierre Antezant. In Antezant, first right.
Michelin Map No: 233-16

Entry no: **434**   Map No: 11

Pierre & Marie-Claude FALLELOUR
Les Moulins
17400 Antezant
Charente-Maritime
Tel: (0)5 46 59 94 52
Fax: (0)5 46 59 94 52
Web: www.sawdays.co.uk

We know why people come back again and again: the Deschamps just love doing B&B and it shows. Madame delights in cooking delicious meals for her guests and Monsieur enjoys talking English. They have enlarged their dining room to take a bigger table and their generosity is legendary (they once delayed a friend's party to dine with late-arriving guests), so what matter a slightly unkempt façade? Huge wardrobes dominate the bright-papered bedrooms – beds and bedding are traditional French, and the recently re-decorated double has three lovely windows.

Rooms: 1 double, 2 suites, all with bath or shower & wc.

Price: 280 Frs for two; suite 380 Frs for four.

Meals: 95 Frs, including wine & coffee.

Closed: November-15 April.

From St Jean d'Angély, D939 direction Matha. About 3km after crossroads to Varaize, D229 towards Aumagne. House 0.8km on left. Michelin Map No: 233-17

Entry no: 435   Map No: 11

Eliane & Maurice DESCHAMPS
La Clé des Champs
17770 Aumagne
Charente-Maritime
Tel: (0)5 46 58 23 80
Fax: (0)5 46 58 23 91
Web: www.sawdays.co.uk

This professional couple left Paris for the country – and what country it is! With nearby Romanesque delights, Cognac at 19km, the beaches of Ile de Ré and Ile d'Oléron not too far, and even the well-known 'free-range' zoo of La Palmyre, you find culture and beauty as well as a warm, relaxing place to stay. The creamy, indigenous stone of the old farmhouse – part 17th, part 19th-century – is a perfect foil for flowers everywhere. Madame, an enthusiastic gardener, grows organic veg; there are hand-painted touches plus a kitchen designed so she can cook and entertain guests at the same time.

Rooms: 2 doubles, each with bath or shower & wc, 1 twin to make family 'suite' with double.

Price: 260-280 Frs for two.

Meals: 110 Frs, including aperitif, wine & coffee.

Closed: Never.

From A10 exit 34 dir. St Jean d'Angély. E on D939 to Matha (20km). In Matha, right dir. Thors. Entering Thors turn left; Le Goulet on right. Michelin Map No: 233-17

Entry no: 436   Map No: 11

Frédérique THILL-TOUSSAINT
Le Clos du Plantis
1 rue du Pont, Le Goulet
17160 Sonnac, Charente-Maritime
Tel: (0)5 46 25 07 91/
          (0)6 81 99 07 98
Fax: (0)5 46 25 07 91
e-mail: auplantis@wanadoo.fr

Madame's *galettes* (biscuits) are famous in the area – enjoy them, and other specialities, in the warm and homely dining room where the television is blessedly hidden in a cupboard. The Forgets are a sweet, welcoming couple who have made great efforts with their French country furniture, pretty curtains and scattered treasures. The rooms are named after flowers in a genuine country family atmosphere. There are bikes for rent, swings to play on, wonderful cookery weekends. One guest found "food, drink and company all excellent".

Rooms: 2 doubles, 1 triple, 1 family room, each with bath or shower & wc.

Price: 215-255 Frs for two.

Meals: 90 Frs, including wine & coffee.

Closed: Never.

From Saintes, N150 direction Niort. After 6km, D129 direction Ecoyeux; signposted (red & white). Michelin Map No: 233-16

Entry no: **437**   Map No: 11

Henri & Marie-Andrée FORGET
Chez Quimand
17770 Ecoyeux
Charente-Maritime
Tel: (0)5 46 95 92 55
Fax: (0)5 46 95 92 55

A very English couple in a very French house. Jenny loves gardening and writing, John is building a boat to sail across the Atlantic in, together they have lovingly restored their *Charentais* farmhouse and they delight in having guests. The atmosphere is sociable and you are welcome to dine *en famille*. Or feel free to go your own way (separate guest entrance). The beautifully-landscaped garden, with its pretty windmill (let separately), has an English feel – and a croquet lawn – but the 'sense of place' remains unmistakably French. And pretty St Savinien is a painters' delight – this really is a lovely part of the country.

Rooms: 1 room for 2-4 with bath & wc.

Price: 260-300 Frs for two (depending on length of stay).

Meals: 90 Frs, including wine & coffee.

Closed: Christmas.

Gîte space for 2 people.

From bridge in St Savinien D114 along river, under railway bridge, left on D124 direction Bords. After 2km, 2nd left after Le Pontreau sign; house 200m on right. Michelin Map No: 233-16.

Entry no: **438**   Map No: 11

John & Jenny ELMES
Le Moulin de la Quine
17350 St Savinien
Charente-Maritime
Tel: (0)5 46 90 19 31
Fax: (0)5 46 90 28 37
e-mail: elmes@club-internet.fr

Your hosts speak no English but are gently welcoming to all nations. They moved south on retirement to enjoy the balmy climate here – guests respond to it as willingly as do all those flowers and... pumpkins. Country-style rooms have big pieces of furniture in smallish spaces, good mattresses and smallish towels. The area is flat – where else could those millions of oysters bed down for their short lives? – but lovely beaches are just 10 minutes away, there are forests for walking or bicycling, birdlife for hours of watching and fortified Brouage on the Ile d'Oléron to visit.

Rooms: 1 double with bath & wc; 1 double with shower & wc.

Price: 250-300 Frs for two.

Meals: Full choice in Marennes, 3km.

Closed: Never.

Gîte space for 5 people.

Take D123 direction Ile d'Oléron. At Marennes, right, towards Château de la Gateaudière then follow signs. Michelin Map No: 233-14

Entry no: 439   Map No: 11

Jean & Jacqueline FERCHAUD
11 rue des Lilas
La Ménardière
17320 Marennes
Charente-Maritime
Tel: (0)5 46 85 41 77
Web: www.sawdays.co.uk

Your hosts love their superb farmhouse and you can tell they have lavished care, money and time on it since they settled here after their years in Morocco. A delightful couple – Anne-Marie is a talented artist whose stylish painted furniture, patchwork, painstakingly-constructed rag rugs and co-ordinated colour schemes adorn the house; her husband is village Mayor. Good breakfasts and dinners are eaten with your hosts in the dining room or by the swimming pool. The gardens are landscaped, the terrace paved, flowers bloom and the bedrooms are big. *Quiet children over six welcome.*

Rooms: 4 doubles, each with bath & wc.

Price: 380 Frs for two.

Meals: 150 Frs, including wine & coffee.

Closed: Never.

From Saintes N150 west for 5km then fork right on N728 for 29km. Right on D118 to St Sornin. In village centre take Rue du Petit Moulin opposite church door. Michelin Map No: 233-15

Entry no: 440   Map No: 11

Anne-Marie PINEL-
PESCHARDIÈRE
La Caussolière, 10 rue du Petit Moulin
17600 St Sornin, Charente-Maritime
Tel: (0)5 46 85 44 62
Fax: (0)5 46 85 44 62
e-mail: caussoliere@wanadoo.fr
Web: www.caussoliere.com

You are clearly in a family home not a guesthouse here – the big antique wardrobes were Madame's mother's, the lacy covers on the lovely antique *lits bateau* (boat beds) are even older, the well-furnished, old-fashioned atmosphere is so comfortable. Madame keeps a good home-produced table; Monsieur organises outings to distilleries and quarries; both enjoy their guests, especially those who help catch escaping rabbits. They are kindly farmers, really worth getting to know – stay a few days, even if the plumbing is a touch noisy.

Rooms: 1 triple on ground floor, 1 suite for 2-4, both with shower & wc.

Price: 260-280 Frs for two.

Meals: 90 Frs, including wine.

Closed: Never.

Madame, a likeable, lively person, interested in people (that includes you), and Monsieur, a wizard on local tourist info, really care for your comfort. Your quarters are a huge, many-beamed barn: there's sitting space with a big log fire, billiards and rocking chairs downstairs, gallery access to bedrooms above. These, called *Agatha Christie*, *Picardie...*, have books, lace bedcovers and garden views. Your hosts love to chat with guests about the best places to explore in this beautiful area. And we have heard of "breakfasts on the sunlit terrace with home-made jams" and you may use Madame's kitchen (leave it tidy!).

Rooms: 3 doubles, 1 twin, each with shower & wc.

Price: 270 Frs for two.

Meals: In village.

Closed: Mid-November-April.

From A10, Saintes exit on N137 towards Rochefort/La Rochelle. After about 11km, D119 to Plassay. House on left on entering village.
Michelin Map No: 233-15

Michelle & Jacques LOURADOUR
La Jaquetterie
17250 Plassay
Charente-Maritime
Tel: (0)5 46 93 91 88

From Saintes N137 towards Rochefort for 6km then left onto D127 to St Georges. Rue de l'Église is in village centre. House on left.
Michelin Map No: 233-15

Anne & Dominique TROUVÉ
5 rue de l'Église
17810 St Georges des Coteaux
Charente-Maritime
Tel: (0)5 46 92 96 66
Fax: (0)5 46 92 96 66
Web: www.sawdays.co.uk

Sue's hobby is painting in watercolours and her sense of style and colour have revitalised this handsome farmhouse. Bedrooms are prettily decorated and furnished with French antique-style pieces. Shower rooms are new and come with sensibly big towels. Beyond the large garden are vineyards and, in summer, fields of sunflowers. This is good walking country and it's a 25 minute drive to the beach and to Cognac. Plenty of choice at breakfast and if you've arranged dinner there will be home-grown vegetables, or there's a barbecue for you to do your own thing.

Rooms: 1 twin, 2 doubles, all with bathroom & wc.

Price: 350 Frs for two.

Meals: 110 Frs, including aperitif & wine.

Closed: Never.

From A10 exit 36 for Pons. After péage bear right, then right dir. Gemozac. Straight on 1.5km, then left dir. Tanzac & Givrezac. In centre of Givrezac left at garage. House last on left.
Michelin Map No: 233-27

Entry no: **443**   Map No: 11

Sue & Phillip CAPSTICK
La Belle Maison
Route de Belluire
17260 Givrezac
Charente-Maritime
Tel: (0)5 46 49 06 66
Fax: (0)5 46 49 06 66
Web: www.sawdays.co.uk

The house dominates this tiny hamlet surrounded by superb walking country and tantalising views. Claude has a ravishing collection of ornaments and antique furniture, which you see displayed in every room. The large bedrooms, one of which has a particularly beautiful ormolu wardrobe, are magnificently decorated and scattered with oriental rugs. The huge hall and staircase give a great feeling of space. Look at the floor tiles in the *salon* which were left to dry outside in the woods where they collected imprints of the footprints of foxes, badgers and birds, before being laid in a church.

Rooms: 2 doubles, 1 twin, each with bath, shower & wc.

Price: 350-400 Frs for two.

Meals: 120 Frs, including wine.

Closed: Never (winter by arrangement)

On A10, exit 37 direction Mirambeau. At roundabout past 'Marché U'; D254 1st right to St Georges des Agouts. At St Georges right at church (D146). First junction left & follow Chambres d'Hôtes signs.
Michelin Map No: 233-27

Entry no: **444**   Map No: 11

Dinah & Claude TEULET
Les Hauts de Font Moure
17150 St Georges des Agoûts
Charente-Maritime
Tel: (0)5 46 86 04 41
Fax: (0)5 46 49 67 18
e-mail: cteulet@aol.com

This is genuine château stuff: gilt, marble, mouldings and period furniture to match the 1850s building. Both house and garden are being brilliantly restored. Monsieur, who was a designer and teaches history of art, has a natural feel for colour and fabric; he loves arches too, and has put one over each bath; rooms are large and finely-proportioned, overlooking the park (where guests can picnic and admire the botanical wonders) – it is all superb and he talks most interestingly about bringing his château back to life. He also plays the piano and serves candlelit dinners of traditional regional cooking in a most congenial atmosphere.

Rooms: 3 doubles, each with bath, shower & wc.

Price: 450-530 Frs for two.

Meals: 200 Frs, including aperitif, wine & coffee.

Closed: Never; open by arrangement in winter.

From A10 exit 37 to Mirambeau Centre. Ave de la République is after & opposite Tourist Office & swimming pool, behind trees on your right. Michelin Map No: 233-27

Entry no: **445**   Map No: 11

René VENTOLA
Le Parc Casamène
95 avenue de la République
17150 Mirambeau
Charente-Maritime
Tel: (0)5 46 49 74 38
Fax: (0)5 46 49 74 38

Our readers wax poetical in their praises of house and owners: "this is 5-star B&B", "close to perfection"… Agathe and Philippe both knew La Loge as children but never imagined they might one day own the big 19th-century house. They've transformed it with sensitivity and flair and clearly have a fine instinct for natural hospitality – people come, are greeted with a cool drink or use of the kitchen, sit chatting while Agathe does her sewing… and never want to leave. Big, comfortable bedrooms and lots of home-grown fruit and vegetables at dinner. The peace is almost monastic beneath the 300-year-old oak trees. Ideal for families.

Rooms: 2 doubles, 1 twin, each with bath, shower & wc.

Price: 270 Frs for two; extra person 60 Frs.

Meals: Self-catering.

Closed: September-Mid-April.

From A10 exit 26 to Pons then D142 to Jonzac. There D134 through Ozillac and Fontaines d'Ozillac. On leaving village, Chaunac is signposted (5km). Michelin Map No: 233-28

Entry no: **446**   Map No: 11

Agathe & Philippe PICQ
La Loge
17130 Chaunac
Charente-Maritime
Tel: (0)5 46 70 68 50
Fax: (0)5 46 86 13 02

A fine family house with beautiful mature gardens – formerly a cognac-making château, really a farm – set in excellent walking country and forest. It has been immaculately restored by the owners, émigrés from Paris, and is well-decorated, beautifully (almost over-) furnished, sparklingly clean; Madame's food is excellent and everything is done properly, without fuss, despite Monsieur's health-imposed rest from helping her. Just relax and enjoy the nearby River Dordogne and the sea. Readers have praised the place and the convivial dinner party atmosphere in the evenings and the road has not caused any problems.

Once a modest inn for train travellers, it still overlooks the former station, now an attractive and lived-in house. Their brochure says: 'La Font Bétou is one of those very rare places in the world that does not pretend but just is.' Both are ex-market researchers, Gordon from London, Laure from Paris, and they thoroughly enjoy people. Laure cooks (rather well) because she loves it. The two big rooms for guests are in the annexe and are pretty and welcoming, with plenty of stone and wood – all kept spotlessly clean. Everyone can use the hosts' sitting room by the pool, and the kitchen door is always open.

Rooms: 2 twins, 1 triple, 1 quadruple, each with shower & wc (1 behind curtain).

Price: 300 Frs for two.

Meals: 115 Frs, including wine & coffee.

Closed: October.

Rooms: 1 split-level double, 1 twin, each with shower & wc + sitting space downstairs.

Price: 300-320 Frs for two.

Meals: 120 Frs, including aperitif, wine & coffee.

Closed: January.

From Paris, A10 Mirambeau exit on D730 direction Montlieu la Garde; then N10 direction Angoulême. After Pouillac, first left after 2nd closed petrol station; signposted after 800m.
Michelin Map No: 233-39

From Angoulême N10 S for 45km then left onto D730 dir. Montguyon. 1km after Orignolles, right to house, signposted.
Michelin Map No: 233-39

Entry no: **447**   Map No: 11

Entry no: **448**   Map No: 11

Denise & Pierre BILLAT
La Thébaïde
Pouillac
17210 Montlieu la Garde
Charente-Maritime
Tel: (0)5 46 04 65 17
Fax: (0)5 46 04 85 38
Web: www.sawdays.co.uk

Laure TARROU & Gordon FLUDE
La Font Bétou
17210 Orignolles
Charente-Maritime
Tel: (0)5 46 04 02 52
Fax: (0)5 46 04 02 52
e-mail: tarrou@la-font-betou.com
Web: www.la-font-betou.com

With Alex fresh from music-publishing, they took on Hélène's family farm and have worked hard to make a go of it. It now produces venison and ostrich meat: if you want to try some, ask for dinner; you will be offered a glass of local *Pineau des Charentes* too. There are wallabies and llamas, of course, and sheep, chickens, dogs and cats; it is a perfect place for family holidays, which the Everitts encourage. Breakfast is in the oak-and-stone kitchen. Bedrooms are in a converted farm outbuilding, clean and fresh, one small, one big, with lake and animal views.

Rooms: 1 quadruple, 1 triple, each with bath or shower & wc.

Price: 240 Frs for two.

Meals: 90 Frs, incl. coffee (wine 40 Frs).

Closed: Never.

Gîte space for 4 people.

From Poitiers D741 S towards Confolens for 50km. 10km after Pressac, left on D168 for St Germain de Confolens; signed after 2km.
Michelin Map No: 233-20

Entry no: 449   Map No: 7

Alex & Hélène EVERITT
Le Pit
Lessac
16500 Confolens, Charente
Tel: (0)5 45 84 27 65
Fax: (0)5 45 85 41 34
e-mail: everitt16@aol.com
Web: www.sawdays.co.uk

A young English farming couple now live in this prosperous-looking country house with their family antiques and their bilingual children (excellent company for small visitors, who are positively welcomed). They grow corn, sunflowers, ostrich and turkey so are busy but happy to sit and talk round the big table too – meals are informal family-style. From the panelled dining hall with its polished wood, soft colours and floor-to-ceiling doors, a splendid staircase leads up to the simple rooms. The big one has a romantic air and a claw-footed bath; others are smaller but all have good lighting and towels and are excellent value.

Rooms: 2 doubles, each with bath or shower & wc; 1 double, 1 twin, each with shower, sharing wc.

Price: 200-250 Frs for two.

Meals: 90 Frs, including wine. Choice in Confolens.

Closed: Never.

From Confolens, D948 direction Limoges for 4km; signposted on road.
Michelin Map No: 233-20

Entry no: 450   Map No: 7

Stephen & Polly HOARE
Lesterie
St Maurice des Lions
16500 Confolens, Charente
Tel: (0)5 45 84 18 33
Fax: (0)5 45 84 01 45
e-mail: polly.hoare@libertysurf.fr
Web: www.sawdays.co.uk

The old house stands proudly on its wooded hill. The guestrooms, in a well-converted stable-block overlooking the garden and the pool-and-waterfall feature, are done with thoughtful taste, antiques and good, tiled shower rooms. Madame, busy with her successful horse breeding (gorgeous foals in summer), always has time to tell guests what to see in the area, arrange cognac-distillery visits or invite.you to relax in a hammock after a game of badminton. Monsieur is most sociable and offers a local aperitif to guests of an evening.

Rooms: 1 double, 1 twin, each with shower & wc.

Price: 300 Frs for two.

Meals: Restaurant nearby. Self-catering possible.

Closed: Never.

Gîte space for 8 people.

From Angoulême, N141 to La Rochefoucauld; right at 3rd traffic light on D162 to St Adjutory; in village 2nd right & follow signs.
Michelin Map No: 233-31

Entry no: **451**   Map No: 7

Sylviane & Vincent CASPER
La Grenouille
16310 St Adjutory
Charente
Tel: (0)5 45 62 00 34
Fax: (0)5 45 63 06 41

This interesting house has an old-fashioned, well-lived-in, much-loved air to it. The bedrooms have parquet floors, old-style wallpapers, pretty old beds (new mattresses); bathrooms have been modernised. Madame's regional cooking is highly appreciated and dinner is worth coming back for. A conservatory has been built to seat more people round a bigger table where your hosts stay and chat if not too busy serving you. They'll also show you the fascinating old cognac still and on winter weekends you may be able to help with the distilling process. *Camping possible too.*

Rooms: 2 triples, 2 doubles, 1 twin, each with shower & wc.

Price: 220 Frs for two.

Meals: 80 Frs, including wine & coffee.

Closed: Never.

From A10, Pons exit on D700 direction Barbezieux Archiac. After Echebrune, D148 (1st left) direction Lonzac-Celles. Right onto D151, then follow signposts.
Michelin Map No: 233-28

Entry no: **452**   Map No: 11

Micheline & Jacky CHAINIER
Le Chiron
16130 Salles d'Angles
Charente
Tel: (0)5 45 83 72 79
Fax: (0)5 45 83 64 80
Web: www.sawdays.co.uk

An exquisitely French neo-Gothic château which Béatrice inherited and lovingly protects from the worst ravages of modernisation (good bathrooms, separate loos). She, a primary school teacher, and Christopher, a lecturer in philosophy, like eating with their guests. Sleep between old linen sheets, sit in handsome old chairs and wallow in a superb bathroom. The sitting room has a most unusual window over the fireplace, the dining room a panelled ceiling studded with plates. This is a gem, perfect for those who definitely do not want a hotel.

Rooms: 1 family suite, 2 doubles, 1 twin, each with bath or shower, sharing 2 wcs on guest room floor & 1 downstairs.

Price: 280 Frs for two.

Meals: 70 Frs, including wine; book ahead.

Closed: Never.

From A10 exit 36 E to Pons, Archiac & Barbezieux (D732/D700/D731); follow D731 towards Chalais for 12km. After Passirac, 1st right at roadside cross and up leafy drive.
Michelin Map No: 233-29

Entry no: **453**   Map No: 12

Mme Béatrice de CASTELBAJAC
Le Chatelard
Passirac
16480 Brossac, Charente
Tel: (0)5 45 98 71 03
Fax: (0)5 45 98 71 03
e-mail: c.macann@wanadoo.fr
Web: www.sawdays.co.uk

A FEW FALSE FRIENDS

Biologique & Organic
Vegetables called 'organic' in English are known as de culture biologique in French, bio for short. If you talk about organique people will imagine you have trouble with your organs.

Biscuit & Gâteau
Biscuit literally means 'twice cooked' and properly applies to dehydrated army rations or the base for some sticky puddings. The usual words for sweet or savoury biscuits are gâteaux secs or petits gâteaux, also gâteaux d'apèritif.
If you are given gâteau maison at breakfast, it will probably be a simple sponge-cake with jam or a French-style fruit cake (also called du cake, just to make things easier).

Tourte *is the closest the French have to 'pie', i.e. with pastry above and below.*
Tarte *is an open tart or flan.*
Tartine *is a half baguette (usually) sliced in half and buttered, i.e. breakfast food.*
Une pie *is a magpie. Un pis (same pronunciation as une pie) is a cow's udder.*
Scotch *means adhesive tape or whisky – the context should help.*
Trouble *You can send a bottle of wine back for this – it means cloudy, murky.*
Mousse *is : froth, foam, lather (beer, sea, soap) or foam rubber or... moss.*
Pomme de pin *is fircone. Pineapple is ananas. Pamplemousse is grapefruit.*
Raisin *Is a fresh grape or grapes.*
Steinbeck's book is called Les Raisins de la Colère. Dried fruit is called : Raisins de Corinthe (currants – see the derivation?); Raisins de Smyrne (sultanas); Raisins secs (raisins!).
Grappe *is a bunch of grapes – une grappe de raisins.*
Prune *is a fresh plum. A prune is pruneau.*
Verger *An orchard : many a greengrocer's shop is called Aux Fruits du Verger.*
Marmelade *means stewed fruit. Marmalade is called confiture d'oranges amères.*

French country cooking enthusiasts, including vegetarians, sing the praises of Mother's meals made with home-grown vegetables, lamb, duck, pigeon and rabbit (delicious pâtés): she just loves to cook (try her tomato jam too). Myriam has lots of time for guests while Pierre looks after the 20 sheep and works hard on house improvement. The 18th-century farmhouse, with its magnificent wooden staircase, original beams and timber framing, has country antiques, functioning fireplaces, peacefully simple bedrooms, a garden full of toys, and... excitement on a microlight(!). Wonderful French value with interesting hosts.

Rooms: 1 double, 1 triple, each with bath or shower & wc; 2 quadruples, each with shower, sharing wc in passage.

Price: 200 Frs for two.

Meals: 80 Frs, including wine & coffee.

Closed: November-February.

Gîte space for 6 people.

In Bellac follow signs to Limoges; just before leaving Bellac right on D3 direction Blond. 4km to Thoveyrat. House signposted on left. Michelin Map No: 233-22

Entry no: 454   Map No: 7

Pierre & Myriam MORICE
Thoveyrat
87300 Bellac
Haute-Vienne
Tel: (0)5 55 68 86 86
Fax: (0)5 55 68 86 86

Limousin-Dordogne

Food and religion already occupied the minds of the prehistoric cave painters all those millenia ago, though there are more geese than bison nowadays to stew with the truffles.

On the site of an ancient fortification, this 18th-century château stands where it can be seen for miles around and the sun sets over the lake. Bedrooms are mostly vast, traditionally-furnished and regally-wallpapered. Bathrooms have all mod cons. Madame had loads of charm and enthusiasm and is re-establishing the formal gardens; she also organises cookery courses. The spectacular west-facing dining room has pale blue and yellow panelling, high-backed tapestry chairs and a fine dining table – the atmosphere is informal but the surroundings do impose civilised dressing for dinner.

Rooms: 2 doubles, 1 twin, each with bath & wc.

Price: 600 Frs for two.

Meals: Dinner 150 Frs, including aperitif, wine & coffee.

Closed: November-June.

From Poitiers N147 towards Limoges, through Bellac, left onto D96 dir. St Junien les Combes. First left in village towards Rancon & approx 1km to Château.
Michelin Map No: 233-22

Entry no: 455   Map No: 7

Comte & Comtesse Aucaigne de
SAINTE CROIX
Château de Sannat
St Junien les Combes
87300 Bellac, Haute-Vienne
Tel: (0)5 55 68 13 52
Fax: (0)5 55 68 13 52
e-mail: labelette@aol.com

Eight centuries ago Knights Templar farmed here; four centuries ago dashing King Henri IV hunted wolves here; the same family has always owned these 750 acres and pilgrims have always passed through on the way to Compostela – such is the tapestry of history that your intelligent, sociable hosts weave for you beneath the Aubusson or across the grand dinner table. They are absolutely the right mix of friendliness and formality. All rooms are properly period-furnished, but pay the extra for the superb suite and enjoy its mighty bathroom (shower rooms smaller).

Rooms: 1 suite for 4, 1 double, 1 twin, each with bath or shower & wc.

Price: 350-400 Frs for two; suite 650 Frs for four.

Meals: 100 Frs, excluding wine (50 Frs).

Closed: November-March.

From A20 exit 24 onto D27 to Bersac. Continue towards Laurière then left after railway bridge and follow signs for 3km to château.
Michelin Map No: 239-1

Entry no: 456   Map No: 7

Éric & Annie PERRIN des MARAIS
Le Château du Chambon
Le Chambon
87370 Bersac sur Rivalier
Haute-Vienne
Tel: (0)5 55 71 47 04
Fax: (0)5 55 71 47 04
e-mail: perrin-desmarais@wanadoo.fr

A really super, nature-loving, chemical-free house where natural materials come into their own: wood everywhere including under the tiles, cork insulation, organic food that includes meat and home-made bread, and they've done it for the last 30 years! The central heating is provided by steam ducts leading from the cooking-pot over the open fire. He is a painter of Italian extraction; she made all the upholstery, bedheads and patchworks. Rooms have soothing, simple, successful colour schemes and lots of wood. And there are more fabulous colours, and walks, to be found outside.

Rooms: 2 doubles, 1 triple, each with shower & wc.

Price: 270-300 Frs for two; minimum 2 nights July-August.

Meals: 90 Frs, excluding wine.

Closed: Never.

From Paris A20 exit 25 on D44 towards St Sylvestre; left on D78 towards Grandmont & St Léger La Montagne; through Grandmont then right towards Les Sauvages after 200m.
Michelin Map No: 239-1

Entry no: 457   Map No: 7

Lorenzo & Edith RAPPELLI
Les Chênes
Les Sauvages
87240 St Sylvestre, Haute-Vienne
Tel: (0)5 55 71 33 12
Fax: (0)5 55 71 33 12
e-mail: les.chenes@wanadoo.fr
Web: www.haute-vienne.com/chenes.htm

Go through your own entrance, covered in wisteria and roses, to your own kitchen area with stairs up to the rather appealing bedroom with its white walls, off-white carpet and sea-grass wallpaper. The other bedroom is useful for overflow. You have your own living room too, with an open fire. (It can all be let as a gîte.) Néline is a wonderful hostess, both gentle and energetic. The house is lovely, splashed with colour and imaginative gestures, and the two-and-a half-acre garden makes further demands upon a willing pair of owners.

Rooms: 1 double/twin, 1 twin, sharing shower, wc & small kitchen with dishwasher & washing machine (same group only).

Price: 300 Frs for two; reduction for 2 nights or more.

Meals: Self-catering.

Closed: Never.

Gîte space for 4 people.

From Limoges, N141 to St Léonard then D39 towards St Priest; after 5km right direction Lajoumard; first left and follow signs.
Michelin Map No: 239-14

Entry no: 458   Map No: 7

Mme Néline JANSEN de VOMÉCOURT
La Réserve
Bassoleil
87400 St Léonard de Noblat
Haute-Vienne
Tel: (0)5 55 56 18 39
e-mail: vomecourt.jansen1@libertysurf.fr

A glorious touch of eccentricity here. The house, once 12th-century, is now entirely 16th/17th and has been in the family for generations. You may share a bath or creep down a floor for the loo, but one room is authentic Charles X and all are deeply evocative. The main house has a spectacular stone staircase with Egyptian vases pillaged from a Pharaoh's tomb, huge bedrooms and modern bathrooms. The great dining hall has wood panelling but breakfast is in a small guest *salon* or in the cottage kitchen. Monsieur, who plays jazz on those two pianos, runs his own model train museum. Definitely different.

There once stood a forge here, producing cannon balls. They now produce pâtés, *confits* and *rillettes* and keep ducks, horses, a pig, dogs, a cat and two children; the latter are very much part of life here and the atmosphere is easy and *familiale*. Nothing fancy about the bedrooms – they are just cosy and comfortable. A huge sitting room with enormous hearth, stone walls, tatty sofa, and the nicest possible people. Stay for dinner; most ingredients are home-grown or home-raised. Boating on the lake. Guests love it all. *Ask about pets when booking.*

Rooms: In gatehouse: 1 double with shower, 2 doubles sharing bathroom, all 3 sharing wc; in main house: 1 triple, 1 suite, each with bath & wc.

Price: 300 Frs for two.

Meals: 90 Frs, including wine & coffee.

Closed: Never.

Gîte space for 6 people.

Rooms: 3 doubles, each with shower & wc.

Price: 240 Frs for two.

Meals: 90 Frs, including wine & coffee.

Closed: Never.

From Limoges, D979 direction Eymoutiers; Fougeolles on left just before entering Eymoutiers, signposted Chambres d'Hôtes.
Michelin Map No: 239-15

From A20 exit 40 to Pierre Buffière; W across river onto D15 then D19 towards St Yrieix la Perche for 15km. At La Croix d'Hervy, left on D57 for Coussac Bonneval. Mill on left after the lake (approx. 4km).
Michelin Map No: 239-13

Entry no: 459   Map No: 7

Entry no: 460   Map No: 12

Jacques & Frédérique du MONTANT
Fougeolles
87120 Eymoutiers
Haute-Vienne
Tel: (0)5 55 69 11 44

Valérie & Renaud GIZARDIN
Moulin de Marsaguet
87500 Coussac Bonneval
Haute-Vienne
Tel: (0)5 55 75 28 29
Fax: (0)5 55 75 28 29

These are real farmers who like to be as bio-dynamic (i.e. respectful of natural life systems) and self-sufficient as possible, so meals are home-grown and nourishing. The four rooms share a living room with kitchen, but dine with your hosts if you can: they are completely unpretentious, very good company and know their region intimately. Two rooms are on the ground floor, two in the roof, with pine-clad sloping ceilings, white walls and roof windows. The farm is surrounded by woods (superb walking), and children love helping to milk the goats and collect the eggs. So do some adults.

Rooms: 3 doubles, 1 triple, all with shower & wc.

Price: 240 Frs for two.

Meals: 85 Frs, including wine, by arrangement. 1 July-15 August only.

Closed: Never.

From A20, exit 41 to Magnac Bourg then D215 (between Total service station & Brasserie des Sports) SW then follow signs 4km to La Chapelle. Michelin Map No: 239-13

Entry no: 461   Map No: 12

Patrick & Mayder LESPAGNOL
La Chapelle
87380 Château Chervix
Haute-Vienne
Tel: (0)5 55 00 86 67
Fax: (0)5 55 00 70 78
e-mail: lespagno@club-internet.fr

The atmosphere is more traditional than the photo suggests, lively yet relaxed. Michel's modern sculptures add magic to the garden and his work is everywhere: handmade door handles, towel rails, shelf supports... mainly in brass and steel. Bedrooms and bathrooms are biggish and the house glories in an extravagant use of materials: opulent floor-length curtains, off-white material instead of wallpaper and a tented ceiling of it in the dayroom (all Madame's work). The living and dining rooms have a studio feel with 'works in progress'. He loves showing his forge and studio, she loves making cakes – a very likeable couple.

Rooms: 2 doubles, each with shower & wc.

Price: 290 Frs for two.

Meals: 90 Frs, including wine & coffee

Closed: January-March.

From Eymoutiers, D30 direction Chamberet. House in village of La Roche, 7km beyond Eymoutiers. Michelin Map No: 239-15

Entry no: 462   Map No: 12

Michel & Josette JAUBERT
La Roche
87120 Eymoutiers
Haute-Vienne
Tel: (0)5 55 69 61 88

A converted school with three fresh and simply-decorated bedrooms (one with a mezzanine) downstairs, sharing a living room and kitchenette. The upstairs suite is more traditional, also with its own living room – the headmistresses study perhaps? A flower-covered loggia leads to the day/dining room; entirely glazed on one side to make the most of the beautiful garden – which also produces vegetables for excellent dinners. Beatrice and Henry are delightful, happy talking in French or English and keen to help you discover their fascinating area. Guided flora and fauna tours and boats for hire too.

If the quaint, quirky and creative appeal, come to this 18th-century house on the edge of town. The bouncy dog, the exquisite handmade patchwork quilts that contrast with fading wallpaper and cluttered terrace (stunning views of medieval Château de Boussac), the jolly, genuine hostess and her delightful husband who live in amiable confusion, all add up to a totally French experience. They both used to be in *haute couture*. Good-sized, clean rooms – ask for one with a view; the new triple has a kitchenette. *Gîte space for 4*.

Rooms: 1 double, 1 twin, 1 quadruple, 1 suite, all with shower or bath & wc.

Price: 275 Frs for two.

Meals: 90 Frs, including wine.

Closed: 15 December-2 January.

From Châteauroux A20 exit 22 for La Souterraine then D951 through Dun le Palestel; right after village D15 to La Celle Dunoise. There, right after tennis courts towards Anzeme; follow signs for approx. 4km.
Michelin Map No: 238-40

Rooms: 2 doubles, 1 triple, 1 suite, all with bath or shower & wc.

Price: 280 Frs for two.

Meals: 80 Frs, including wine & coffee.

Closed: October.

From A71, exit 10 onto D94 W (15km), right on D916 to Boussac. On main square, take road to left of Mairie, left again at butchers; house on right.
Michelin Map No: 238-42

Entry no: **463**   Map No: 7

Entry no: **464**   Map No: 8

Beatrice & Henry NGUYEN
L'École Buissonnière
23800 La Celle Dunoise
Creuse
Tel: (0)5 55 89 23 49
Fax: (0)5 55 89 27 62

Françoise GROS &
David COLSENET
La Courtepointe, 3 rue des Loges
23600 Boussac, Creuse
Tel: (0)5 55 65 80 09
Fax: (0)5 55 65 80 09
e-mail: courtepointe@wanadoo.fr
Web: www.sawdays.co.uk

Jacquie, half-French, and Ian, half-Hungarian, are fervent Francophiles: it's all very cosmopolitan. Their renovation of this old village house is an achievement to be proud of, with remarkable bathrooms and Laura Ashley-style décor. They are very organised and will tell you everything about the locality and its people, history, flora and building regs. A professional chef, Ian produces superb food which he serves with a flourish and wines from his own cellar. Aperitifs and dinner *en famille* are occasions for stimulating conversation – not a time for shrinking violets.

Rooms: 2 doubles/twins, 1 twin, each with bath or shower & wc.

Price: 185-205 Frs for two.

Meals: 85 Frs, including wine & coffee, by arrangement.

Closed: Never.

From Tulle N120 to Forgès. Left into Place de la Mairie and park in church square behind.
Michelin Map No: 239-27

Entry no: 465   Map No: 12

Ian & Jacquie HOARE
La Souvigne
1 impasse La Fontaine
19380 Forgès, Corrèze
Tel: (0)5 55 28 63 99
Fax: (0)5 55 28 65 62
e-mail: ianhoare@wanadoo.fr
Web: perso.wanadoo.fr/souvigne

You will be part of life on the farm while you stay and you'll understand why Madame, born in the area, has no desire ever to move away. Ideal for families, with its expanse of grass within eyesight, canoes for hire and fishing down on the River Dordogne (ask about their own piece of river bank) in what is now a conservation area, and a proper kitchen for guests, Saulières has a superbly 'family, friends and farming' atmosphere. They are a highly likeable couple – he raises beef cattle and grows walnuts while she makes pretty curtains, soft bedcovers and paints pictures for the guest rooms in the modern extension.

Rooms: 1 quadruple, 1 triple, 1 double, 1 twin, all with shower & wc.

Price: 250 Frs for two.

Meals: Self-catering possible or good choice 2km.

Closed: Never.

Gîte space for 8 people.

From Tulle, N120 to Argentat then D12 along River Dordogne direction Beaulieu; past Monceaux to Saulières (6km from Argentat).
Michelin Map No: 239-27

Entry no: 466   Map No: 13

Marie-Jo & Jean-Marie LAFOND
Saulières
Monceaux sur Dordogne
19400 Argentat
Corrèze
Tel: (0)5 55 28 09 22
Fax: (0)5 55 28 09 22
Web: www.sawdays.co.uk

They have been given "10/10 for welcome, comfort, food - everything". The kitchen is a wonderful place with its display of farm things and Anne's sunny presence - she delights in texture, smell and colour, her cooking reflects her pleasure and you catch the vibes easily. Their house restoration job is (extremely well) finished and Jim can spend time coaching the village football team; many local farmers are the Lardners' friends so visits can be arranged; regional dinners are served with good wine - all proof of thorough integration among the rolling hills of rural France. Excellent value, plus deep peace.

Rooms: 1 twin with bath & wc. Extra room for children.

Price: Price: 200 Frs for two.

Meals: 95 Frs, including wine & coffee.

Closed: Never.

Gîte space for 2 people.

From Argentat, N120 direction Tulle then left onto D921 direction Brive. Pass sign to Albussac; 300m on, left to Le Prézat, through hamlet; house on right with lawn.
Michelin Map No: 239-27

Entry no: **467**   Map No: 12

Anne & Jim LARDNER
Le Prézat
19380 Albussac
Corrèze
Tel: (0)5 55 28 62 36
Fax: (0)5 55 28 62 36

Come to this deliciously rustic hamlet to experience true French *paysan* hospitality in the Durieux's converted barn. Furniture is properly dark, bathrooms authentically simple, Madame's regional cuisine (you can watch her cook) a daily marvel. She uses fine ingredients, many home-produced: vegetables, nuts, honey, fruit and free-range chickens. The history-charged area has ancient caves and stately châteaux; add spice to sightseeing with a sprinkling of local folklore, available courtesy of Monsieur who acts, if requested, as a knowledgeable guide and plies guests with his own fruit liqueurs when they return.

Rooms: 2 triples, each with shower and basin behind screens, sharing a wc.

Price: 390 Frs for two, half-board only.

Meals: Dinner with aperitif, wine & coffee included in price.

Closed: Never.

From Angoulême, D939 south. After Dignac D23 to Villebois Lavalette, D17 to Gurat then D102 towards Vendoire for 2km; left for Le Bouchaud.
Michelin Map No: 233-30

Entry no: **468**   Map No: 12

André & Pierrette DURIEUX
Le Bouchaud
24320 Vendoire
Dordogne
Tel: (0)5 53 91 00 82

Once a lovers' retreat, this peaceful, long-viewed stone cottage stands in two acres of woods and fields. Your hostess paints, plays the flute, teaches French, shares her library and her talent for good conversation, drawing on a long and interesting life. Her house, filled with Belgian antiques and exceptional paintings, has a split-level sitting room opening onto a sun terrace, modest but adequate bedrooms, big open fires and a large heated pool. Madame welcomes single visitors for week-long rest cures, or French immersion, and excellent guided tours of the area – enquire about full-board terms.

We love this place – the bright, rustic dining room with its limed walls, white tablecloths and ticking chair covers, the level changes upstairs, the bedrooms with their berugged wooden floors and simple furnishings (good taste and African throws), the inviting bathrooms. The cool, overflowing stone plunge pool in the green and pleasant garden is unforgettable (there's a shallow one for children). Delightful, energetic Jane creates a relaxed atmosphere, offers superb and imaginative food and early supper for children in this lovely tranquil spot. And John "is a joy to be with".

Rooms: 1 double, 1 twin, sharing bath, shower & wc (2nd wc on ground floor).

Price: 250 Frs for two; min. 2 nights.

Meals: 80 Frs, including wine.

Closed: Never.

Gîte space for 4 people.

Rooms: 2 doubles, 1 twin each with shower & wc; 1 double, 1 twin sharing bath & wc.

Price: 290-325 Frs for two.

Meals: 110 Frs, including coffee.

Closed: Never.

Gîte space for 4 people.

From Angoulême D939 S 29km, right on D12/D708 for 22km to Bertric Burée. D106 W dir. Allemans for 3km, right for Chez Marty for 1km, left at junction; house at end of lane on left. Michelin Map No: 233-41

From Ribérac dir. Verteillac for 2km. At La Borie right on D99 for 4km, through Celles dir. La Tour Blanche for 2km. Right after small vineyard and down into hamlet. House first on right. Michelin Map No: 233-41

Entry no: **469**   Map No: 12

Entry no: **470**   Map No: 12

Anne HART
La Fournière
Chez Marty
24320 Bertric Burée
Dordogne
Tel: (0)5 53 91 93 58
Fax: (0)5 53 91 93 58
Web: www.sawdays.co.uk

Jane & John EDWARDS
Pauliac
Celles
24600 Ribérac, Dordogne
Tel: (0)5 53 91 97 45
Fax: (0)5 53 90 43 46
e-mail: pauliac@infonie.fr
Web: www.sawdays.co.uk

David and Alison are keen vegetarians producing their own vegetables, eggs, honey and jam. (Carnivores should try the good choice of restaurants in Brantôme, 15 minutes away). Despite dreadful storm damage when they lost 35 trees in December '99, they have created a pretty garden – you eat under a wooden pergola covered in roses, honeysuckle and vines. This is a great place for children, they usually adore the donkeys, goats, chickens and cats. The two large uncluttered bedrooms with sloping ceilings and massive beams are on either side of a dayroom with furniture made by David, a first-rate carpenter.

Rooms: 1 double, 1 twin, each with bathroom & wc.

Price: 300 Frs for two.

Meals: Dinner (vegetarian only) 90 Frs, including wine & coffee.

Closed: Christmas.

Gîte space for 8 people.

From la Dorl Nontron to Brantôme road, take D83 onto La Roche is on the right about 1km past the D675.
Michelin Map No: 233-31

Entry no: 471   Map No: 12

David ALLISON & Alison
COUTANCHE
La Roche
24530 Champagnac de Belair
Dordogne
Tel: (0)5 53 54 22 91
e-mail: allisons@club-internet.fr
Web: perso.club-internet.fr/allisons/

In a really pretty hamlet, this is a civilised place for the independently-minded to stay. You sleep and breakfast in the well-converted barn where original beams and stones are married with white walls, plain furniture and good old cupboard doors. Beds and bathrooms are all good too, breakfast is served until late and the Rubbens enjoy chatting to their guests. The fine big pool, out of sight or hearing of the guest quarters, is inviting with its diving board and barbecue, service is excellent and well-behaved children are tolerated!

Rooms: 1 triple, 2 doubles, each with bath or shower & wc.

Price: 390 Frs for two.

Meals: Restaurant in village.

Closed: By arrangement November-Easter.

From Périgueux, D939 to Brantôme. There, D78 & D83 towards Champagnac de Belair; D82 & D3 to Villars and 'Grottes de Villars'. Left to Lavergne; signposted.
Michelin Map No: 233-32

Entry no: 472   Map No: 12

Mme Eliane RUBBENS
L'Enclos
Lavergne
24530 Villars
Dordogne
Tel: (0)5 53 54 82 17
Fax: (0)5 53 54 82 17
Web: www.sawdays.co.uk

There is an island for loners, a dream of a garden (all John's work), a swimming pool in the walled garden and superb, light, airy rooms with pretty soft furnishings and bathrooms across the corridor. Diana, a passionate and excellent cook (readers have confirmed), is happy for people to come into her marvellous great kitchen to enjoy her company and the views from all four sides of this very finely converted 17th-century millhouse on the banks of the Auvezère river. They have been here for eight years and will happily direct you towards the many nearby treasures and pleasures. *Children over 12 welcome.*

Your interesting hosts are in the peasant heritage movement... and go to Glyndebourne whenever they can. The sensitive restoration of this lovely, listed group of ancient buildings, with a shingle-roofed bread oven, illustrates their commitment. Bedrooms, at opposite ends of the long building, have odd bathroom layouts: one has the shower in a (big) cupboard next to the fireplace, an antique washbasin that tips straight into the drain (genuine period feature) and a 120cm brass bed. They founded the local music/dance festival and are very involved in the cultural life of the community.

Rooms: 1 double, 1 twin, both with bath or shower & wc.

Price: 700 Frs for two.

Meals: 200 Frs, including coffee.

Closed: Never.

Rooms: 1 suite for 4 with bath & wc; 1 double with shower & wc.

Price: 320-350 Frs for two; min. 2 nts.

Meals: 2 restaurants within 1.5km. Picnic possible.

Closed: Never.

From Périgueux, N21 dir. Limoges. About 2km on, right over bridge dir. airport. Left at next r'bout on D5 dir. Hautefort. 1.5km after Tourtoirac, left dir. La Crouzille. Cross the Auvezère. 1st drive on right.
Michelin Map No: 233-44

From Périgueux N21 N to Sarliac sur l'Isle; D705 to Coulaures; right on D73 to Tourtoirac. Right after bridge, left on D67 towards St Orse; house 1km on left.
Michelin Map No: 233-44

Entry no: 473   Map No: 12

Entry no: 474   Map No: 12

John & Diana ARMITAGE
Le Moulin de la Crouzille
Tourtoirac
24390 Hautefort
Dordogne
Tel: (0)5 53 51 11 94
Fax: (0)5 53 51 11 94
Web: www.sawdays.co.uk

Danièle & Jean-Pierre MOUGIN
Bas Portail
Tourtoirac
24390 Hautefort
Dordogne
Tel: (0)5 53 51 14 35
e-mail: bestofperigord@perigord.com

A little bit of Alsace in the Dordogne. This *moulin* in a valley is like a Swiss mountain inn. Levels change, steep original stairs rise, brilliantly chosen colours give huge character, Alsace rugs and antiques warm the atmosphere – as does the sitting room fireplace – and if bedrooms are on the small side the welcome from your easy-going hostess is huge. The whole effect is rich and brave. Add fully organic home-grown ingredients for delicious dinners and you have excellent value.

With a brand new pool in the garden this place really is a bargain. The Gay family are all involved with the property; Madame has recently handed over the running of the auberge and B&B to her two daughters, while her husband runs the mixed farm 'growing' fruit, vegetables, poultry, and wine. People drive from quite a distance to eat here – the food is so good (open every day for lunch and dinner). The two bedrooms are in the grandmother's old house over the road from the auberge. They are fairly spartan but it would be a good spot for two couples travelling together, as you would have the whole house.

Rooms: 1 twin (& child's room), 1 double, each with shower & wc.

Price: 250 Frs for two.

Meals: 80 Frs, excluding wine (price according to quality chosen).

Closed: November-February.

Rooms: 2 doubles, each with own shower & wc.

Price: 250 Frs for two.

Meals: 90-160 Frs, including aperitif & wine.

Closed: October-April.

From Périgueux N89 SW dir. Mussidan/Bordeaux. At end of dual carriageway, follow blue signs: left/right on D39e dir. St Séverin for 3km; house on right after small lake. Michelin Map No: 233-41

From Perigueux take N21 towards Bergerac. 4km after Bordas left to St Maime. Leave village towards Vergt. Then immediately left towards Castagnol. Follow Auberge signs. Michelin Map No: 233-42

Entry no: 475   Map No: 12

Entry no: 476   Map No: 12

Jacques & Ginette KIEFFER
Le Moulin de Leymonie du Maupas
24400 Issac
Dordogne
Tel: (0)5 53 81 24 02

Laurence & Ghislaine GAY
La Petite Auberge
Castagnol
24380 St Maime de Péreyrol
Dordogne
Tel: (0)5 53 04 00 54
Fax: (0)5 53 04 00 54

Staying as guests of Robert and Stuart in this charming watermill, where they serve their own spring water, is a delight. Views over a perfect landscape of deep, willow-dotted meadow, green lawns, stream coursing under the house and a reedy lake, can be enjoyed from all the smallish, ever-immaculate rooms in the separate guest house and there's a good dayroom with a white piano. Breakfast tables are set out here or on the idyllic, vine-shaded little terrace beside the old bread oven. It is all lovingly tended, nearby is unspoilt Paunat with its huge church and peace, perfect peace. *Small pets by arrangement; careful children only (unfenced water).*

Rooms: 3 doubles, 2 twins, 1 triple, all with bath or shower & wc.

Price: 434 Frs for two.

Meals: Good choice in nearby towns/villages.

Closed: Never.

From Le Bugue D703 towards Limeuil, left on D31 through Limeuil. At crossroads D2 towards Ste Alvère. After 100m fork left; house is on left 2km along; drive leads down from small crossroads.
Michelin Map No: 233-43

Entry no: 477   Map No: 12

Robert CHAPPELL & Stuart SHIPPEY
Le Moulin Neuf, Paunat
24510 Ste Alvère, Dordogne
Tel: (0)5 53 63 30 18
Fax: (0)5 53 73 33 91
e-mail: moulin-neuf@usa.net
Web: www.sawdays.co.uk

Carine is half-Greek, easy-going and helpful and really makes you feel welcome in the sunny kitchen of her restored farmhouse. All the bedrooms in the converted barn will be newly decorated by 2001, each has its own terrace overlooking the shady garden – the pool is far enough away not to disturb snoozers – and the style is unfussy with exposed stonework and beams, fresh paintwork, local country furniture and good, modern bathrooms. Madame likes cooking, both French and International, uses locally produced food where possible and organises barbecues around the pool on some evenings. Spend two or three nights and get to know the area.

Rooms: 2 doubles, each with shower & wc; 2 twins, each with bath & wc.

Price: 280-295 Frs for two.

Meals: 85 Frs, including wine.

Closed: January.

From Le Bugue to Ste Alvère, at main crossroads in village take D30 direction Trémolat. House is 2nd right, 500m after sign Lemaine at top of hill.
Michelin Map No: 233-43

Entry no: 478   Map No: 12

Carine SOMERITIS
Les Hirondelles
Le Maine
24510 Sainte Alvère
Dordogne
Tel: (0)5 53 22 75 40
Fax: (0)5 53 22 75 40

Claire and Marc are from the Alps where she teaches ski-ing. He works in tourism; both are experienced cooks, keen to make their new home a relaxing, easy place to be. It's in a particularly lovely area and the tiny hamlet is calm and simple. La Licorne is three old buildings; a stream bounds the pretty courtyard. Clutter-free rooms, one in the 13th-century barn overlooking the nut trees and garden, are small, white, with modern furniture and the occasional old carved cupboard door. The dining room is superb with its big fireplace and gallery at each end; food is light and vegetable-orientated. *Please arrive after 5pm.*

A brilliant site, with lovely wide rural views, carefully chosen as the new position for this re-constructed barn – as the garden matures, you'd think it had been there for centuries. Marie-Ange and Phillipe's country furniture looks just right between the oak beams and tiled floor of the kitchen. The 'feel' is bright and uncluttered, a good mix of ancient and modern. Bedrooms are fresh and pleasant, with views, stylish fabrics and superior mattresses. Sit on the rose-covered terrace and contemplate a spot of fishing – they have their own lake – horse riding or driving; another member of the family runs stables nearby.

Rooms: 2 doubles, 1 suite for 4, each with bath or shower & wc.

Price: 350-380 Frs for two.

Meals: 120 Frs, excluding wine (carafe 36 Frs), by arrangement.

Closed: Mid-November-March.

Rooms: 2 doubles, 1 twin, each with shower & wc.

Price: 260 Frs for two.

Meals: Good choice 3km.

Closed: Never.

Gîte space for 12 people.

From Montignac D65 south for 6km then left on minor road towards Valojoulx. House in centre of hamlet to left of Mairie.
Michelin Map No: 233-44

From Monpon Ménestérol on N89 Bordeaux-Perigueux take D708 towards Ste Foy la Grande for 8km. Right in St Rémy, opposite CHEZ SAM, on D33 towards St Martin/Villefranche and follow signs Gîtes/Chambres d'Hôtes la Mouthe.
Michelin Map No: 233-41

Entry no: 479   Map No: 12

Claire & Marc BOSSE
La Licorne
Valojoulx
24290 Montignac Lascaux
Dordogne
Tel: (0)5 53 50 77 77
Fax: (0)5 53 50 77 77

Entry no: 480   Map No: 12

Marie-Ange & Philippe CAIGNARD
Domaine de la Mouthe
24700 Saint Rémy Sur Lidoire
Dordogne
Tel: (0)5 53 82 15 40
Fax: (0)5 53 82 15 40
e-mail: hebergement@pays-de-bergerac.com

All power to this deeply united family and their desire to keep local tradition alive, raising poultry and hand-crafting pâtés and foie gras. Marie-Jeanne and her son and daughter-in-law (a brilliant cook and teacher, though not for vegetarians) now share the B&B tasks. Marie-Jeanne will welcome you with her natural good humour, settle you into your genuinely French Rustic room, give you time to admire the view then drive you the 7km across the Dordogne River to her son's lovely old house for a memorable dinner. One of France's most exquisite areas and an exceptional experience of genuine French country warmth.

Rooms: 1 double, 1 triple, 1 quadruple, all with shower & wc (1 curtained).

Price: 260-290 Frs for two; minimum 2 nights.

Meals: 125 Frs, including wine & coffee.

Closed: December-February.

Gîte space for 5 people.

From Bergerac, D32 direction St Alvère. After 10km, look for signpost 'Périgord – Bienvenue à la Ferme'. Michelin Map No: 234-4

Entry no: 481   Map No: 12

Marie-Jeanne & Marie-Thérèse
ARCHER
La Barabie
Lamonzie Montastruc
24520 Mouleydier
Dordogne
Tel: (0)5 53 23 22 47
Fax: (0)5 53 22 81 20

This Belgian couple know their adopted region 'like their pocket' and are keen that you discover the hidden treasures of the Dordogne not just the oversubscribed star sights. Their fine set of Périgord buildings sits high on a wooded, hawk-hunted hill, the big, solar-heated pool is at a decent distance and the house has been beautifully restored (the garden is taking shape too). In the biggest room, you sleep under a soaring timber canopy supporting a crystal chandelier... Easy décor, good furniture, a friendly welcome and the run of the kitchen. You may even be able to paint your own souvenir tile.

Rooms: 1 double, 1 triple, 1 quadruple, all with bath and wc.

Price: 250-325 Frs for two.

Meals: Auberge 4km; choice in Bergerac, 9km; use of kitchen possible.

Closed: 30 October-14 March.

Gîte space for 6 people.

From Bergerac N21 N direction Périgueux. 4km after Lembras, Les Rocailles sign on right. Michelin Map No: 234-4

Entry no: 482   Map No: 12

Marcel VANHEMELRYCK & Nicole DENYS
Les Rocailles de la Fourtaunie
24520 Lamonzie Montastruc
Dordogne
Tel: (0)5 53 58 20 16
Fax: (0)5 53 58 20 16
e-mail: lesrocailles@wanadoo.fr

The curvy roof, the entrance arch, the rough old beams and the wafer bricks round the fireplaces are well-preserved old friends that we are always happy to see again; the first-floor alcove enclosing the original long-drop privy is rarer. Splendid main rooms combine simplicity and taste, antique and modern furniture; smaller, tempting bedrooms have hand-stencilled doors. Your hosts, two easy, articulate former *Parisiennes,* may offer you their irresistible chocolate courgette cake, a browse in their library and a chance to share their genuine pleasure in people.

Rooms: 3 doubles, 1 twin & 1 family suite, all with bath or shower & wc.

Price: 350 Frs for two.

Meals: 120 Frs, incl. wine & coffee.

Closed: Never.

Gîte space for 6 people.

From Bergerac D660 W dir. Lalinde & Sarlat. Right across River Dordogne at Pont de Couze (still D660). At Bayac right onto D27 towards Issigeac; at top of hill house on left after 2km. Michelin Map No: 235-5

Entry no: 483   Map No: 12

Francine PILLEBOUT & Odile
CALMETTES
Le Relais de Lavergne
Lavergne
24150 Bayac, Dordogne
Tel: (0)5 53 57 83 16
Fax: (0)5 53 57 83 16
Web: www.sawdays.co.uk

It's not all truffles and romance, y'know – here are French country people still working the land with their priorities and values still intact. They are busy, capable farmers living in an utterly typical French farmhouse, down to that very special colour of orangey-brown wallpaper and those highly-polished *lits bateau.* There are walnuts galore, dairy cows, a vegetable garden and you can visit the prune ovens. Succulent regional dishes are eaten with the family and the house is altogether an excellent and welcoming stopping place. One reader says it's "huge fun but don't talk while the weather report is on."

Rooms: 2 doubles, 1 triple each with bath or shower & wc.

Price: 230 Frs for two. Half-board 410 Frs for two.

Meals: 90 Frs, including wine.

Closed: Never.

Gîte space for 5 people.

From Beaumont du Périgord, D660 5km direction Montpazier; second farm on right after sign for Petit Brassac. Michelin Map No: 235-5

Entry no: 484   Map No: 12

Gilbert & Reine MARESCASSIER
Petit Brassac
Labouquerie
24440 Beaumont du Périgord
Dordogne
Tel: (0)5 53 22 32 51
Fax: (0)5 53 22 32 51

Hard by medieval Sarlat, this much-visited château (free tour for B&B guests!) is a dream. Painted beams draw the eye, the carved stone staircase and the ancient floors are utterly lovely, history oozes from every corner (there may be a ghost). All furniture is authentic 17th-century Perigordian – no concessions to 20th-century chic. The twin? two four-posters; the suite? one room perfect Louis XVI with claw-footed bath behind curtains and loo in an archer's turret, the other classic red Jouy fabric-clad (slightly showing its age). Madame is elegant, friendly, very French; her son, who helps in the château, speaks good English; both are delightful.

Rooms: 1 twin (& single), 1 suite, both with bath, shower & wc.

Price: 750 Frs for two.

Meals: Good restaurant 5km away; choice in Sarlat, La Métairie.

Closed: November-March.

Gîte space for 10 people.

From Sarlat D47 direction Les Eyzies for 8km. Château signposted regularly. Michelin Map No: 235-6

Entry no: 485   Map No: 12

Comte & Comtesse de MONTBRON
Château de Puymartin
24200 Sarlat la Canéda
Dordogne
Tel: (0)5 53 59 29 97
Fax: (0)5 53 29 87 52
e-mail: ch.puymartin@lemel.fr
Web: www.sawdays.co.uk

Come for the opulent 'marbled halls' feel of the main rooms, for the poolside set-up, for Richard, half-Spanish, half-Bordelais, who encourages deer, has hens running loose, grows fruits and nuts to bursting point (they make their own oil). He's a young, enthusiastic, ex-hotelier; he paints too. Breakfast consist of own eggs and anything you want. Isabelle is a part-time air-hostess and they will share their imaginatively-cooked dinner with you if you are a small group. Simple bedrooms with plain beds and white walls are in calming contrast to the spectacular style below.

Rooms: 3 doubles, 2 twins, each with shower or bath & wc (2 connect for family use).

Price: 340-440 Frs for two.

Meals: 95 Frs, including aperitif.

Closed: Never.

Gîte space for 5 people.

From Périgueux D710 S towards Belvès. Do NOT take right fork up into Belvès, stay on D710 for 500m then left towards Sagelat Église. House 600m on left. Michelin Map No: 235-5

Entry no: 486   Map No: 12

Richard & Isabelle GINIOUX
Le Branchat
24170 Belvès
Dordogne
Tel: (0)5 53 28 98 80
Fax: (0)5 53 28 90 82
e-mail: le.branchat@wanadoo.fr
Web: www.perigord.com/belves/lebranchat

Once a wreck, now a village manor-house again, transformed by the Orefices and given a touch of easy elegance. Warm, bright colours in the living room, overlooking the sweeping lawn, reflect Madame's sunny, Latin personality and you're welcome to play the piano and read the books. The tower suite and small double have a modern feel, the three other rooms are more traditional, huge and high-ceilinged; all have very good 'fixtures and fittings'. There are children's games, a free 'beach' nearby on the Dordogne, riding stables next door, good food (neighbours' produce) in and plenty of choice out.

Rooms: 3 doubles, 1 double/twin, 1 suite, all with bath or shower & wc.

Price: 410-560 Frs for two.

Meals: 100 Frs, by arrangement.

Closed: Never.

From Sarlat D57 towards Beynac, then D703 through St Cyprien. After 7km right to Coux et Bigaroque. Up through village, turn left after the Mairie. House is on right after approx. 1km, just after wayside cross.
Michelin Map No: 235-5

Entry no: 487   Map No: 12

Ghislaine et Marc OREFICE
Manoir de la Brunie, La Brunie
24220 Le Coux et Bigaroque
Dordogne
Tel: (0)5 53 29 61 42
Fax: (0)5 53 28 62 35
e-mail: marc.orefice@wanadoo.fr
Web: www.abscisse.com

On a quiet road with its land stretching behind it, the château is mostly 14th and 17th-century with a superb 12th-century tower. The four château bedrooms are very fine with antiques and old paintings mixed with more contemporary pieces. Shower rooms are less grand but perfectly adequate. There's a baronial-style dining room – Monsieur prepares dinner for four or more guests – and a dignified *salon* with red brocade chairs and Chinese pieces. The gardens below the swimming pool are very pretty, you can cycle or walk through the woods and there's much to visit close by.

Rooms: 4 doubles, each with shower & wc.

Price: 490-690 Frs for two.

Meals: 150 Frs, excluding wine.

Closed: December & January.

Gîte space for 18 people.

From Sarlat dir. Gourdon for 3.5km. Left on D704, Souillac to Cazoulès. Opposite bakery turn left beside restaurant; Château is up hill on left.
Michelin Map No: 235-6

Entry no: 488   Map No: 12

Michele & William VIDAL D'HONDT
Château du Pas du Raysse
24370 Cazoulès, Dordogne
Tel: (0)5 53 29 84 41
Fax: (0)5 53 59 62 16
Web: www.pageszoom.com/chateau-du-raysse

Knights Templar lived here and pilgrims hostelled en route to Santiago de Compostella. It's now a family home, full of personal treasures: reflecting the Nevilles' travels and interests. Christopher is a writer and can tell many tales about this ancient house. The large, comfortable upstairs rooms share a living room and views of the walled gardens. The ground floor 'studio' has a more functional feel, its own entrance (from the wonderful old village street), kitchen and living area. The freshest breads for breakfast from the bakery next door. *Children over 12 welcome.*

Rooms: 1 quadruple, 1 family suite both with bath or shower & wc.

Price: 400-500 Frs for two.

Meals: Good choice in town.

Closed: Rarely.

From Brive take A20 & exit at Cressenac. Then N140 to Martel. Bear right down from Place Gambetta, Rue Droite is 2nd on left. Pass pharmacy, house on right, green door.
Michelin Map No: 235-2

Entry no: 489	Map No: 12

Christopher & Sigrid NEVILLE
La Maison du Silence
Rue Droite
46600 Martel, Lot
Tel: (0)5 65 37 40 09
Fax: (0)5 65 37 40 09
e-mail: christopher.neville@fnac.net

With its steep roofs and light-coloured stone, and now that the Bells have accomplished that labour of love called restoration, the old farmhouse is quaint and inviting. The original character of beams, old floors and twisty corners has been preserved and furnishing is simple with cast-iron beds, original paintings and, in the huge living-kitchen, an open hearth and a closed stove. It's not smart just family-comfortable and relaxed. Gavin, an artist and potter, and Lillian, a happy (and excellent) cook, left South Africa to bring up their son in this quiet setting and they'll give you a great welcome.

Rooms: 1 triple, 1 double & bunks, 1 suite (3), all with bath or shower & wc.

Price: 240 Frs for two.

Meals: 90 Frs, including wine & coffee.

Closed: Never.

Gîte space for 10 people.

From Brive, N20 S for 10km then N140 dir. Rocamadour; D36 left to Rignac; at church, left then right; D36 dir. Lavergne for 50m; left for Pouch. 2km; first house, blue shutters.
Michelin Map No: 235-6

Entry no: 490	Map No: 12

Gavin & Lillian BELL
Pouch
46500 Rignac
Lot
Tel: (0)5 65 33 66 84
Fax: (0)5 65 33 71 31
e-mail: lilianbel@aol.com
Web: www.sawdays.co.uk

You instantly feel at home in this converted 18th-century barn with its great Lot views. Madame, who spent many years in America, is an avid patchworker and her creative touches are everywhere, including the garden and terrace area, full of shrubs and ferns and secluded spots. The open-plan living room, where old skylights deliver splashes of sky, is full of artistic character with its oak floors, stove and pretty antiques beneath paintings of all periods. The airy ground-floor guest room has its own antique writing table, watercolours and a glazed stable door onto the garden. A privilege for two – and an extra room for children is occasionally available.

Rooms: 1 twin with bath & wc.

Price: 270 Frs for two.

Meals: Occasionally with advance notice. Restaurant within walking distance.

Closed: Never.

From Figeac N140 NW 24km towards Gramat; before Thémines exit, right for Le Bout du Lieu; house 200m on left with large wooden gates in stone wall & blue sign.
Michelin Map No: 235-6

Entry no: 491   Map No: 12

Élisabeth de LAPÉROUSE-COLEMAN
La Buissonnière
Le Bout du Lieu
46120 Thémines, Lot
Tel: (0)5 65 40 88 58
Fax: (0)5 65 40 88 58
Web: www.sawdays.co.uk

The owners have restored this lovely ancient mill, to make space for you and space for them. It stands in colourful gardens, the stream runs round it. Nearly all the guestrooms, with their sand/lime-rendered or old stone walls and fine wall hangings, lead off a ground-floor corridor and have French windows onto the garden. A new barn conversion includes kitchen, TV room, *salon* and dining conservatory for guests. Here, you will eat Madame's fine food while Monsieur's paintings of typical local houses are on view. Their near-professional welcome is superb, the area full of fascinating treasures such as Rocamadour and the Gouffre du Padirac.

Rooms: 4 doubles, 1 family room, all with shower & wc.

Price: 320-430 Frs for two.

Meals: 120 Frs, including wine.

Closed: November-February.

From Gramat, N140 direction Figeac; after 500m, left onto a small road leading to the mill.
Michelin Map No: 235-6

Entry no: 492   Map No: 12

Gérard & Claude RAMELOT
Moulin de Fresquet
46500 Gramat
Lot
Tel: (0)5 65 38 70 60
Fax: (0)5 65 38 70 60

A multi-talented, cosmopolitan couple keep house here in the summer and live in Japan in the winter. Charles cooks – the huge kitchen/entrance hall is his domain and meals, French or Franco-Japanese, are memorable. Kako paints – even the wooden coat hangers bear her flowers. The house is French and spotless. All bedrooms, in the older, lower part of the house, have an exceptionally tranquil view of rolling meadows, superb mattresses and lush bathrooms; the oldest has an ancient stone fireplace and traditional stone sink. They are delightful people and Figeac is said to be "one of the best-renovated towns in Europe".

Rooms: 2 twins, 1 suite for 3, each with bath or shower & wc.

Price: 290 Frs for two. If you book for 6 nights the 7th night is free.

Meals: 110 Frs, including aperitif & wine.

Closed: November-May.

From Gramat SE on N140 towards Figeac for 17km, through Le Bourg, sharp left immediately after small bridge on edge of village. House signed on left, 1km.
Michelin Map No: 235-11

Entry no: 493   Map No: 13

Kako & Charles LARROQUE
Mas de la Feuille
46120 Le Bourg
Lot
Tel: (0)5 65 11 00 17
Fax: (0)5 65 11 00 17
Web: www.sawdays.co.uk

In the hills between Figeac and Rocamadour, Isabelle and her son live in a beautiful barn, with one of those plunging rooflines. The superb conversion, with very green bathrooms, has created a wonderful beamed living/eating area which opens out through big barn doors onto a pretty garden. Isabelle is an open-hearted person with great energy and enthusiasm. Meals at the big convivial table are good Périgord style and she grows her own vegetables. A relaxed atmosphere, intelligent conversation and guidance on things to see in the Lot.

Rooms: 1 double, 3 triples, each with shower & wc.

Price: 250 Frs for two.

Meals: 90 Frs, including wine.

Closed: Never.

From Figeac, N140 NW dir. Gramat for 21.5km, left on D38 to Théminettes. House signed, 1st left 400m after N140.
Michelin Map No: 235-11

Entry no: 494   Map No: 13

Isabelle N'GUYEN
La Gaoulière
Friaulens Haut
46120 Théminettes
Lot
Tel: (0)5 65 40 97 52
Fax: (0)5 65 40 97 52

There are five hectares of garden with a huge swimming pool (where you can make yourself lunch in the 'summer kitchen') a tennis court and swings for children. (Guy and Gilou are up for a game of tennis with you if you wish). There is a beautiful terrace with wonderful views, perfect for dining out in warm weather. Everything has been newly done for B&B so the mattresses are good and the comfort is perfect. There is even a children's bedroom in the pigeonnier with two beds and a platform. You will be made hugely welcome.

Rooms: 2 doubles, each with shower & wc; extra room for children available.

Price: 250 Frs for two; 90 Frs per child in tower room.

Meals: 100 Frs, including wine.

Closed: Never.

Gîte space for 4 people.

From Gourdon D673 dir. Fumel; left on D6 to Dégagnac. In town square follow SNCF station. After football ground on left, 2nd right. At top of hill right to Domaine de Montsalvy.
Michelin Map No: 235-10

Entry no: 495   Map No: 12

Guy & Gilou NODON
Domaine de Montsalvy
Montsalvy
46340 Dégagnac
Lot
Tel: (0)5 65 41 51 57
Fax: (0)5 65 41 51 57

Once the laundry house to the château that rises above it, in a perfect medieval village, it is old, tiny, three-levelled, and space is brilliantly used: convertible sofa beds, miniature kitchen. The bedroom under the eaves is decorated with French antiques and treasures from faraway places. Fish in the river – which also has a 'beach' – chat to Françoise in the sitting room, also full of travel mementoes. Breakfast when you like on fresh bread and croissants from the local bakery.

Rooms: Cottage for 8: 2 doubles & 2 twins, shower & wc, kitchen.

Price: 250 Frs for two; reductions for children.

Meals: Self-catering (+50 Frs) or in village.

Closed: Never.

Gîte space for 4 people.

From Cahors W on D911 to Puy l'Évêque. At r'bout take road towards bridge; before bridge, right in Rue des Teinturiers. Park by river between 2 plane trees & take steps up to house.
Michelin Map No: 235-13

Entry no: 496   Map No: 12

Mme Françoise PILLON
4 rue des Mariniers
46700 Puy l'Évêque
Lot
Tel: (0)5 65 36 56 03
Fax: (0)5 65 36 56 47
e-mail: fanfan2.@wanadoo.fr
Web: www.sawdays.co.uk

Built in the 1850s by Dr Rouma, a distinguished local figure and Consul General, the house was almost a ruin before the Arnetts found it on their return from Japan. In restoring it, they kept as much of the original as possible including the wallpaper in the hall, where the winding staircase is a delight. Much of the décor has an oriental theme, particularly in the enormous dining room. The setting just couldn't be better; there are stunning views over the river and the pretty old town – famous for its medieval music festival which climaxes, by the way, with the largest firework display in France.

Rooms: 2 doubles, 1 twin, each with bath, shower & wc.

Price: 300 Frs for two.

Meals: Choice nearby.

Closed: Never.

A heart-warming and very French experience, staying with this lovely cheerful couple who are always ready for a drink and a chat (in French) – their wonderful love of life is infectious. Use the peaceful terrace where your hosts are happy for you to sit all day over your breakfast, revelling in the setting, the vast views and the flowering garden. Inside, the décor is in keeping with the farmhouse, with floral papers and family furniture. No dinner but lots of home-grown wine and aperitif, fruit from their trees and *gâteau de noix* (walnut cake) with their own honey – flowing as if you were in paradise.

Rooms: 1 double with curtained-off shower & wc.

Price: 250 Frs for two.

Meals: Good restaurant 2km.

Closed: Never.

Gîte space for 6 people.

From Cahors D911 towards Fumel & Villeneuve sur Lot. At Puy l'Eveque take Rue du Dr Rouma to bridge. House is last on right before bridge.
Michelin Map No: 235-13

Entry no: 497　　　　　Map No: 12

Bill & Ann ARNETT
Maison Rouma
2 rue du Docteur Rouma
46700 Puy l'Evêque, Lot
Tel: (0)5 65 36 59 39
Fax: (0)5 65 36 59 39
e-mail: williamarnett@hotmail.com
Web: www.sawdays.co.uk

From Cahors take D8 direction Pradines for 8km. At sign for Flaynac, follow Chambres d'Hôtes sign on right, then right and right again.
Michelin Map No: 235-14

Entry no: 498　　　　　Map No: 12

M & Mme Jean FAYDI
Flaynac
46090 Pradines
Lot
Tel: (0)5 65 35 33 36

On a balustraded terrace overlooking the river, this house was built in 1805 by the Italian ambassador, homesick for Florence. It has a beautiful garden, with a swimming pool in a flowery corner of the lawn but the first word that springs to mind inside is 'dramatic'. The library is raspberry with a zebra throw over the black leather sofa, while the big, white beamed dining room – once the kitchen perhaps? – is dominated by a vast fireplace, bold still lifes and red and white checks. A teacher, who loves to talk to people, Claude is about to retire and thought B&B the perfect solution.

Rooms: 3 doubles, each with shower & wc.

Price: 300 Frs for two.

Meals: Choice available locally.

Closed: Never.

From Cahor D8 direction Pradines. 5km into village right at roundabout. House 100m downhill on right. Enter through large metal gates.
Michelin Map No: 235-14

Entry no: 499   Map No: 12

Claude FAILLE
Valrose – Le Poujal
46090 Pradines
Lot
Tel: (0)5 65 22 18 52

Built of Lot stone, the 17th-century farmhouse (a gîte in summer, extra B&B in winter) and barn (where the first B&B rooms are) with stunning views over two valleys, are being restored by the Scotts to look like the old characters they are, with modern comforts too. The bedrooms are small and storage space is limited but the pool (solar-heated, salt-purified) and sunbeds beckon you out. Friendly, busy hosts who want you to have a good time; breakfast served any time; dinner, sometimes a poolside barbecue, is fun, relaxed and informal. Pool-house kitchen and fridge for picnic lunches.

Rooms: 1 double with bathroom; 1 suite for 2 with bathroom and wc.

Price: 250-360 Frs for two.

Meals: 100 Frs, including aperitif, wine & coffee, by arrangement.

Closed: Never; please telephone to book.

Gîte space for 22 people.

Bypass Cahors direction Toulouse; at roundabout D653 direction Agen; at fork right on D656. Pass Villeseque, Sauzet, Bovila then take 3rd left on straight stretch; signposted.
Michelin Map No: 235-13

Entry no: 500   Map No: 12

Peter & Zoé SCOTT
Mondounet
46800 Fargues
Lot
Tel: (0)5 65 36 96 32
Fax: (0)5 65 31 84 89
e-mail: scotsprops@aol.com

Walk through the entrance hall into the handsome country kitchen and thence onto the lawns that roll towards those views. Or stop in it and dine; it has a large fireplace, pottery pieces and sculpture – and a lot of flowers. The living room has terracotta tiles and kilim rugs, a fireplace and grand piano. Adriana is Swiss, Jocelyn South African, and they tend to do things well. They are new to it all and hugely committed, creating 'lush' bedrooms and a touch of luxury in the bathrooms. The abiding memory will be of terracotta tiles, great food, and attention to detail.

Rooms: 2 suites, each with bathroom & wc.

Price: 350-450 Frs for two.

Meals: 80-150 Frs, including wine.

Closed: Never.

Gîte space for 8 people.

From Saintes A10 motorway (Paris-Bordeaux), exit St Andre de Cubzac, towards Ste Foy La Grande. There take D708 to Duras; 5km after Duras left on the C1 to St Pierre sur Dropt. Michelin Map No: 234-8

Entry no: **501**   Map No: 12

Jocelyn & Adriana CLOETE
Manoir de Levignac
St Pierre sur Dropt
47120 Duras
Lot-et-Garonne
Tel: (0)5 53 83 68 11
Fax: (0)5 53 93 98 63

A distinguished house, once a ladies' music school, in an unspoilt, ungentrified village. It fronts onto the market square and backs onto lovely, long countryside views. Fiona is Scottish, Leif is Danish, with a background in film, advertising and interior design. They've lived in London, New York and the Middle East and the house is full of fascinating things: antique pieces, masks, relics from the set of the English National Opera – a brave and successful mix. The beige and white theme extends to the bedrooms, with their white-painted floors and sumptuous raw Irish linen bedspreads and curtains. *No guest sitting room. Canoeing and horse-riding nearby.*

Rooms: 1 double, 2 twins, each with own bath or shower & wc.

Price: 450-500 Frs for two.

Meals: 100-120 Frs, including wine, by arrangement; picnic basket possible.

Closed: Never.

From Marmande D708 to Levignac. Left in Levignac & follow signs for centre ville. House has white front door & is on left behind market hall. Michelin Map No: 234-12

Entry no: **502**   Map No: 12

Leif & Fiona PEDERSEN
La Maison de la Halle
47120 Lévignac de Guyenne
Lot-et-Garonne
Tel: (0)5 53 94 37 61
Fax: (0)5 53 94 37 66
e-mail: maison.de.la.halle@wanadoo.fr
Web: www.lamaisondelahalle.com

Fed up with working too hard, in Monte Carlo and New York, the Peyres moved here for a quieter life then thought of B&B as a way of sharing their love of the place. The double rooms are not large but have French windows onto their own terrace and splendid views down the valley to a small lake. The twin is huge and very *vieille France* – rugs on original wood floor and *lits bateau*. Then there are the glorious public rooms, corridors and vast yellow-tiled kitchen. Stunning furniture, a remarkable solid brass candelabra, a piano, a billiard room, handmade carpets... the list goes on. Very casual yet civilised.

Rooms: 2 doubles, 1 twin, all with shower & wc.

Price: 390-550 Frs for two.

Meals: By arrangement.

Closed: 15 December-March.

Gîte space for 4 people.

From Bergerac D933 S towards Marmande. Approx. 1.5km after Eymet left on C1 towards Agnac-Mairie; Château 500m on left.
Michelin Map No: 234-12

Entry no: **503**   Map No: 12

Françoise & Henri PEYRE
Château de Péchalbet
47800 Agnac
Lot-et-Garonne
Tel: (0)5 53 83 04 70
Fax: (0)5 53 83 04 70

A house as beautiful as the surrounding countryside; this is a 17th-century 'family château' which the Babers, who are British, fell for some years ago. They brought their fine family furniture which sits most graciously in the bedrooms (the double beds are king-sized) overlooking 15 hectares of gardens, parkland, woods and fields. You can roam, relax or play: there's a large, carp-stocked lake you can fish, a hard tennis court and a 16m child-friendly pool. Breakfast in the huge kitchen, or on the terrace, on Patricia's excellent home-made jams and marmalades (maybe bread too). Good local markets, restaurants and wines.

Rooms: 2 doubles, 1 family suite, each with bath & wc.

Price: 500-700 Frs for two.

Meals: Several good restaurants in Castillonès (5 mins).

Closed: December-February.

From Bergerac N21 dir. Villeneuve. 1.5km after Castillonès, pass 'Terres du Sud' on left. After 50m, drive signposted on right before crest of hill.
Michelin Map No: 234-12

Entry no: **504**   Map No: 12

Patricia BABER
Domaine des Rigals
47330 Castillonnès
Lot-et-Garonne
Tel: (0)5 53 41 24 21
Fax: (0)5 53 41 24 79
e-mail: babersrig@aol.com
Web: www.ecu.co.uk/rigals

Deep in the Périgord countryside, Salarial is a typical local farmhouse unexpectedly furnished with the fruits of an informed traveller's choice: antiques, wall-hangings and paintings from distant lands bring sophisticated originality to rustic beams, old country doors and low ceilings. Madame has lived in China, can tell many a tale of the Orient (the Chinese Room is witness) whilst being extremely knowledgeable about what to see and do just here – you're in walled town territory. Breakfast, when you're ready, on the terrace in summer; embroidered sheets and spotless bathrooms; good conversation or bucolic peace – you choose. An ideal getaway.

Rooms: 1 duplex for 2/4 with bath & wc; 1 double with shower & wc.

Price: 300-350 Frs for two.

Meals: In Villeréal 3.5km, Monflanquin 9km.

Closed: Never.

From Bergerac N21 S for 9.5km. Fork left on D14 to Villeréal (24km). D676 S towards Monflanquin for 2.5km, left towards St Etienne de Villeréal. House signed on right after 800m.
Michelin Map No: 235-9

Entry no: 505　　　　Map No: 12

Jacqueline DELLETERY
Salarial
47210 St Etienne de Villeréal
Lot-et-Garonne
Tel: (0)5 53 36 08 71/
　　　(0)6 07 14 09 05
Web: www.sawdays.co.uk

Horses are a passion with this family and you will often find them out riding. Within striking distance of three famous *bastides*, this old farm grows tobacco, maize and sunflowers and there's a château thrown in for the view. The house is a converted pigeon tower (h and owls nest in the holes outside); t are good bedrooms, a log-fired, cou style sitting room, highchair, bottle-warmer and games for children, a fin swimming pool for all. Madame has a infectious energy and speaks fluent English; her affable husband is quiete Readers are enthusiastic.

Rooms: 2 doubles, each with shower wc, 1 with mini-kitchen.

Price: 320 Frs for two.

Meals: 100 Frs, including wine & coff Self-catering 60 Frs per day.

Closed: Never.

Gîte space for 8 people.

From Villeneuve sur Lot, D676 to Monflanquin and D272 dir. Monpazier. 1.5km after crossroads to Dévillac, left before bridge; house is 2nd on right.
Michelin Map No: 235-9

Entry no: 506　　　　Map No: 12

Michel & Maryse PANNETIER
Colombié
47210 Dévillac
Lot-et-Garonne
Tel: (0)5 53 36 62 34
Fax: (0)5 53 36 04 79

The brash modernity of the telephone is hidden behind a model ship; no TV either. The triumphant five-year restoration Paul and Pippa did mostly themselves, with two small children and a passionate commitment to the integrity of the (13th and 16th centuries) building. It is breathtaking: the great hall with its elaborate floor set in cabalistic patterns and lit only with candles, two stone staircases and patches of fresco. The Tower room is unforgettable, as is the pool. Paul and Pippa are vegetarian-friendly and pro-organic; dinner is an elaborate affair (may feature home-reared lamb), and often lasts hours; people clearly love it.

Rooms: 3 doubles & 2 suites, each with bath, shower & wc.

Price: 450-650 Frs for two.

Meals: 110 Frs, including wine & coffee.

Closed: Never.

Gîte space for 26 people.

From Tournon D656 dir. Agen; after 1km left dir. Courbiac past church; turn right at the cross dir. route de Montague. 1km house on left.
Michelin Map No: 235-13

Entry no: 507 Map No: 12

Paul & Pippa HECQUET
Château de Rodié
47370 Courbiac de Tournon
Lot-et-Garonne
Tel: (0)5 53 40 89 24
Fax: (0)5 53 40 89 25
e-mail: chateau.rodie@wanadoo.fr

Ann knows her design – she and Alain have clearly enjoyed doing the conversion using interesting paint techniques. There are lovely gardens and three acres of ancient trees around the château. It has salmon-coloured shutters, open fires, lots of high windows, brightly-coloured walls, palm trees, polished wooden floors, some Empire furniture. The superb bedrooms are very plush and well-mattressed, one with a Rice Bed from Ann's native South Carolina. Dinner is delicious and your hosts are gregarious yet efficient. *Security is assured by electronically operated park gates.*

Rooms: 1 duplex for 5 with 2 bathrooms; 4 doubles, each with bath or shower & wc.

Price: 690 Frs for two.

Meals: 150 Frs, including wine & coffee.

Closed: December & January.

From A62 exit 6 towards Aiguillon. Take 2nd right, D642, towards Buzet. Château on right, signposted, shortly before Buzet.
Michelin Map No: 234-16

Entry no: 508 Map No: 12

Ann & Alain Doherty GELIX
Château de Coustet
47160 Buzet sur Baïse
Lot-et-Garonne
Tel: (0)5 53 79 26 60
Fax: (0)5 53 79 14 16
e-mail: c.coustet@csi.com
Web: www.coustet.com

A wonderfully welcoming hostess (Monsieur runs the farm), brilliant big bedrooms in the best French provincial (unflouncy) style looking across the garden to meadows and woods, opulent but unostentatious white bathrooms, acres of parkland for walks from your door, space for 8,000 free-range chickens and myriad other animals: sheep, horses, ducks, dogs (but no cats). Despite its size, the 17th-century château is a comfortable, informal home, ideal for children. You can play billiards, table tennis, croquet, *boules.* Breakfast – with the inevitable eggs – and dinner are very much *en famille.* French B&B *par excellence.*

Rooms: 1 double, 1 twin, 1 suite, all with bath or shower & wc.

Price: 320-380 Frs for two.

Meals: 120 Frs, including wine & coffee.

Closed: Never.

Peaceful at the end of a long drive, this is a wonderful place, albeit more formal than some. The Montaignacs are elegant, immaculate and gracious, like their dining room with its panelling and breakfast silver – the epitome of Old France. Choose the ground-floor, original-parqueted, fireplaced suite or glide up the fine staircase past the ancestors to the double room. Both welcome you with antiques, old engravings, personality. Monsieur know books-worth of fascinating history; Madame is quietly attentive. Very special.

Rooms: 1 suite for 2-4 people, 1 twin, both with bath or shower & wc.

Price: 580 Frs for two, including breakfast.

Meals: Good choice within 9km.

Closed: Never , but advance bookings only.

From Marmande, D933 S direction Casteljaloux for 10km. Château signposted on right opposite D289. Michelin Map No: 234-16

Entry no: **509**   Map No: 12

M & Mme de LA RAITRIE
Château de Cantet
Samazan
47250 Bouglon
Lot-et-Garonne
Tel: (0)5 53 20 60 60
Fax: (0)5 53 89 63 53

From Montluçon, N145 direction Chamblet; signposted on the right. Michelin Map No: 238-44

Entry no: **510**   Map No: 8

Yves & Jacqueline de
MONTAIGNAC
Château du Plaix
03170 Chamblet
Allier
Tel: (0)4 70 07 80 56

Visitors eat round a 10ft-diameter table made from an outsize wine barrel, in a 19th-century barn with beams, cantilevered gallery and a magnificent two-storey fireplace. Antoine teaches cookery and still loves to whip up regional feasts in his own sensational stainless steel kitchen then serve rather special wines from his contacts in the trade. Children have a sandpit, climbing frame and pool (and the company of Claire and Antoine's three children). Canoeing, canal trips, fishing, riding and cycling are available locally. Readers write reams of praise.

Rooms: 4 doubles, 1 twin, each with bath and/or shower & wc.

Price: 300 Frs for two.

Meals: 120 Frs, including wine & coffee.

Closed: Never.

A62 Toulouse-Bordeaux take exit 4 'La Réole'. D9, then take left direction Bazas-Grignols. Over motorway bridge & take 1st left, 250m after bridge. Follow signs Chambres d'Hôtes for 3km. Michelin Map No: 234-11

Entry no: **511**   Map No: 12

Claire & Antoine LABORDE
La Tuilerie
33190 Noaillac
Gironde
Tel: (0)5 56 71 05 51
Fax: (0)5 56 71 05 51
e-mail: claire.laborde@libertysurf.fr
Web: www.sawdays.co.uk

Aquitaine

Stilted shepherds once herded their flocks in swamps but pine plantations drained the land so stilts just dance at country fairs where northern neighbours sell the fermented juice of the world's best grapes.

Don't be fooled by the modest exterior – go through the main buildings, and splendour strikes! Discover delightful gardens and a great pool enclosed by charming guest quarters: your dynamic hosts have done a brilliant conversion of the old stables. They have kept much of the original wood and added elegant antique furniture to each of the large, individually-styled bedrooms. Attention to detail includes armoires lined with sophisticated fabrics that match curtains and wallpaper, good bathrooms, superb breakfasts. Overall, excellent value. *Gîte space for 6.*

Rooms: 2 doubles, 1 twin, each with bath or shower & wc.

Price: 450 Frs for two.

Meals: Restaurant 300m.

Closed: Never.

From Libourne D670 S 45km to La Réole; left on N113 towards Agen. House on left on edge of town opp. Automobile Museum.
Michelin Map No: 234-11

Entry no: 512   Map No: 12

Christian & Danielle HENRY
Les Charmettes
Henry's Lodge
33190 La Réole
Gironde
Tel: (0)5 56 71 09 23
Fax: (0)5 56 71 25 13
Web: www.sawdays.co.uk

Such kind, courteous people. Food and wine buffs love it here as Madame is an excellent cook who willingly (with advance warning) caters for special diets (and guests can buy her conserves) and Monsieur is a wine expert. Their 19th-century farmhouse, surrounded by fields and vineyards, is attractively furnished and the beamed, wallpapered guestrooms are big and comfortable – the family room is particularly lovely and has a more contemporary feel, with a mezzanine floor and a sitting area overlooking the garden. The dining room is decorated in Art Deco style with modern pictures and *two* fireplaces. *No payment by credit card.*

Rooms: 1 double, 1 triple, 1 family room; all with bath, shower & wc.

Price: 350 Frs for two.

Meals: 120-200 Frs, excluding wine & coffee.

Closed: 16 October-31 December.

From Libourne, D670, then left on D230 to Rimons. Just outside Rimons, at sawmill on right, take first left; signposted.
Michelin Map No: 234-12

Entry no: 513   Map No: 12

Dominique & Patrick LÉVY
Grand Boucaud
Rimons
33580 Monségur
Gironde
Tel: (0)5 56 71 88 57
Fax: (0)5 56 71 88 57

This spotlessly clean and comfortable 1750s farmhouse was Monsieur's family holiday home for years. Born in Senegal, he has been in Madagascar, Tahiti and many other places: quantities of fascinating souvenirs tell the tale. Madame, pleasant and attractive, was a nursery school teacher and is very keen to please her guests: we were naturally offered coffee and cakes on the terrace. Beautiful bedrooms, simple yet not stark, have white or clean stone walls, built-in cupboards often with genuine wall-to-wall doors. Excellent for fishing, canoeing or riverside walking (50m to the River Dordogne) and St Emilion just 7km away.

Rooms: 1 double/twin, 1 suite for 2/4, each with bathroom.

Price: 280-320 Frs for two.

Meals: In village or choice 500m.

Closed: Never.

Gîte space for 4 people.

From Bordeaux D936 E for 36km. 4km after Branne right on D670 towards Agen. At Lavagnac (1km) left after Boucherie/Charcuterie; house on left. Michelin Map No: 234-7

Entry no: **514**   Map No: 12

France PRAT
3 chemin de Courbestey
Lavagnac
33350 Ste Terre, Gironde
Tel: (0)5 57 47 13 74
Fax: (0)5 57 47 13 74
e-mail: france.prat@wanadoo.fr
Web: perso.wanadoo.fr/france.prat

Tradition has deep, proud roots here; you sense it in the ancient walls. The *Girondin* farmhouse has stood for three centuries, the vines are mature, the wine superb; the lovely linen, pretty patchwork and lace bedcovers are family heirlooms, the family itself is busy, lively, full of character, all three generations have a strong presence. The stone-walled, old-furnished guest rooms and their small bathrooms are immaculately kept. There's a guest sitting room and useful kitchenette but the beautiful breakfast table in the cosy family dining room make it special indeed. St Emilion and Libourne are each just 4km away.

Rooms: 2 doubles, 2 twins, 1 triple, all with bath or shower & wc.

Price: 300-320 Frs for two.

Meals: Choice locally.

Closed: January.

From Libourne, D243 direction St Emilion. 3km before St Emilion, D245 direction Pomerol; signposted. Michelin Map No: 234-3

Entry no: **515**   Map No: 11

Claude BRIEUX
Château Millaud-Montlabert
33330 St Emilion
Gironde
Tel: (0)5 57 24 71 85
Fax: (0)5 57 24 62 78

Parts of this priory are 12th-century, when it provided rest for pilgrims. Susie now sees that 20th-century guests are also refreshed. Her warm personality (she does personal development workshops) and the serenity of the setting are worth coming for. Lie in a hammock under the walnut tree, let the fantail pigeons coo you into a blissful siesta, the nightingales serenade your dawn. The house is decorated with a sophisticated combination of good antiques and modern pieces, opulent curtains and cheerful bedcovers. No routine – breakfast served whenever it suits, candlelit dinners on request.

Rooms: 2 doubles with shower, bath & wc, 1 apartment with 2 doubles.

Price: 440-550 Frs for two (min. 2 nights July-August).

Meals: Ask if chef is around or restaurant 3km.

Closed: Never.

Gîte space for 6 people.

From Bordeaux D936 dir. Bergerac. Exactly 1km after St Quentin de Baron, house signed on right. Michelin Map No: 234-7

Entry no: 516   **Map No: 11**

Susie de CASTILHO
Le Prieuré
33750 St Quentin de Baron
Gironde
Tel: (0)5 57 24 16 75
Fax: (0)5 57 24 13 80
e-mail: stay@stayfrance.net
Web: www.stayfrance.net

Both simple and sophisticated, this self-contained barn conversion attached to the cottage has a 'holiday home' feel in the best sense in that it also has some lovely and characterful bits and pieces from the main house that are too good, useful or well-loved to throw away. The living area has an old woodburning stove and *coin cuisine* corner kitchen with open-tread stairs leading to the charming bedroom with patchboard ceiling, a fresh yellow and white colour scheme and an enchanting little window at floor level. Outside there are wonderful old roses, an organic vegetable garden and a swimming pool surrounded by lavender.

Rooms: 1 double with shower & wc.

Price: 450 Frs for two.

Meals: Occasionally by arrangement & choice in Branne (6km).

Closed: Never.

From Bordeaux take D936 direction Bergerac (or exit 24 from A10 motorway) for approx. 20km to Tizac de Curton. Through village then left on D128 direction Moulon, after 1km turn left at crossroads. House 5km on right. Michelin Map No: 234-7

Entry no: 517   **Map No: 11**

Mme Laurence GEOFFROY
Beyrin
33240 Tizac de Curton
Gironde
Tel: (0)5 57 24 18 62
Fax: (0)5 57 24 18 62
e-mail: laurencegeoffroy@yahoo.fr

A hard-working young couple in an 18th-century château, without quite enough money to make it over-stylish; but they have three good and very big bedrooms, a stone entrance hall, a wrought-iron balcony terrace for a glass of (their own dry white Semillon) château wine, and decorative bantams all over the garden. It is relaxed and easy – even busy – with three young children, and deer in the woods. Breakfast is on the terrace, wine-tasting in the magnificent *salle de dégustation*. The small pool is for evening dippers rather than sun-worshippers.

Rooms: 3 triples, each with shower & wc.

Price: 300 Frs for two.

Meals: Choice in Bourg.

Closed: February & 1 week in August.

From A10 exit 40a or 40b through St André de Cubzac, W on D669 through Bourg towards Blaye and very soon right on D251 towards Berson for 1km; signed on right up lane/drive.
Michelin Map No: 233-38

Entry no: 518   Map No: 11

M & Mme BASSEREAU
Château de la Grave
33710 Bourg sur Gironde
Gironde
Tel: (0)5 57 68 41 49
Fax: (0)5 57 68 49 26
e-mail: chateau.de.la.grave@wanadoo.fr
Web: www.sawdays.co.uk

For wine-lovers! There are five comfortable, old-furnished guest rooms in this generous 18th-century mansion, built on the foundations of a medieval château in a place loaded with history. It surveys vineyards (the fulsome Côtes de Blaye are here), fields and forest. The Chartiers keep about a dozen horses and ponies and their daughters might give your children rides. The large, quiet, sunny rooms have their own entrance, kitchen and living room. This is well-organised, 'no-nonsense' hospitality and Monsieur will arrange vineyard tours for you.

Rooms: 4 triples, 1 double all with shower & wc.

Price: 240 Frs for two.

Meals: Self-catering; restaurants nearby.

Closed: Never.

From A10, exit 38 on D132 and D115 to St Savin. There, D18 to St Mariens. Left just before village; signposted.
Michelin Map No: 233-38

Entry no: 519   Map No: 11

Daniel & Yvonne CHARTIER
Château de Gourdet
33620 Saint Mariens
Gironde
Tel: (0)5 57 58 05 37

The New Hebrides, Brazil, New Zealand, the Sahara... Michèle has lived in them all; it is enough to make one feel parochial. But her family has been here for five generations and they built this hacienda-style house where the old farm crumbled away. The imitation zebra and tiger-skin upholstery in the living room pales into insignificance beside all the memorabilia and African sculptures. Bedrooms are traditional, with fine views across oceans of vines. Their own wine comes with dinner and the nearby ferry comes from Blaye and Royan.

Rooms: 1 double with bath & wc; 1 twin with shower & wc.

Price: 300-320 Frs for two.

Meals: 150 Frs, including aperitif, wine & coffee.

Closed: Never.

From Bordeaux Rocade (bypass) exit 7 on D1 to Castelnau; N215 through St Laurent; 4km on, right for St Sauveur & Vertheuil. Through village, leave abbey on right, over level crossing, white house approx. 1km on left.
Michelin Map No: 233-37

Entry no: 520   Map No: 11

Michèle TARDAT
Cantemerle
9 rue des Châtaigniers
33180 Vertheuil Médoc, Gironde
Tel: (0)5 56 41 96 24/mobile: (90) 6 08 98 71 02
Fax: (0)5 56 41 96 24

Ideal for wine buffs! Old meets new here – the house is a successful mixture of both. The rooms have modern fabrics alongside fine old pieces of furniture, Philippe is Cellar Master for a *Grand Cru Classé* steeped in tradition, and is also an Internet convert; Monika, who is German and nursed in Vietnam for a while, may give you home-baked bread and muesli for breakfast. They are urbane, helpful, well-travelled polyglots and can obtain entry to most big wine châteaux for their guests. The large fish and-lily pond adds a note of serenity. You may breakfast on the terrace and the beach is just 20 minutes away.

Rooms: 1 double/twin, 1 double, 1 suite, each with bath or shower & wc.

Price: 260-380 Frs for two; 380 Frs for cottage without breakfast.

Meals: Restaurant 7km.

Closed: Never.

Gîte space for 4 people.

From Bordeaux ring road exit 7 on D1 towards Le Verdon, past Castelnau & St Laurent. 4km after St Laurent right on D104 to Cissac. In village, right at War Memorial into Rue du Luc. House 1km on left, after water tower.
Michelin Map No: 233-37

Entry no: 521   Map No: 11

Philippe & Monika ACHENER
Le Luc
6 route de Larrivaux
33250 Cissac Médoc, Gironde
Tel: (0)5 56 59 52 90
Fax: (0)5 56 59 51 84
e-mail: ph.achener@gmx.net
Web: www.TRAVEL.TO/MEDOC

Madame is a gem, gracious and charming, her husband is more reserved, Braco the dog loves company. In its secluded setting, their miniature château rejoices in a fine chestnut staircase with iron banister, a veranda paved with rare Bidache stone, high ceilings, old prints, a glimpse of the Pyrenees and the call of a peacock. Madame teaches yoga, paints, is a long-distance walker and a committed vegetarian. Children can freely roam the 20 hectares of parkland – they love it. The rooms, large and properly decorated, have gorgeous parquet floors and relatively little 'château' furniture. We think the smaller ones give better value.

Rooms: 3 doubles, 1 twin, each with shower or bath & wc.

Price: 300-500 Frs for two.

Meals: Vegetarian dinner 100 Frs, including wine & coffee (min. 3 nights).

Closed: November-March, except by arrangement.

From A10 or A63 motorways: exit St Geours de Maremne to Orist. Or, from A64 exit Peyrehorade to Dax. In both cases, 10km to Monbet.
Michelin Map No: 234-30

Entry no: 522   Map No: 16

M & Mme Hubert de LATAILLADE
Château du Monbet
40300 St Lon les Mines
Landes
Tel: (0)5 58 57 80 68
Fax: (0)5 58 57 89 29

"The whole place is special! The furniture is astounding, the house captivating. I love it." Our inspector was obviously moved. The house (1610) and contents have been accumulated by Colette's family for 14 generations: there are portraits from the 12th-century onwards. The bedrooms are spectacular: antique beds with canopies and drapes, strong colours, wonderful old furniture; three have open fireplaces. Dining room and *salon* are handsome, too: antiques, terracotta tiles and huge stone fireplace. Colette is elegant, attentive, helpful and hugely resourceful.

Rooms: 4 doubles, each with bath or shower & wc.

Price: 280-350 Frs for two.

Meals: 110 Frs, including wine & coffee.

Closed: Never.

From Dax D947 for Pau/Orthez for 10km. Stay on D947, ignoring sign for Mimbaste and take NEXT right onto D16 then follow discreet little yellow signs to house.
Michelin Map No: 234-26

Entry no: 523   Map No: 16

Colette DUFOURCET-ALBERCA
Maison Capcazal de Pachioü
40350 Mimbaste
Landes
Tel: (0)5 58 55 30 54
Fax: (0)5 58 55 30 54
Web: www.sawdays.co.uk

All the floors of this grand and appealing old French country house are original oak and it has an atmosphere of dream-like tranquillity. Just outside the park gates is the beautiful River Adour, rich in bird and wildlife – every 10 years or so it comes up and kisses the terrace steps. The two south-facing bedrooms overlook the river and a great spread of communal meadows where animals graze freely. There is a vast choice for 'flexitime' breakfast on the terrace or in the dining room. Madame, an attractively energetic and interesting hostess, was a publisher in Paris for many years and also speaks Spanish.

Rooms: 3 doubles, 1 triple, all with bath or shower & wc.

Price: 350 Frs for two.

Meals: Wide choice 2-5km.

Closed: Never.

From A63 exit 8 to St Geours de Marene then south on D17 for 5km to Saubusse. Right just before bridge; Château 800m on right.
Michelin Map No: 234-26

Entry no: 524   **Map No: 16**

Claude DOURLET
Château de Bezincam
Route de l'Adour
Saubusse les Bains
40180 Dax
Landes
Tel: (0)5 58 57 70 27
Fax: (0)5 58 57 70 27

Lost in a forest its windows onto endless young oaks and pines, with duck pond and river beyond, this house will satisfy your soul. Madame, a lovable person, teaches yoga (for guests too, and she's trilingual); her artist son's hand-painted decoration (marbling, stencilling, *tromp l'œil*) brings originality without offence to old stone and brickwork (he also teaches); grandchildren live next door, all in harmony with nature, and summer walks yield wildflower treasures. The simple rooms are not large but there is real family space at the piano or around the huge kitchen fireplace during delicious dinners.

Rooms: 1 double, 1 twin, 1 triple, all with shower & wc (& 2 small 'dormitories')

Price: 220-250 Frs for two.

Meals: 80 Frs, incl. wine; children 60 Frs.

Closed: Never.

From Mont de Marsan N134 NW to Garein (20km); left on D57 towards Ygos & Tartas then follow signs; 1km of lane before arriving at house.
Michelin Map No: 234-18

Entry no: 525   **Map No: 16**

Mme Liliane JEHL
Moulin Vieux
40420 Garein
Landes
Tel: (0)5 58 51 61 43

An exceptional couple: Heather, warmly communicative, Desmond, a retired architect with a great sense of fun, have brilliantly restored Agnos and still do all the cooking. Bedrooms come in various sizes, the most impressive being Henri IV (antique gilt beds) and François I (black and white bathroom + antique cast iron bath). Admire the high ceilings framing remarkable mirrors, paintings set into panelling, fine period furniture, the black marble dining room fountain... François I is said to have escaped by a secret tunnel (can you find it?), there's a medieval kitchen and an old prison. It's huge and you will feel completely at home.

Basque – SW Pyrenees

Rooms: 3 suites, 1 double, 1 twin, each with bath and/or shower & wc.

Price: 380-650 Frs for two.

Meals: 100-120 Frs, excluding wine (60 Frs).

Closed: February.

Gîte space for 14 people.

From Pau N134 for 35km to Oloron Ste Marie; through town and S on N134 towards Zaragoza for 1km. In Bidos, turn right for Agnos.
Michelin Map No: 234-38

Entry no: 526   **Map No: 16**

Heather & Desmond NEARS-CROUCH
Château d'Agnos
64400 Agnos
Pyrénées-Atlantiques
Tel: (0)5 59 36 12 52
Fax: (0)5 59 36 12 52

The Basques still play Pelote against a finely-shaped wall,
the eagle still reigns high over the Pyrenees,
the shaggy sheep graze the pastures and beret-wearers grow old interestingly.

From the terrace you can see for ever into the great Pyrenees – sunlit snowy in winter, awesomely coloured in summer: the Brownes own the land around so no danger of encroaching uglies and it's ideal for landscape painters. They have converted the old gîte into three delightful cosy rooms – exposed stonework, beams, living room – with a fourth in the main house, all with good bathrooms. Your hosts are multinational (Polish, French, South African), they and their children are a happy, relaxed and thoroughly integrated family. It is not smart, just easily friendly – and the food is delicious.

Rooms: 2 doubles, 2 twins, all with bath or shower & wc.

Price: 310 Frs for two.

Meals: 130 Frs, including wine & coffee.

Closed: Never.

This grand 18th-century village house and its owners are quiet, elegant, sophisticated. Dinner is a chance to talk with your hosts about the region; you can delve into their extensive library (she binds books). They have completely renovated the house since finding it and this sleepy village in the foothills of the Pyrenees. The bedrooms are light and airy with interesting old furniture and lovely wooden floors. *La Rose* is very chic and *La Verte* is a dream – enormous, beautifully furnished, with views out to the mountains and a 'waltz-in' bathroom. Readers are ecstatic.

Rooms: 2 doubles, each with shower or bath & wc.

Price: 300 Frs for two.

Meals: 100 Frs, including wine & coffee.

Closed: Never.

From Pau N134 S dir. Saragosse for 10km. At Gan right on D24 dir. Lasseube for 9km then left on D324. Follow Chambres d'hôtes signs, cross 2 small bridges. House on left up hill. Michelin Map No: 234-39

Entry no: 527   Map No: 16

Simon & Isabelle BROWNE
Maison Rancès
Quartier Rey
64290 Lasseube
Pyrénées-Atlantiques
Tel: (0)5 59 04 26 37
Fax: (0)5 59 04 26 37
Web: www.sawdays.co.uk

From Navarrenx D2 towards Monein to Jasses. There D27 towards Oloron Sainte Marie. In Lay Lamidou turn left then first right; 2nd house on right. Michelin Map No: 234-34

Entry no: 528   Map No: 16

Marie-France DESBONNET
Chambres d'Hôtes
64190 Lay Lamidou, Pyrénées-Atlantiques
Tel: (0)5 59 66 00 44/
    (0)6 86 22 02 76
Fax: (0)5 59 66 00 44
e-mail: desbonnet.bruf@infonie.fr
Web: www.sawdays.co.uk

These Béarn houses are 'sturdy', with solid old furniture and traditional decoration. Marie-Christine has added her own good furniture and decorative touches over the years and everything is kept immaculate. There are colourful wallpapers in the bedrooms and small, modern bathrooms. Madame is elegant and energetic... doing nearly all the work here herself and longing to show you her remarkable garden. It has huge old trees, magnolia, azalea, rhododendron, with benches discreetly placed for quiet reading... and the Pyrenees as a backdrop. There's now a table tennis table and the new spa centre in Salies is good for swimming all year.

A huge hall leads to the *salon*; leather chairs wait round the open fireplace. You are up above the village in a 14th-century Basque farmhouse: the vast lintel stones, the original heart-of-oak staircase, the split levels, nooks and crannies speak of great age, the distant hills echo the message. The former attic, restored with imagination and colour by Isabelle, successfully combines ancient and modern. Indulge in daughter Charlotte's delicious desserts, hear tales of yore from Isabelle, who has adopted her new land by training as a native storyteller, and visit the prehistoric caves of Isturitz for a taste of things more ancient still.

Rooms: 2 twins, 1 double, 1 suite, each with bath or shower & wc.

Price: 295-345 Frs for two.

Meals: 95 Frs, including coffee (carafe of wine from 18 Frs).

Closed: Never.

Gîte space for 10 people.

From A64 exit 7; right for Salies '<>5 tonnes' then next right signed to Le Guilhat for 1.8km. House on left beside nurseries at x-roads with Chemin des Bois.
Michelin Map No: 234-30

Rooms: 2 doubles, 3 triples, each with shower & wc.

Price: 270-350 Frs for two.

Meals: 100 Frs, including wine.

Closed: 1-15 February.

From A64, Briscous exit on D21 S to Hasparren. There, left on D10 towards Labastide Clairence for 3km then right on D251 through Ayherre to Isturitz. Signposted.
Michelin Map No: 234-33

Entry no: 529   Map No: 16

Entry no: 530   Map No: 16

Marie-Christine POTIRON
La Closerie du Guilhat
64270 Salies de Béarn
Pyrénées-Atlantiques
Tel: (0)5 59 38 08 80
Fax: (0)5 59 38 08 80
e-mail: guilhat@club-internet.fr
Web: www.sawdays.co.uk

Isabelle & Charlotte AIROLDI
Urruti Zaharria
64240 Isturitz
Pyrénées-Atlantiques
Tel: (0)5 59 29 45 98
Fax: (0)5 59 29 14 53
e-mail: urruti.zaharria@wanadoo.fr
Web: www.urruti-zaharria.fr

This 16th-century Basque farmhouse in a superb listed village has had new life breathed into it by its French/Irish owners who run the place with well-organised informality. Dinners around the enormous oak table are lively; food is excellent and local. Rooms are big, light and well decorated with hand-stencilling and pretty fabrics, beams and exposed wafer bricks (and bottled thoughtful 'extras' like good books and water). Breakfast is on the terrace in warm weather.

Rooms: 1 triple, 4 doubles, all with bath or shower & wc.

Price: 280-360 Frs for two.

Meals: 90 Frs, excl. wine or coffee; 130-150 Frs (gastronomic), with wine & coffee, by arrangement.

Closed: Never; please phone to book.

From A64 junc. 4 dir. Urt/Bidache; right on D123 to La Bastide Clairence. House on main street, opp. bakery. Michelin Map No: 234-29

Entry no: 531   Map No: 16

Valerie & Gilbert FOIX
Maison Marchand, Rue Notre Dame
64240 La Bastide Clairence
Pyrénées-Atlantiques
Tel: (0)5 59 29 18 27
Fax: (0)5 59 29 14 97
e-mail: valerie.et.gilbert.foix@wanadoo.fr
Web: perso.wanadoo.fr/maison.marchand

A 17th-century house, largely Victorianised, especially the three main bedrooms which have ornate wooden furniture, striped wallpaper and drapes, old linen and embroidered pillow cases – they're fun and spotless and bathrooms 'no-nonsense modern'. The smaller double is on the mezzanine above the tiled and beamed living room where Luc serves five-course meals; both he and Marie-Françoise love sitting and chatting with guests. There's a good deal of cosy knick-knackery: dried flowers, gingham and floral fabrics, brasses and ornaments but it's all rather comforting and your hosts so warm and friendly. Son Luc is a guide – mountaineering, caving and canoeing.

Rooms: 1 double, 3 triples, each with bath & wc.

Price: 220-250 Frs for two.

Meals: 125 Frs, including aperitif, wine & coffee.

Closed: Never.

From Lourdes D937 dir. Pau 8km to St Pé de Bigorre. Facing Mairie take road on right. Le Caleche 100m on right. Michelin Map No: 234-39

Entry no: 532   Map No: 12

Luc & Marie-Françoise L'HARIDON
Le Caleche
65270 Saint Pé de Bigorre
Hautes-Pyrénées
Tel: (0)5 62 41 86 71
Fax: (0)5 62 94 60 50
e-mail: turonimmobilier@wanadoo.fr

Cedar and sequoia shade this imposing 400-year-old house. The large bedrooms, with old, uneven, stained wooden floors and curtained four-posters, have regal titles and modern bathrooms. Buffet breakfast and formal dinner are at separate tables set with silver, linen and candelabras. Besides restoring house and garden (including a French-style kitchen garden), Monsieur's passions are computers (games for children), music (he has an excellent CD collection) and receiving guests. Rafting and canoeing close by.

Rooms: 3 doubles, 1 triple, all with bath or shower & wc (1 behind curtain).

Price: 350 Frs for two.

Meals: Available locally.

Closed: Never.

Monsieur is both ski instructor and mountain guide so there's good advice on hand. He's also in charge of breakfasts, although it's Madame who prepares dinners (both like to eat with their guests) and cooks the local speciality *gâteau à la broche* (cake on a spit), in the big open fireplace. She was a costume designer for the Paris Opera House and her needlework makes the cosy, perfectly decorated bedrooms, complete with electric blankets, exceptional; brilliant bathrooms too. All this in a traditional Pyrenean building in the oldest part of the village. Perfect in summer or winter.

Rooms: 3 doubles, each with bath & wc.

Price: 330 Frs for two.

Meals: 100 Frs, including wine.

Closed: November-15 January.

From Pau D938/937 for 31km towards Lourdes. In St Pé, facing Mairie, take road to its right; house 50m up on right. Michelin Map No: 234-39

Entry no: 533   Map No: 12

From Lourdes N21 towards Argelès-Gazost. After 3km right onto D13 towards Ossen & Omex. House signposted. Michelin Map No: 234-39

Entry no: 534   Map No: 12

Christian PETERS
Le Grand Cèdre, 6 rue du Barry
65270 St Pé de Bigorre
Hautes-Pyrénées
Tel: (0)5 62 41 82 04
Fax: (0)5 62 41 85 89
e-mail: chp@grandcedre.com
Web: www.grandcedre.com

Mme Murielle FANLOU
Les Rocailles
65100 Omex
Hautes-Pyrénées
Tel: (0)5 62 94 46 19
Fax: (0)5 62 94 33 35
Web: www.sawdays.co.uk

English Nick is a wonderful host, full of life, ideas and love of good food – he wears his chef's hat magnificently and talks all the time he's cooking, which is all the time he's indoors. He and his wife, who is French, really belong in Fontrailles: they run the local music festival. Their farmhouse is a good mix of 17th-century architecture and new comforts (including good mattresses), the food a delicious mix of traditional French and exotic, the rooms cosy, fresh and neat. This is 'Foothills Country' surrounded by rolling farmland – a haven for birds, wildlife and walkers – the mountains are an hour's drive away.

Rooms: 2 doubles, 1 triple, each with shower & wc.

Price: 320 Frs for two.

Meals: 120 Frs, including wine; children 60 Frs.

Closed: Never.

From Tarbes D632 NE to Trie sur Baïse (about 30km). Through village to junction with D17; there take tiny D939 N for 1.5km. House signposted on left. Michelin Map No: 234-36

Entry no: 535   Map No: 12

Nick & Dominique COLLINSON
Jouandassou
65220 Fontrailles
Hautes-Pyrénées
Tel: (0)5 62 35 64 43
Fax: (0)5 62 35 66 13
e-mail: nick@collinson.fr
Web: www.collinson.fr

The Hindu greeting *namaste* to name it, star-spangled, moonstruck beams and furniture to fill it – there are exotic touches here. Architecture buffs will like the impressive barn with walls containing sections of the original earth construction. The Fontaines have spent two years restoring their lime-rendered 18th-century farmhouse, polishing wooden floors and creating a balance between the traditional and the modern. The guest rooms both have doors leading to semi-secluded corners of the garden. In cold weather, enjoy the huge open fire in the comfortable *salon*.

Rooms: 1 quadruple with bath & wc; 1 triple with shower & wc.

Price: 280 Frs for two.

Meals: 100 Frs, including wine.

Closed: Never.

From A64 exit 16 onto D939 through Lannemezan to Galan. From village square/church, take Rue de la Baïse towards Recurt; house 500m on left. Michelin Map No: 234-40

Entry no: 536   Map No: 12

Jean & Danielle FONTAINE
Namaste
13 rue de la Baïse
65330 Galan, Hautes-Pyrénées
Tel: (0)5 62 99 77 81
Fax: (0)5 62 99 77 81
e-mail: namaste_65@libertysurf.fr
Web: www.namaste-pyrenees.com

Madame is heavenly, a person of enormous grace; her *domaine* is an oasis of calm where peace reigns and you may make a lifelong friend, sharing her delight in playing the piano or golf (good course 3km). Built during the Napoleonic Wars, the house has a coolly elegant hall, big, airy bedrooms and superb bathrooms, while fine furniture and linen sheets reflect her pride in her ancestral home. A beautifully-presented breakfast is further enhanced by civilised conversation. Come to unwind – you may never want to leave for this is a remarkable place.

Rooms: 1 double, 1 triple, 1 quadruple, all with bath & wc.

Price: 280 Frs for two.

Meals: Restaurant 2km.

Closed: Never.

Once a professional cook, Rosie still clearly loves cooking – French and 'foreign' – and is knowledgeable about local food. Sam was in the Navy but now battles only with the high pH content of his clay soil; he's succeeding in establishing a really excellent vegetable and flower garden. The house is late 19th-century, with woodburning stoves, comfortable, unpretentious furniture, and a good piano. Bedrooms have polished wooden floors, big windows and impeccable bathrooms. Beautiful, gently rolling, wooded and brooked countryside to explore; wild orchids and woodpecker thrive in the clean air.

Rooms: 1 triple, 1 double, 1 twin, each with shower & wc.

Price: 330 Frs for two; reduction for 4 nights or more.

Meals: 100 Frs including wine.

Closed: Never.

From A64 exit 16 to Lannemezan; there, D117 towards Toulouse for 5km. In Pinas, at church, take road towards Villeneuve. House on right after 1km.
Michelin Map No: 234-40

From Agen D931 SW for Condom then D15 W to Castelnau. Turn right for 'Centre Ville' and right again at Post Office onto D43 towards St Pé and Sos. House first on left past landslip after approx 5km.
Michelin Map No: 234-24

Entry no: 537   Map No: 12

Entry no: 538   Map No: 12

Mme Marie-Sabine COLOMBIER
Domaine de Jean-Pierre
20 route de Villeneuve
65300 Pinas, Hautes-Pyrénées
Tel: (0)5 62 98 15 08
Fax: (0)5 62 98 15 08
e-mail: marie.colombier@wanadoo.fr

Rosie & Sam BENNETT
Les Colombiers
Bournic
32440 Castelnau d'Auzan, Gers
Tel: (0)5 62 29 24 05
Fax: (0)5 62 29 24 05
e-mail: rabennett@talk21.com
Web: www.sawdays.co.uk

An 18th-century townhouse built snug against the 13th-century hilltop village fortifications. A lovely terraced garden, perfect for breakfasting, shaded by masses of scented old-fashioned climbing roses; Madame is a keen gardener. She has also done a great job of preserving original features like the planed wooden floors, fireplaces, and door fittings. Colour schemes are mostly pale, with plenty of blue and grey; rooms are elegant and unpretentious. There's a kitchenette for longer-stay guests and it is worth settling in to explore this historic, little-visited area. Good footpaths close by.

Rooms: 1 double, 1 twin, 1 triple, each with shower & wc. 1 twin with bath & wc.

Price: 270-350 Frs for two.

Meals: Available locally.

Closed: 4 January-4 February.

From Auch N21 towards Tarbes. At le Trouette take D2 to L'Isle de Noé; then D943 to Montesquiou. Through village past church on left; house on right. Michelin Map No: 240-22

Entry no: **539**   Map No: 12

Mme KOVACS
Maison de la Porte Fortifieé
32320 Montesquiou
Gers
Tel: (0)5 62 70 97 59
Fax: (0)5 62 70 97 59
Web: www.france-bonjour.com/gascogne/

This splendid 18th-century Gascon farmhouse in its large lush garden has heart-stopping views south to the Pyrenees and west down the valley to the setting sun. Restored with comfort a priority (roll-top baths, saltwater swimming pool) by its friendly and interesting English owners, it breathes charm and peace from cool arched terra and antique-furnished rooms. Your host enjoy entertaining and Christine's local dishes are made with fresh garden ingredients. This is hidden France still, with old villages, *bastides* (fortified farmhouses), and fascinating architectur as well as vineyards and fabulous food. A highly civilised place to stay.

Rooms: 1 suite for 4, 1 double, 1 twin, each with bath, shower & wc.

Price: 600-700 Frs for two.

Meals: 250 Frs, excluding wine.

Closed: 2 weeks December-January.

Gîte space for 10 people.

From Auch N124 W dir. Vic Fézenac for 5km; left on D943 through Barran, Montesquiou, Bassoues. After Bassoues follow D943 left dir. Marciac. Scieurac et Fl signed off this road. In village bend left by church; house 1st on right. Michelin Map No: 234-32

Entry no: **540**   Map No: 12

Michael & Christine FURNEY
Setzères
Scieurac et Flourès
32230 Marciac, Gers
Tel: (0)5 62 08 21 45
Fax: (0)5 62 08 21 45
e-mail: setzeres32@aol.com
Web: www.sawdays.co.uk

Madame has lived here all her life and her son now runs the busy farm. The house has plenty of French *paysan* warmth and is as genuine as your kindly hostess. Breakfast is outside or at a long table by a huge open hearth and there's a useful guests' kitchen area too. It is all down-to-earth and clean with proper country charm. The bedrooms open onto the balcony overlooking the courtyard, have super old rickety wooden floors and some endearing features like Granny's wedding furniture (beds are old as well but have first class mattresses). It all rejoices in a very French and delightfully secluded setting of gentle hills, grain fields and pastures.

Rooms: 1 double, 1 triple, 1 suite ideal for families, all with bathroom.

Price: 230 Frs for two.

Meals: Self-catering possible.

Closed: Never.

From Auch, N21 towards Tarbes. 6km after Mirande, house signposted on left.
Michelin Map No: 234-32

Entry no: 541   Map No: 12

Marthe SABATHIER
Noailles
32300 Saint Maur
Gers
Tel: (0)5 62 67 57 98

On a clear day you can see the Pyrenees... and every day the rolling fields beyond the wooden terrace outside your window. Youthful and natural, Mireille is an inspired cook and a delight to be with; Olivier, though disenchanted somewhat with farming in the modern age, still enjoys his smallholding. They grow Christmas trees and cereals, fill their cosy house with antique plates, prints, pictures and furniture and create a relaxed and happy family home with the essential dogs and cats and now a swimming pool. Perfect for children.

Rooms: 1 double (+ 1 small double for 2 children) with bathroom.

Price: 240-270 Frs for two; reduction for 3 nights or more.

Meals: 90 Frs, including wine & coffee.

Closed: Never.

Gîte space for 10 people.

From Auch N21 dir. Tarbes for 2km; left on D929 dir. Lannemezan. In Masseube, left dir. Simorre for 4km; left dir. Bellegarde. House 1st turning on left, before church and castle.
Michelin Map No: 234-36

Entry no: 542   Map No: 12

Mireille & Olivier COUROUBLE
La Garenne
Bellegarde
32140 Masseube
Gers
Tel: (0)5 62 66 03 61
Fax: (0)5 62 66 03 61

A blue valentine on a quiet lane: the happy family who live here have decorated their 18th-century manor in quiet good taste with antiques (every piece chosen because it is the right one), lovely bed linen, pretty bath tiles and that blue-and-white theme – not sky or baby or royal but Brigitte's favourite French (Williamsburg to Americans) blue. It is soft, mellow, uncluttered; she is smiling, enthusiastic, young; the daughters are adorable and helpful. A dreamy, comfortable, happy house, where you appreciate the reality of the hard-working kitchen gardener when you sit down to dinner.

Rooms: 1 twin, 1 suite, each with shower & wc; 1 double sharing shower & wc.

Price: 250 Frs for two.

Meals: 80 Frs, including wine.

Closed: Last week in August.

From Toulouse N117 SW past Muret for approx. 50km. Exit S on D6 to Cazères. Cross River Garonne, right on D62, follow signs for Camping Planturel. House is 2nd left after camping site. Michelin Map No: 235-37

Entry no: 543   Map No: 12

Brigitte & Bruno LEBRIS
Les Pesques
31220 Palaminy
Haute-Garonne
Tel: (0)5 61 97 59 28
Fax: (0)5 61 98 12 97

Steve is a wonderful cook, Kris a man of the theatre, together they have achieved the splendid restoration of their remote old mill where fire roars and stream flows, bedding and bathrooms are excellent, furniture is country French, rugs are oriental and colours simple. They are deeply involved in the local environment, preserving trees, encouraging wildlife, helping farmers and still waiting for a turbine to make heat from the river (so rooms may be a little chilly in winter). A very special spot, great value... and so near the Pyrenees.

Rooms: 2 triples, each with bath/shower & wc; 1 double & 1 triple sharing shower & wc.

Price: 245 Frs for two.

Meals: 85 Frs, including wine & coffee.

Closed: Never.

From Toulouse A64 to Boussens (exit 21) on D635 to the edge of Aurignac and D8 direction Alan, turning left through Montolieu to Samouillan, then D96; signposted. Michelin Map No: 235-37

Entry no: 544   Map No: 12

Stephen CALLEN & Kris
MISSELBROOK
Le Moulin, Samouillan
31420 Aurignac, Haute-Garonne
Tel: (0)5 61 98 86 92
Fax: (0)5 61 98 86 92
e-mail: kris.steve@free.fr
Web: www.moulin-vert.net

Madame Fieux gets full marks for the beauty of her reception rooms: they are big, warm and dignified in the elegant patina of age. Her house is full of old pictures, books, comfortable chairs and antiques, her visitors are immersed in the French way of life, sleep in fine rooms with views across the green oaks, enjoy her warm and genuine interest in people, manifested in "a mix of the formidable and the lovable, the dignified and the mischievous". Step out on a summer's morning and enjoy your breakfast – often with home-made cakes – in the large, lush garden. When the temperature soars head for those oaks. Lake and tennis court next door.

Rooms: 3 doubles, 2 twins, all with bath or shower & wc.

Price: 500 Frs for two.

Meals: Restaurant 4km.

Closed: Never.

From Toulouse A68 direction Albi exit 3 direction Montastruc la Conseillère. After 1km right on D30 direction Lavaur for 4.5km; right on D30E direction Verfeuil & follow signs for Stoupignan; 1km on left. Michelin Map No: 235-30

Entry no: 545   Map No: 12

Claudette FIEUX
Stoupignan
31380 Montpitol
Haute-Garonne
Tel: (0)5 61 84 22 02
Fax: (0)5 61 84 22 02

An exceptional working farm/B&B where quiet Gilbert will take you egg-hunting or goose-feeding of a morning. Smiling, big-hearted Michèle has won prizes for her recipes, invents sauces and makes her own aperitif. Rooms are comfortable (beware waist-low beams) but food is definitely the priority here. Fishing rods on loan for use in the pond; footpaths out from the gate; proper hiking trails a bit further away; the treasures of Moissac, lovely villages, caves, are within easy reach. *Well-behaved children and small pets welcome.*

Rooms: 2 doubles, 2 twins, all with bath, shower & wc.

Price: 250 Frs for two; 240 Frs after the third day.

Meals: 90 Frs, including wine & coffee.

Closed: Never.

Gîte space for 4 people.

From Moissac, D7 direction Bourg de Visa for about 14km. Before Brassac and just before a bridge, right direction Fauroux. Farm 2km along; signposted. Michelin Map No: 235-17

Entry no: 546   Map No: 12

Gilbert & Michèle DIO
La Marquise
Brassac
82190 Bourg de Visa
Tarn-et-Garonne
Tel: (0)5 63 94 25 16

The Sellars, warm country people, left big-scale farming in Sussex for a smallholding in deepest rural France where they breed sheep, goats, poultry and rabbits using natural, traditional methods (no pesticides, no heavy machines). Their guts and enthusiasm have earned them the respect of the local community and their recipe for a simple, rewarding way of life includes receiving guests under the beams and by the open hearth. Julie will welcome you to her kitchen, too, where she creates feasts fit for farmers (organic veg and home-made goodies of course).

Rooms: 1 family room for 3/4, 1 double, each with shower & wc.

Price: 220 Frs for two.

Meals: 100 Frs, including aperitif, wine & coffee.

Closed: Never.

It's hard to find fault here! The rooms could grace the pages of a magazine – lovely prints, old wardrobes, terracotta tiles. All is fresh, light and a happy marriage of old and new. Varied breakfasts and delicious dinners – regional and exotic dishes and an excellent cheeseboard. Sunflowers, farmland and a dreamy hamlet surround the 19th-century farmhouse which has been lovingly restored by its present owners, a Franco-Dutch family who enjoy sharing their summers here with guests. Madame is vivacious and energetic, Monsieur is calm and diplomatic, their children are delightful. Not to be missed.

Rooms: 1 suite for 2-4, 1 double, each with shower & wc.

Price: 250 Frs for two.

Meals: 90 Frs, including wine & coffee.

Closed: September-June.

From A62 exit 8 on D953 N dir. Cahors (round Valence d'Agen) for 21km; at Lamothe left on V4 signed Castelsagrat; Tondes 1.6km on left. Michelin Map No: 235-17

Entry no: 547   Map No: 12

Julie & Mark SELLARS
Tondes
82400 Castelsagrat
Tarn-et-Garonne
Tel: (0)5 63 94 52 13
Web: www.sawdays.co.uk

From Agen, A62 east, exit 8 towards Gramont. After Mansonville, follow signs to Lachapelle; house on right on entering village. Michelin Map No: 235-21

Entry no: 548   Map No: 12

M & Mme VAN DEN BRINK
Au Village
82120 Lachapelle
Tarn-et-Garonne
Tel: (0)5 63 94 14 10 or
        (0)1 39 49 07 37
e-mail: cvandenbrink@ctr.fr

The best reason for being here is the Gorges de l'Aveyron – a paradise of clear water, cliffs, wildlife, canoeing and wild scenery. Johnny and Véronique, suitably, are sports teachers – all tan and dynamism, they encourage the active-holiday idea with great enthusiasm. They have renovated their house beyond the constraints of its origins – its rooms are simple, modern and functional, with little that is memorable or quintessentially French. But the food is good and generous and so are your friendly hosts. Very busy in summer so don't expect family intimacy then.

Rooms: 2 doubles, 3 twins, each with bath or shower & wc.

Price: 260-340 Frs for two.

Meals: 100 Frs, including wine & coffee.

Closed: Never.

Ideas by Nathalie, action by Sean, result: the elegant simplicity of their renovated 13th-15th-century townhouse with its great sense of light and space in the airy hall, large spiral staircase, views through into the garden courtyard, stone walls and original old tiles. It has large, beautifully-decorated rooms, one with its own sun terrace, all with en suite bathrooms. He, a natural host full of charm and unflappability, is enthusiastic about being here; she, originally from Belgium, quietly looks after their two children; both delight in providing extraordinary attention to their guests – some come for one night and stay for seven!

Rooms: 3 doubles, 2 twins, each with bath & wc.

Price: 350-450 Frs for two.

Meals: 110 Frs, including wine & coffee.

Closed: Never.

From Cahors, N20 to Caussade then D964 direction Gaillac. At Montricoux, D115 towards Nègrepelisse; after 500m, signposted.
Michelin Map No: 235-22

Entry no: **549**   Map No: **12**

From Montauban N20 NE to Caussade (22km); right on D926 for 7km; right on D5 to St Antonin Noble Val (12km); in town centre, follow signs.
Michelin Map No: 235-18

Entry no: **550**   Map No: **12**

Johnny & Véronique ANTONY
Les Brunis
82800 Nègrepelisse
Tarn-et-Garonne
Tel: (0)5 63 67 24 08
Fax: (0)5 63 67 24 08

Nathalie & Sean O'SHEA
La Résidence, 37 rue Droite
82140 St Antonin Noble Val
Tarn-et-Garonne
Tel: (0)5 63 68 21 60
Fax: (0)5 63 68 21 60
e-mail: laresidence@compuserve.com
Web: www.la-residence.homepage.com

With the loveliest smile, Madame takes guests in as family; her dogs and cats are as friendly as she is and she greeted us from the milking shed, her hands dripping with the evidence: Le Gendre is a working farm with roaming chickens, ducks and pigs. Go lightly on lunch: dinner is uncompromisingly, deliciously 'farmhouse' with portions suitable for a hard-working farmer. Your hosts are lively and empathetic, sharing their home easily, without fuss; the rustic, cluttered dayroom has a warm open fire; bedrooms are simply furnished, pleasing and spotless, breakfast coffee is in a bowl – you've found real rural France.

Rooms: 1 double, 1 suite for 4, each with shower & wc.

Price: 220 Frs for two.

Meals: 80 Frs, including wine.

Closed: Never.

N20 south from Cahors to Caussade. Left on D926 through Septfonds. 3km beyond, left direction Gaussou. Farm is 1km on; signposted.
Michelin Map No: 235-18

Entry no: 551   Map No: 12

Françoise & Jean-Louis ZAMBONI
Ferme du Gendre
82240 Lavaurette
Tarn-et-Garonne
Tel: (0)5 63 31 97 72

So close to skiing, golfing, fishing and Toulouse's new opera house – but why go anywhere when Soulès (meaning 'sun') is here? Set among 300-year-old cedars, it has majestic gardens, a pond-blessed orchard attracting woodpeckers owls, hoopoes and deer, a new heated swimming pool, big breakfasts till noon and *haute cuisine* dinners. The higher things in life are worshipped too: there's a baby grand, an elegant library and a fabulous antique clock collection. Denise is Swiss and a fine French cook; Arnold is English and was 'in clocks'. They are good company, their rooms are big and comfortable and they love having guests.

Rooms: 3 triples, 1 double, each with bath or shower & wc; some connecting for families.

Price: 385 Frs for two.

Meals: 125 Frs, including wine.

Closed: New Year.

Gîte space for 8 people.

From Toulouse N20 S to Pins Justaret (10km); fork right on D4 for 26km to Lézat sur Lèze. Continue 3km after Lézat; château entrance on right.
Michelin Map No: 235-38

Entry no: 552   Map No: 12

Denise & Arnold BRUN
Château de Soulès
09210 St Ybars
Ariège
Tel: (0)5 61 69 20 12
Fax: (0)5 61 69 21 68
e-mail: arnold.brun@wanadoo.fr
Web: www.sawdays.co.uk

A renovated farmhouse/hamlet that looks towards the Pyrenees. You may plan your stay during one of your hostess's weekend art courses. You could stop a while, forget the maps and itinerary – you are in a world of ceramics, watercolours, weaving and sculpture... and wide-open spaces. The rooms feel right, light, not over-decorated and adorned with Dutch Jeanne's handiwork. Guests have their own living room and fridge but dinner – cooked rather well by Guy – is served *en famille* in a very friendly atmosphere. *Ask about summer art courses.*

Rooms: 1 double, 2 triples, all with bath or shower & wc.

Price: 250 Frs for two.

Meals: 90 Frs, including wine & coffee.

Closed: Never.

Gîte space for 7 people.

From Toulouse A66/N20 South, exit Belpech. D11 for 8km, right for La Bastide de Lordat, through village dir. Gaudies. Before Gaudies bear right, cross the river. Certes farm near top on left.
Michelin Map No: 235-38

Entry no: 553   Map No: 12

Jeanne & Guy GOSSELIN
Certes
09700 Gaudies
Ariège
Tel: (0)5 61 67 01 56
Fax: (0)5 61 67 42 30

Nick lists about 200 different birds and over 50 orchids though people do come to look for just one type. He, a fauna and flora guide who really knows his stuff, and Julie, a midwife, are a thoroughly likeable pair. This tiny hamlet has breathtaking views up to the mountains and across miles of fields, farms and forests; it is ineffably lovely. The simple and pretty renovated house has smallish rooms, and a cosy family living room. They'll collect you from the airport as part of a week's package. Great value.

Rooms: 2 doubles, 1 twin, each with shower & wc.

Price: 240 Frs for two.

Meals: 85 Frs, including wine & coffee.

Closed: Never.

From St Girons D117 E for 7km. Just before fork for Mas d'Azil see Chambres d'Hôtes sign on left. Follow signs up this tiny, metalled track for 2km.
Michelin Map No: 235-42

Entry no: 554   Map No: 12

Nick & Julie GOLDSWORTHY
La Baquette, Lescure
09420 Rimont, Ariège
Tel: (0)5 61 96 37 67
Fax: (0)5 61 96 37 67
e-mail: goldsnj@aol.com
Web: www.ariege.com/lodging/goldsworthy.html

You don't have to like horses to enjoy yourself here, but if you do you'll love it: the daughter of the family has a riding school on the spot. Guests stay in an independent ivy-clad house at this old farm in the foothills of the Pyrenees. A staircase leads from a little living room (fires in winter) to clean, simple rooms – one has stone walls – with pine furniture (plus more basic rooms for groups of up to 19). Beautiful views and plenty of invigorating walks for those who prefer to use Shanks's pony. Children are made very welcome by the warm, friendly and relaxed hosts who work well together and are very interesting about local lore.

Rooms: 3 doubles, 1 twin, all with bath or shower & wc.

Price: 210-220 Frs for two.

Meals: 65 Frs, including wine & coffee.

Closed: Never.

Gîte space for 9 people.

From Foix, D117 direction St Girons; at top of hill, left on small D45 for 6km then left again for 1km; Cantegril drive is on the left, signposted.
Michelin Map No: 235-42

Entry no: **555**   Map No: 17

Édith & Jean-Michel PAGÈS
École d'Équitation de Cantegril
09000 St Martin de Caralp
Ariège
Tel: (0)5 61 65 15 43
Fax: (0)5 61 02 96 86
Web: www.sawdays.co.uk

Don't expect silver or lace but bring your hiking boots. This old mill in its magical valley was once a *cloutier*: nails were made here. The beds are made of softer stuff and the water rushing past will lull you to sleep after that great walk. The room isn't large but there's a lovely terrace and you'll want to be out by the stream, catching trout in the right season. Your hosts will gladly harness their horse and cart to take you for a day trip in the mountains with picnic lunch on board. A simple, honest welcoming place in a magnificent setting with a river nearby for swimming. Small pets welcome and a private kitchen you can use.

Rooms: 1 twin with shower & wc. Kitchenette available.

Price: 200 Frs for two.

Meals: Restaurant 2km or self-catering.

Closed: January.

Gîte space for 4 people.

From Foix, D21 to Ganac. After 5km take route to Micou 'Les Carcis'; right just after small bridge.
Michelin Map No: 235-42

Entry no: **556**   Map No: 17

Sylviane PIEDNOËL & Guy DROUET
Les Carcis
09000 Ganac
Ariège
Tel: (0)5 61 02 96 54

"It is enchanting!" The setting is spectacular, the reception rooms are generously fireplaced, the antique chests, tables and desks are genuine and in superb condition, the bedrooms are big, airy and elegant and the bathrooms excellent. Michel, a restaurateur for 30 years, is still the finest chef within 100km and loves cooking for half a dozen. He takes his daily inspiration from the market, has twinkling eyes, says he is temperamental but may let you into his sanctum. What a welcome! And moreover, Unac church, just next door, is superb – an early Romanesque jewel. *Well-behaved children over 5 welcome.*

Rooms: 1 double, 1 triple, each with bath & wc.

Price: 390 Frs for two.

Meals: 180 Frs, including aperitif, wine & coffee.

Closed: Never.

It is unusual to find B&Bs in the Ariège run by locals, but Josiane has lived in the area all her life and Pierre used to farm nearby. She is justifiably proud of the elegant bedrooms she has created with carefully orchestrated fabrics, lovely old furniture and sturdy beds. The views up and down the magnificent Vicdessos valley are splendid, with a tumbling stream right in front of you. Skiers should come here in the early spring to test their skill on the Massif de Montcalm, a few kilometres up the road. *If you're tall ask for the 'Chambre Bleu'.*

Rooms: 1 double & 1 twin each with shower & wc; 1 double with shower & separate wc.

Price: 240 Frs for two.

Meals: Good auberge in Niaux.

Closed: 30 September-31 March.

Gîte space for 6 people.

From Foix N20 S for 33km through Tarascon to Luzenac. There, left on D2 & follow signs to Unac. Take 2nd entrance into Unac. House just down from church, 100m on right.
Michelin Map No: 235-46

Entry no: 557   Map No: 17

Michel & Simone DESCAT
L'Oustal
09250 Unac
Ariège
Tel: (0)5 61 64 48 44

From Foix, N20 direction Tarascon. After Tarascon, right direction Vallée Vicdessos, after 5.5km, right at Junac & Chambres d'Hôtes sign. Cross river then immediately left. House on right.
Michelin Map No: 235-46

Entry no: 558   Map No: 17

M & Mme Pierre DA SILVA
Le Pré de la Forge
09400 Capoulet et Junac
Ariège
Tel: (0)5 61 05 93 57

Walkers! Once you've reached the house, you'll never need to get into your car again: there are 80km of hiking trails, from easy to tough, straight from the door. It is a paradise for botanists, bird-watchers and tree insect fanatics, and your kindly hosts know those paths intimately. Layrole's most memorable features are the greenery, the riot of flowers all round the south-facing terrace and the sound of water in the background. The guest room has an immaculate new bed, a mass of books and central heating while the Orient Express loo will appeal to train buffs. A very pretty village and good homely dinners.

Rooms: 1 double with shower & wc.

Price: 220 Frs for two.

Meals: 90 Frs, including wine.

Closed: Mid-October-mid-April.

From Foix, N20 S to Tarascon then D618 W through Saurat. 2.5km after the café/bar at Saurat, right up steep road towards Cabus. House on right after 700m, signposted.
Michelin Map No: 235-46

Entry no: 559   **Map No: 17**

Roger & Monique ROBERT
Layrole
09400 Saurat
Ariège
Tel: (0)5 61 05 73 24

The setting is out of this world, the house has tons of character – local stone, beams, low windows, uneven ceilings, all excellently renovated – and your hosts know what real *chambre d'hôtes* means. High up at a remote edge of the world, surrounded by 70 hectares of breathtaking forested Pyrenean foothills, they raise horses and Newfoundlands, will let you join their picnics, ride their horses (if you are an experienced rider), live in their space for a while and hear their stories, in several languages, of sailing the Atlantic or the Caribbean: don't miss dining with them. Good rooms and excellent value.

Rooms: 2 doubles, 1 twin, 1 triple, 1 quadruple (summer only), all with shower & wc.

Price: 230-250 Frs for two. Book early.

Meals: 75 Frs, including wine & coffee.

Closed: 2 October-28 February.

Gîte space for 6 people.

From Foix, D17 dir. Col de Marrous. After 9km, in La Mouline left at Chambres d'Hôtes sign for 1.5km, right on C6, tiny but easy track, to house.
Michelin Map No: 235-42

Entry no: 560   **Map No: 17**

Bob & Jenny BROGNEAUX
Le Poulsieu
Serres sur Arget
09000 Foix
Ariège
Tel: (0)5 61 02 77 72
Fax: (0)5 61 02 77 72
Web: www.sawdays.co.uk

After years of renovation your weaver hosts have made this rural idyll what it is today. Samples of their work, they use only natural dyes from local plants, are everywhere and fit well with the exposed stone and woodwork of the old house. Bedrooms are rustic-warm with good views. Dine *en famille* in a huge living/dining room (village dances were held here!) and share the Loizances' local knowledge. They are a delightful family and their home has real heart. Perfect country for summer walking and winter cross-country skiing – the tiny hamlet is perched 900m up on the side of a National Park valley and the valley above is virtually unpopulated.

Rooms: 3 doubles, 1 triple, all with shower & wc.

Price: 240 Frs for two.

Meals: 80 Frs, including wine & coffee.

Closed: Never.

Beauty without: from the lovely dining room you look straight across to a great snowy peak; breakfast is wholemeal bread and home-made jam with this spectacular view. Beauty within: pretty fabrics and your hosts' own works (from mid-July to September they stage a special exhibition). Teresa was educated in England and paints; Alpine-born, Paris-educated Bernard is an expert on water mammals, sculpts and draws. A very special couple and this tiny village (pop. 60!) has an almost Alpine feel. *Children over five or babies only (ladder to mezzanine). Gîte space for 4.*

Rooms: 1 double, 1 single, with bath & wc.

Price: 250 Frs for two; reduction for long stays.

Meals: Choice 1.5km.

Closed: Never.

From Foix D17 direction Col des Marrous for 15km, do not follow sign for Le Bosc on left. 'Hameau de Madranque' signposted on right. Michelin Map No: 235-42

Entry no: 561   Map No: 17

From A64 exit 20 S to St Girons. There right on D618 towards Castillon for 12km then tiny D404 on left to Cescau. Park below church on left. Michelin Map No: 235-41

Entry no: 562   Map No: 17

Birgit & Jean-Claude LOIZANCE
Madranque
09000 Le Bosc
Ariège
Tel: (0)5 61 02 71 29
Fax: (0)5 61 02 71 29
Web: www.sawdays.co.uk

Teresa & Bernard RICHARD
Chambres d'Hôtes
09800 Cescau
Ariège
Tel: (0)5 61 96 74 24

Chantal's excellent Catalan cuisine gathers lively mixed nationality groups (sometimes 20-odd) for dinner in the shade of the kiwi trees. This energetic young farming couple grow organic kiwi fruit, have vineyards and peach trees too and have converted their farmhouse so that it now has six large functional guest rooms. Floors are tiled, furnishings are simple – almost basic – and practical; showers small and modern. Hedges are growing but there is still some road noise. Luis is a good-natured host and this place remains good value, not far from the coast and close to the ever-beautiful Pyrenees.

Rooms: 5 doubles & 1 suite, all with shower & wc.

Price: 230 Frs for two.

Meals: 85 Frs, including aperitif & wine.

Closed: Never.

Languedoc

Rugby rouses great passions here, as do corridas and high dramas enacted beneath the Roman arches; down on the coast, traditional water-jousters get less emotional but much wetter.

From Perpignan, N114 to Elne. In village take D612 to Bages; signs after 500-600m.
Michelin Map No: 235-52

Entry no: 563   Map No: 18

Louis & Chantal TUBERT
Mas de la Couloumine
Route de Bages
66200 Elne
Pyrénées-Orientales
Tel: (0)4 68 22 36 07

This ancient *ferme-auberge* combines austerity and comfort to suit both backpacker and motorist: rooms like Fra Angelico's cells, views that go on forever with maybe an eagle circling, a swimming hole in the dammed river, owners who also raise animals and are passionate about their mountains. Sunday lunch (Catalan and French) is a riotously convivial affair; everything except the bread is home-made or home-grown and served by the two teenage children before a magnificent stone fireplace. Exceptional!

Rooms: 2 triples, each with shower & wc.

Price: 290 Frs for two.

Meals: Lunch 160 Frs, including wine & coffee

Closed: Mid-November-mid-March.

Gîte space for 12 people.

Kim is an exceptionally warm and lovely person. This well-travelled, cosmopolitan Scottish family, have turned their house into a perfect Pyrenean haven among some of Europe's wildest, remotest landscapes. It has a magical garden full of lush vegetation and intimate sitting areas among the trees, dazzling views past snow-capped mountains down to the sea, romantic and comfortable rooms decorated with original works of art and bright scatter cushions. Two rooms offer the private bliss of walking from bed to terrace for breakfast, delivered by Kim. *Children welcome with parental supervision (pool).*

Rooms: 3 doubles, 3 twins, each with shower & wc.

Price: 500-700 Frs for two.

Meals: Excellent restaurant 400m or choice in village; barbecue available.

Closed: December-January.

On French-Spanish border. From A9 exit 43 onto D115 W through Prats de Mollo and 10km beyond to Col d'Arès. Farm on left.
Michelin Map No: 235-56

Entry no: **564**   Map No: 18

Michelle & Gilbert LANAU
Ferme Auberge La Costa de Dalt
Route du Col d'Arès
66230 Prats de Mollo
Pyrénées-Orientales
Tel: (0)4 68 39 74 40
Fax: (0)4 68 39 74 40
e-mail: ferme.auberge@free.fr

A9 to Spain, last exit before border. Drive into Céret; follow signs for 'Centre Ville' then signs for Hôtel La Terrasse au Soleil. House 300m after hotel, on left.
Michelin Map No: 235-56

Entry no: **565**   Map No: 18

Kim BETHELL
La Châtaigneraie
Route de Fontfrède
66400 Céret, Pyrénées-Orientales
Tel: (0)4 68 87 21 58
Fax: (0)4 68 87 68 16
e-mail: kimmie@club-internet.fr
Web: www.ceret.net

For 200 years, this Catalonian farmhouse has stood dramatically on its hillside of Mediterranean *maquis* and vineyards. Your hosts have built an extension and made it a perfect place for all lovers of nature, walking and good food. Lucie is a passionate cook with a repertoire (lots of organic in it) that reflects her cosmopolitan, polyglot background. Breakfast is remarkable, too. She and Jacques radiate warm, intelligent hospitality and the common rooms in the old house reflect their personalities. The superbly-equipped bedrooms are in the modern block – less romantic but utterly comfortable.

Rooms: 1 double, 1 twin, 2 triples, 1 quadruple, all with shower & wc.

Price: 350 Frs for two.

Meals: 130 Frs, including wine.

Closed: October-March.

Gîte space for 14 people.

From A9 exit 42 onto D612 W to Thuir then D615 W for 5km; left just before D58 for 1.5km. Drive on right (1km, steep, winding, paved).
Michelin Map No: 235-52

Entry no: 566   **Map No: 18**

Lucie & Jacques BOULITROP
Le Mas Félix
66300 Camelas
Pyrénées-Orientales
Tel: (0)4 68 53 46 71
Fax: (0)4 68 53 40 54
e-mail: lucie.boulitrop@wanadoo.fr
Web: www.sawdays.co.uk

Impossible to capture in one photo – there's an almost Moroccan feel as this old Catalan house unfolds, showing off its exposed stone and beams, pine floors and terracotta tiles. The walled pool is perfect; the surrounding wild hills are the garden. Big, airy, well-equipped bedrooms look out on those great hills, to the sea, or the vineyards – so does the impressive upstairs *salon*. Your host, an ex-professional trumpet player, really knows his regional wines; which are served with dinner – perfect after the delights of Collioure, Céret, Cathar castles and cloisters. *Main house occasionally available to rent.*

Rooms: 1 double, 1 triple, 1 family, each with shower or bath & wc. Garden House for 2/3 (2 rooms, 2 bathrooms, kitchen).

Price: 300-500 Frs for two; Garden House 500 Frs, for two.

Meals: 100 Frs, including aperitif, wine & coffee. Wine-tasting menu 150 Frs.

Closed: Never.

From A9 exit Perpignan Sud to Thuir. Dir. Elne for 2km; right dir. Céret for 5.5km to Fourques; D2 right to Caixas (11km). Follow Mairie/Eglise; house by church.
Michelin Map No: 235-52

Entry no: 567   **Map No: 18**

Ian MAYES
Mas Saint Jacques
66300 Caixas
Pyrénées-Orientales
Tel: (0)4 68 38 87 83
Fax: (0)4 68 38 87 83
e-mail: masstjacq@aol.com
Web: www.sawdays.co.uk

The drive from Perpignan is historical and gorgeous and Mont Louis has changed very little since the time of Louis XIV. La Volute is on/in the entrance arch to this 17th-century citadel and even has a little garden. One room is a tribute to someone's talent with the fretsaw and there is a dramatic black and white bathroom. All rooms are simple, attractive, in good taste. Young and relaxed, Martine neatly combines taking good care of her guests and her two children and has concocted a fantastically complete guide to things to do. It's a perfect base for visiting this fascinating area with its 3,000 hours of sunshine a year (do visit the solar-powered kiln).

Rooms: 2 doubles, 1 twin, each with shower & wc.

Price: 310 Frs for two.

Meals: Choice in village.

Closed: 2 weeks in June & November.

From Perpignan N116 SW for 80km. Chambres d'Hôtes signposted at entrance to Mont Louis. Michelin Map No: 235-55

Entry no: 568   Map No: 18

Martine SCHAFF
La Volute
1 places d'Armes
66210 Mont Louis
Pyrénées-Orientales
Tel: (0)4 68 04 27 21
Fax: (0)4 68 04 27 21

Beautifully restored, with elegant old features including a mosaic tiled hallway, fine wooden chevron floors, old radiators and wood-panelled ceilings, this is a 'dream' house. The enormous and spotless bedrooms have been renovated and decorated in individual styles with tremendous attention to detail and the finer creature comforts, such as candles in the bathrooms. The multi-lingual owners, originally from Belgium, adore meeting people, making them feel at home and chatting around the dinner table. The lovely walled tree and shrub-filled garden is exquisitely peaceful. No wonder people keep returning for more.

Rooms: 4 doubles, 1 suite each with shower &/or bath & wc.

Price: 290-350 Frs for two; breakfast 35 Frs p.p.

Meals: 100 Frs excluding wine (20 Frs), by arrangement.

Closed: Never.

From A61-E80, take Lezignan-Corbieres exit, dir. Fabrezan (6km). In village follow yellow signs to Chambres d'Hôtes. Michelin Map No: 235-40

Entry no: 569   Map No: 13

Mieke MACHIELS & Jan WOUTERS
Lou Castelet, Place de la République
11200 Fabrezan, Aude
Tel: (0)4 68 43 56 98
Fax: (0) 4 68 43 56 98
e-mail: lou.castelet@bigfoot.com
Web: lou.castelet.free.fr

Tea-lovers will be happy here, for bubbly, energetic Martine has more than 40 types on offer. Art-lovers too for she and her husband are passionate about art and the house is full of his paintings and sculptures. It's a comfortable place, endearingly faded around some edges. Strong colours and dark furniture in the bedrooms. Meals on the terrace or in the kitchen with its massive marble-topped open fireplace. There's tennis in the village and the Canal du Midi 200m away. *Gîte space for 4.*

Rooms: 2 doubles, each with shower & wc.

Price: 300 Frs for two.

Meals: 100 Frs, including wine & coffee, by arrangement.

Closed: Mid-October-Easter.

From Narbonne, N113 to Capendu. Left at 1st traffic lights to Marseillette. Right after bridge over the Aude. House 100m on right.
Michelin Map No: 235-40

Entry no: **570**   Map No: 13

Martine de ROULHAC
Demeure La Fargue
16 avenue de la Belle Aude
11800 Marseillette
Aude
Tel: (0)4 68 79 13 88
Fax: (0)4 68 79 13 88
Web: www.sawdays.co.uk

Sally was born in England, lived in America and now, having adopted France completely, has thrown her energies into turning this 17th-century coaching inn into a well-balanced marriage of solid old French base and modern inspiration. She was an interior designer and her sense of style permeates the house which has a comfortable mix of antique and contemporary pieces. She is also a trained cook – delicious Mediterranean-inspired cooking using the best local produce – provides all possible goodies in her big, well-furnished bedrooms and loves to share her passion for, and books on, history and travel.

Rooms: 2 doubles, 1 suite for 4, each with bath & wc.

Price: 400 Frs for two.

Meals: 150 Frs, including wine & coffee, by arrangement.

Closed: Never.

From Beziers take D11, then right to Olonzac, follow signs to Pépieux. From Carcassonne go to Treves, left on D610, through 2 villages, left to Olonzac, follow signs to Pépieux. House has blue shutters and is next to church.
Michelin Map No: 235-40

Entry no: **571**   Map No: 13

Sally WORTHINGTON
Le Vieux Relais
1 rue de l'Etang
11700 Pépieux, Aude
Tel: (0)4 68 91 69 29
Fax: (0)4 68 91 65 49
e-mail: sally.worthington@wanadoo.fr
Web: perso.wanadoo.fr/carrefourbedbreakfast/

The 'House on the Hill' overlooks medieval Carcassonne, just a short kilometre through the vines. A quiet haven from bustling postcard sellers, this sumptuous house, ablaze with colour inside and out, is full of pictures, lovely old furniture and treasures (hats, handmade pots, straw sandals). The wonderfully festooned bedrooms have bathrooms to match (one with a two-body shower!). Madame is open and generous, serves a fantastic array of home-made jams at breakfast on the terrace and is helped by her daughter who also made the striking coffee table of polished cement and iron.

Rooms: 4 doubles, 1 apartment for 4, each with shower or bath & wc.

Price: 330-450 Frs for two.

Meals: 140 Frs, including aperitif, wine & coffee.

Closed: Never.

Gîte space for 4 people.

Go to Carcassonne cité main gate, pass cemetery on right & follow Chambres d'Hôtes signs for 1km along narrow lane through vineyards. Well signposted.
Michelin Map No: 235-39

Entry no: 572   Map No: 13

Mme Nicole GALINIER
La Maison sur la Colline
Sainte Croix
11000 Carcassonne, Aude
Tel: (0)4 68 47 57 94
Fax: (0)4 68 47 57 94
e-mail: nicole.galinier@wanadoo.fr
Web: www.sawdays.co.uk

You could never feel cramped in this 19th-century gentleman-farmer's house and there's space to hide in bad weather – the bedrooms are vast, comfortably furnished and impeccably clean. Breakfast and dinner are served on the terrace in fine weather. On cold days you can make the most of a lovely open fire in the drawing room. Madame, open and welcoming, chats to guests in her attractive kitchen/dining room and enjoys their travellers' tales. Her freshly-decorated house is full of character (and good mattresses) and the huge, restful park beckons, as do nearby Carcassonne, the dreamy Canal du Midi, and the vineyards.

Rooms: 1 double, 1 triple, 1 suite for 4/5, all with shower & wc.

Price: 330-380 Frs for two.

Meals: 120 Frs, including wine & coffee.

Closed: Never.

Gîte space for 5 people.

From Carcassonne direction Salvaza airport; stay on D119 for approx. 4km more; house signposted on left.
Michelin Map No: 235-39

Entry no: 573   Map No: 13

Isabelle CLAYETTE
Domaine des Castelles
11170 Caux et Sauzens
Aude
Tel: (0)4 68 72 03 60
Fax: (0)4 68 72 03 60

The beautifully-converted farmhouse, which rejoices in huge beams, an open fireplace and impeccable taste throughout, has five pretty rooms (one for disabled), utter quiet to relax into and wonderful walks around. Diana is lively, attentive and a superb cook, though meals, served in the enormous dining room or outside, have been known to run late. She and Chris revel in the area, its birdlife, wild flowers, history and wine. They have lovely children (and well-behaved large dogs) and give language courses in winter. And all this just 5km from Carcassonne, 10km from an 18-hole golf course.

Rooms: 3 doubles, 1 twin, 1 triple, all with bath or shower & wc.

Price: 350-400 Frs for two; minimum 2 nights May to September.

Meals: 155 Frs, including wine & coffee, by arrangement.

Closed: January & November.

From Carcassonne, D142 to Cazilhac. Left in front of Mairie on D56 direction Villefloure (bear left at cemetery). La Sauzette signposted to left after 2km. Michelin Map No: 235-39

Entry no: 574   Map No: 13

Chris GIBSON & Diana WARREN
Ferme de la Sauzette
Route de Villefloure
Cazilhac
11570 Palaja, Aude
Tel: (0)4 68 79 81 32
Fax: (0)4 68 79 65 99
Web: www.sawdays.co.uk

You are definitely in Cathar country now: there are donkeys and goats roaming around; the rooms are named after Cathar castles. They are ordered rather than cosy and the cool impression of alarm clocks and televisions is dispelled by the warm personal attention to your needs and the library of 1,000 books, many on the Cathars, many on cookery. Breakfast is hearty, with several types of bread, honey, cheese, home-made cakes and jams. Supper could be grilled salmon with lemon sauce and Madame's crème caramel. Nearby are fortified Carcassonne, medieval Foix and Mirepoix. Wonderful setting. *Discount on stays of more than three days.*

Rooms: 2 doubles, 1 twin, each with shower & wc (& children's room).

Price: 350-370 Frs for two.

Meals: 130 Frs, including aperitif, wine & coffee.

Closed: November-Easter.

From Limoux, D620 direction Chalabre for 7km, then fork right on D626 (signposted Mirepoix) to Peyrefitte. Signposted from village. Michelin Map No: 235-43

Entry no: 575   Map No: 13

Jean-Pierre & Marie-Claire ROPERS
Domaine de Couchet
11230 Peyrefitte du Razès
Aude
Tel: (0)4 68 69 55 06
Fax: (0)4 68 69 55 06
e-mail: jean.pierre.ropers@fnac.net
Web: www.sawdays.co.uk

Your hosts have transformed the buildings of this charming stone-built farm into a series of wonderfully comfortable rooms. There's a real family atmosphere, lots of places to curl up with a book in house or garden and masses of interest for children when the pool palls (including lambs or foals in season). On summer evenings, parental peace is ensured by a resident babysitter so you can enjoy Michèle's delicious French cuisine and the fascinating conversation round her table. Want a cup of tea? Just "pop your head round the kitchen door and ask – any time".

Rooms: 3 doubles, 3 twins, each with bath or shower & wc.

Price: 480 Frs for two.

Meals: 139 Frs, including aperitif, wine & coffee; children 50-65 Frs.

Closed: Mid-November-March.

From Carcassonne D118 S for 40km. At Couiza left on D613 12km to Arques then left on D54 towards Valmigère for 4km. At fork, right on D70 towards Bouisse for 2km; signposted on right. Michelin Map No: 235-43

Entry no: 576   Map No: 13

Michèle & Michel DELATTRE
Domaine des Goudis
11190 Bouisse
Aude
Tel: (0)4 68 70 02 76
Fax: (0)4 68 70 00 74
e-mail: delattre-goudis@mnet.fr

You will be serenaded by birds, bees and sheep in this lovely and largely undiscovered part of France, so close to Albi and its fascinating red-brick Cathedral. Your Anglo-French hosts are welcoming and helpful – the bright, unfussy rooms may be small but the hospitality is great and their deeply converted 200-year-old farmhouse is a deliciously secluded place to stay and walk or bike out into the country. Local sheep farmers (who supply Rocquefort with milk) will show you their milking sheds if asked. The Wises grow their own vegetables and summer dinners are on the terrace overlooking the lovely Tarn valley.

Rooms: 1 twin, 1 triple, each with shower & wc; 1 twin sharing bathroom.

Price: 230 Frs for two.

Meals: 95 Frs, including aperitif, wine & coffee.

Closed: Never.

From Albi, D999 dir. Millau. At La Croix Blanche (25km), left to Cambon du Temple and up to La Barthe on D163. Turn right; house 1st on left. Michelin Map No: 235-27

Entry no: 577   Map No: 13

Michèle & Michael WISE
La Barthe
81430 Villefranche d'Albigeois
Tarn
Tel: (0)5 63 55 96 21
Fax: (0)5 63 55 96 21
e-mail: mx2wise@aol.com
Web: www.angelfire.com/la/wise

Aurifat has new owners – not for the first time since the Middle Ages (the watchtower is 13th-century). Ian & Penelope have installed their good furniture, books and paintings and all is serene and inviting. Each freshly-decorated room has its own private entrance, balcony or terrace and stupendous views. The house is on the southern slope of the hilltop village of Cordes (only five minutes from both the top and the bottom), the swimming pool is big enough for real exercise and there's a poolside barbecue, kitchen and dining area. Cosy in winter too. Enough to entice you to stay a while and try the special three-day deal?

Rooms: 1 suite for 4, 1 double, 2 twin, all with bath or shower & wc.

Price: 320-400 Frs for two, reduction 3 nights or more.

Meals: Wide choice in Cordes. Barbecue & summer kitchen available.

Closed: End December-April.

From Albi D600 to Cordes. There take upward 'Cité' road on right of 'Maison de la Presse' for 500m; fork left dir. Le Bouysset; left at hairpin bend and right 200m on at 2nd hairpin bend to Aurifat.
Michelin Map No: 235-23

Entry no: 578   Map No: 13

Ian & Penelope WANKLYN
Aurifat
81170 Cordes sur Ciel
Tarn
Tel: (0)5 63 56 07 03
Fax: (0)5 63 56 07 03
e-mail: aurifat@wanadoo.fr
Web: www.jcjdatacomm.co.uk/france

A small corner of delight on the edge of Cordes, this old house glows with the sensitive, loving care it has received. A magnificent hallway, a sweeping staircase bring you to fine, airy rooms that have original fireplaces, beams, interesting pictures, views of Cordes and are beautifully furnished (matt satin is very fitting). Your hosts are a gentle couple, maybe a little reserved at first but their dry humour warms up over dinner – most of which they'll proudly tell you they produced themselves. Children are welcome; there are games, a small park where you can picnic if you wish, and Leonard the friendly donkey.

Rooms: 1 twin, 2 doubles, 1 triple, 1 quadruple, all with shower & wc.

Price: 300 Frs for two.

Meals: 105 Frs, including wine & coffee

Closed: Never.

From Albi D600 to Cordes. There follow signs 'Parking 1 & 2'. Then signposted.
Michelin Map No: 235-23

Entry no: 579   Map No: 13

Annie & Christian RONDEL
Les Tuileries
81170 Cordes sur Ciel
Tarn
Tel: (0)5 63 56 05 93
Fax: (0)5 63 56 05 93
e-mail: christian.rondel@wanadoo.fr

Mas de Sudre is a warm friendly house, just like its owners. George and Pippa are ideal B&B folk – relaxed, good-natured, at ease with people, adding lots of little extras to make you comfortable, enthusiastic about their corner of France. Dinners are delicious and convivial, *dégustations* (wine-tastings) can be arranged and there's a large shady garden set in rolling vineyards and farmland where you can sleep off any excesses. For the more energetic there are bikes, a pool, a tennis court, badminton and table tennis. Children are welcome and guests are encouraged to treat the house as their own.

Rooms: 2 doubles, 2 twins, all with shower & wc.

Price: 350 Frs for two.

Meals: Good choice locally.

Closed: Never.

Gîte space for 10 people.

From Gaillac dir. Cordes. Cross railway; fork immed. left on D964 dir. Castelnau de Montmiral for 1km; left on D18 dir. Montauban 400m; right on D4 1.5km; 1st left, 1st house on right. Michelin Map No: 235-27

Entry no: 580   Map No: 13

Pippa & George RICHMOND-
BROWN
Mas de Sudre
81600 Gaillac, Tarn
Tel: (0)5 63 41 01 32
Fax: (0)5 63 41 01 32
e-mail: georgerbrown@free.fr
Web: www.sawdays.co.uk

Looking for the complete French bourgeois experience? The huge cool entrance hall and the massive stone staircase winding up through four floors, the *trompe-l'œil* 'marble' alcoves, the high ceilings and southern colours – deep blue shutters, white walls – make it almost colonially grand. Add the owners' passion for Napoleon III furniture, oil paintings and gilt-framed mirrors and the mood is formal rather than family but above all unmistakably French. Bedrooms are antique-furnished, breakfast is on the terrace overlooking the square – good to be in a town with friendly, utterly French people.

Rooms: 1 suite, 4 doubles, 1 twin, all with bath or shower & wc.

Price: 280 Frs for two; suite 360 Frs.

Meals: Plenty of places in town.

Closed: Never.

In centre of Gaillac, directly opposite St Michel abbey church as you come in across bridge from A68 Toulouse-Albi road. Michelin Map No: 235-27

Entry no: 581   Map No: 13

Lucile & Jean-Luc PINON
8 place Saint-Michel
81600 Gaillac
Tarn
Tel: (0)5 63 57 61 48
Fax: (0)5 63 41 06 56

Madame is a delight, runs this family château with boundless energy and infectious *joie de vivre*, serves breakfast in her big kitchen in order to chat more easily to you while preparing dinner. The comfortable, lived-in bedrooms still have their original 19th-century charm, including a rare 1850s wallpaper, and turning walk-in cupboards into shower rooms or wcs was a stroke of brilliance. The antique-filled sitting rooms are totally French and the little reading room holds hundreds of books. A country house in the style of days gone by, now comfortably worn around the edges and with a tennis court you're welcome to use.

Rooms: 1 suite, with shower & wc; 1 double with shower, sharing wc.

Price: 400-420 Frs for two.

Meals: 120-130 Frs, including wine & coffee.

Closed: Never.

From Revel, D622 towards Castres. 9km along, left on D12 to Lempaut. At Lempaut, right on D46 towards Lescout. La Bousquétarié is on your left. Michelin Map No: 235-31

Entry no: 582   Map No: 13

Monique & Charles SALLIER
La Bousquétarié
81700 Lempaut
Tarn
Tel: (0)5 63 75 51 09
Web: www.sawdays.co.uk

The sort of home we all dream of – on a hill in a beautiful corner of the Tarn, approached by an avenue of old oaks. Your heart will stir to the beauty of house and setting – and the startlingly-positioned pool. Huge dayrooms, heavy ancient doors, beams, open fires and some Louis XIII furniture. One of the rooms is richly furnished with a bathroom in the tower, the other is in brighter, simpler, Mediterranean style – both are worthy of the praise heaped upon them by visitors. And equally elegant, civilised hosts with much charming enthusiasm for the house they have lived in for 40 years and guests they have received for 30!

Rooms: 2 doubles, each with bath or shower & wc.

Price: 300 Frs for two; minimum 2 nights July & August.

Meals: 3 restaurants in village 4km. Mini-kitchen for hire in summer.

Closed: October-March.

From Gaillac D964 direction Caussade. 4km before Larroque, turn left on D1 for 3km. House signposted on right. Michelin Map No: 235-22

Entry no: 583   Map No: 12

Minouche & Christian JOUARD
Meilhouret
81140 Larroque
Tarn
Tel: (0)5 63 33 11 18
Fax: (0)5 63 33 11 18

Named after their years in Africa the Zidi's villa which they genuinely love to share, is full of reminders of their travels: art and artefacts. It's fascinating to talk to them and they have an impressive range of languages. All is immaculate, but not clinically so; bedrooms are extremely comfortable – one has an *enormous* bathroom (inc. Jacuzzi), and its own terrace. There's an unusual mix of styles throughout – a lot of modern with dashes of antique – and there *are* gnomes in the garden. There are also lovely views, a great pool, dogs, cats, and donkeys.

Rooms: 3 doubles, each with bath or shower & wc.

Price: 470-670 Frs for two.

Meals: 135-200 Frs, by arrangement.

Closed: Never.

A68 exit 9 Gaillac. D964 dir. Castelnau de Montmiral. After 8km D15 dir. Le Verdier for 4km. At foot of village left dir. Castelanu de Montmiral. After 300m take road on right signed Ste Cecile de Cayrou. House signed after 1.5km.
Michelin Map No: 235-22

Entry no: 584   Map No: 12

Raymond & Monique ZIDI
Villa Akwaba
81140 Le Verdier
Tarn
Tel: (0)5 63 33 94 72
Fax: (0) 5 63 33 96 58
e-mail: akwaba@wanadoo.fr
Web: www.sawdays.co.uk

Catherine runs her 19th-century manor farmhouse with charm and efficiency – nothing is too much trouble; picnics can be arranged. There's table tennis, *pétanque*, a swimming pool and a big, peaceful garden to roam or relax in. Bedrooms are immaculate with prettily co-ordinated colour schemes, good linen and mattresses. Meals are served either in the bright, pleasant dining room or on the terrace. Perfectly placed for visits to the extraordinary Cathedral at Albi, for walking, cycling and riding in the Gresigne forest, or for outings to the nearby lake complex with all its sporting possibilities.

Rooms: 1 double, 2 triples, all with bath or shower & wc.

Price: 310 Frs for two.

Meals: 110 Frs; gastronomic 150 Frs, including wine; children 40 Frs.

Closed: Never.

From Gaillac D964 N to Castelnau de Montmiral, right at bottom of village for 100m. Right at sign La Croix du Sud, fork left towards Mazars; house on left.
Michelin Map No: 235-22

Entry no: 585   Map No: 12

Catherine SORDOILLET
La Croix du Sud, Mazars
81140 Castelanau de Montmiral
Tarn
Tel: (0)5 63 33 18 46
Fax: (0)5 63 33 18 46
e-mail: guillaume.sordoillet@libertysurf.fr
Web: www.sawdays.co.uk

The moment you drive through the imposing gates and up the gravelled drive you know you are in for something special. This magnificent house, which has been painstakingly restored, is shamelessly luxurious. The dining room has wonderful stained-glass windows and the house is full of interesting paintings, pottery and exotic rugs. Each bedroom has been stylishly decorated with unusual attention to detail; superb furnishings, linens, embroidered towels, bathrobes and modern, well-equipped bathrooms. The sprawling gardens are filled with birdsong and the large swimming pool is at a discreet distance from the house.

Rooms: 2 doubles, 2 twin, 1 suite, each with bath or shower & wc.

Price: 350-475 Frs for two.

Meals: 125 Frs, excluding wine (from 45 Frs).

Closed: Never.

From A68 Toulouse-Albi exit 6. At Saint Sulpice take direction Couffouleux on the D13, for about 3km. House on left clearly signed.
Michelin Map No: 235-25

Entry no: 586   Map No: 12

Tony & Marianne SILVER
Le Manoir de la Maysou
81800 Couffouleux
Tarn
Tel: (05) 63 33 85 92
Fax: (05) 63 40 64 24
e-mail: tonysilver@compuserve.com
Web: www.manoir-maysou.8m.com

A sense of refined luxury, even opulence, pervades this beautifully-restored house where 43 large ebony beams (brought from Madagascar as repatriation luggage when the family moved back...) were used for the job. There is a happy, humorous family atmosphere with many traces of those years on exotic shores, in the cooking as well as the bathrooms. The large, pretty bedrooms are immaculate, the warm-hearted, people-loving owners are most unusual, both refined and down-to-earth, country-comfortable and artistic. *If they haven't heard from you by 8pm they may re-let the room.*

Rooms: 1 double, 1 twin, both with bath or shower & wc.

Price: 300 Frs for two.

Meals: 95 Frs, including wine & coffee

Closed: Mid-December-mid-January.

From Rabastens, D12 direction Coufouleux. Cross river Tarn then imm'ly left on D13 direction Loupiac. Just before village right by cemetery; skirt cemetery, fork right, follow signs for La Bonde for 1km.
Michelin Map No: 235-26

Entry no: 587   Map No: 12

Maurice & Bernadette CRÉTÉ
La Bonde-Loupiac
81800 Rabastens
Tarn
Tel: (0)5 63 33 82 83
Fax: (0)5 63 33 82 83

All is light, sun and simplicity here in superbly wild surroundings (good walks and rock climbing). Madame is gentle, welcoming and most proud of her restored barn and of the guest quarters created within it. They are furnished with old country pieces, fitted with pretty curtains and new bedding; rejoice in a fireplace and a fully-equipped kitchen. She will even come to the rescue with fresh eggs for your supper. There is a lovely terrace for breakfast, which includes a different kind of bread every day, or cheese, or walnuts, or honey. Really lovely people.

New Dutch owners here used to visit as B&B guests, fell in love with the place and have bought it, lock, stock and barrel. Albert used to practise as a solicitor and together they ran a rather famous restaurant. Their plan now is that Honorah will cook occasionally but they have an arrangement for guests with a nearby restaurant. Breakfast is served in the soft yellow-painted, green-panelled dining room. A proud old staircase sweeps up to the bedrooms which are not overdone but just right: light, roomy, marble-fireplaced, old-furnished, with super views of hills and the truly lovely garden.

Rooms: 1 double, 1 twin, each with bath & wc.

Price: 270 Frs for two.

Meals: Self-catering. Restaurants nearby.

Closed: November-March.

Rooms: 3 doubles, 1 twin, 1 suite for 2 with kitchenette, each with bath or shower & wc.

Price: 340-420 Frs for two.

Meals: Good restaurant just down the road.

Closed: 1 November-Easter.

Gîte space for 4 people.

From A9 Béziers Ouest exit on D64 then N112 dir. Castres/Mazamet/St Pons. 1km before St Pons right on D908 dir. Riols/Bédarieux. House signed on left leaving Riols.
Michelin Map No: 240-25

From Mazamet, N112 direction St Pons de Thomières. At Courniou, left to Prouilhe; farm on left.
Michelin Map No: 240-25

Entry no: 588   Map No: 13

Entry no: 589   Map No: 13

Eliane & Jean-Louis LUNES
La Métairie Basse
Hameau de Prouilhe
34220 Courniou
Hérault
Tel: (0)4 67 97 21 59
Fax: (0)4 67 97 21 59

Honorah & Albert JAN KURSTEN
La Cerisaie
1 avenue de Bédarieux
34220 Riols, Hérault
Tel: (0)4 67 97 03 87
Fax: (0)4 67 97 03 88
e-mail: cerisaie@wanadoo.fr
Web: www.sawdays.co.uk

Sarah, who has just written a cookery book and Denis, an accomplished photographer, have decorative flair too, clearly visible within these golden rag-painted walls. The fine townhouse has lovely spaces, just enough antiques, careful use of light and fabrics, inviting guest rooms. You can walk, ride, climb rocks; swim, canoe in the river; follow Denis's wine trail; visit the town's unusual succulent garden – and return drunk with exertion and beauty for a superb, civilised meal on the terrace. Very special.

Rooms: 2 doubles, 1 twin, 1 suite, all with shower & wc.

Price: 395-475 Frs for two.

Meals: 155-175 Frs, including coffee.

Closed: Never.

Gîte space for 4 people.

From Béziers N112 W direction St Pons for 1-2km; then right on D14 through Maraussan, Cazouls lès Béziers, Cessenon to Roquebrun. House signposted in village.
Michelin Map No: 240-26

Entry no: 590   Map No: 13

Denis & Sarah LA TOUCHE
Les Mimosas
Avenue des Orangers
34460 Roquebrun, Hérault
Tel: (0)4 67 89 61 36
Fax: (0)4 67 89 61 36
e-mail: la-touche.les-mimosas@wanadoo.fr
Web: perso.wanadoo.fr/les-mimosas/

"The exotic appearance of the vegetation matches the anachronism of the architecture adding to the impression of a theatrical décor". How's that for a start? "Vast, amazing" – the brochure lies not. Towers, turrets – yet at the same time a very simple welcome from Marie-France and her children; she is a remarkable and courageous woman. Crystal chandeliers, grand piano, original wallpapers, cavernous rooms with great beamed ceilings, lovely inner courtyard, delightful gardens, "defensive" walls – it is all 18th-century has adopted the comforts of this century and retained the traditions of hospitality of another. Worth every penny.

Rooms: 2 doubles, 1 twin, each with bath & wc.

Price: 600-650 Frs for two.

Meals: From 95 Frs, including wine.

Closed: Never.

Gîte space for 7 people.

Leave A75 at exit 35 Béziers. Le Château de Grézan is on D909, 20km south of Bédarieux.
Michelin Map No: 240-22

Entry no: 591   Map No: 13

Mme Marie-France LANSON
Château de Grezan
34480 Laurens
Hérault
Tel: (0)4 67 90 28 03
Fax: (0)4 67 90 05 03
e-mail: chateau-grezan.lanson@wanadoo.fr
Web: www.sawdays.co.uk

The famous, tree-lined Canal du Midi runs through the charming old village and your friendly Australian hostess gives a genuinely warm welcome to visitors to her striking 15th to 18th-century 'terraced château' – which climbs the hillside, in terraced steps. Lovingly restored, the house has handsome panelling, a magnificent *trompe-l'œil* tiled hall and fine painted ceilings. The big, comfortable rooms include two metre-long beds, power showers and much attention to authentic detail. And you are only 5km from the sea.

Rooms: 2 doubles, 2 twins, all with bath or shower & wc.

Price: 270 Frs for two.

Meals: 90 Frs, including wine & coffee.

Closed: Never.

Gîte space for 2 people.

From Béziers, N112 towards Agde. Under motorway then right on D37 into Villeneuve; house in centre opposite Hôtel de Ville. Michelin Map No: 240-30

Entry no: 592   Map No: 13

Jennifer-Jane VINER
7 rue de la Fontaine
34420 Villeneuve lès Béziers
Hérault
Tel: (0)4 67 39 87 15
Fax: (0)4 67 32 00 95
e-mail: anges-gardiens@wanadoo.fr
Web: www.sawdays.co.uk

Madame, an artist and sculptor, is an open, fun person who loves getting to know her guests and showing them her work. Her modern house has lots of artistic atmosphere and big, simply-furnished rooms, each with a few lovely things, good fabrics and a private outside space onto the green garden. The surroundings are worth the trip too: you are up on the hillside, protected by umbrella pines, above the magnificent Salagou lake – perfect for sailing, swimming on those long, hot summer's days, wonderful biking, walking and riding in winter. Definitely worth staying two nights or more.

Rooms: 2 doubles, each with bath or shower & wc.

Price: 270-320 Frs for two; minimum 2 nights.

Meals: Choice within 3-5km; barbecue & picnic possible.

Closed: Never.

From A9 exit 34 onto D13 N then N9 to Clermont l'Hérault . In Clermont D156 towards Lac du Salagou for 3km. Fork left for Liausson; 700m along last house on right before woods. Michelin Map No: 240-22

Entry no: 593   Map No: 13

M & Mme NEVEU
La Genestière
Route de Liausson
34800 Clermont l'Hérault
Hérault
Tel: (0)4 67 96 30 97/
          (0)4 67 96 18 46
Fax: (0)4 67 96 32 56

Not a pelican in sight, nothing out of place either on this superb estate with its mulberry-lined drive, woods, hills, vineyards and wonderful family atmosphere (the couple have an active child and an above-ground swimming pool). The large *auberge* dining room gives onto a covered terrace and rows of vines – just the place to try a glass of estate wine followed by delicious regional cooking. The fresh-coloured bedrooms are new and mezzanined and the delightful, hard-working owners have decorated their family house with the utmost care.

Rooms: 4 double/quadruples, each with shower & wc.

Price: 300-330 Frs for two.

Meals: 100-120 Frs, including wine.

Closed: Last week in October.

Leave Gignac centre eastwards towards Montpellier. At the edge of town: 'Hérault Cuisines' on right; turn right (signed) and follow signs for 3km. Michelin Map No: 240-22

Entry no: 594   Map No: 13

Isabelle & Baudouin THILLAYE de BOULLAY
Domaine du Pélican
34150 Gignac
Hérault
Tel: (0)4 67 57 68 92
Fax: (0)4 67 57 68 92

The big gates open off the typical sun-drenched sleepy village street with its arched doorways and shuttered windows. At the back, your eye leaps straight out into the parallel vineyards and uneven hills – a festival of flaming colour in autumn. Monsieur is English; Madame is French and an artist. She is good company and has done her house with great sympathy for its stone floors and original spaces. Her works are a bonus on the walls. It is a privilege to be her only guests, enjoy the big ground-floor bedroom that opens onto the garden and step out into the morning light for home-made fig jam.

Rooms: 1 double with bathroom.

Price: 350 Frs for two.

Meals: Choice 5km.

Closed: Never.

From A9 exit 27 Lunel dir. Sommière. Left towards Saint-Christol. In village follow main road to right of post office, towards 'cave coopérative'; left at r'bout before small bridge, right for 800m, left into Ave des Bruyères which becomes rue de l'Église. Michelin Map No: 240-19

Entry no: 595   Map No: 14

Monique SYKES-MAILLON
La Ciboulette
221 rue de l'Église
34400 St Christol, Hérault
Tel: (0)4 67 86 81 00
Fax: (0)4 67 86 81 00
e-mail: cibou@aol.com
Web: www.sawdays.co.uk

This fine old *bastide* (fortified farmhouse), built 200 years ago by Madame's great-grandfather, stands on the Ardèche River with its own private 'beach'. Rooms, some reached by the superb stone staircase, look over the romantic and much-painted ruined bridge or the squirrelly, tall-treed park where shade invites summer lingerers. Madame paints furniture, most prettily, and one room has hand-painted frieze and ceiling; Monsieur can accompany you on canoe trips (you may spot an otter) – an attractive, sociable couple who enjoy their guests. There's a small campsite on the property, but plenty of room for all.

This fine rambling house, built in the 18th century as a silkworm farm, has old stones, arches, a lovely shady courtyard. Antoine and Isabelle have created a home for themselves and their three children in their own informal and friendly image: Isabelle is an artist, her touch evident in the imaginative decoration of indoor and outdoor spaces. Breakfast is home-made jams and delicious breads on the shady terrace in summer; dinner is also served on the terrace. Isabelle is interested in cookery from all round the Mediterranean and includes North African and Greek dishes in her repertoire – all very exciting.

Rooms: 1 quadruple, 1 triple, 2 doubles, 1 twin, all with shower & wc.

Price: 300 Frs for two.

Meals: In village.

Closed: Never.

Gîte space for 8 people.

Rooms: 2 twins, 1 triple, 1 quadruple, each with shower & wc.

Price: 300 Frs for two.

Meals: 100 Frs, including aperitif, wine & coffee.

Closed: Never.

From A7, Bollène exit onto D994 to Pont St Esprit. N86 dir. Bourg St Andéol; signed before bridge across river. Michelin Map No: 240-12

From Alès D16/D579 NE to Barjac, through Barjac dir. Vallon Pont d'Arc, 300m after Gendarmerie; house on right, arched doorway. Michelin Map No: 240-8

Entry no: 596 Map No: 14

Entry no: 597 Map No: 14

Mme de VERDUZAN
Pont d'Ardèche
30130 Pont St Esprit
Gard
Tel: (0)4 66 39 29 80
Web: www.sawdays.co.uk

Antoine & Isabelle AGAPITOS
Le Mas Escombelle
La Villette
30430 Barjac, Gard
Tel: (0)4 66 24 54 77
Fax: (0)4 66 24 54 77
e-mail: mas-escombel@wanadoo.fr
Web: perso.wanadoo.fr/mas.escombel/

Climb the steps straight into the huge old kitchen to find a long wooden table on an uneven stone floor, an old sideboard along one whitewashed wall, the old stone sink along another. Touches of bright blue and splashes from pretty ochre-yellow plates punctuate the picture. This happy, intelligent couple chat easily, are warm, informal and welcoming. Bedrooms are big and uncluttered; the house is family-relaxed; dinner is good value and a chance to talk about lots of things including local culture and... wine!

Rooms: 2 doubles, 1 suite, each with shower & wc.

Price: 320 Frs for two.

Meals: 100 Frs, including aperitif, wine & coffee.

Closed: Never.

From Alès D6 E for 27km then left on D979 beyond Lussan towards Barjac for 1km; left on D187 to Fons sur Lussan. Entering village right at old fountain; house up street on left opposite church. Michelin Map No: 240-12

Entry no: 598   Map No: 14

Michèle DASSONNEVILLE
La Magnanerie
30580 Fons sur Lussan
Gard
Tel: (0)4 66 72 81 72

Madame is delightful and an excellent cook. Monsieur is a very competent potter – lovely pottery around the house and a little gallery to buy from. They run a pottery workshop as well as their *chambres d'hôtes* so the atmosphere is busy and creative with lots of interesting people about. The guest rooms, separate from the main house, are simply furnished and guests have a sitting room with a fireplace. Breakfast and dinner (on request) are served on the terrace or in the dining room. Lovely landscape of rolling hills and woods, music festivals and theatrical happenings locally: it's ideal for hikers and culture vultures as well as potters.

Rooms: 1 twin, 1 double, each with shower & wc.

Price: 270-290 Frs for two.

Meals: 80 Frs, including wine, by arrangement.

Closed: Never.

Gîte space for 16 people.

From Alès, D16 through Salindres; after Salindres, left onto D241 direction St Julien de Cassagnes; signposted. Michelin Map No: 240-11

Entry no: 599   Map No: 14

Michel & Françoise SIMONOT
Mas Cassac
30500 Allègre
Gard
Tel: (0)4 66 24 85 65
Fax: (0)4 66 24 80 55
e-mail: mas.cassc@online.fr
Web: www.ceramique.com/Mas-Cassac

Warm sandstone outside, golden light inside washing over old white-painted beams, pretty coloured walls, easy furnishings and the amiable clutter of a family's lifetime. The heart of this rambling house is the kitchen/diner where Marie-Laure marries Mediterranean and Oriental magic to create artistic dinners for evenings of intelligent conversation. They have gifts of hospitality, humour and interior design; a Banksia rose shades the table, the olive grove is perfect for a good read and a Roman path runs by the house and up into the hills. *Good river swimming. Gîte space for 8.*

Rooms: 1 apartment (for 4) with shower, wc & kitchen; 1 suite (for 4) in main house sharing bath, shower, wc, *salon* & kitchen.

Price: 280-350 Frs for two.

Meals: 100 Frs, including wine & coffee. *Use of kitchen extra.*

Closed: Never.

From Alès D50/D129 SW to Anduze then D907 dir. Nîmes for 4km. Right on D35 dir. Quissac. 400m after Bouzène fork right; 2km to Aspères, turn right, 2nd house on left. Michelin Map No: 240-15

Entry no: 600   Map No: 14

Marie-Laure & John MARSH
Mas des Loriots
Aspères
30140 Tornac, Gard
Tel: (0)4 66 61 88 25
Fax: (0)4 66 61 88 25
e-mail: loriots@club-internet.fr
Web: www.sawdays.co.uk

The pool and the flower-filled garden are reason enough to stay here, so is the shady pergola for reading beneath... and the sense of having got away from it all. Edna has created something utterly English – books, pictures, trinkets, a certain kind of comfort – but it is so well done, the colours and space so carefully thought out, the day/dining room so big and pleasant, that we think you will like La Fauguière too. Breakfast is worth being on time for: it is as good as the rooms are comfortable and children are as welcome as you are.

Rooms: 2 doubles, each with bath, shower & wc; 1 double, 1 twin each with shower & basin, sharing wc.

Price: 375-475 Frs for two.

Meals: Wide choice 10km.

Closed: Never.

From Alès, N110 S, right on D910 towards Anduze; after 500m, left on D24 to Canaules. There, right on D149 to St Nazaire des G., right at railway bridge, up hill to Mairie, turn left. House at bottom of hill on left. Michelin Map No: 240-15

Entry no: 601   Map No: 14

Edna & Ted PRICE
Mas de la Fauguière
30610 St Nazaire des Gardies
Gard
Tel: (0)4 66 77 38 67
Fax: (0)4 66 77 11 64

Where to sit in the château's large drawing room where over a dozen French chairs open their arms? Or you might wander onto the balcony with its panoramic views across river, dramatic viaduct and red-roofed village to the terraced hills beyond. The large elegant bedrooms have a perfect château feeling with their dark-coloured walls. Madame, one of an old French family in the silk industry who have lived here for several generations, is delightful and practical and will show you where to find really good walks, exciting canoeing, tennis, riding, interesting wildlife spots and ancient buildings to visit nearby.

Rooms: 2 twins, 1 double, each with bath or shower & wc.

Price: 350-450 Frs for two.

Meals: 100 Frs, including wine & coffee.

Closed: Never.

From Millau S on N9 for 19km. At La Cavalerie left on D7 direction Le Vigan for about 50km to Bez. Before bridge, little château signposted on left.
Michelin Map No: 240-14

Entry no: 602   Map No: 13

Françoise du LUC
Château Massal
Bez et Esparon
30120 Le Vigan, Gard
Tel: (0)4 67 81 07 60
Fax: (0)4 67 81 07 60
Web: www.sawdays.co.uk

This ancient abode, with flower-filled terrace, large private orchard and views of the Cévennes mountains, is home to an artist/designer couple. Supremely quiet (the only passer-by is the local winegrower) it has a choice of styles: an 11th-century vaulted ground-floor room with private courtyard or a first floor room remodelled in the 1920s, all ice-cream colours, long, elegant windows and patterned tiled floors with private balcony. The lovely blue, big-tabled kitchen and the living room with its display of David's work add to the welcoming atmosphere. Dinner – regional or exotic – may be rounded off with organic, home-grown fruit. Art classes too.

Rooms: 2 doubles, each with bath or shower & wc.

Price: 320 Frs for two.

Meals: 120 Frs, including wine & coffee.

Closed: Never.

From Nîmes D999 direction Le Vigan for 27km then right to Bragassargues. House in village centre.
Michelin Map No: 240-15

Entry no: 603   Map No: 14

David & Patricia CHAPMAN
La Maison des Rêves
Le Village
30260 Bragassargues, Gard
Tel: (0)4 66 77 13 45
Fax: (0)4 66 77 13 45
e-mail: chapreves@aol.com
Web: www.sawdays.co.uk

A *hôtel particulier* is a private mansion and Philippe 'receives' at his with warm refinement. His rooms, all very separate and private, each named after a different local luminary (including our own Lawrence Durrell) are in traditional Provençal style: highly-polished floors, white bedcovers, a different and beautiful wall-hanging over each bed; super big bathrooms too. The magic secluded terrace garden with views over the roofs of the old town is where you have breakfast, which to Philippe is a very important moment of the day. Guests have filled the visitors' book with ecstatic comments; yours to come?

Marion has made something very special of this 17th-century house: there is a slightly Moorish feel to the rooms she has lovingly put together, placing beautiful pieces of furniture and paintings to enhance their generous proportions. Her cooking also has a North African influence as well as the Provençal specialities one would expect. Candlelit dinner under the pergola in a lovely walled garden, huge breakfast the next morning including cold meats, cheese and local *fougasse* (a soft delicate bread), and the usual French delicacies – bliss!

Rooms: 4 doubles, 1 twin, 1 triple, all with bath or shower & wc.

Price: 380-500 Frs for two.

Meals: 120 Frs, including wine.

Closed: Never.

Rooms: 1 double, 1 twin, sharing bathroom; 1 suite with bath & wc.

Price: 350-500 Frs for two.

Meals: 140 Frs, including aperitif, AOC wine & coffee.

Closed: Never.

From Nîmes D40 W 28km to Sommières. House clearly signed in town centre; park in front.
Michelin Map No: 240-19

From A9 exit 26 S to Aimargues Centre. Cross roundabout with fountain down lane of plane trees for 300m. Entrance Rue de la Violette (3 cypresses behind garden wall).
Michelin Map No: 240-23

Entry no: 604   Map No: 14

Entry no: 605   Map No: 14

Philippe de FRÉMONT
Hôtel de l'Orange
Chemin du Château Fort
30250 Sommières, Gard
Tel: (0)4 66 77 79 94
Fax: (0)4 66 80 44 87
e-mail: philippe.de.fremont@wanadoo.fr
Web: www.sawdays.co.uk

Marion ESCARFAIL
26 boulevard St Louis
30470 Aimargues
Gard
Tel: (0)4 66 88 52 99
Fax: (0)4 66 88 52 66
e-mail: marionmais@aol.com
Web: members.aol.com/marionmais

A path through the woods leads from the house to the river by the Pont du Gard, a World Heritage site – the setting is truly wonderful. Indoors, the décor is fulsome, almost whacky – a net canopy over one of the beds, hanging hats, splayed fans, silk flowers, etc. The rooms are themed. *La Provençale* has a small connecting room with bunk beds and soft toys for the younger guest. Monsieur works in Nîmes but gives all his remaining time to welcoming and caring for his guests. The new swimming pool is now an added enticement and bedrooms have air-conditioning.

Rooms: 1 suite, 3 doubles, 1 twin with bath or shower & wc.

Price: 500-700 Frs for two.

Meals: Auberges at Pont du Gard 500m.

Closed: October-March.

Gîte space for 11 people.

From Remoulins follow signs for Pont du Gard 'Rive Droite'. Signposted on right.
Michelin Map No: 240-16

Entry no: 606   Map No: 14

Gérard & Catherine CRISTINI
La Terre des Lauriers
Rive Droite – Pont du Gard
30210 Remoulins
Gard
Tel: (0)4 66 37 19 45
Fax: (0)4 66 37 19 45

John, who will welcome you with exuberance to the 19th-century *maison de maître* he has restored with Michel, is a joiner who also has an excellent eye for interior design and decoration while Michel does the cooking and the garden. They are a delightful couple. From the classic black and white tiles of the entrance hall to the carefully-planned lighting in the bedrooms, every detail has been attended to. A very generous breakfast is served under the chestnut trees or by the pool; afterwards you can wander off to join in lazy Provençal village life, visit Avignon, Uzès or nearby Lussan, the fortified Cévenol village.

Rooms: 1 double, 2 twins, each with bath or shower & wc.

Price: 500 Frs for two.

Meals: 160 Frs, including aperitif, wine coffee.

Closed: Never.

From A9 exit 23 W to Uzès 19km. There D979 N for 7.5km then right on D238 to La Bruguière. House on big square next to Mairie (vast Micocourier tree in front).
Michelin Map No: 240-12

Entry no: 607   Map No: 14

John KARAVIAS & Michel COMAS
Les Marronniers
30580 La Bruguière
Gard
Tel: (0)4 66 72 84 77
Fax: (0)4 66 72 85 78
e-mail: les.marronniers@hello.to
Web: hello.to/les.marronniers

This magical 17th-century moated château (parts of it even 12th-century) has its very own ghost, *la Dame à la Rose*. Towers overlook the monumental courtyard where Mary Stuart (later Queen of Scots) once walked. Madame runs a cultural centre and stages a summer music festival in this beautiful setting. Breakfast is in the courtyard or in the dining room. The exceptional bedrooms, with round tower bathrooms, have just been renovated with colourful details such as bright new satin canopies. The pool and sauna set up is a seductive addition.

Rooms: 3 doubles, 2 quadruples, 1 twin, all with bath & wc.

Price: 500 Frs for two.

Meals: Choice 5-10km.

Closed: Never.

A simple village home where guests have lots of space in their vaulted ground-floor suite and, although it's right on the street, there's very little traffic in enchanting Pujaut. Helen and Jacques met while working in Africa, where she was a nurse and Jacques an agriculturist – they are an interesting and concerned couple (10% of their B&B income goes to development projects) and the house has many African mementoes and lots of pine. The pretty, peaceful, terraced garden now has a summer kitchen for guests but is not really suitable for adventurous toddlers. Super folk with whom to share good conversation over delicious suppers.

Rooms: 1 suite for 4 with shower & wc.

Price: 250 Frs for two.

Meals: 80 Frs, including wine & coffee. Summer kitchen.

Closed: Never.

From Avignon, N580 direction Bagnols sur Cèze. At junction in L'Ardoise, left along D9 direction Laudun; signposted. Michelin Map No: 240-12

Entry no: 608   Map No: 14

Gisèle & Jean-Louis BASTOUIL
Château de Lascours
30290 Laudun
Gard
Tel: (0)4 66 50 39 61
Fax: (0)4 66 50 30 08
e-mail: chateau.de.lascours@wanadoo.fr
Web: www.sawdays.co.uk

From Avignon & Villeneuve N580 direction Bagnols sur Cèze then right on D377 & D177 to Pujaut. In village follow signs to Mairie; Saba'ad is 300m into the old village from Mairie and church. Michelin Map No: 240-16

Entry no: 609   Map No: 14

Helen THOMPSON & Jacques SERGENT
Saba'ad
Plage des Consuls
30131 Pujaut, Gard
Tel: (0)4 90 26 31 68
Fax: (0)4 90 26 31 68

Elevated by his experiences as a caterer to the British army after the war, the owner of this fine example of an expatriate 'bungaloid' set up shop in the Languedoc as a gastronome – and failed. Rumour has it that his taste in food was a mirror of his architectural taste, and that the area was not ready for him. This is an unusual place to spend the night, and affordable, too, if you live in horror of inflationary prices. So, a special place in the financial sense, if in no other. One of those characteristic British 'faces' that once seen are never remembered.

Rooms: 4 bunk beds (16 max) sharing a cold shower.

Price: 50 Frs for two. Reduction for groups.

Meals: 25 Frs including wine, by arrangement every 4 hours.

Closed: Always open to the elements.

Gîte space for 50 people.

For security reasons these will be supplied on application.

Entry no: **610**   Map No: 14

Gen. DUN CATRYN
Pensées de l'Angleterre
Rue des Martyrs
81701 Balbi
Tarn
Tel: (0)5 70 77 07 70
e-mail: Bungal-oid@sawdays.com

In a peaceful Provençal village, go through the high double doors to find this converted barn and small house. The Rousseaus are warm, friendly people and really enjoy having guests to stay. Joel paints watercolours and Michèle is a keen and good cook. Meal times are flexible, the atmosphere relaxed and the sheltered courtyard or cosy dining room very conducive to lingering chat. The cottagey, beamed bedrooms have good solid furniture, wooden floors, plants, patchwork counterpanes and sensible bathrooms. An easy place to be, 10 minutes from Avignon, 20 minutes from Nimes and in excellent rosé wine, olive and fruit country.

Rooms: 2 doubles, each with bath & wc.

Price: 280 Frs for two.

Meals: 80 Frs, including wine, by arrangement.

Closed: Never.

From autoroute du Nord, exit Orange, direction Mims-Montpellier; 1st exit to Roquemaure; Pujaut 6km. House opposite town hall with large wooden door.
Michelin Map No: 240-16

Entry no: **611**   Map No: 14

Joel & Michèle ROUSSEAU
Les Bambous
Rue de la Mairie
30131 Pujaut
Gard
Tel: (0)4 90 26 46 47
Fax: (0)4 90 26 46 47
e-mail: rousseau-michele@wanadoo.fr

In a beautiful, unsung part of France, cross the lovely old bridge over the Tarn into Quézac. You'd never guess Marius was a new house, it fits in so perfectly with its old stones, beams and doors and its warm, lived-in feel. Inside, if you could decorate it, it's been decorated, including a delightful mural of birds flying up the stairs. Dany and Pierre clearly adore embellishing their home, and spoiling their guests with an amazing array of delicacies from home-made brioche to home-grown organic veg to their speciality: *gâteau de noix* made with their own walnuts.

Rooms: 3 doubles, each with shower & wc; 1 twin with bath, shower & wc.

Price: 280-400 Frs for two.

Meals: 100 Frs, including wine.

Closed: Never.

Gîte space for 12 people.

From A75 exit 39 on N88 E for 25km then right on N106 towards Alès for 25km; at Ispagnac right to Quézac and follow signs in village.
Michelin Map No: 240-6

Entry no: 612   Map No: 13

Danièle MÉJEAN & Pierre
PARENTINI
La Maison de Marius
8 rue du Pontet
48320 Quézac
Lozère
Tel: (0)4 66 44 25 05
Fax: (0)4 66 44 25 05

Auvergne

On the wild plateau, protected by a multitude of medieval castles, the ancient hardwoods share the land with mild cows, hardy sheep and a few farmers – their ancestors ate those chestnuts, their pigs those acorns.

A mini-hamlet in the calm green Aveyron where there is so much space. Two rooms, in the main house, each with a little terrace, look out over a typical old medieval château; the third, in an outbuilding, has a mezzanine; all are welcoming, two have cooking facilities. The garden is full of flowers, the view stupendous, your hosts solicitous and keen to help, providing for all your needs. The food is "outstanding and imaginative" – Pierre and Monique used to run a restaurant. *Well-behaved children and pets welcome.*

Rooms: 2 doubles, each with bath or shower & wc. In separate house: 2 doubles, bath & wc.

Price: 250-300 Frs for two.

Meals: 100 Frs, including wine & coffee; self-catering possible.

Closed: Never.

Gîte space for 8 people.

From Villefranche, D922 south direction Albi; at entrance to Sanvensa, follow signs on right to Monteillet Chambres d'Hôtes.
Michelin Map No: 235-15

Entry no: 613   Map No: 13

Monique & Pierre BATESON
Monteillet-Sanvensa
12200 Villefranche de Rouergue
Aveyron
Tel: (0)5 65 29 81 01
Fax: (0)5 65 65 89 52
e-mail: pbc@wanadoo.fr

Here is a simple unpretentious home with a real family feel. The house is modern, the rolling Languedoc hills are wild and very ancient. You can put on your wings and join the paragliders and hang-gliders who launch themselves off a nearby cliff, or you can watch them from the safety of your breakfast table in the garden. It matters little that Henriette speaks no English: she is kind and welcoming and you can get a long way with smiles and sign language. The immaculate, simply and attractively furnished bedrooms include a suite which is perfect for a family.

Rooms: 1 double, 1 suite for 4, each with shower & wc.

Price: 240-260 Frs for two.

Meals: Choice in Millau, 3km.

Closed: Never.

From Millau D911 towards Cahors. Just after leaving city limits right at 'Chenil' and 'Auberge' crossroads. Signposted. Follow small road for about 2km.
Michelin Map No: 240-14

Entry no: 614   Map No: 13

Mme Henriette CASSAN
Montels
12100 Millau
Aveyron
Tel: (0)5 65 60 51 70
Web: www.sawdays.co.uk

What a setting! Ideal for wildlife and outdoors lovers – orchids and other rare species plus canoeing, rock-climbing, hang-gliding – this is a *Gîte Panda* (providing detailed info. on local fauna and flora). The restored 16th-century farmhouse with terracotta floors, old beams and white walls throughout. Jean made much of the pine furniture. The dining room has tapestries on the walls and antique farm furniture with the fragrance of years of polish. Home-produced organic meat and veg are used in excellent regional meals. *Reductions for longer stays.*

Rooms: 5 doubles, 1 room for 4/5, each with bath or shower & wc.

Price: 280 Frs for two.

Meals: 95-110 Frs, excluding wine.

Closed: Mid-November-March.

Your young hosts escaped from heaving, stressful Paris to this rural paradise. Their brilliant conversion of an old Cantal farmhouse has preserved the original scullery ledge and sink, made of vast slabs of stone, the beams, the inglenook fireplace. They now aim to convert their neighbours to better environmental (get the scrap metal off the hillside) and social (more respect for your woman?) attitudes. The rooms are well and simply done with good colours and fabrics and no unnecessary frippery, the meals are feasts, the Balleux a most interesting and happy couple.

Rooms: 1 double, 1 twin, 1 suite for 4 in main house; 2 suites & 1 double in cottage; all with bath or shower & wc.

Price: 250-280 Frs for two; half-board 195-215 Frs p.p.

Meals: 80 Frs, including wine & coffee.

Closed: Never.

From Millau N9 N to Aguessac. Leaving village right on D547 to Compeyre; left in village and follow signs for 2km.
Michelin Map No: 240-10

From Aurillac D920 to Arpajon; left on D990 for 10km (DON'T go to St Etienne de Carlat) then left direction Caizac; signposted.
Michelin Map No: 239-41

Entry no: 615   Map No: 13

Entry no: 616   Map No: 13

Jean & Véronique LOMBARD-PRATMARTY
Quiers
12520 Compeyre
Aveyron
Tel: (0)5 65 59 85 10
Fax: (0)5 65 59 80 99

Francine & Jacky BALLEUX
Lou Ferradou
Caizac
15130 St Etienne de Carlat
Cantal
Tel: (0)4 71 62 42 37

The lava of the surrounding volcanoes provided the stone flags for the dining room floor of this handsome, family house. Élisabeth is bright and enthusiastic, her interior is uncluttered, sober and furnished with antiques and soft textiles. Each room is named after an ancestor; we liked *Guillaume* best – canopied bed, Japanese grass paper, lovely Louis XV armoire, cabinet full of old *objets* – but they are all superb, the garden a treat for sunlit breakfasts, the cast-iron *Godin* stove warming in winter, the outbuildings full of character.

A dream! Vaulx, a fairy-tale castle that was English during the Hundred Years' War, has been in the family for 800 years. Creak along the parquet, pray in the chapel, swan around the *salon*, sleep in one tower, bath in another. Room names are as evocative as furnishings are romantic – worthy of Sleeping Beauty, who would surely have woken up for breakfast of home-hive honey, brioche, yoghurt, eggs, cheese. Get to know your delightfully entertaining hosts, visit the donkey or, if you're feeling homesick, have a drink in Guy's *petit pub* with its impressive collection of beer mats.

Rooms: 3 doubles, all with shower & wc.

Price: 320-380 Frs for two.

Meals: Wide choice 5-8km.

Closed: Never; open by arrangement Nov-March.

Rooms: 2 triples, 1 double, each with bath or shower & wc.

Price: 300-350 Frs for two.

Meals: 100-120 Frs, including aperitif & wine.

Closed: Never.

Gîte space for 5 people.

From A71, Riom exit, N144 direction Combronde & Montluçon. 2.5km after Davayat, right onto D122 to Chaptes. Michelin Map No: 239-7

From A72 exit 3 on D7 through Celles sur Durolle to Col du Frissonnet. Château is the first right after the Col. Michelin Map No: 239-21

Entry no: 617   Map No: 8

Entry no: 618   Map No: 8

Mme Élisabeth BEAUJEARD
8 route de la Limagne
Chaptes
63460 Beauregard Vendon
Puy-de-Dôme
Tel: (0)4 73 63 35 62
Web: www.sawdays.co.uk

Guy & Régine DUMAS de VAULX
Château de Vaulx
63120 Sainte Agathe
Puy-de-Dôme
Tel: (0)4 73 51 50 55
Fax: (0)4 73 51 50 55

A thoroughly restored old stone-walled, stone-shingled house, Manou is typical of these Auvergne hills – ancient volcanoes where great rivers rise. She is a delight, as generous with her time as with her breakfasts: ham, cheese, three kinds of bread, brioches, croissants, home-made jam – the embroidered napkins give an idea of her attention to detail – served in the impressive dining room or the garden. Bedrooms are hung with silk, writing tables wait for you to be inspired to pen deathless prose, hairdryers hide in bathrooms; in short, every modern comfort against a timeless backdrop of drama and character. *Book ahead.*

Perched on top of a rocky outcrop, Le Chastel has eye-stretching views towards the snow-capped Mont Dore. Most of the Auvergne seems to be lying at your feet. The château was an almost total ruin when the Sauvadets moved here and began the painful task of restoration. Michel is an architect, Anita a designer. Through sheer hard work, dedication and attention to detail they have recreated a masterpiece, searching far and wide to find authentic furniture, tapestries and other pieces to fit the mood exactly. The bedrooms are all absolutely magnificent. This is spectacular, high-class stuff. You simply have to visit!

Rooms: 2 doubles, 1 twin, 2 triples, all with shower & wc.

Price: 350 Frs for two.

Meals: Restaurant in village.

Closed: November–mid-February.

Rooms: 3 doubles, each with bath/shower & wc.

Price: 550-700 Frs for two.

Meals: Restaurants 4km.

Closed: January-February.

From A71/75 exit 6 on D978/D996 W to Le Mont Dore (53km). Continue D996 W past Mairie then 5km to Le Genestoux. House signposted in village. Michelin Map No: 239-18

From Clermont Ferrand A75 south exit 6 onto D978 towards Champeix & Besse. From Champieux D996 to Montaigut le Blanc. Château on hill; signposted from town. Michelin Map No: 239-19

Entry no: 619   Map No: 13

Entry no: 620   Map No: 13

Françoise Marie LARCHER
La Closerie de Manou
Le Genestoux
63240 Le Mont Dore
Puy-de-Dôme
Tel: (0)4 73 65 26 81
Fax: (0)4 73 81 11 72

M & Mme SAUVADET
Le Chastel Montaigu
63320 Montaigut le Blanc
Puy-de-Dôme
Tel: (0)4 73 96 28 49
Fax: (0)4 73 96 21 60

Acres of parkland, a walled garden, a 12th-century vaulted chapel. The splendid rooms are utterly in keeping, from the vast, panelled, period-furnished drawing and dining rooms to big, beautiful bedrooms, with here a canopied bed, there an exquisite little dressing room, everywhere shimmering mirrors, fabulous views of ancient trees or the Puy-de-Dôme. A perfect hostess, Madame makes you feel immediately at ease and helps you plan your day over a most delicious breakfast. She can also show you how to make lace (*dentelle du Puy*).

Rooms: 3 doubles, 1 twin, 1 suite, all with bath and/or shower & wc.

Price: 385-555 Frs for two.

Meals: 150 Frs, including wine & coffee, by arrangement (not July/August); choice nearby.

Closed: November-March.

The 14th-century origins of this gloriously isolated house, once a fortified manor, are still evident but it is a far cry from the ruin your hosts bought some 30 years ago. They have restored it beautifully, making big, cosy, subtly-lit rooms that are lovingly decorated with family antiques and memorabilia and reached by a delicious spiral staircase – a treat. Their sheep graze safely in the the fields which surround the house – here, you can walk, fish and hunt mushrooms in season. The easy, good-natured Raucaz open their hearts and dining table to all this is really somewhere you can feel at home and relax.

Rooms: 1 double, 1 twin, 2 triples, all with bath or shower & wc.

Price: 220-260 Frs for two.

Meals: 100 Frs, including wine.

Closed: Never.

From Clermont Ferrand, A75 exit 13 to Parentignat; D999 direction St Germain l'Hermite for 6km; signposted on right. (8km from A75 exit.)
Michelin Map No: 239-20

Entry no: 621   Map No: 13

Henriette MARCHAND
Château de Pasredon
63500 St Rémy de Chargnat
Puy-de-Dôme
Tel: (0)4 73 71 00 67
Fax: (0)4 73 71 08 72
Web: www.sawdays.co.uk

From Nevers N7 S 22km; right on D978a to Le Veudre; there D13 then D234 to Pouzy Mésangy. Signposted.
Michelin Map No: 238-32

Entry no: 622   Map No: 8

Claire RAUCAZ
Manoir Le Plaix
Pouzy Mésangy
03320 Lurcy Levis
Allier
Tel: (0)4 70 66 24 06
Fax: (0)4 70 66 25 82

Once upon a time, kindly Anne-Marie lived in a big town. One day she found her dream house in the Auvergne near deep mysterious woods and babbling brooks so she left the city, lovingly restored her house, installed her old family furniture and opened the door so that visitors could share her dream. So, after a delicious supper, before the roaring fire, Anne-Marie may treat you to a fairy tale of her own making. (She also offers breathing and relaxation courses.) Thus you will all live happily ever after and never forget this exceptional woman.

Rooms: 2 triples, 2 twins, 1 double, each with shower & wc.

Price: 270-350 Frs for two.

Meals: 95 Frs, including wine & coffee; children 70 Frs.

Closed: Never.

From A72 exit 4 onto D53 E to Champoly. Here D24 E to St Marcel d'Urfé then D20 S towards St Martin la Sauveté and follow signs.
Michelin Map No: 239-22

Entry no: 623   Map No: 8

Anne-Marie HAUCK
Il fut un temps, Les Gouttes
42430 St Marcel d'Urfé, Loire
Tel: (0)4 77 62 52 19/
      (0)6 86 96 59 67
Fax: (0)4 77 62 52 19
e-mail: anne-marie.hauck@wanadoo.fr
Web: www.eazyweb.co.uk/ilfut

Do stay a few days in this charmingly typical Napoleon III manor house, square and confident in its five acres of parkland (with tennis court) and the famous Troisgros restaurant just 8km away. There are fine walks (all levels of difficulty) to help work up an appetite for the local gastronomy. You are guests in a family home, your antique-furnished bedroom has its own character, the bath is a claw-footed marvel (plenty of towels and bathrobes to go with it) and Madame a gentle friendly widow. She loves sharing a welcome cup of something with new people and guiding them to the hidden delights of this lovely area. *Ask about pets.*

Rooms: 1 double with shower & wc; 1 suite for 3/4 with bath & wc.

Price: 350 Frs for two; suite 500 Frs for three.

Meals: Choice within 3km or in Roanne, 8km.

Closed: Mid-November-mid-March, except by arrangement.

From Roanne D53 for 8km. Right into village & follow signs.
Michelin Map No: 239-10

Entry no: 624   Map No: 8

Mme GAUME
Domaine de Champfleury
42155 Lentigny
Loire
Tel: (0)4 77 63 31 43
Fax: (0)4 77 63 31 43
Web: www.sawdays.co.uk

Once part of the ramparts of this ancient city, the old townhouse has been furnished and decorated by mother and daughter in classically French manner with proper antiques on stylish parquet floors. Dinner both looks and tastes good – true Gallic cuisine enhanced by bone china, family silver and Bohemian crystal. Hear the great organ nearby and the famous music festival (August), walk the excellent hiking paths from the back door, then return to wallow in the gentle, floral, boudoir-like comfort of La Jacquerolle.

Rooms: 2 triples, 1 double, 1 twin, each with bath or shower & wc.

Price: 300 Frs for two.

Meals: 120 Frs, including wine & coffee.

Closed: Never.

Catherine, Bill and *Valentin* – a rare trio awaits you in this fairy-tale spot where the forest laps up to the edge of the hilltop village and its once-abandoned inn. The Hays left the bright lights of entertaining – he directed, she acted (opposite Peter Sellers, 007,...) – for the old *auberge* whose name was/will be Bill's in another life (they can tell you all over dinner, in several languages). He, with great painting talent, has waved his magic wand over walls, furniture, bathtubs; she receives magnificently. Their combined sensitivities make staying here truly memorable.

Rooms: 1 suite for 4, 3 doubles, 1 twin each with bath or shower & wc.

Price: 290-320 Frs for two.

Meals: 110 Frs, including wine (low season only; super restaurant next door)

Closed: Never.

From Brioude D19 to La Chaise Dieu. Follow signs to Centre Ville; in front of Abbey turn right to Place du Monument. Park here; house is just off the square at bottom left-hand corner. Michelin Map No: 239-33

Entry no: 625   Map No: 13

Jacqueline & Carole CHAILLY
La Jacquerolle
Rue Marchédial
43160 La Chaise Dieu
Haute-Loire
Tel: (0)4 71 00 07 52
Web: www.sawdays.co.uk

From Clermont Ferrand, A75 to Issoire exit 13 on D999 to La Chaise Dieu, then S on D906 towards Le Puy; after 100m left on D20 & follow signs for 6km. Michelin Map No: 239-34

Entry no: 626   Map No: 13

Bill & Catherine HAYS
Chambres d'Hôtes 'Valentin'
Le Bourg
43160 Bonneval
Haute-Loire
Tel: (0)4 71 00 07 47
Web: www.sawdays.co.uk

Lively, intelligent Béatrice took over this gorgeous old farmhouse and moved from Lyon in May; she's German, speaks excellent English and French, adores cooking and plans international menus (dance and language courses are in the pipeline too). The character and individuality of the bedrooms are unchanging; the décor simply freshened. Bathrooms are excellent. Walk out and explore those remote, green-wooded hills and secret streams; maybe you'll return to a blazing log fire in the great stone fireplace and dinner in the former stables (a magnificent 15m tree carries the ceiling).

Rooms: 3 doubles, 2 twins, all with shower & wc (2 adjoining, 3 separate).

Price: 300 Frs for two.

Meals: 120 Frs, including apéritif, wine & coffee. Picnic possible.

Closed: Never.

From Le Puy en Velay N102 dir. Brioude, then D906 dir. La Chaise Dieu, then D1 through Craponne onto D498 dir. Pontempeyrat for 3km; follow signs, left up hill, house 1st on left. Michelin Map No: 239-46

Entry no: 627   Map No: 13

Béatrice KNOP
Paulagnac
43500 Craponne sur Arzon
Haute-Loire
Tel: (0)4 71 03 26 37
Fax: (0)4 71 03 26 37
e-mail: celivier@infonie.fr
Web: www.sawdays.co.uk

Walkers! Join a circuit here and walk from B&B to B&B in this superbly unspoilt area; or cross-country ski it in winter. Simple, unaffected people will love Rosa, her somewhat dated décor and her fabulous home-grown, home-made food which oozes genuine natural goodness. A real old soldier, she manages the flock of milk-producing sheep, is surrounded by grandchildren and welcomes all-comers with a 'cup of friendship' before her great granite hearth. The house is warm, the rooms perfectly adequate, the hostess unforgettable.

Rooms: 1 double, 1 twin, 1 triple, all with shower & wc.

Price: 200 Frs for two; reduction for children.

Meals: 70 Frs, including wine & coffee.

Closed: January & February.

From Le Puy en Velay, D589 to Saugues then D585 direction Langeac, turning left onto D32 to Venteuges. Michelin Map No: 239-45

Entry no: 628   Map No: 13

Rosa DUMAS
Le Bourg
43170 Venteuges
Haute-Loire
Tel: (0)4 71 77 80 66

Take your time: the drive up is spectacular. Then you arrive for a drink on the terrace, a gasp at the view across the valley and time to stay and unwind. Judas trees enchant, bright flowers tumble over terraces, the 400-year-old house has nooks and crannies around a small courtyard, cosy bedrooms, a magnificent vaulted sitting room, PLUS heated pool, sauna, telescope, music system, stupendous walking... Henri is smiling and positive, Jacote quieter and twinkly; they are good, interesting hosts and provide excellent food (home-made sorbets to die for) with locally-made ingredients (also for sale).

Rooms: 3 doubles, 1 twin, 2 quadruples, all with shower & wc.

Price: 290-390 Frs for two.

Meals: 110 Frs, including wine & coffee.

Closed: December-April, except by arrangement.

From Joyeuse D203 towards Valgorge. At Pont du Gua cross bridge and take narrow paved road up hillside to La Roche (10 hairpins in 3km!). Michelin Map No: 240-3

Entry no: 629   Map No: 14

Rhone

This valley flows past the greatest chefs of France, the woods where wild boar (and tame pigs) hunt big black truffles, and the hills where the Gauls fought so bravely their last fight against the Roman legions.

Henri & Jacote ROUVIÈRE
La Petite Cour Verte
07110 La Roche Beaumont
Ardèche
Tel: (0)4 75 39 58 88
Fax: (0)4 75 39 43 00
e-mail: henri.rouviere@wanadoo.fr

How to describe paradise in one short paragraph? The setting: high, rural, hidden, silent. The views: long, of mountain peaks, inspiring. The house: lovingly restored, of stone, and wood from the surrounding chestnut forests, light, open, lovely. Bedrooms: just right. Food: organic, home-grown, imaginative... and there's lots of honey. Your hosts are warm and trusting, quickly your friends. Gil is a carpenter in winter and a beekeeper in summer. Come up the long narrow road to walk, talk, and believe us.

Rooms: 1 suite for 5, 1 triple, 1 double, each with shower & wc.

Price: 280 Frs for two.

Meals: 100 Frs, including wine & coffee.

Closed: Christmas.

Jean-Michel is inexhaustible: having virtually rebuilt the old mill (part of the château) on its spectacular ravine site where basalt prisms shimmer and the falling stream sings (and powers his generator), he is extending his walkers' dormitories, improving his superb hiking/biking itineraries, keeping donkeys to clear the land and carry small children (over five only) or hikers' packs, making lovely wooden toys and apple juice; Madame cares for five good sober rooms, serves local honey and yoghurt at one long breakfast table and the fire glows. They long for you to STAY and discover the beauty at the heart of their lovely mountain.

Rooms: 5 twins, all with bath & wc.

Price: 250-270 Frs for two.

Meals: Restaurants 3-6km.

Closed: Never.

Gîte space for 15 people.

From Aubenas N102 W towards Le Puy for 8.5km. At Lalevade left to Jaujac. By Café des Lorsirs, cross river & follow signs 4km along narrow mountain road.
Michelin Map No: 239-48

Entry no: 630   Map No: 14

Marie & Gil FLORENCE
Les Roudils
07380 Jaujac
Ardèche
Tel: (0)4 75 93 21 11
Fax: (0)4 75 93 21 11
Web: www.sawdays.co.uk

From Aubenas D104 to Vals les Bains. D578 towards Le Cheylard. Leaving Vals, left on D243 to La Bastide sur Besorgues. D254 towards Aizac, past tennis courts; 300m after bridge right down sharp bend.
Michelin Map No: 239-48

Entry no: 631   Map No: 14

Bernadette & Jean-Michel FRANÇOIS
Le Château
07600 La Bastide sur Besorgues
Ardèche
Tel: (0)4 75 88 23 67
Fax: (0)4 75 88 23 67
e-mail: jean-michel.francois4@wanadoo.fr

In this glorious setting, let the wild Ardèche landscape be your playground or the backdrop for total relaxation. Take walking boots, jodhpurs, bike, canoe, hang-glider, or just yourselves, and you'll be warmly welcomed. Surrounded by almond trees, fields of lavender and mountains, this peaceful farmhouse is truly lost in the countryside. Monsieur has elevated 'home brew' onto a new plane, making aperitifs and *digestifs* to go with Madame's local dishes, eaten *en famille*. Simply-furnished rooms, each with its own entrance, vary in size and style and there's a charming stone-vaulted dayroom.

Rooms: 1 quadruple, 1 triple, 2 doubles, all with bath or shower & wc.

Price: 280 Frs for two.

Meals: 95 Frs, including wine & coffee (not Sundays).

Closed: Never.

Madame alone is worth the detour: her kindliness infuses her home – one that, at first glance, is coy about its age or charms; her eventful life has nourished a wicked sense of humour but no bitterness and she is a natural storyteller (she'll show you the photographs too). The slightly fading carpets and small shower rooms become incidental after a short while. Enjoy, instead, the pretty bedrooms, the peace of the lush leafy garden, which shelters the house from the road, and relish breakfast – home-made jams and cake, organic honeys, cheese – where the table is a picture in itself.

Rooms: 2 twins, 1 single/twin, each with shower & wc.

Price: 255-280 Frs for two.

Meals: Restaurant 2km.

Closed: Never.

From Bourg St Andéol D4 to St Remèze then D362 direction Gras. Signposted on right.
Michelin Map No: 240-8

Entry no: 632   Map No: 14

From A7 Valence Sud exit onto A49 direction Grenoble. At exit 33 right on D538a direction Beaumont. After 2.6km, right at sign Chambres d'Hôtes/Chambedeau; house 800m along on right.
Michelin Map No: 244-36

Entry no: 633   Map No: 14

Sylvette & Gérard MIALON
La Martinade
07700 St Remèze
Ardèche
Tel: (0)4 75 98 89 42
Fax: (0)4 75 04 36 30
e-mail: sylvetlm@aol.com
Web: www.angelfire.com/la/lamartinade/

Mme Lina de CHIVRÉ-DUMOND
Chambedeau
26760 Beaumont lès Valence
Drôme
Tel: (0)4 75 59 71 70
Fax: (0)4 75 59 75 24
e-mail: linadechivredumond@minitel.net
Web: www.sawdays.co.uk

There's a time-warp feel to this 1970s villa high above the valley outside Valence: dark floral wallpaper covers hall, stairs and bedrooms, animal skins cover floors and modern sofas, interesting modern sculptures call from *salon* and stairs. Your hostess is interesting, enthusiastic and hugely welcoming, a gift inherited from Armenian parents. Breakfast (hot croissants and home-made organic jam) on the terrace and admire the magnificent chalk escarpments of the Vercors range (beyond less attractive St Marcel). Little traffic noise can be heard. Careful: this is the B&B on the LEFT-hand side of the road.

Rooms: 1 twin with shower & wc; 1 double with bath & wc.

Price: 280-320 Frs for two.

Meals: Vast choice in Valence, 5km.

Closed: Never.

From A7 exit 14; through Bourg lès Valence; left on N532 towards Romans/Grenoble; exit to St Marcel. At 'Place de la Mairie' left to Stop, straight across, under bridge, straight on up hill (total 400m) – house on LEFT round hairpin.
Michelin Map No: 244-36

Entry no: 634   Map No: 14

Marie-Jeanne KATCHIKIAN
La Pineraie
383 chemin Bel Air
26320 St Marcel lès Valence
Drôme
Tel: (0)4 75 58 72 25
e-mail: marie.katchikian@club.francetelecom.fr

They are a perfect team in their shimmeringly lovely house and garden. Renée's garden is a horticultural delight where colours run rife. Jacques wears the chef's hat; breakfast on home-made muffins, dine on refined regional dishes with fresh-picked herbs – he may join you for dessert on the covered terrace where plants flower in big pots. Bedrooms – large, luminous and immaculate – have antique headboards, open out onto the terrace or garden and have good modern bathrooms. Welcoming, life-loving people who will put fresh fruit in your room every day.

Rooms: 3 doubles, each with bath or shower & wc.

Price: 350 Frs for two; babies free; 2-14 yrs 60 Frs.

Meals: Available locally.

Closed: Mid-November-March, except by arrangement.

From A7 exit 15 towards Grenoble then exit 34 towards Chabeuil for 6km. In Alixan right at 'Epicerie' on D101 towards Besayes for 500m, then left; 1st house on right.
Michelin Map No: 244-37

Entry no: 635   Map No: 14

Jacques & Renée CRAMMER
L'Eygalière
Quartier Coussaud
26300 Alixan, Drôme
Tel: (0)4 75 47 11 13
Fax: (0)4 75 47 13 35
e-mail: jcrammer@easynet.fr
Web: www.sawdays.co.uk

Sample the simple country life at this friendly farm which has been in the family for more than a century and has returned to *biologique* (organic) methods which Madame calls "acupuncture for the land". Meals of regional food are served family-style and include home-produced vegetables, fruit and eggs. Madame, although always busy, finds time to spend with guests and is happy to share recipes,. The bedrooms are in a separate wing with unfussy modern interiors, interesting antique beds and pretty floral linen. The setting, at the foot of Mont Vercors, is very peaceful.

Rooms: 2 doubles, 1 triple, each with shower or bath & wc.

Price: 260 Frs for two.

Meals: 80 Frs, including wine & coffee.

Closed: Never.

Gîte space for 8 people.

From Romans D538 dir. Chabeuil.Leaving Alixan left by Boulangerie, left again & follow Chambres d'Hôtes Les Marais St Didier signs for 3km; farm on left. Michelin Map No: 244-37

Entry no: 636   Map No: 14

Christiane & Jean-Pierre IMBERT
Le Marais
26300 St Didier de Charpey
Drôme
Tel: (0)4 75 47 03 50/
    (0)6 68 92 74 16

Madame is the grandmother we all dream of, a sprightly, delightful woman who cossets her guests, putting sweets and fruit in the bedrooms. This old stone farmhouse facing the Vercors mountains is definitely a family home (the family has been here since 1680!), so meals of regional dishes with local wine can be very jolly with family, friends and guests all sharing the long wooden table in the kitchen. The roomy, old-fashioned bedrooms have lovely walnut armoires and the bright, new suite has a tiny single attached for children.

Rooms: 3 triples, both with bath or shower & wc.

Price: 230 Frs for two.

Meals: 85 Frs, including wine & coffee

Closed: Never.

From A6 exit Valence Sud on D68 to Chabeuil. There, cross river and turn left on D154 direction Combovin for 5km; signposted. Michelin Map No: 244-37

Entry no: 637   Map No: 14

Mme Madeleine CABANES
Les Péris
D154 – route de Combovin
26120 Châteaudouble
Drôme
Tel: (0)4 75 59 80 51
Fax: (0)4 75 59 48 78
Web: www.sawdays.co.uk

This artistic, caring couple are deeply concerned with social and ecological issues. They have renovated their farmhouse with sensitivity and an eye for detail, using nothing but authentic materials. Art-lovers will enjoy Madame's beautifully-made china dolls, the summer exhibitions and courses (it's a great place for seminars for up to 15 who can self-cater or be catered for). Guest quarters, in a separate building, have good rooms and handsome carpentry by Mado's son. Organic meals with home-grown vegetables and fruit in season are served in the vaulted guest dining room or on the terrace. A special house with a very special atmosphere.

Rooms: 3 doubles, 1 suite for 4, all with bath or shower & wc.

Price: 250-380 Frs for two: minimum 2 nights.

Meals: 95 Frs, including wine & coffee.

Closed: Never.

From Chabeuil, D538 direction Crest for 5km (ignore signs for Montvendre). Left at sign Les Dourcines; house 700m on right next to Auberge-Restaurant sign.
Michelin Map No: 244-37

Entry no: 638   Map No: 14

Mado GOLDSTEIN & Bernard DUPONT
Les Dourcines
26120 Montvendre
Drôme
Tel: (0)4 75 59 24 27
Web: www.sawdays.co.uk

Walk in the enchanting park, designed by Le Nôtre, swim in the nearby river, drink in the shining views of the Vercors. Evelyne is an artist who loves people, has a permanent exhibition of well-known contemporary artists and also opens her busy, lively château to groups studying meditation, music and massage. All the food is organic and vegetarian dishes no problem. The big simply-furnished, wood-floored bedrooms have some fine antiques though the bathrooms, across the corridor, seem a little basic. The house can sleep large groups during courses but never when B&B guests are there.

Rooms: 3 twins: 1 with shower & wc; 1 with shower, sharing wc; 1 sharing shower & wc.

Price: 290-340 Frs for two; minimum 2 nights.

Meals: Occasionally, 90 Frs, including table wine & coffee.

Closed: Never; bookings only.

From Crest, D93 to Mirabel et Blacons. Château on left as you leave village with sign Galerie Arbre de Vie on wall.
Michelin Map No: 245-4

Entry no: 639   Map No: 14

Evelyne LATUNE
Château de Blacons
Mirabel et Blacons
26400 Crest
Drôme
Tel: (0)4 75 40 01 00
Fax: (0)4 75 40 04 97

Perched 2,000 feet up in *Drôme Provençale*, you have glorious views of the foothills of the Alps from this happy, relaxed house (from which you can stride straight out for a day's walking). The Fortunatos (Italian/Spanish) love having guests and are flexible and enterprising – in winter they organise special weekends: such as cooking in their bread oven. If you collect wild mushrooms, strawberries or chestnuts they'll prepare them to go with their home-grown chemical-free veg on the menu for dinner. Rooms are 'refined country-style' – fresh, colourful and warm with big windows. And it's quiet.

Rooms: 3 doubles, 2 triples, all with shower & wc.

Price: 330 Frs for two.

Meals: 125 Frs, including wine.

Closed: Never.

Gîte space for 13 people.

The stone cross-vaulting in the dining room is wonderful and Francis has renovated the rest of the house with loving care. He has poured his energy into giving new life to old beams and tiles. He was once an engineer and knows about structures, old and new. Jackie is an artist... "and it shows", says a reader. There is a huge organic vegetable garden, producing the basics, plus fruit and eggs, for some superb meals. The rooms are perfectly simple, not a frill too many. Lively and charming people living in lovely countryside.

Rooms: 2 triples, 1 double, 1 twin, each with bath or shower & wc.

Price: 295-325 Frs for two.

Meals: 100-115 Frs, including coffee.

Closed: Never.

From Crest D538 through Bourdeaux & towards Dieulefit for 5km. Right on D192 towards Truinas. House on right.
Michelin Map No: 245-4

Entry no: **640**   Map No: 14

Pilar & Carlo FORTUNATO
Les Volets Bleus
26460 Truinas
Drôme
Tel: (0)4 75 53 38 48
Fax: (0)4 75 53 49 02
Web: www.sawdays.co.uk

From Montélimar D540 E to La Batie Rolland (10km). In village left onto D134 towards St Gervais; signposted on right.
Michelin Map No: 240-4

Entry no: **641**   Map No: 14

Francis & Jackie MONEL
La Joie
26160 La Batie Rolland
Drôme
Tel: (0)4 75 53 81 51
Fax: (0)4 75 53 81 51
e-mail: f.monel@infonie.fr
Web: www.sawdays.co.uk

The ever-delightful Prothons are still renovating their 17th-century coaching inn. The great high hay barn has been put to superb use: each guest room has a and views through one normal and one roof window to the magnificent countryside, though stairs are VERY steep. Lots of friendly old furniture, and one room has one of the antique loos from the old house. Meals, in the family dining room or outside, are made with products from the younger Prothons' farm; there are truffle weekends in winter and a welcoming fireplace. A hard-working and wonderfully friendly place.

Rooms: 3 triple/quadruples, each with shower & wc.

Price: 280-300 Frs for two.

Meals: 90-120 Frs, including wine.

Closed: 15 December-15 January.

Gîte space for 5 people.

From A7 exit 18, N7 S dir.Avignon for 2km left on D133 dir. Grignan for 5km. Just before Valaurie, right dir. St Paul 3 Châteaux (D133) 2km; house on right 200m from road.
Michelin Map No: 240-8

Entry no: 642   Map No: 14

Marie-Claire (Mick) & François
PROTHON
Val Léron
26230 Valaurie
Drôme
Tel: (0)4 75 98 52 52
Fax: (0)4 75 98 52 52
e-mail: ls.vacher@ free.fr

The Cornillons bought this ruined 1769 farmhouse in the 1960s and have worked hard to create their beautiful property and the surrounding vineyards. Bedrooms have dark beams, lovely old doors and views out across lavender fields or the chestnut-shaded courtyard. One double has a fab bathroom, a Jacuzzi and an extra-big bed. The dining room, with an open fire for winter warmth after a truffle expedition, is very snug and everyone eats together at the long wooden table. There is a cleverly-hidden swimming pool and Vaison la Romaine, Orange and Avignon are not far away.

Rooms: 4 doubles, 1 twin, 1 triple, all with bath & wc.

Price: From 400 Frs for two; 600 Frs deluxe room.

Meals: 150 Frs, excluding wine.

Closed: Never.

Gîte space for 5 people.

From Bollène D995 to Suze la Rousse. D59 for St Paul 3 Châteaux; right on D117 to La Baume de Transit; signposted.
Michelin Map No: 240-8

Entry no: 643   Map No: 14

Ludovic & Eliane CORNILLON
Domaine de Saint-Luc
26790 La Baume de Transit
Drôme
Tel: (0)4 75 98 11 51
Fax: (0)4 75 98 19 22
Web: www.sawdays.co.uk

If you enjoy people who have long experience of country life and are without pretension, then go and stay with the well-educated, happy and relaxed Pagis family in their creeper-clad, wisteria-hung farmhouse in this forgotten corner of the Drôme. A fountain titters in the courtyard, breakfast and dinner include home-made jams and goats' cheese, eggs, and vegetables from their superb kitchen garden and, in season, truffles hunted in their own secret ways. They are generous and off-beat, guest rooms share a kitchen and, Jean-Jacques plays trumpet in the local salsa band.

Rooms: 1 double, 1 quadruple, sharing kitchen, bath & wc.

Price: 200 Frs for two.

Meals: 75 Frs, including wine, by arrangement. Self-catering possible.

Closed: December-February.

From Vaison la Romaine, D938 dir. Malaucène for 4km. Left on D13 8km. Right on D40 to Montbrun les Bains, right dir. Sault. House 1km on left. Michelin Map No: 245-18

Entry no: **644**   Map No: **14**

Jean-Jacques & Agnès PAGIS
Le Chavoul
Reilhanette
26570 Montbrun les Bains
Drôme
Tel: (0)4 75 28 80 80
e-mail: antoine3@wanadoo.fr

The ground floor of the tower is the original 17th-century kitchen complete with wood-fired range, stone sink and cobbled floor. Hélène makes her own bread, honey and jams and prepares meals using vegetables from her garden; she even makes her own aperitifs (the *vin d'orange* is superb). You will also be offered wine from the Rossis' own vineyard near Montpellier. The house has loads of character with enormous rooms, high heavy-beamed ceilings and large windows overlooking the valley, and the bedrooms are reached up an ancient stone spiral staircase, which sets the imagination reeling.

Rooms: 2 doubles, 2 twins, 1 family room, each with bath or shower & wc.

Price: 320 Frs for two.

Meals: 90 Frs, including wine.

Closed: 2 November-28 February.

Take A51 from Grenoble towards Sisteron for 2km to roundabout then follow signs to St Martin de la Cluze. Château is signed in village. Michelin Map No: 244-39

Entry no: **645**   Map No: **14**

Jacques & Hélène ROSSI
Château de Paquier
38650 St Martin de la Cluze
Isère
Tel: (0)4 76 72 77 33
Fax: (0)4 76 72 77 33
e-mail: hrossi@club-internet.fr
Web: perso.club-internet.fr/hrossi/

Satin cushions, swags and curly legs: your fun-loving hosts brought their standards from their previous home on the Riviera, which means you will want for nothing. Such care, attention and unbridled luxury, including superb beds and great bathrooms, may not make for a 'homely' atmosphere but the meals... Madame is not only charming, she's a stupendous cook (*bouillabaisse* a speciality). Breakfast is a banquet of home-made jams, brioche, cake, and more. The half-acre garden provides rest and... flowers for indoors.

Rooms: 3 doubles, 1 twin, 2 suites, all with bath and wc.

Price: 450-550 Frs for two.

Meals: 200 Frs, including wine & coffee.

Closed: Never.

Although this is not a working farm, it might as well be. The Garniers adore animals. They have seven Camargue horses (for stroking, not riding), ducks, chickens, turkeys, guinea fowl, a pig, two dogs and a cat! Albert is French, Margaret is English, she loves cooking and grows all her own vegetables. She also has a large collection of dolls from around the world. The classic Dauphinoise house is a thoroughly welcoming family home decorated in French country style with some modern pieces and a pretty garden; all this near a ramblingly attractive old village in rolling wooded countryside.

Rooms: 1 double, 1 twin, each with shower & wc.

Price: 260 Frs for two.

Meals: 90 Frs, including wine & coffee.

Closed: Never.

Exit A43 La Tour du Pin, direction N6, right at roundabout, then direction Aix le Bains. Left at lights at St Clair de la Tour, 3km direction Dolomieu, then follow signs for Chambres d'Hotes. Michelin Map No: 244-27

From Lyon, A43 Chimilin/Les Abrets exit towards Les Abrets & follow signs. Michelin Map No: 244-28

Entry no: 646   Map No: 14

Entry no: 647   Map No: 14

Christian & Claude CHAVALLE REVENU
La Bruyère
38490 Les Abrets, Isère
Tel: (0)4 76 32 01 66
Fax: (0)4 76 32 06 66
e-mail: carbone38@aol.com
Web: members.aol.com/carbone38/

Margaret & Albert GARNIER
Le Traversoud
38110 Faverges de la Tour
Isère
Tel: (0)4 74 83 90 40
Fax: (0)4 74 83 90 40

The Barrs are English and Irish but have lived in France for 25 years so are pretty well French too. Mary, an easy, relaxed person, loves flowers and helps Greig with his wooden-toy business in winter. They have renovated their old farmhouse to give it an English feel yet preserve its utterly French character: the atmosphere is light, airy and warm as well as solid and reassuring. In the big guest rooms, the beds have excellent mattresses, the views are rural, the super bathroom (across the landing but private) is blue and white with lots of pretty china bits. A very civilised place to stay.

Rooms: 2 twins with bath & wc.

Price: 300 Frs for two.

Meals: 110 Frs, including wine. Wide choice 12km.

Closed: September-December.

Come here to experience the charming, authentically aristocratic lives of your hosts: no pretence or prissiness (two screened-off bathrooms), just unselfconscious style. The richly-decorated *salon* has a piano, books and open fireplace. The richly-stocked garden has a pool, a summerhouse, a large terrace, 150 species of trees, an organic vegetable garden and a statue of Grandad. Madame is too busy cooking to eat with guests but welcomes company as she's preparing dinner. Children love it – there are toys and the hosts' children to play with.

Rooms: 2 doubles, each with bath or shower & wc; 2 twins, each with shower & wc.

Price: 400 Frs for two.

Meals: 120 Frs, excluding wine (80 Frs).

Closed: Never.

From A43 exit 8 on N85 to Nivolas. Exit Nivolas, left on D520 for Succieu. After 2km left again on 56D for Succieu. Through Succieu follow signs for St Victor. After 3km sign for Longeville, last house at top of steep hill. Michelin Map No: 244-27

Entry no: 648   Map No: 14

Mary & Greig BARR
Longeville
38300 Succieu
Isère
Tel: (0)4 74 27 94 07
Fax: (0)4 74 92 09 21
e-mail: mary.barr@free.fr

From A6 exit Macon Sud or Belleville, then N6 to Romaneche and Lancié. In village take road towards Fleurie into Square Les Pasquiers. Michelin Map No: 244-2

Entry no: 649   Map No: 9

Jacques & Laurence GANDILHON
Les Pasquiers
69220 Lancié/Belleville
Rhône
Tel: (0)4 74 69 86 33
Fax: (0)4 74 69 86 57
e-mail: ganpasq@aol.com

An Egypto-Roman obelisk amid the topiary in the garden, wine from the vines which surround the château and beautiful 17th-century beams to sleep under. What more could you want? Your hosts, much-travelled, polyglot and sophisticated, are genuinely keen to share their enthusiasm for the area and its wines (and will organise wine-tastings). The vast rooms, some with fine carved door frames, are eclectically and elegantly furnished (Olivier's brother is an antique dealer) and breakfast, with home-made jams, can be followed by a visit to the winery. If you want to sample *le grand style*, this is for you.

An amazing avenue of lime trees conducts you to this wholly exceptional house and hostess. Madame is a live wire, laughing, enthusing, giving – unforgettable. The house is as elegant as she is. Climb the old wooden stairs to your splendidly decorated and furnished room, revel in Persian carpets, *trompe-l'œil*, antiques, fresh flowers. Beside the complete works of Shakespeare, Madame pours tea from silver into porcelain, artfully moves the breakfast table butter as the sun rises; at night she'll light your bedside lamp, leaving a book open at a carefully chosen page for you to read after a game of (French) Scrabble. Inimitably fine.

Rooms: 3 doubles, 2 suites, each with bath & wc.

Price: 600-700 Frs for two.

Meals: 200 Frs, including château's own wine; by arrangement.

Closed: Never.

Rooms: 1 double with bathroom & wc; 1 double, 1 twin, sharing shower & wc.

Price: 500 Frs for two. Child under 8 in same room free.

Meals: Good restaurant 3km.

Closed: Never.

From A6 exit 'Belleville', then N6 towards Lyon for 10km, then right on D43 to Arnas. Go through village; château on right after 1.5km.
Michelin Map No: 244-13

From Bourg en Bresse, N83 direction Lyon. At Servas right on D64 direction Condeissiat for 5km, then left at sign Le Marmont into tree-lined avenue. Don't go as far as St André.
Michelin Map No: 244-4

Entry no: 650 Map No: 9

Entry no: 651 Map No: 9

Alexandra & Olivier du MESNIL
Les Jardins de Longsard
Château de Longsard
69400 Arnas, Rhône
Tel: (0)4 74 65 55 12
Fax: (0)4 74 65 03 17
e-mail: longsard@wanadoo.fr
Web: www.sawdays.co.uk

Geneviève & Henri GUIDO-ALHERITIERE
Manoir de Marmont
01960 St André sur Vieux Jonc
Ain
Tel: (0)4 74 52 79 74

Stone and wood, white paint, dried flowers and good furniture combine to give this 200-year-old Savoyard farmhouse a light, harmonious air that matches Madame's smartly energetic presence. She keeps a kitchen garden which provides fresh vegetables for her good and varied dinners and will do anything for you. Monsieur shares his extensive wine knowledge and interest in mushroom-collecting. There is an upstairs sitting room for guests with an unusual half-moon window at floor level, big light bedrooms with antique, new-mattressed, lace-covered beds and spotless glass-doored showers.

Rooms: 1 double, 2 twins, each with shower & wc (1 behind curtain).

Price: 310 Frs for two.

Meals: Available locally.

Closed: Mid-November-February.

From Annecy, N201 direction Geneva. 1km after Cruseilles, left on D27 to Copponex. Through village, left at cemetery; signs to Chambres d'Hôtes Châtillon. House on left. Michelin Map No: 244-7

Entry no: 652   Map No: 9

Suzanne & André GAL
La Bécassière
Châtillon
74350 Copponex
Haute-Savoie
Tel: (0)4 50 44 08 94
Fax: (0)4 50 44 08 94

Alps

Up there among the pointy peaks, the Savoyards don't mix their delicious cheeses into gooey *fondue* for the sake of the furry marmot alone – there's enough for all.

This is a no-frills place, simple and clean, with relaxed hosts (locals who know their area well), the possibility of baby-sitting and a kind micro-climate: the nearby mountains apparently attract the clouds, leaving the sun to beat a clear path to your door. Breakfast only is provided but the Martins recommend restaurants and provide a kitchen for the two rooms in the guest chalet. The rooms are fairly small and furnishings plain and simple but the garden is a pleasant surprise with swings and ropes for youngsters and there are fabulous walks to be taken. Only 10km from Annecy.

Rooms: 2 doubles (& sofa bed) in cottage, each with shower & wc.

Price: 250 Frs for two.

Meals: Self-catering possible in cottage.

Closed: Never.

Gîte space for 6 people.

From A41 exit for Annecy (sud), then head for Chamberry. At crossroads take right onto D16 for Rumilly. After 10km enter Marcellaz Albanais and go immediately left on D38 towards Chapeiry for 1km. Right towards Chaunu; house 200m up on right. Michelin Map No: 244-18

Entry no: 653   Map No: 9

Claudie & Jean-Louis MARTIN
Chemin de Chaunu
74150 Marcellaz Albanais
Haute-Savoie
Tel: (0)4 50 69 73 04

This house flourishes with the loving care its owners lavish upon it. "Luxury without ostentation" is their aim and their passion for antiques, interior decorating, gourmet cuisine and entertaining ensures just that. A vast brunch for all and four- or five-course dinners on request: French-Canadian Denyse is a food journalist. The rooms are all different: the blue *Albanaise*, the raspberry *Aixoise*, the oak-beamed, four-postered *Écossaise*. You choose. Bathrooms are superb too. Beautiful Annecy with its gleaming lake, Chamonix-Mont Blanc, the towering Alps, swinging Geneva, are all nearby.

Rooms: 2 doubles, 1 twin, each with bath or shower & wc.

Price: 700 Frs for two.

Meals: 225 Frs, including wine & coffee, by arrangement.

Closed: Never.

Gîte space for 3 people.

From A41 exit Alby/Rumilly, N201 direction Chambéry. In St Félix, at church onto D53: pass cemetery, go 300m then left (sign for Mercy) to statue, right and immediately left, past farm and through gate. Michelin Map No: 244-18

Entry no: 654   Map No: 9

Denyse & Bernard BETTS
Les Bruyères
Mercy
74540 St Félix
Haute-Savoie
Tel: (0)4 50 60 96 53
Fax: (0)4 50 60 94 65
Web: www.sawdays.co.uk

Wood, wood and more wood, outside and in, plus lovely fabrics and furniture, make this brand new traditional-style chalet warm and reassuring. It has panoramic views south across the valley to rising green Alpine pastures and great rocky mountains. Guests have the privacy of a floor to themselves, a room with doors to the garden and that fabulous view. Your hosts, retired contented travellers, are great fun, energetic and enthusiastic about their house, the 135km of marked mountain trails, and their lovely Labradors who enjoy the walking too. Delightful Annecy is just two dozen kilometres and a few bends away. And there's great ski-ing.

Rooms: 1 twin with shower & wc.

Price: 300 Frs for two.

Meals: 110 Frs, including aperitif wine & coffee.

Closed: Never.

From Annecy, D909 to Thones then D12 towards Serraval & Manigod; very shortly after, take D16 to Manigod. Through village then follow signs. House is 4th on right.
Michelin Map No: 244-19

Entry no: 655   Map No: 10

Colin & Alyson BROWNE
Les Murailles
74230 Manigod
Haute-Savoie
Tel: (0)4 50 44 95 87
Fax: (0)4 50 44 95 87

Hospitality is a family tradition; Anne-Marie speaks fluent English, keeps horses and organises rides or walks to the Alpine pastures above the valley. The walking is indeed exceptional and you may see chamois and marmots if you go far enough. The chalet has a 'museum' depicting life on an Alpine farm in the old days. Dinner (served late to allow guests time to settle) is eaten at the long wooden table, with grand – mama's recipes cooked on a wood-fired stove: "simple ingredients well prepared delicious cheeses". Readers love it and the half-board formula includes absolutely everything.

Rooms: 1 triple with shower & wc; 5 doubles sharing 3 showers & 3 wcs.

Price: 210 Frs PER PERSON: half-board only.

Meals: Half-board: dinner with aperitif wine & coffee included in price.

Closed: Never.

From Thonon les Bains, D26 direction Bellevaux. House is 2km before Bellevaux on the left; signposted.
Michelin Map No: 244-9

Entry no: 656   Map No: 10

Anne-Marie FELISAZ-DENIS
Le Chalet
La Cressonnière
74470 Bellevaux
Haute-Savoie
Tel: (0)4 50 73 70 13
Fax: (0)4 50 73 70 13
Web: www.sawdays.co.uk

Greet the gentle giant Danes, admire the scale of La Terrosière as you arrive – *la vie de château* is yours. In the luxuriously converted stable block there are vast antique-furnished bedrooms (you may need a mounting block for the four-poster), brilliant bathrooms, a softly embracing living room with open fire, staff to wait on you and a *châtelaine* of charm and wit to make fine food, bring superb wines from her cellar and keep you company at table. Horses exercise in the school, a tennis court, fishing lake and heated spring-water pool beckon on the 100-acre estate. Worth every centime. Oh, and it's brunch, not breakfast.

They are a lively, friendly, happy young family – so refreshing! Myriam adores having people to stay and everyone joining in the lighthearted atmosphere. Their typical 19th-century farmhouse is welcoming but not smart and the family room, the hub of life at La Touvière, is cosy and pleasing. Marcel is part-time farmer (he just has a few cows now), part-time home improver. One guest room has a properly Alpine view across the valley, the other overlooks the owners' second chalet, let as a gîte; both are small but not cramped and this is a perfect place whence to set out into the walkers' paradise that surrounds it. Remarkable value.

Rooms: 2 suites, 1 twin, each with bath, shower, double basin & wc.

Price: 800-900 Frs for two.

Meals: 260-300 Frs including wine ; self-catering possible.

Closed: August & Christmas, except by arrangement.

Rooms: 2 doubles, each with shower & wc.

Price: 200 Frs for two.

Meals: 90 Frs, including wine.

Closed: Never.

Gîte space for 5 people.

From Chambéry N504 N via Le Bourget du Lac through small tunnel to Chevelu; left on D921 to St Paul. After r'bout, 1st left. House on right approx. 1km along (large iron gates).
Michelin Map No: 244-17

From Albertville N212 NE towards Megève for 21km. Shortly after Flumet, left at Panoramic Hotel & follow signs to La Touvière.
Michelin Map No: 244-20

Entry no: 657   Map No: 9

Entry no: 658   Map No: 10

Mme Jeannine CONTI
La Terrosière
73170 St Paul sur Yenne
Savoie
Tel: (0)4 79 36 81 02
Fax: (0)4 79 36 81 02
Web: www.sawdays.co.uk

Marcel & Myriam MARIN-CUDRAZ
La Touvière
73590 Flumet
Savoie
Tel: (0)4 79 31 70 11

This is a year-round Alpine dream. In summer it's all flowers, birds and rushing streams. In winter ski cross-country, snow-walk or take the ski lift, just 500m away, to the vast ski field of les Arcs. La Plagne and Val d'Isère are quite close too. Cooking takes place in the outside wood oven and the cuisine is as good and honest as the young hosts. Children are catered for with early suppers, son Boris and daughter Clémence are playmates for them and Claude will baby-sit in the evening. Guests have their own comfortable dayroom with a refrigerator. *Discount on ski hire and passes.*

Rooms: 1 suite for 4/5, 1 double for 2/3, each with shower & wc.

Price: 250 Frs for two; reduction for children & long stays.

Meals: 90 Frs, including wine & coffee.

Closed: Never.

From Albertville N90 to Moutiers then on towards Bourg St Maurice. Right on D87E to Peisey Nancroix; left to Peisey Centre then follow green arrows. 9km from main road to house.
Michelin Map No: 244-32

Entry no: 659   Map No: 15

Claude COUTIN & Franck CHENAL
Maison Coutin, T12 Peisey
73210 Peisey Nancroix, Savoie
Tel: (0)4 79 07 93 05/
  (0)6 14 11 54 65
Fax: (0)4 79 04 29 23
e-mail: maisoncoutin@aol.com
Web: www.maison-coutin.fr.st

Blazing fires, natural wood – all pure *Savoyard*; big rooms and luxury bathrooms – such a treat. The televisions and the cardphone in the hall give a slight 'hotelly' feel, but what matter? Perched on the edge of a mountain, you have a superb view of peaks above and villages below, be you in your room, in the jacuzzi, or rolling in the snow after your sauna. After a hearty breakfast your Franco-American hostess will gladly help you map out your itinerary – mountain-lake fishing in summer, skiing in winter, superb walking all year.

Rooms: 2 suites for 4, 3 doubles (queen or king-size beds), all with bath or shower & wc.

Price: 650-950 Frs for two.

Meals: 195 Frs, including aperitif, wine & coffee.

Closed: October-November & May-June.

Gîte space for 9 people.

From Bourg St Maurice D902 direction Val d'Isère through Ste Foy Tarentaise. After La Thuile left direction Ste Foy Station and follow wooden signposts.
Michelin Map No: 244-21

Entry no: 660   Map No: 15

Nancy TABARDEL
Yellow Stone Chalet
Bonconseil Station
73640 Ste Foy Tarentaise
Savoie
Tel: (0)4 79 06 96 06
Fax: (0)4 79 06 96 05
e-mail: yellowstone@limelab.com

You can walk (or ski) straight out onto the mountains from this dramatically-set house with its wonderful views over to Italy. Jean-Marc and Jacqueline are keen walkers, quite able to plan a whole walking holiday for you. Jean-Marc designed and built the house (he's a retired architect) with the bedrooms snugly under the eaves. There is a self-contained apartment with its own garden; the third person does have to sleep in the kitchen/living room, but has sole use of the microwave and the magnificent view. *Advance booking essential.*

Rooms: 2 doubles, sharing shower & wc; 1 twin with shower & wc; 1 apartment with bath & wc.

Price: 320-350 Frs for two; min. 2 nights.

Meals: Town centre 4km.

Closed: 1 April-31 May; 9 September-21 December & 5 January-2 February.

From Gap N94 NE to Briançon. Entering town, left at first traffic light dir. Puy St André. In village, house 3rd on left.
Michelin Map No: 244-43

Entry no: 661   Map No: 15

J & JM LABORIE
Le Village, Puy St André
05100 Briançon, Hautes-Alpes
Tel: (0)4 92 21 30 22/
     (0)6 84 04 11 72
Fax: (0)4 92 21 30 22
e-mail: sudalp@club-internet.fr
Web: www.sawdays.co.uk

Your first taste of magnificence is the drive up. Come, to ski across country or down hills, rent your snow shoes on the spot, do some exceptional summer walks, hang-glide or just bathe in splendour. Michel, who took a half-ruined farmhouse and turned it into this atmospheric, country-warm house of welcome with small, no-frills rooms that have all you could want, is a burly, good-natured host who loves the convivial evenings around the communal table. Claude's artistry is seen in the décor, her kindness is in the air.

Rooms: 1 double, 2 quadruples, 2 twins, 1 suite, all with shower & wc.

Price: 260-300 Frs for two.

Meals: 100 Frs, incl. wine & coffee.

Closed: Never, but telephone to check.

From Gap N94 E dir. Briançon for 36km; right just before Embrun on D40 for 10km. Follow 'Station des Orres' down hill; house in hamlet, on left just before bridge.
Michelin Map No: 245-9

Entry no: 662   Map No: 15

Michel & Claude HURAULT
La Jarbelle
Les Ribes
05200 Les Orres, Hautes-Alpes
Tel: (0)4 92 44 11 33
Fax: (0)4 92 44 11 23
e-mail: lajarbelle@wanadoo.fr
Web: www.sawdays.co.uk

The ancient bits of this village château ooze history and mystery. Plays based on high spots of French history as seen from Montmaur are enacted on summer Fridays, the exhibition room has a five-metre-high fireplace, the dining room, where you breakfast with family silver on a magnificent Provençal cloth, has superb old beams and your energetic hostess is kindness itself – she will give you a guided tour. Guest rooms, not in the château proper, are somewhat dim and cramped with unremarkable furnishings. But romantics at heart come for the ghostly splendour of it all.

Rooms: 3 triples, each with shower & wc.

Price: 450 Frs for two.

Meals: Choice 1.5-6km.

Closed: October-April.

From Gap, D994 towards Veynes. 4km before Veynes, take D320 towards Superdévoluy; Montmaur is 2km on, visible from road. Drive along château wall then towards church.
Michelin Map No: 245-6

Entry no: 663   Map No: 14

Raymond & Élise LAURENS
Château de Montmaur
05400 Veynes
Hautes-Alpes
Tel: (0)4 92 58 11 42
Fax: (0)4 92 58 11 42

MORE FALSE FRIENDS

En-suite *can lead to terrible confusions in France as it is not an expression used for 'with own bathroom'. One booking for two 'en-suites', made with B&B owners who speak good English, became a disaster when the owners reserved their only suite for these guests: the two adult couples were unhappy at having to fit into a double room leading to a 'children's' twin room leading to a shared bathroom.*
Cheminée *is French for fireplace, flue or chimney stack (the flue is also called le conduit de cheminée). Un feu dans la cheminée does not mean you need to call the fire brigade but un feu de cheminée does.*
Une Commode *is a chest of drawers. A commode is une chaise percée.*
Grange simply means barn, not a big country house.
Actuel - Actuellement
A great pitfall this one – it means current, present - currently, presently, NOW and not As a Matter of Fact.
Eventuel *– eventuellement Possible – should the occasion arise.*
Un Christmas *is a Christmas card. The French used only to send each other visiting cards with hand-written New Year greetings. The English and American custom of sending decorative cards for Christmas only caught on fairly recently and the object was naturally given the (truncated) English name.*
Correspondance *applies to travel connections between flights, trains and metro lines.*

Esparron has been in the same family since the 1400s. Vast bedrooms, reached by a superb stone staircase, are lovingly decorated: plain walls and fresh flowers, tiles and fine designer fabrics, good antiques and lots of lamps. The garden is small – for a château – but prettily planted. Slender, apple-blossom Charlotte-Anne and her two beautiful children come straight from a Gainsborough portrait (she IS English). She is attentive to everyone: husband, children, staff and guests. Bernard, with suntan, impeccable clothes and manners and pipe, adds a touch of 1930s glamour. Wonderful family, splendiferous house, vast breakfast...

Rooms: 3 doubles, 1 twin, 1 suite, each with bath & wc.

Price: 700-1300 Frs for two.

Meals: 5 minutes walk.

Closed: November-March.

From Aix en Provence A51 exit 18 onto D907 then D82 to Gréoux les Bains; follow signs on D952 & D315 to Esparron. Stop and ring at château gates (once past, it's impossible to turn).

Michelin Map No: 245-33

Entry no: 664   Map No: 14

Bernard & Charlotte-Anne de CASTELLANE
Château d'Esparron
04800 Esparron de Verdon
Alpes-de-Haut-Provence
Tel: (0)4 92 77 12 05
Fax: (0)4 92 77 13 10
e-mail: bernard.de.castellane@wanadoo.fr
Web: www.provenceweb.fr/04/ukEsparron.htm

Provence-Riviera

The best *bouillabaisse* ingredients swim among the white Mediterranean horses; on shore, the native white ponies carry their dashing *gardians* over the Camargue, herding the great black bulls.

Set among vineyards below the Montmirail hills, this simple, Provençal farmhouse has a courtyard shaded by a lovely linden tree. The views across the surrounding country and unspoilt villages are wonderful. Madame grows organic vegetables and fruit and considers dinners with her guests, in dining room or courtyard, as the most interesting part of doing B&B. Meals are also showcases for local specialities. The interior decoration is a bright version of traditional French country style with old family furniture.

Rooms: 1 suite for 4, 1 double, 3 twins, each with shower & wc.

Price: 250 Frs for two.

Meals: 80 Frs, including wine (not Thurdays & Sundays).

Closed: End October-March.

The big old house, surrounded by its vineyards, and within harmless earshot o a road, is very handsome and Madame brings it to life with her special sparkle and enthusiasm for what she has created here. The decoration is all hers – more 'evolved French farmhouse'-comfortable than 'designer'-luxurious. She loves cooking, herbs and flowers; you may be offered her elderflower aperitif and have home-made cakes at breakfast. Nothing is too much trouble – walkers' luggage can be transferred, picnics can be laid or so can wine or honey tastings. A great spot for exploring Provence.

Rooms: 2 doubles, 1 triple, 1 suite (4), 1 suite (6), all with bath or shower & w

Price: 450 Frs for two.

Meals: 120 Frs, including aperitif, wine & coffee.

Closed: Never.

From Carpentras D7 N through Aubignan & Vacqueyras, fork right, still on D7, towards Sablet. 500m after 'Cave des Vignerons de Gigondas' turn right; signposted.
Michelin Map No: 245-17

Entry no: 665   Map No: 14

Sylvette GRAS
La Ravigote
84190 Gigondas
Vaucluse
Tel: (0)4 90 65 87 55
Fax: (0)4 90 65 87 55

A9 exit at Bollène, dir. Carpentras. On road out of Cairanne take turning for Carpentras. House is 1.5km on corner of right-hand turn.
Michelin Map No: 245-16

Entry no: 666   Map No: 14

Elizabeth & Jerry PARA
Domaine du Bois de la Cour
Route de Carpentras
84290 Cairanne, Vaucluse
Tel: (0)4 90 30 84 68
Fax: (0)4 90 30 84 68
e-mail: infos@boisdelacour.com
Web: www.boisdelacour.com

Narrow, cobbled streets lead to this fascinating, impeccably-furnished house that was once part of the 17th-century Bishop's Palace. The Verdiers are charming, cultivated people – he an architect/builder, she a teacher – with a keen interest in antiques and in protecting medieval Vaison from the predations of 'progress'. The guest rooms and cosy *salon* have a warm, Provençal feel. Well-presented breakfasts on the terrace come complete with French and English newspapers and, best of all, the magnificent view over to the Roman bridge.

Rooms: 2 doubles, 2 twins, all with bath or shower & wc.

Price: 420-470 Frs for two.

Meals: Choice in Vaison.

Closed: 2 weeks in November.

From Orange, D975 to Vaison. In town, follow 'Ville Médiévale' signs.
Michelin Map No: 245-17

Entry no: 667   **Map No: 14**

Aude & Jean-Loup VERDIER
L'Évêché
Rue de l'Évêché
84110 Vaison la Romaine, Vaucluse
Tel: (0)4 90 36 13 46
Fax: (0)4 90 36 32 43
e-mail: eveche@aol.com
Web: www.avignon-et-provence.com/eveche

There is great character here and the chapel includes part of the Roman town wall. Monsieur has done much of the restoration himself, reproducing some of the 18th-century grandness. The wonderful entrance hall has its own grand piano and the family coat of arms – this is Madame's family home but she is not in the least daunting. The very large guest rooms feature antiques, old tiles and fireplaces and two of the bathrooms, with their old-fashioned claw-footed baths, are built into the restored tower. The swimming pool is discreetly tucked away. *It's a Big house so let the telephone ring at length.*

Rooms: 4 triples, each with bath & wc; 1 apartment/suite: 2 bedrooms, bath & wc, shower & wc, *salon*, kitchen.

Price: 550 Frs for two.

Meals: Available locally. Self-catering apartment available.

Closed: Never.

From Roman theatre in Vaison follow signs for Malaucène/Mt Ventoux. Left onto 'Chemin de Planchettes'. Signposted.
Michelin Map No: 245-17

Entry no: 668   **Map No: 14**

Rémy & Cécile DAILLET
Château de Taulignan
St Marcellin lès Vaison
84110 Vaison la Romaine, Vaucluse
Tel: (0)4 90 28 71 16
Fax: (0)4 90 28 75 04
e-mail: chateau@pacwan.fr
Web: www.sawdays.co.uk

There is a fine acacia over the terrace, the garden rambles in and out of shade; inside, there are fireplaces and decorative platters of fruit. One bedroom has lavender colour-washed walls, stripped wooden floors and good country furniture, with a rolled-edge cast-iron bath and period basin. Now to breakfast: served under mature trees with vineyards and distant mountains... local bread, of course, and home-made jam. Dinner is delicious too; Michael is English and an imaginative chef.

Rooms: 1 suite for 4, 3 doubles, all with bath or shower & wc.

Price: 420 Frs for two.

Meals: 175 Frs, including aperitif, wine & coffee.

Closed: November-March.

Gîte space for 2 people.

The solid old aristocratic *bastide* (manor farmhouse) was built on the foundations of a 12th-century watermill and the thick stone walls keep rooms cool in the fiercest heat. There is also a big pool, with fountains, in the landscaped, tree-filled garden surrounding it. The house is full of interesting mementoes of the owners' time in various North African countries; bedrooms are traditionally furnished with good mattresses and bathrooms. Breakfast includes home-made jam out on the terrace or in the dining room and dinners feature Madame's Provençal specialities. She and her family create a very relaxed, easy atmosphere here.

Rooms: 2 doubles, 2 family suites, all with bath or shower & wc.

Price: 370 Frs for two.

Meals: 130 Frs, including wine.

Closed: Never.

From Vaison la Romaine D938 N towards Nyons for 5km then right on D46 towards Buis les Baronnies for 4km. On entering Faucon, house on right at crossroads with D205 (blue gate & shutters).
Michelin Map No: 245-17

Entry no: 669   Map No: 14

From Carpentras, D974 direction Bédoin/Mont Ventoux; stay on this road, do NOT enter Crillon village. The mill is on the left below signpost.
Michelin Map No: 245-17

Entry no: 670   Map No: 14

Michael BERRY
Les Airs du Temps
84110 Faucon
Vaucluse
Tel: (0)4 90 46 44 57
Fax: (0)4 90 46 44 57

Bernard & Marie-Luce RICQUART
Moulin d'Antelon
Route de Bedoin
84410 Crillon le Brave, Vaucluse
Tel: (0)4 90 62 44 89
Fax: (0)4 90 62 44 90
e-mail: moulin-dantelon@wanadoo.fr
Web: www.art-vin-table.com

A genuine, long-established Provençal family: seven generations of wine-growers have breathed their first in this 17th-century farmhouse. Silkworms were bred on the estate that looks across vineyards to Mont Ventoux and Madame organises tastings of her own *Coteaux du Ventoux* wine. She also produces olive oil, tomatoes, beans and melons. The link between where you sleep and where you eat and swim is her very tempting kitchen. Rooms are cosy, clean and functional with tiled floors and a proper patina on walls and friezes. The old family recipes are made with wine – naturally.

Rooms: 4 doubles, 1 twin, each with shower & wc.

Price: 320 Frs for two.

Meals: 145 Frs, including aperitif, wine & liqueur.

Closed: Never.

Gîte space for 4 people.

From Carpentras D974 NE dir. Bedoin. 175m after sign to St Pierre de Vassols, right on D224 dir. Mormoiron; signposted on left.
Michelin Map No: 245-17

Entry no: 671   Map No: 14

Mme Marie-José EYDOUX
Domaine la Condamine
84410 Crillon le Brave, Vaucluse
Tel: (0)4 90 62 47 28/
        (0)6 08 45 26 70
Fax: (0)4 90 62 47 28
e-mail: christellemasclaux@yahoo.com
Web: domainelacondamine.here.de

Set in great walking country among spectacular fields of lavender with vast views, this fine 19th-century farmhouse is built around a courtyard shaded by a spreading linden tree. The family living/dining room is homely and warm with a large table and a fireplace for cooler weather. The comfortable, light-filled rooms are carefully decorated in an unpretentious mix of new and old. Monsieur is a keen cook and prepares Provençal dishes using local produce and herbs while charming, enthusiastic Madame makes the desserts and also gives Feldenkrais (conscious movement) sessions. Stay long enough to taste ALL these pleasures.

Rooms: 1 suite for 4, 1 suite for 3, 3 triples, each with bath or shower & wc.

Price: 390-500 Frs for two; minimum 3 nights.

Meals: 135 Frs, including coffee.

Closed: January & February.

From Carpentras, D941/D1 to Sault (41km) then D942 direction Aurel. Just before Aurel, left at signpost.
Michelin Map No: 245-18

Entry no: 672   Map No: 14

Christian & Visnja MICHELLE
Richarnau
84390 Aurel
Vaucluse
Tel: (0)4 90 64 03 62
Fax: (0)4 90 64 03 62
e-mail: c.richarnau@accesinter.com
Web: richardnau.free.fr

An open-hearted welcome and a real guest room in a real home where the friendly Lawrences thoroughly enjoy their role as hosts. The room has its own dressing room and a newly-tiled shower. The new house is built of old stone in traditional local style and surrounded by hills, woods, fields and vineyards with lovely views across the valley towards Bonnieux and the Lubéron. The Lawrences worked overseas for 40 years, he in public works, she in the diplomatic, and the house is full of attractive *objets* from their travels.

Rooms: 1 triple with shower & wc.

Price: 280 Frs for two.

Meals: Good choice 5km.

Closed: Never.

Gîte space for 16 people.

We need pages to do justice to this gem. The Gouins, a real Provençal family, grow grapes and cherries and Madame is a renowned cook. For breakfast she may serve her special *galette de pomme* and her evening meals are outstanding. The beauty of the interior – sunshine yellows, fresh flowers, natural stone, charming furniture – is partnered by the stunning exterior, a well-planted garden offering shade, a field of sunflowers (in July) and views of the Lubéron. The new apartment is ideal for families, with three rooms and a Jacuzzi! (It also brings numbers up quite a lot.) Simply arrive, absorb and wonder what on earth you did to deserve it.

Rooms: 1 suite, 2 quadruples, 2 doubles, 1 apartment for 6, all with shower & wc.

Price: 500-800 Frs for two.

Meals: 160 Frs, including wine, coffee, and more...

Closed: November & February.

From Avignon N100 for Apt. At Coustellet, D2 for Gordes. After Les Imberts right on D207 & D148 to St Pantaléon. Pass church, stay on D104 for 50m, left onto small uphill road; THIRD drive on the right. Michelin Map No: 245-80

Entry no: 673   Map No: 14

From Avignon, N7 then D22 direction Apt (approx. 29km total). After 'Le Petit Palais', signposted on right. Michelin Map No: 245-30

Entry no: 674   Map No: 14

Pierrette & Charles LAWRENCE
Villa La Lèbre
St Pantaléon
84220 Gordes
Vaucluse
Tel: (0)4 90 72 20 74
Fax: (0)4 90 72 20 74
Web: www.sawdays.co.uk

Isabelle & Rolland GOUIN
La Ferme des 3 Figuiers
Le Petit Jonquier
84800 Lagnes
Vaucluse
Tel: (0)4 90 20 23 54
Fax: (0)4 90 20 25 47
Web: www.sawdays.co.uk

The dining room, with its tile floors and old beams, used to be the carthorse stable and country simplicity is the theme throughout this recently-restored farmhouse. Its clean and basic rooms include good beds with Provençal covers and views over the fields. According to one of our readers, "Madame is a star with a lovely sense of humour"; fortunately she is up and shining during the daytime as well. She and her family – a gently shy husband and two teenage children – create a genuine Provençal atmosphere round the table. The fare is traditional, with home-grown vegetables.

Rooms: 5 doubles, all with bath or shower & wc.

Price: 290 Frs for two.

Meals: 80 Frs, including wine & coffee.

Closed: 1 January-9 February.

From Apt, N100 towards Avignon. At Lumières, D106 towards Lacoste, then D218 to Ménerbes; second farm on the left.
Michelin Map No: 245-31

Entry no: 675   Map No: 14

Maryline & Claude CHABAUD
Mas Marican
84220 Goult
Vaucluse
Tel: (0)4 90 72 28 09

Genuine country class is here. Michel, who lives in another house 500m away, is part of a true Provençal country community: his family has lived here for generations, his father runs the farm (vineyards and cherry trees march past, honey is combed for breakfast), a friend deals with the wine, Sophie looks after guests. The irrigation pond at the front has rippled with southern light for 250 years, the old house has been lovingly restored with properly colour-washed walls, old doors and floor tiles and is refreshingly uncluttered. But modernity takes a bow with superb bathrooms and a streamlined pool.

Rooms: 2 doubles, 2 twins, 1 triple, each with bath & wc.

Price: 420-520 Frs for two.

Meals: Choice 2-5km.

Closed: December-February.

From Cavaillon D973 E for 30km. Left then right, through Lauris on D27 and on towards Puyvert/Lourmarin; signposted after 1km.
Michelin Map No: 245-31

Entry no: 676   Map No: 14

Michel CUXAC
La Carraire
84360 Lauris
Vaucluse
Tel: (0)4 90 08 36 89
Fax: (0)4 90 08 40 83
e-mail: infos@lacarraire.com
Web: www.lacarraire.com

Everyone's dream of what a house in Provence should be: wonderful furniture, fabrics, tiles and beams, it is all exquisite refinement. It is a former 17th-century staging post, yet its garden is an oasis of coolness, right in the centre of pretty Lourmarin. Madame, a cultivated and interesting person and a keen cyclist, is ready to advise on routes and leads such an active life that she may just not be there to greet you or dust your room! She is now running the Villa with her daughter – and granddaughter, who speaks perfect five-year-old English. There are bikes for guests' use and for the less athletic or the saddle-sore there's that shady garden.

Rooms: 2 doubles, 3 twins, all with bath or shower & wc.

Price: 350-450 Frs for two.

Meals: Choice locally.

Closed: Never.

From Aix en Provence, N96 and D556 to Pertuis. There, D973 to Cadenet and then D943 towards Bonnieux until you reach Lourmarin.
Michelin Map No: 245-31

Entry no: 677　　　　　Map No: 14

M & Mme LASSALLETTE
Villa Saint Louis
35 rue Henri de Savornin
84160 Lourmarin
Vaucluse
Tel: (0)4 90 68 39 18
Fax: (0)4 90 68 10 07

The gentle sound of the millstream pervades the whole house, which is decorated in Provençal style and filled with the aroma of incense and flowers. The big rooms are simply, and appropriately decorated with fresh white linen, pastel shades and fine old furniture. An ample breakfast is served at the long oak table beside the large open fire. There are two lovely dogs, one a big soft St. Bernard, and two horses. Outside, the terrace stretches the length of the house overlooking the pretty garden filled with flowers and home-grown vegetables; a lovely place to sit and sense the space around you.

Rooms: 4 doubles, each with bath, shower & wc.

Price: 680-850 Frs for two.

Meals: Ask for hosts' recommendations.

Closed: 1 November-1 March.

From the Tourist Office in Apt, take the D943 towards Lourmarin. At roundabout take road to Lourmarin. After 800m turn left at the electric transformer. Then follow lane for 600m.
Michelin Map No: 245-31

Entry no: 678　　　　　Map No: 14

Manuèle & Frédéric MIOT
Le Moulin de Mauragne
Route de Marseille
84400 Apt, Vaucluse
Tel: (0)4 90 74 31 37
Fax: (0)4 90 74 30 14
e-mail: info@moulin-de-mauragne.com
Web: www.moulin-de-mauragne.com

Don't pick up that broken saucer – it's part of an artist's installation. A fascinating contemporary arts centre run by a Franco-Polish couple who offer artists a spell of creative peace and sympathetic B&B guests a chance to share the privilege of an art-centred atmosphere. Pierre will even take you sketching. The old Provençal house has an authentic patina and lovely worn tiles, the sparse furniture is designer-perfect, the new apartment (bookable daily or weekly) a sheer delight, the artwork everywhere, the garden reached by a bridge across the street, the hospitality exceptionally generous and the whole feel incomparably special.

Rooms: 2 doubles, 1 twin, 1 apartment (with kitchen) for 2, each with bath or shower & wc.

Price: 380-530 Frs for two.

Meals: 140 Frs, including wine.

Closed: January.

Gîte space for 2 people.

Saignon is 3km SE of Apt. In Saignon, park near PTT Post Office. On main street, house is on right, 30m after PTT. Michelin Map No: 245-31

Entry no: 679　　　　Map No: 14

Kamila REGENT & Pierre JACCAUD
Chambre de Séjour avec Vue
Rue de la Bourgage
84400 Saignon en Luberon, Vaucluse
Tel: (0)4 90 04 85 01
Fax: (0)4 90 04 85 01
e-mail: chambreavecvue@vox-pop.net

On an old cobbled street right in the heart of old Tarascon, this *maison de maître* has really ancient origins. It has been beautifully, artistically renovated without losing any of the lovely patina of stone walls and old tiles. Built round a typical ochre-hued courtyard where breakfast is served, it exudes Mediterranean age and history. The rooms have fine old furniture, beams, stone flags. Your charming hosts, new to B&B, have slipped with perfect ease into a relaxed, friendly way of receiving guests and are enjoying it immensely. Madame plans to open a little *brocante* in her generous porch entrance.

Rooms: 4 doubles, 1 twin, each with bath or shower & wc.

Price: 450 Frs for two; 420 Frs for 3 nights or more.

Meals: Choice in town.

Closed: November-February, except by arrangement.

In Tarascon centre take Rue du Château opposite the château (well signposted); No 24 is along on right. Michelin Map No: 245-28

Entry no: 680　　　　Map No: 14

Yann & Martine LARAISON
24 rue du Château
13150 Tarascon
Bouches-du-Rhône
Tel: (0)4 90 91 09 99
Fax: (0)4 90 91 10 33
e-mail: ylaraison@wanadoo.fr
Web: www.sawdays.co.uk

Marie-Pierre is passionate about art and books while Christian loves music and making furniture. They organise concerts in the barn, and painting classes. Both were journalists travelling the world before settling here. This elegant manor house has a calmness enhanced by the refined pastel, almost Baroque décor reflecting Marie-Pierre's personal taste. The simply-furnished, comfortable bedrooms in the tower wing have exposed stone walls and beams, polished wooden floors and wonderful views of the countryside and hills beyond. *Gîte space for 6.*

Madame, who owns an antique shop, has used her knowledge and imagination to furnish this townhouse in one of Fontvieille's busy main streets with great taste. Everything here is refined and in impeccable order. Both bedrooms have beautiful antiques as well as thick woollen carpets, fine linens and large bathrooms; both overlook the small garden. There is a large, very handsome guest *salon*. Breakfast is served on old silver, a typically elegant touch. Your enthusiastic hosts enjoy sharing their love of music and Provence. *On-street parking.*

Rooms: 2 doubles, 1 triple, 1 suite, each with shower or bath & wc.

Rooms: 1 double, 1 triple, each with bath, shower & wc.

Price: 550-600 Frs for two.

Price: 500 Frs for two.

Meals: 150 Frs, incl. aperitif & wine.

Meals: Choice within walking distance.

Closed: Never.

Closed: Never, (book ahead).

Take D970 Avignon to Tarascon, after junction with road to Arles on left, carry on under bridge. After 1.6km white fence on left. On bridge, turn left & through white gate.
Michelin Map No: 245-28

From Arles, D17 to Fontvieille; follow signs to 'Regalido' Hotel. House is 50m beyond on right.
Michelin Map No: 245-29

Entry no: 681   Map No: 14

Entry no: 682   Map No: 14

Marie-Pierre CARRETIER &
Christian BILLMANN
Le Mas D'Arvieux, Route d'Avignon
13150 Tarascon, Bouches-du-Rhône
Tel: (0)4 90 90 78 77
Fax: (0)4 90 90 78 68
e-mail: mcarretier@aol.com
Web: www.sawdays.co.uk

Jean-Marie & Édith-Claire RICARD
DAMIDOT
Le Mas Ricard
107 avenue Frédéric Mistral
13990 Fontvieille
Bouches-du-Rhône
Tel: (0)4 90 54 72 67
Fax: (0)4 90 54 64 43

The interior of this manicured farmhouse is as cool as the welcome is warm from its French/Irish owners – John is big and relaxed, Christiane is trim and efficient. Natural stone, oak beams, terracotta floors and cool colours give a wonderfully light and airy feel to the house while bedrooms are carefully elegant with small, functional shower rooms. Outside, centuries-old plane trees, a vine tunnel, three hectares of cypresses and horses (why not head for the *Alpilles* mountains?) add to the magic. An oft-tinkled piano is there for you to play.

Rooms: 4 doubles, 2 twins, all with shower & wc.

Price: 500-550 Frs for two.

Meals: Choice in St Rémy.

Closed: November-Easter.

From St Rémy D571 direction Avignon. After 2 r'bouts, left just before 2nd bus stop (Lagoy), opp. 2nd yellow Portes Anciennes sign, onto Chemin de Velleron & Prud'homme. House is 6th on right.
Michelin Map No: 245-29

Entry no: 683   Map No: 14

Christiane & John WALSH
Mas Shamrock
Chemin de Velleron & du
Prud'homme
13210 St Rémy de Provence
Bouches-du-Rhône
Tel: (0)4 90 92 55 79
Fax: (0)4 90 92 55 80

Photographs do little justice to the sheer beauty of the garden, nurtured by Astrid. The homely little cottage is packed with furniture, oriental carpets and ornaments. Most rooms open directly onto the terrace, the self-contained, 'romantic' chalet in the garden, with its soft yellow patina on the walls and interesting fireplace is very popular too. The suite is ideal for six with four children sleeping in a dormitory (with piano), and a separate room for the parents. Breakfast in the bright and cheery salon. Very cosy.

Rooms: 1 family suite, 1 double, each with shower & wc; 1 twin, 1 double sharing shower & wc; 1 twin with bath.

Price: 400-500 Frs for two.

Meals: By arrangement 150-200 Frs, including wine & coffee.

Closed: Christmas & New Year.

From D99 to St Rémy right after Place de la Republique into Chemin de la Combette. After 960m left onto Chemin de Servières & Cadernières, on for 600m. House signed on right.
Michelin Map No: 245-29

Entry no: 684   Map No: 14

Mme Astrid REBOUL
L'Harmas
Chemin de Servières et Cadenières
13210 St Rémy de Provence
Bouches-du-Rhône
Tel: (0)4 90 92 11 35
Fax: (0)4 90 92 47 61

Cats sit like kings on cushions in corners of this restored *mas*, but only downstairs. In an area of seething tourism and synthetic welcomes, this is proper B&B of genuine warmth and character. The owners are easy, natural, chatty and patient. The house has lots of bits and pieces – an old water pump, a royalist carving on the façade where the 1788 coin was found, an oil painting of the house by Monsieur's father, lots of local info. Simple pink or mauve rooms; copious breakfasts under plane trees or in the stupendously high old horse barn, its stone trough worn to a sculpture. Unpretentious Provence at its best.

Rooms: 1 twin with shower & wc; 1 double, 1 double/twin, each with shower & washbasin & wc.

Price: 280 Frs for two.

Meals: Restaurant in village.

Closed: 21 September-March.

Float in the pool and watch the sun set over the Alpilles before strolling to the large, picture-hung kitchen where Madame's mother may be imparting her knowledge of Provençal food and gardening – home-made cakes are always available. Built by great grandfather in 1897, up a quiet lane and surrounded by fields and fruit trees, this *mas* blends modern with rustic Provence. Quarry-tiled rooms with colourful local fabrics open onto the terrace and garden. Madame, a former teacher, will help you choose the ideal walk or the restaurant to suit your appetite.

Rooms: 1 double, 1 suite for 4, each with shower & bath.

Price: 380-400 Frs for two.

Meals: Good restaurants nearby.

Closed: Never.

From St Remy, D571 to Avignon. In Eyragues take small road behind pharmacie signposted about 1.5km on left.
Michelin Map No: 245-29

Entry no: 685   Map No: 14

Christiane & Robert POLI
Le Mas des Chats qui Dorment
1671 chemin des Prés
13630 Eyragues
Bouches-du-Rhône
Tel: (0)4 90 94 19 71
Fax: (0)4 90 94 19 71

From Avignon, take RN7 for Aix-Marseille, exit for Plan d'Orgon – Cavaillon. House is shortly before church on left (look out for arrow signposts).
Michelin Map No: 245-30

Entry no: 686   Map No: 14

Magali RODET
Mas de la Miougrano
447 route des Ecoles
13750 Plan D'Orgon
Bouches-du-Rhône
Tel: (0)4 90 73 20 01
Fax: (0)4 90 73 20 01
e-mail: lamiougrano@net-up.com

The Latin above the door says it all: "What you seek is here". Receiving strangers comes naturally to Michael: he began with 15 Bosnian refugees and finds endless time for his guests, providing home-made croissants, cookery classes with olive oil straight from his trees, jogging companionship, airport pick-up. His fine pink villa is filled with Provençal antiques, Berber carpets, crocheted bedcovers, sculptures by local artists and piles of books – a discovery at every turn. Plus tennis and croquet on the spot, sailing, swimming, trekking, bicycling a step away. Superior prices for superior attention.

Rooms: 2 triples, each with bath & wc.

Price: 700 Frs for two.

Meals: 180 Frs, including aperitif & wine; lunch 130 Frs.

Closed: Never.

From A54 exit 13 towards Miramas on D19 to Grans 6km. Right on D16 to St Chamas 9km;. Just before railway bridge, sharp left towards Cornillon, up hill 2km; house on right before tennis court. Detailed map faxed on request.
Michelin Map No: 245-30

Entry no: 687   Map No: 14

Michael FROST
Mas de la Rabassière
Route de Cornillon
13250 St Chamas, Bouches-du-Rhône
Tel: (0)4 90 50 70 40
Fax: (0)4 90 50 70 40
e-mail: michaelfrost@rabassiere.com
Web: www.rabassiere.com

You may have thought this intelligent elderly couple would be slowing down – they are opening more rooms! Their 1960s house (designed by Monsieur) on the beautiful, residential side of Aix, just 10 minutes walk from the centre, is modern inside, with Mackintosh-style furniture and lots of cool tones of grey, blue and white in the smallish rooms. There's a pool and the big garden has tall pines and squat olive trees from which your helpful, cheerful hosts make their own oil (though the 1997 frost was painful). Children are welcome. Extra rooms may be available.

Rooms: 3 doubles, each with bath or shower & wc; 1 double and 1 twin, sharing shower & wc.

Price: 300-450 Frs for two; 2 nights or more preferred.

Meals: Wide choice in Aix.

Closed: Never.

In Aix, from Pl. de la Rotonde, pass Tourist Information, onto Bd. Victor Hugo. At top of road, left on Bd. du Roi René. At 9th traffic light after Pl. de la Rotonde, turn into Rte du Tholonet direction piscine/stade; house at 2nd r'bout, tall gateposts on right.
Michelin Map No: 245-31

Entry no: 688   Map No: 14

Mauricette & René IUNG
L'Enclos
2 avenue du Général Préaud
(rte du Tholonet)
13100 Aix en Provence
Bouches-du-Rhône
Tel: (0)4 42 96 40 52

This enormous farmhouse is decorated in the manner of the 19th-century Aixoise bourgeoisie, notably the authentic painted ceiling in the huge dining room attributed to Coulange. Monique is quite an expert in Provençal culture, custom and dress. Her special talent is making nativity cribs and there is a wonderful *santons crèche* in the living room which she redecorates every Christmas. Bedrooms are comfortable, very peaceful and simply furnished. Everywhere there are hints of the house's aristocratic past including a number of family portraits, furniture and vases of dried and silk flowers.

Rooms: 2 doubles, each with shower & wc; 1 suite for 4 with bath, shower & wc.

Price: 350 Frs for two; suite 600 Frs for four.

Meals: 100 Frs, including wine, by arrangement.

Closed: October-April.

From De Gaule square, Aix, R N8 towards Marseille. Through Luynes, at large roundabout turn tight towards Gardanne. After 600m turn right D59 towards Bouc Bel Air. House on left approx. 1200m after crossroads.
Michelin Map No: 245-44

Entry no: **689**   Map No: 14

Monique & Henri MORAND
La Lustière
442 Petit Chemin d'Aix
13320 Bouc Bel Air
Bouches-du-Rhône
Tel: (0)4 42 22 10 07
Fax: (0)4 42 94 13 42

This modern, Provençal-style house sits high above the surrounding vineyards and orchards as if in a Cézanne: the view of the Montagne Sainte Victoire is loaded with breathtaking references. It's also a good base for a family holiday: guests have a large room with mezzanine and kitchenette in a separate little house (illustrated); there is a fine pool, table tennis, boules for all, the sea 45 minutes away and lovely old Aix within easy reach. The Babeys, with four sons, are relaxed and easy. One reader wrote: "A favourite – such caring and phlegmatic hosts".

Rooms: Cottage for 4: 1 double/twin on ground floor, 1 double on mezzanine, bathroom and kitchenette.

Price: 360 Frs for two.

Meals: Self-catering; restaurants in village, 2km.

Closed: Never.

From Aix, N7 direction Nice for approx. 15km. Left just after Château de La Bégude direction Puyloubier; Chemin des Prés is 20m along on right. House at end.
Michelin Map No: 245-32

Entry no: **690**   Map No: 14

Jean-Pierre & Sophie BABEY
Les Bréguières
Chemin des Prés
13790 Rousset
Bouches-du-Rhône
Tel: (0)4 42 29 01 16
Fax: (0)4 42 29 01 16

The 18th-century manor farmhouse dominates its little hilltop on the edge of pretty Peynier. Pull the old cowbell, pass the big wooden doors and its solid red-shuttered mass surges up from its rose-filled garden. Beautifully restored *à la Provençale*, it once belonged to painter Vincent Roux and memories of Cézanne live on. 'Roux' room (the best) has a delicious garden view, beams, terracotta tiles, a fantastic ochre/green bathroom down the corridor. The others are good too, though more functional, but the *salon* is a lovely spot. The atmosphere created by your gracious hostess is much praised. Older children welcome.

Rooms: 2 doubles, 1 triple, each with bath or shower & wc.

Price: 360-400 Frs for two; minimum 2 nights May to September.

Meals: In village. Summer kitchen available for lunches.

Closed: First 3 weeks in August.

From Aix on D6, 4km before Trets, right on D57 to Peynier. There, up hill to Trets/Aubagne road; left on D908; right between Poste & Pharmacie. House 50m along.
Michelin Map No: 245-45

Entry no: 691   Map No: 14

Mme Jacqueline LAMBERT
Mas Sainte Anne
3 rue Auriol
13790 Peynier
Bouches-du-Rhône
Tel: (0)4 42 53 05 32
Fax: (0)4 42 53 04 28

A village or not a village? It feels like one and is a perfect place to stay when Avignon itself is heaving with people. A former stable block, the property is next door to *La Grande Chartreuse*, a beautiful 13th-century monastery, now a European Centre for Literature and Theatre. Pascale runs the Ecuries as a B&B but you really have a fully equipped studio, so can opt to be independent. But don't think Pascale doesn't want you! She is on hand with breakfast, information and magazines you can borrow, and an aperitif before you head out for the evening.

Rooms: 2 doubles, 1 suite, each with bath, shower & wc.

Price: 390-545 Frs for two.

Meals: Choice nearby.

Closed: Never.

Gîte space for 4 people.

From Avignon cross the Rhône towards Nîmes/Villeneuve lès Avignon. Just after the bridge right towards Villeneuve centre, you are then on Rue de la République. House is next to La Grande Chartreuse.
Michelin Map No: 240-16

Entry no: 692   Map No: 14

Pascale LETELLIER
Les Ecuries des Chartreux
66 rue de la République
30400 Villeneuve lès Avignon, Gard
Tel: (0)4 90 25 79 93
Fax: (0)4 90 25 79 93
e-mail: ecuries-chartreux@avignon-et-provence.com
Web: www.avignon-et-provence.com/ecuries-chartreux

These are happy, civilised people who enjoy having guests in their beautiful rambling stone property, leaving them in peace and cooking them delicious dinners. You sleep in rooms of timeless simplicity in the ancient tower (once a dovecote): exposed stones and old tiles breathe in the coolness, smart bedcovers glow, each room has its own entrance – it's almost monastic. Meals, with home-grown fruit and vegetables, are in the family dining room (separate tables) or on the terrace. There is a majestic peacock, a friendly dog, lots of pure-bred Arab ponies and... a child. Botanic walks, riding and visits to local wine cellars can be arranged.

Rooms: 3 suites for 3, 1 triple, 1 twin, all with bath or shower & wc.

Price: 330 Frs for two.

Meals: 120 Frs, including wine & coffee.

Closed: Never.

From Ginasservis D23 direction Rians for 1.5km then left on D22 direction Esparron for 1km. Signposted Aubanel on left.
Michelin Map No: 245-33

Entry no: 693   Map No: 14

Fatia & Michel LAZÈS
Aubanel
83560 Ginasservis
Var
Tel: (0)4 94 80 11 07
Fax: (0)4 94 80 11 04

Brand new owners and a brand new touch of style to a house already much enjoyed by our readers. Jean-Yves and Alain have tackled their new careers with panache, adding a noble black Labrador and some lovely new furniture and *objet* to an already fine house, a bust of Marie-Antoinette to the dining room and a touch of freshness to the uncluttered, stylish bedrooms. The gardener has stayed to care for the lavender, herbs and organic vegetables in front of the house. Breakfast can be brought to your room between 8am and midday; dinners are imaginative and delicious.

Rooms: 4 triples, 2 doubles, all with shower & wc.

Price: 400-450 Frs for two.

Meals: 150 Frs, including aperitif, wine & coffee.

Closed: November.

In St Maximin take D28 direction Bras for 3km to signpost on right. From here follow narrow road for further 3km.
Michelin Map No: 245-33

Entry no: 694   Map No: 14

Jean-Yves SAVINA &
Alain VAN'T HOFF
Domaine de Garrade, Route de Bras
83470 St Maximin la Ste Baume, Var
Tel: (0)4 94 59 84 32
Fax: (0)4 94 59 83 47
e-mail: garrade@aol.com
Web: www.provenceweb.fr/83/garrade

The Mediterranean garden is spectacularly beautiful with its tall trees, flowering shrubs and manicured lawn. Indeed, the whole place is thoroughly manicured. Monsieur, an architect, designed the large, luxurious family villa, thoughtfully integrated into its surroundings – the pool is well concealed. Rooms are decorated in Provençal style with lovely Salernes bathroom tiles and are extremely comfortable; one has its own garden with table and chairs. Monsieur is shyly welcoming, Madame smilingly efficient and the nearby medieval village of Castellet is definitely worth a visit.

Rooms: 2 doubles, 1 twin, 1 suite for 4, all with bath or shower & wc.

Price: 380 Frs for two; suite 500 Frs.

Meals: In village.

Closed: Never.

Gîte space for 4 people.

From Toulon N8 towards Aubagne. Enter Le Beausset, cross 2 r'bouts then right opp. Casino supermarket & immediately into Chemin de la Fontaine de 5 Sous; house signposted on left after 1.5km.
Michelin Map No: 245-46

Entry no: 695   Map No: 14

Charlotte & Marceau ZERBIB
Les Cancades
Chemin de la Fontaine
83330 Le Beausset, Var
Tel: (0)4 94 98 76 93
Fax: (0)4 94 90 24 63
e-mail: charlotte.zerbib@wanadoo.fr
Web: www.sawdays.co.uk

Your hosts were born in this unspoilt part of the Var where beautiful views of the Alps across vineyards and hills – and genuine human warmth – await you at their modernised farmhouse (19th-century foundations). The smallish bedrooms feature typical Provençal fabrics and antiques, the bathrooms are new and spotless. Breakfast is brought to you on the private terrace or in the dining room. Monsieur, a tenant farmer, loves to talk about his work and his village. Madame is a kindly hostess. Readers have amply confirmed this.

Rooms: 1 triple, 1 double, 1 twin, all with shower & wc.

Price: 295-320 Frs for two.

Meals: In village (1km) or 3km away. Barbecue available.

Closed: Never.

From Aups, D9 and D30 to Montmeyan. There, D13 direction Quinson. House is on left of road, 1km along; signposted.
Michelin Map No: 245-34

Entry no: 696   Map No: 15

Dany & Vincent GONFOND
Mas Saint Maurinet
Route de Quinson
83670 Montmeyan
Var
Tel: (0)4 94 80 78 03
Fax: (0)4 94 80 78 03

"SUCH delightful, cultivated people". Here is a chance to stay with a warm, lively family (four children) on a working farm/vineyard with a timeless feel to it. The first-class bedrooms, impeccably decorated in authentic Provençal style, and the guests' dayroom (with mini-kitchen) are in a separate wing; weather permitting, breakfast is on the terrace. Monsieur, an historian, is happy to share his encyclopaedic knowledge of the monuments and sights of the area and readers simply write: "Armelle is wonderful". And this is superbly varied walking country.

Rooms: 2 twin/doubles & 1 suite for 4, all with bath or shower & wc.

Price: 300-350 Frs for two.

Meals: Self-catering; restaurant nearby.

Closed: November-March.

Gîte space for 4 people.

From A8, Saint Maximin/La Sainte Baume exit onto D560 through Barjols. There, continue on D560 for 2km towards Draguignan; entrance opposite D60 turning for Pontevès. Michelin Map No: 245-33

Entry no: 697   Map No: 15

Guillaume & Armelle de JERPHANION
Domaine de Saint Ferréol
83670 Pontevès
Var
Tel: (0)4 94 77 10 42
Fax: (0)4 94 77 19 04
Web: www.sawdays.co.uk

"What a lovely lady!" wrote our visitor; "sweet-natured and generous". The old farmhouse, with outbuildings grouped around an olive grove (the Gros make their own oil) has bright colours and painted walls, artistic quirks which 'work': bulrushes in a vase, wrought-iro wall-brackets for candles. Bedrooms are very attractive and immaculate, bathrooms too. The garden is rather busy, with individual tables and there is bit of noise from the road, but the overall impact is delightful. There is an enormous artist's workshop for Didier's painting courses, a pool among the olives, and chat with your hosts – all ver informal.

Rooms: 1 triple & 3 doubles, each with shower & separate wc.

Price: 400-450 Frs for two.

Meals: Several restaurants in Cotignac (3km) and Carcès (4km).

Closed: Never.

Gîte space for 3 people.

From Cotignac D13 direction Carcès. Pass turning on right direction Brignoles, continue 300m after crossroads. Signposted. Michelin Map No: 245-34

Entry no: 698   Map No: 15

Didier & Chantal GROS
Mas de Canta-Die
Routes de Carcès
83570 Cotignac
Var
Tel: (0)4 94 77 72 46
Fax: (0)4 94 77 79 33
e-mail: mas-de-canta-die@wanadoo.fr

Half of this gorgeous, well-restored 18th-century *bastide* (manor farmhouse) is yours: yours the light, airy, vineyard-view bedrooms, simply Provençal-furnished with a happy mix of antique and modern, yours the big bourgeois sitting room (little used because it's too lovely outside), yours the kitchen for picnic-making and laundry, yours a share in the great spring-watered tank for delicious natural swims. Gently confident, Jean-François runs the vineyard and the tastings. Enthusiastic and efficient, Nathalie cares for three children – and you – with sweet-natured ease. Very close to perfection, we thought.

Rooms: 3 doubles and 1 twin, all with bath or shower & wc.

Price: 350 Frs for two; minimum 3 nights July & August.

Meals: 110 Frs, including wine (not Saturday or Sunday).

Closed: November-February.

From A8, Brignoles exit north onto D554 through Le Val; then D22 through Montfort sur Argens, direction Cotignac. 5km along, turn left; signposted.
Michelin Map No: 245-34

Entry no: 699   Map No: 15

Nathalie & Jean-François ROUBAUD
Domaine de Nestuby
83570 Cotignac
Var
Tel: (0)4 94 04 60 02
Fax: (0)4 94 04 79 22

Panache in heaps here – sitting at the terrace table, you would wish to be nowhere else. In a quiet narrow street in the heart of the old town, one side of the house is château-like; another overlooks the walled garden and its trees. Enter on original floor tiles and under a grand, arched, white, embossed ceiling. All the rooms are big, most with 17th-century features. In winter you can nestle by a log fire and read in peace. The Counts of Provence lived here in the 12th century – and had style, as does Michel Dyens.

Rooms: 1 twin/double, 2 doubles, 1 twin, each with bath/shower & sep. wc; 1 family suite with shower, bath & wc.

Price: 400-500 Frs for two.

Meals: 150 Frs, including wine.

Closed: November-February.

Gîte space for 12 people.

Leave A8 at exit 35 Brignoles. Cross river dir. town centre. Right at Hotel de Clavier. At Palais de Justice straight ahead 300m. Rue des Cordeliers on left.
Michelin Map No: 245-47

Entry no: 700   Map No: 15

Michel DYENS
La Cordeline
14 rue des Cordeliers
83170 Brignoles, Var
Tel: (0)4 94 59 18 66
Fax: (0)4 94 59 00 29
e-mail: lacordeline@ifrance.com
Web: lacordeline.ifrance.com

The sea you can see has a good beach only 400m from this quiet 1960s villa. The warm-hearted, enthusiastic and tireless Didiers seem to have been born to run a happy and hospitable B&B. Two spotlessly clean bedrooms with real attention to comfort – good cupboards and bedside lights, for example – share the modern shower room. The dining room leads to a private outside terrace and thence to the garden – and guests have a key and are welcome to sit and have breakfast or a drink with the family. The hut at the bottom of the large pretty garden is Amélie's painting studio.

Rooms: 1 suite (1 double, 1 twin), sharing bath, shower & wc.

Price: 400 Frs for two; 650 Frs for four.

Meals: Simple places nearby; choice in Le Lavandou.

Closed: Never.

In winter Madame has walking or golfing parties. At other times she gives you the chance to gasp at the beautiful views from the beautiful rooms of her beautiful house. Built with ancient stones 50 years ago, looking lots older, it stands in three hectares where she clearly enjoys both her solitude and your company. Bedrooms are Edwardian, with antique and retro furniture, or Provençal, or Modern with original paintings (some her own). Breakfast simply (home-made jam, toast and butter), alone or at a big communal table, in the delicious garden, or in the glorious 100m² *salon* if it's cold. *Children over five welcome.*

Rooms: 3 doubles, 1 triple, all with bath & wc.

Price: 380 Frs for two.

Meals: Good auberge 800m.

Closed: January.

Gîte space for 9 people.

From Le Lavandou D559 E to La Fossette. Arriving in village, left Ave Capitaine Thorel, left again into Chemin des Marguerites. If lost, telephone for help!
Michelin Map No: 245-48

Entry no: 701   Map No: 15

Robert & Amélie DIDIER
21 chemin des Marguerites
La Fossette
83980 Le Lavandou
Var
Tel: (0)4 94 71 07 82
Fax: (0)4 94 71 07 82

From A8 exit 'Le Luc' onto D558 direction La Garde Freinet & St Tropez; house signposted on right after 4km.
Michelin Map No: 245-48

Entry no: 702   Map No: 15

Mme Monique FAUVET
La Githomière
Route de St Tropez
83340 Le Cannet des Maures
Var
Tel: (0)4 94 60 81 50
Fax: (0)4 94 60 81 50

This delicious old manor house was built in 1760 as a silkworm farm – mulberry trees still shade the wonderful terrace that gives onto a mature walled garden, a meadow area with children's games, a summer pool and a stupendous view to the distant hills. Inside it is just as authentic: old tiles with good rugs, beams, white walls and simple, comfortable antique furniture. Unlike our other owners, organised, warm-hearted Nicola is here four months of the year only; her vivacious, multi-lingual Norwegian friend, Randi, receives you, in perfect English, at other times. *Min. 2 nights June-August.*

Rooms: 1 double, 1 twin, each with shower & wc; 1 double, 1 twin, sharing shower/bath & wc.

Price: 520-580 Frs for two.

Meals: Wide choice within walking distance.

Closed: Never.

From A8, exit 13, N7 E to Vidauban, left on D48 to Lorgues. In main street, post office on right: right and right again. At T-junction left into Place Arariso. Leave square on left into Rue de la Canal; house on left. Michelin Map No: 245-35

Entry no: 703   Map No: 15

Nicola D'ANNUNZIO
La Canal
477 rue de La Canal
Quartier le Grand Jardin
83510 Lorgues
Var
Tel: (0)4 94 67 68 32
Fax: (0)4 94 67 68 69

We wanted to stay for a week! Georges, retired, does most of the B&B work, with enthusiasm and warmth. He keeps the house, with its surprising touches of colour and imagination, immaculately. The bedrooms are indisputably pretty; one, the much larger of the two, has floral curtains on a brass rod, peach-coloured 'dragged' walls and painted bed. Hard to imagine anyone not liking it, especially the doors onto the private terrace. It is all immensely peaceful (half a mile up a rough stony track), there's a splendid pool, views across the tree-laden countryside and generous windows to let the Provençal light stream in.

Rooms: 2 doubles, each with shower or bath & wc.

Price: 300-400 Frs for two.

Meals: Good restaurants nearby.

Closed: Never.

Gîte space for 4 people.

Exit autoroute at Le Muy, follow direction Sainte Maxime & St Tropez. Approx 5km before Sainte Mazime right on D74 to Plan de la Tour. Entering village turn left onto D44 direction Grimaud. Michelin Map No: 245-48

Entry no: 704   Map No: 15

M & Mme Georges PONSELET
Le Petit Magnan
Quartier St Sébastien
83120 Plan de la Tour
Var
Tel: (0)4 94 43 72 00
Fax: (0)4 94 43 72 00
Web: www.sawdays.co.uk

A modern house looking out over ancient hillsides studded with gnarled olive trees, this is a place to rest between sophisticated Monte Carlo and the wild Verdon gorges. Your kindly, hospitable hosts are doing B&B for the sheer pleasure of it – feel the difference. Monsieur will tell you all about everything (in French), and will then take you walking in the 'red' hills of Esterel if you like. Madame is quieter with the sweetest smile. The double room is excellent, simply but thoughtfully furnished, has good storage space and lighting and shares the large shower room with the much smaller twin room. Very good value.

Rooms: 1 twin, 1 double, sharing bathroom & wc.

Price: 250-290 Frs for two.

Meals: Choice in Montauroux, 2.5km.

Closed: Never.

From A8 exit 39 onto D37 N for 8.5km; cross D562, continue for 200m then Chemin Fontaine d'Aragon on right; signposted.
Michelin Map No: 245-36

Entry no: 705   Map No: 15

Pierre & Monique ROBARDET
Fontaine d'Aragon
Quartier Narbonne
83440 Montauroux
Var
Tel: (0)4 94 47 71 39
Fax: (0)4 94 47 71 39
e-mail: p.robardet@wanadoo.fr

On sunny summer days, breakfast is eaten and life is lived on the peaceful terrace beside the pool of this modern villa. Monsieur, a very able watercolourist, personally designed the house in the Provençal style, adding extensions over the years. The spotlessly clean, if somewhat impersonal, guest rooms are named *Papillon* and *Provence* They are light and airy and have direct access to the flower-filled garden and the swimming pool. An excellent base and there are many good local beaches.

Rooms: 1 double, 1 twin, each with shower & wc.

Price: 400 Frs for two.

Meals: 120 Frs, including wine & coffee.

Closed: October-April.

In Fréjus N7 towards Cannes; pass memorial to 'Morts en Indochine' on right. After 1km enter Les Jardins de César development on left; 1st left is Pline l'Ancien; No 7 on left.
Michelin Map No: 245-36

Entry no: 706   Map No: 15

Yvette BERTIN
Les Jardins de César
7 allée Pline l'Ancien
83600 Fréjus
Var
Tel: (0)4 94 53 17 85
Fax: (0)4 94 53 17 85
Web: www.sawdays.co.uk

Near the top of one of those stunning hilltop villages, the house itself is nothing spectacular but it has a sheer rock face rising above it (where mountaineers practise) and incredible views down to the sea 10km below. The terraced garden is alive with subtropical vegetation, the old Provençal house has later additions and is decorated with old furniture and good taste. Your host is a retired colonel who enjoys having guests, Madame is a management consultant of charm and intelligence and they love children.

Rooms: 2 doubles, 1 twin, each with bath, shower & wc.

Price: 500 Frs for two; under 10s free.

Meals: In village.

Closed: Never.

Cascades of bougainvillea and blushes of pelargonium beloved by colour-loving Riviera gardeners tumble over this modern townhouse. Antibes' sea front is an easy 15-minute walk and vibrant, fashionable Juan les Pins just a few minutes more. Madame, who fills the rooms with fresh flowers, took a crash course in English before opening her rooms and takes great care of her guests: she took the trouble to walk to the Place de Gaulle to meet us to guard against any wayward wanderings. The house, garden and terrace are remarkably quiet for the area.

Rooms: 1 double with *salon*, shower & wc.

Price: 400 Frs for two.

Meals: Wide choice in Antibes.

Closed: Never.

From A8 St Laurent du Var exit on D118 then D18/D2210 to St Jeannet. Into village along narrow (2-way) street; fork right into Rue St Claude; No 136 is 300m along. Or park in car park at entrance and walk (10 mins). Michelin Map No: 245-37

Entry no: 707   Map No: 15

Guy & Michelle BENOIT SÈRE
L'Olivier Peintre
136 rue Saint-Claude
06640 St Jeannet
Alpes-Maritimes
Tel: (0)4 93 24 78 91
Fax: (0)4 93 24 78 77
Web: www.sawdays.co.uk

In Antibes centre, from Place de Gaulle take Rue Aristide Briand; left at roundabout and follow railway 600m; right into impasse with barrier, marked 'Privé'; house at end on right. Michelin Map No: 245-37

Entry no: 708   Map No: 15

Martine & Pierre MARTIN
Villa Maghoss
8 impasse Lorini
06600 Antibes
Alpes-Maritimes
Tel: (0)4 93 67 02 97
Fax: (0)4 93 67 02 97

Panko is a riot of colour: the sheltered (no-smoking) garden has clumps of orange, yellow, mauve and scarlet flowers; real and fake flowers invade every bit of the living room and fight with the cheerful pictures filling every inch of the variegated walls; upstairs are rainbow sheets, patchwork bedcovers, painted furniture and *objets* galore, fine big towels and myriad toiletries. Big outdoor breakfasts come on colourful china. Madame's energy drives it all – she will organise your stay to a tee. It is quiet, exclusive, six minutes from the beach – superb! *Children over five; pets by arrangement; book EARLY.*

Rooms: 1 double/twin, 1 double/twin & 1-2 children's beds, each with bath & wc.

Price: 500-730 Frs for two; minimum 3 nights; reservations only.

Meals: Good choice in town.

Closed: Christmas & New Year.

From Antibes centre towards Cap d'Antibes. At palm-tree r'bout, towards Cap d'Antibes 'Direct'. At next junction, towards Cap d'Antibes. 1st right into Chemin du Crouton; 1st left. At end of cul-de-sac left on drive. At No 17, Panko is 2nd house on right. Michelin Map No: 245-37

Entry no: 709   Map No: 15

Clarisse & Bernard BOURGADE
Villa 'Panko'
17 chemin du Parc Saramartel
06160 Cap d'Antibes
Alpes-Maritimes
Tel: (0)4 93 67 92 49
Fax: (0)4 93 61 29 32

Geographically, it's not far from the tourist shops, potteries and madding fleshpots of Vallauris but it's a world away in atmosphere. Your hosts restored this old building on a terraced vineyard when they retired from the hectic life of running a *brasserie* in Paris 15 years ago, so they understand the value of peace. The house is light, well furnished and eclectically decorated with collections of antique glass and mugs. The fabulous garden with its swimming pool is a place to pamper yourself and relax to the sound of chirruping cicadas.

Rooms: 1 double with shower & wc; 1 twin with bath & wc.

Price: 420-450 Frs for two.

Meals: Choice in town.

Closed: Never.

From A8 Antibes exit towards Vallauris. There follow signs Route de Grasse from centre; go through 2 roundabouts then hairpin bend; at next crossroads left into forest (signed Mas du Mûrier); 50m up track. Michelin Map No: 245-37

Entry no: 710   Map No: 15

M & Mme G. RONCÉ
Mas du Mûrier
1407 route de Grasse
06220 Vallauris
Alpes-Maritimes
Tel: (0)4 93 64 52 32
Fax: (0)4 93 64 23 77

These two are really worth getting to know. Eve, a fascinating Medieval History specialist, has decorated her large and spotlessly clean, cool villa in her own personal 'retro' style. She and her doctor husband, Henri, provide a generous breakfast that is usually served in the lovely garden under the spreading palm tree (self-service before 8am); one of the ground-floor rooms actually opens onto the garden and the top bedrooms have a big private balcony. The house is only 15 minutes walk from old Cannes and its famous star-crossed Croisette (they close during The Festival to avoid the curling faxes strewn on the floor at 4am).

Rooms: 1 double, 2 twins, 1 triple, all with bath & wc.

Price: 480-620 Frs for two.

Meals: 15 minutes walk to town centre.

Closed: During film festival.

From A8 exit 'Cannes Centre' onto Bd Carnot. At 69 Bd Carnot (Le Kid café) right into Rue René Vigieno; up hill for 150m; house on right on small roundabout.
Michelin Map No: 245-37

Entry no: 711   Map No: 15

Eve & Henri DARAN
L'Eglantier
14 rue Campestra
06400 Cannes
Alpes-Maritimes
Tel: (0)4 93 68 22 43
Fax: (0)4 93 38 28 53

The setting is entrancing, with umbrella pines, palms, the southern skies and Mediterranean heat – and this very appealing Provençal-type villa is a happy marriage of modern technique and traditional design. In the cool interior all is well-ordered, and smart. Your charming, efficient and enthusiastic hosts have created old out of new, paved their generous terrace with lovely old squares, and furnished the rooms with an appropriate mix of the antique and the contemporary. There is an excellent dayroom/kitchen for guests and a beautifully tended green garden (and 10 golf courses within a 5k radius!)

Rooms: 2 doubles/twins, 1 double, all with bath & wc.

Price: 350-430 Frs for two; under 2s free.

Meals: In village.

Closed: Never; please book ahead.

From A8 Antibes exit on D103 towards Antibes. Across Les Bouillides r'bout towards Valbonne village for 3km. 100m after Bois Doré restaurant before La Petite Ferme bus stop, right up private lane (begins at No 205). House on left at top.
Michelin Map No: 245-37

Entry no: 712   Map No: 15

Alain & Christine RINGENBACH
Le Cheneau
205 route d'Antibes
06560 Valbonne, Alpes-Maritimes
Tel: (0)4 93 12 13 94
Fax: (0)4 93 12 91 85
e-mail: ringbach@club-internet.fr
Web: www.sawdays.co.uk

Annick is a well-travelled former riding instructress, good with horses (though she rides less now) and good with people. The garden has awesomely ancient olive trees, like old men with a few wisps of hair, dotted about on the terraces. Over this looks the garden suite, a treat for those who want to self-cater: its most delightful kitchen is light-filled, quarry-tiled and attractive. The blue room is charming, smaller, with its own entrance, a vast antique wardrobe and an old wooden bed.

Rooms: 2 doubles, each with shower & wc.

Price: 300-400 Frs for two.

Meals: In village; self-catering in suite.

Closed: January & February.

Twenty years ago there was just a little stone sheepshed on 5,000m² of land. Then an open-plan villa took one wall of the shed as its attractive fireplace surround and the rest became a semi-independent 'cottage', now your beautifully-equipped quarters, in total contrast to the vast living and terrace areas of the villa itself. Marianne told her dogs and cat to "say *bonjour* to the lady" and all four smiled in greeting. Utterly welcoming, bubbling with joy and radiating serenity, Marianne's breakfasts are a feast. Éric will initiate longer stayers into scuba diving. Wonderful people; lovely house. Sensible dogs welcome.

Rooms: Duplex with sitting room, double bedroom, shower & wc.

Price: 400-450 Frs for two.

Meals: Choice within easy drive.

Closed: Never.

From A8 exit 47 on D2085 towards Grasse for 17km. About 1km after Le Rouret, turn hard back left before Mercedes garage, immediately right into Chemin Reinards for 800m, right into Chemin Clamarquier, right to No 34 in cul-de-sac.
Michelin Map No: 245-37

Le Rouret is on D2085 between Grasse & Cagnes. South of village, left on D7 La Colle sur Loup / Roquefort Notre Dame road. On leaving village, right down lane signed Chambres d'Hôtes.
Michelin Map No: 245-37

Entry no: 713   Map No: 15

Mme Annick LE GUAY
Les Coquelicots
30 route de Roquefort
06650 Le Rouret
Alpes-Maritimes
Tel: (0)4 93 77 40 04
Fax: (0)4 93 77 40 04
Web: www.sawdays.co.uk

Entry no: 714   Map No: 15

Marianne & Éric PRINCE
34 chemin de Clamarquier
06650 Le Rouret
Alpes-Maritimes
Tel: (0)4 93 77 42 97
Fax: (0)4 93 77 42 97

Dinners are amazing and Alain claims they charge "the lowest prices on the Côte d'Azur". Both Alain and Michelle, a delightfully happy and enthusiastic couple, are fiercely proud of this very pretty old house which they saved up for while working for *France Télécom*. In an ideal setting on the upper fringe of a very pretty village, the house and garden have been lovingly renovated to create a really super place to stay. A good feature is that the bedrooms, each with its own terrace onto the garden, are entirely separate from, yet cleverly integrated with the rest of the house. Ask Alain about his vintage wines.

Escape from the sometimes hectic Côte d'Azur to this big modern villa, in its olive grove. The large, simply but effectively decorated studio has its own entrance, French windows onto a private terrace with the pool beyond, a small corner kitchen and a good bathroom. Philippe, who works at *the* perfume house is Grasse, will eagerly provide armfuls of his organic vegetables for a barbecue and there's s a bowl of fresh fruit to welcome guests. His energy and charm are invigorating, but never overwhelming. A superb combination of self-catering privacy and gracious family welcome and a civilised place to stay.

Rooms: 1 double & 1 suite for 4, each with shower, bath & wc.

Price: 280-330 Frs for two.

Meals: 100 Frs, including aperitif, wine & coffee.

Closed: Mid-December-mid-January.

Rooms: 1 studio for up to 4 (double on mezzanine plus sofa bed).

Price: 500-600 Frs for two.

Meals: Restaurants in St Paul de Vence.

Closed: October-March and possibly August.

From centre of Cagnes sur Mer take direction La Gaude D18; left 600m after 'La Gaude' sign & the cupola. Park if possible in Place des Marroniers. Walk uphill behind grocers along Rue de Marroniers to house. (Alain will fetch your luggage).
Michelin Map No: 245-37

Leave autoroute exit 47 Cagnes sur Mer, follow signs towards Vence. On dual carriageway towards Vence at first roundabout, right at 2nd r'bout towards Vence. Continue 500m, take cul-de-sac Impasse des Figuiers uphill on right. House near the top on left.
Michelin Map No: 245-37

Entry no: 715   **Map No: 15**

Entry no: 716   **Map No: 15**

Alain & Michelle MARTIN
13 Montée de la Citadelle
06610 La Gaude
Alpes-Maritimes
Tel: (0)4 93 24 71 01
Fax: (0)4 93 24 71 01

Colette & Philippe RUIZ
Lieu-dit St Jean
254 chemin des Blaquières
06570 St Paul de Vence, Alpes-Maritimes
Tel: (0)4 92 13 23 05
Fax: (0)4 92 13 23 05
e-mail: phruiz@hotmail.com
Web: www.sawdays.co.uk

Madame radiates enthusiasm and generosity – her breakfast of cheese, cereals, stewed and fresh fruit, various breads and jams is not for picking at. You can see the sea from this huge, Italianate villa smothered in bougainvillea and set in a big, peaceful garden way up above Nice. The drive up is part of the adventure and your reward is a warm welcome; Monsieur will park your car for you in the tiny space. Rooms are big, each one individually decorated with comfort unmatched by any hotel I know. The sparkling bathrooms sport lots of toiletries and a chocolate appears on your pillow at night.

Madame, an elderly, lively and talented painter, inherited this house from an uncle, loves it to bits and wants to share it with others. It is like a dolls' house; indeed, the small single room is full of antique dolls. The main bedroom, also quite small, looks across the large, lushly Mediterranean, statue-decorated, terraced garden to the Alps and has delightful French antiques, a well-equipped kitchenette and a modern shower room. Amazing peace so near the centre of Nice, and there are good walking and biking paths nearby.

Rooms: 2 doubles, 1 suite for 4, each with bath, shower & wc.

Price: 600 Frs for two; suite 1000 Frs.

Meals: Vast choice in town, 2km (walk down, taxi back?).

Closed: Never.

Not far from Nice railway station. From Place St Philippe, under expressway & left into Ave Estienne d'Orves for 600m, over level crossing & after sharp right-hand bend, turn hard back left into private track climbing steeply to house. Telephone if lost. Michelin Map No: 245-38

Entry no: 717   Map No: 15

Mme Jacqueline OLIVIER
Le Castel Enchanté
61 route de St Pierre de Féric
06000 Nice
Alpes-Maritimes
Tel: (0)4 93 97 02 08
Fax: (0)4 93 97 13 70
e-mail: castel.enchante@wanadoo.fr

Rooms: 1 suite (double & single) with shower & wc.

Price: 390 Frs for two; single 190 Frs.

Meals: In village.

Closed: Never.

From A8 exit 54 Nice Nord on D14 to Gairaut. After village follow towards Aspremont. Pass Auberge du Mas Fleuri on left. Ave Panéra is 1km along on left; house a few metres down hill. Michelin Map No: 245-38

Entry no: 718   Map No: 15

Mme Pia MALET-KANITZ
Villa Pan 'É' Râ
8 avenue Panéra – Gairaut Supérieur
06100 Nice
Alpes-Maritimes
Tel: (0)4 92 09 93 20
Fax: (0)4 92 09 93 20
Web: www.sawdays.co.uk

This large and slightly faded Italianate villa (imagine 80 shutters to paint) set in splendid isolation among tall trees, is home to a trio of highly cultured, interesting, English-fluent people, just a dramatic drive up from the hot vulgarity of the coast. No clutter, either of mind or matter here. Breakfast is in the atmospheric old kitchen. White bedrooms have pretty fabrics, simple furniture, good bathrooms, lots of pine-slatted cupboards and views over the great park where Marcel Mayer's superb sculptures await your visit. Above his studio in the garden is the suite, perfect for a family of four. It's fine walking, riding, bird-watching country.

Rooms: 1 twin, 3 doubles, each with shower & wc; 1 suite (1 double, 1 twin), with shower, sharing wc.

Price: 280-400 Frs for two.

Meals: Sospel 3km.

Closed: Never.

From Menton, D2566 to Sospel; at Mairie, left towards Col de Turini for 1.9km then left towards 'La Vasta' & 'Campings'. Domaine is 1.3km along, hard back on right after ranch & sharp bend.
Michelin Map No: 245-26

Entry no: 719   Map No: 15

Marie MAYER & Marcel MAYER
Domaine du Paraïs
La Vasta
06380 Sospel
Alpes-Maritimes
Tel: (0)4 93 04 15 78

Paul is French and very proud of his building work; his latest creation is a Japanese-style bridge over the water garden. He and his English wife Dorothy have been here since the '60s and have made the most of every square inch of the steep site. The views – of wooded valley leading to the distant sea – are stupendous which makes it entirely worth braving the narrow approach roads through the outskirts of Old Menton. Bedrooms all open off a south-facing terrace, have satin bedspreads, simple furniture and functional bathrooms. Breakfast may be on the pretty shaded terrace and it's deliciously breezy by the pool in summer.

Rooms: 4 doubles, each with bath & wc.

Price: 320 Frs for two.

Meals: Wide choice in Menton.

Closed: December & January, except by arrangement.

Gîte space for 13 people.

From Menton D24 towards Castellar (NOT Ciappes de Castellar). Follow numbers (odds on left) and park above house.
Michelin Map No: 245-39

Entry no: 720   Map No: 15

M & Mme Paul GAZZANO
151 route de Castellar
06500 Menton
Alpes-Maritimes
Tel: (0)4 93 57 39 73
e-mail: natie06@yahoo.fr
Web: www.sawdays.co.uk

A warmly human refuge from the fascinating excesses that are Monaco: looking east over the yacht-studded bay and south over the onion domes of a *fin de siècle* Persian palace. Michelle's sober, white-painted flat is decorated with wood, marble and lots of contemporary art, her own and friends'. Living room: arched doors, little fireplace, little breakfast table, wide balcony; guest room: white candlewick bedcover, big gilt-framed mirror, sea view; bathroom: gloriously old-fashioned beige. Space everywhere, and Michelle's as good a hostess as she is an artist.

Rooms: 1 double/twin with bath & wc.

Price: 490 Frs for two. Children under 2 free.

Meals: Wide choice in Monaco.

Closed: August.

From A8 exit 56 Monaco, through tunnel towards centre. Past Jardin Exotique then on right-hand bend, pharmacie on corner, turn left. Left at end into Malbousquet; park opposite number 26 to unload.
Michelin Map No:

Entry no: 721   Map No: 15

Michelle ROUSSEAU
Villa Nyanga
26 rue Malbousquet
98000 Principauté de Monaco, Monaco
Tel: 03 77 93 50 32 81
Fax: 03 77 93 50 32 81
Please note this includes code for Monaco.
e-mail: michelle.rousseau@mageos.com

TABLE D'HÔTES - DINNER

Please remember that dinner is NEVER automatic at a Chambre d'Hôte. It must always be booked ahead and may not be available every day.

Quick reference indices

Quick reference indices

French words and expressions

French words and expressions used in this book

Types of property:

Chambre d'hôtes - B&B

(*Table d'hôtes* - Dinner with the owners of the house).

Gîte - May be *de Séjour* or *Rural* self-contained holiday houses or *d'Etape*: overnight stops for cyclists or walkers (usually catered for). A *Gîte Panda*: may be either a *Chambre d'Hôtes* or a self-catering house in a national or regional park; owners provide information about flora and fauna, walking itineraries, sometimes guided walks and will lend you binoculars, even rucksacks.

Château - a mansion or stately home built for aristocrats between the 16th and 19th centuries. A 'castle', with fortifications, is a *château fort*.

Bastide has several meanings : it can be a stronghold, a small fortified village or, in Provence, it can simply be another word for *mas*.

Longère - a long, low farmhouse made of Breton granite.

Maison bourgeoise and *maison de maître* are both big, comfortable houses standing in quite large grounds and built for well-to-do members of the liberal professions, captains of industry, trade, etc.

Maison paysanne - country cottage.

Mas - a Provençal country house, usually long and low and beautifully typical in its old stone walls, pan-tiled roof and painted shutters.

Maison vigneronne can be anything from a tiny vine-worker's cottage to a comfortable house owned by the estate manager or proprietor.

Dépendance - outbuilding of château, farm etc

Other words and expressions:

Brocante - secondhand (furniture)

Le confit/ magret /rillettes - parts of goose or duck, preserved in their own fat, then fried/duck cutlet/potted meat made from pork or goose

Châtelain/e - Lord/lady of the manor

Grand-père - Grandfather

Jouer aux boules, pétanque - bowling game played with metal balls on a dirt surface

Mairie and *Hôtel de Ville* mean town and city hall respectively.

Marais means marsh or marshland.

Objets/objets trouvés - objects/finds (lost property)

Potage/potager - vegetable soup/vegetable garden

Pommeau - alcoholic drink made from apples

Pressoir - Press for olives/grapes/apples

Déguster means to taste, sample or savour and *une dégustation* is a tasting - of wine, oysters, any speciality. Note that it is NOT necessarily free.

A volonté means 'as much as you want'.

La toile de Jouy - classic French fabrics and wallpapers depicting romantic scenes

Viennoiserie - literally 'things from Vienna' - covers all those relatively plain flaky-pastry concoctions served for breakfast or tea: *croissants, pains au chocolat*, etc.

Tips for travellers in France

- If you are not wedded to a mobile phone buy a phonecard (*télécarte*) on arrival; they are on sale at post offices and tobacconists' (*tabac*).

- Be aware of public holidays; many national museums and galleries close on Tuesdays, others close on Mondays (e.g. Monet's garden in Giverny) as do many country restaurants, and opening times may be different on the following days:

New Year's Day (1 January)   **May Day** (1 May)
Liberation 1945 (8 May)   **Bastille Day** (14 July)
Assumption (15 August)   **All Saints** (1 November)

2001 dates:

Easter Sunday	16 April
Ascension	24 May
Whit Sunday & Monday (Pentecost)	3 & 4 June

- Beware also of the mass exodus over public holiday weekends, both the first day - outward journey - and the last - return journey.

Medical and Emergency procedures

- If you are an EC citizen, have an E111 form with you for filling in after any medical treatment. You will subsequently receive a refund for only part of your payment, so it is advisable to take out private insurance.

- French emergency services are: - the public service called SAMU or the Casualty Department - Services des Urgences - of a hospital;- the private service is called SOS MÉDECINS.

Roads and driving

- Current speed limits are: Motorways 130 kph (80 mph), RN National trunk roads 110 kph (68 mph), other open roads 90 kph (56 mph), in towns 50 kph (30 mph). The road police are very active and can demand on-the-spot payment of fines.

- One soon gets used to driving on the right but complacency leads to trouble; take special care coming out of car parks, private drives, narrow one-lane roads and coming onto roundabouts.

Directions in towns

The French drive towards a destination and use road numbers far less than we do. Thus, to find your way *á la française*, know the general direction you want to go, i.e. the towns your route goes through, and when you see *Autres Directions* or *Toutes Directions* in a town, forget road numbers, just follow towards the place name you're heading for or through.

Avoiding cultural confusion

En suite

'En suite' is not used in France to describe bathrooms off the bedroom and to do so can lead to confusion. To be clear, simply ask for a room *'avec salle de bains et wc'*

Greetings and forms of address

We drop far more easily into first-name terms than the French. This reluctance on their part is not a sign of coldness, it's simply an Old National Habit, to be respected, we feel, like any other tribal ritual. So it's advisable to wait for the signal from them as to when you have achieved more intimate status.

The French do not say "*Bonjour Monsieur Dupont*" or "*Bonjour Madame Jones*" - this is considered rather familiar. They just say "*Bonjour Monsieur*" or "*Bonjour Madame*" - which makes it easy to be lazy about remembering people's names.

A table

Breakfast

There may be only a bowl/large cup and a teaspoon per person on the table. If so, you are expected to butter your bread on your hand or on the tablecloth (often the kitchen oilcloth) using the knife in the butter dish, then spread the jam with the jam spoon.

A well-bred English lady would never dream of 'dunking' her croissant, toast or teacake in her cup - it is perfectly acceptable behaviour in French society.

Lunch/Dinner

Cutlery is laid concave face upwards in 'Anglo-Saxon' countries; in France it is proper to lay forks and spoons convex face upwards (crests are engraved accordingly). Do try and hold back your instinctive need to turn them over!

To the right of your plate, at the tip of the knife, you may find a knife-rest. This serves two purposes : to lay your knife on when you are not using it, rather than leaving it in your plate; to lay your knife *and* fork on (points downwards) if you are asked to *'garder vos couverts'* (keep your knife and fork) while the plates are changed - e.g. between starter and main dish.

Cheese comes *before* pudding in France - that's the way they do it! Cut a round cheese as you would cut a round cake - in triangular segments. When a ready-cut segment such as a piece of Brie is presented, the rule is to 'preserve the point', i.e. do not cut it straight across but take an angle which removes the existing point but makes another one.

Alastair Sawday
Special Places to Stay series

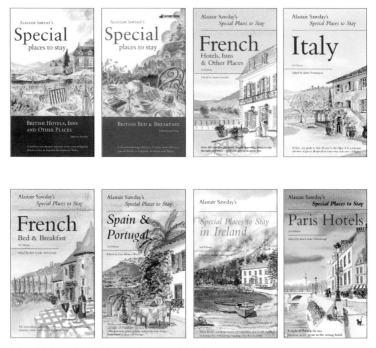

Tel: 01275 464891 Fax: 01275 464887
www.sawdays.co.uk

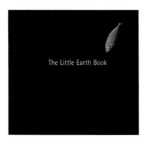

The Little Earth Book

Tough, stimulating, provocative and original - this collection of mini-essays will set you alight. The environment is THE issue of this century, and with *The Little Earth Book* you can now understand it - and do something about it.

"The Little Earth Book is different. And instructive. And fun!"

Jonathon Porritt

Order Form UK

All these books are available in major bookshops or you may order them direct. Post and packaging are FREE within the UK.

	price	qty
Special Places to Stay: **French Bed & Breakfast**		
Edition 6	£13.95	
Special Places to Stay: **British Hotels, Inns** and other places		
Edition 2	£10.95	
Special Places to Stay: **British Bed & Breakfast**		
Edition 5	£12.95	
Special Places to Stay: **French Hotels, Inns** and Other Places		
Edition 1	£11.95	
Special Places to Stay: **Italy** (from Rome to the Alps)		
Edition 1	£9.95	
Special Places to Stay in Spain & Portugal		
Edition 3	£11.95	
Special Places to Stay in Ireland		
Edition 2	£10.95	
Special Places to Stay: **Paris Hotels**		
Edition 2	£8.95	
The Little Earth Book	£4.99	

Please make cheques payable to: **Alastair Sawday Publishing**   **Total** [   ]

Please send cheques to: Alastair Sawday Publishing, The Home Farm, Barrow Gurney, Bristol BS48 3RW. **For credit card orders call 01275 464891 or order directly from our website www.sawdays.co.uk**

Name:

Address:

Postcode:

Tel: Fax:

If you do not wish to receive mail from other companies, please tick the box ❑

FBB6

Order Form USA

All these books are available at your local bookstore, or you may order direct. Allow two to three weeks for delivery.

	Price	No. copies
***Special Places to Stay:* British Hotels, Inns & other places**		
Edition 2	$17.95	
***Special Places to Stay:* British Bed & Breakfast**		
Edition 5	$19.95	
***Special Places to Stay:* French Hotels, Inns and Other Places**		
Edition 1	$19.95	
***Special Places to Stay:* Paris Hotels**		
Edition 2	$14.95	
Special Places to Stay in Ireland		
Edition 2	$19.95	
Special Places to Stay in Spain & Portugal		
Edition 3	$19.95	
***Special Places to Stay:* Italy** (from Rome to the Alps)		
Edition 1	$14.95	

Shipping in the continental USA: $3.95 for one book, $4.95 for two books, $5.95 for three or more books. Outside continental USA, call (800) 243-0495 for prices. For delivery to AK, CA, CO, CT, FL, GA, IL, IN, KS, MI, MN, MO, NE, NM, NC, OK, SC, TN, TX, VA, and WA, please add appropriate sales tax

Please make checks payable to: The Globe Pequot Press   **Total**

To order by phone with MasterCard or Visa: (800) 243-0495. 9 a.m. to 5 p.m. EST; by fax: (800) 820-2329, 24 hours; through our Website: www.globe-pequot.com; or by mail: The Globe Pequot Press, P.O. Box 480, Guilford, CT 06437.

Name: Date:

Address:

Town:

State: Zip code:

Tel: Fax:

Report Form

Comments on existing entries and new discoveries.

If you have any comments on entries in this guide, please let us have them. If you have a favourite house, hotel, inn or other new discovery, please let us know about it.

Report on:

Entry no: _____ Edition: _____

New Recommendation: _____

Name of property: _____

Address: _____

_____ Postcode: _____

Tel: _____

Comments: _____

_____

_____

_____

_____

_____

_____

_____

_____

From: _____

Address: _____

_____ Postcode: _____

Tel: _____

Please send the completed form to: **Alastair Sawday Publishing, The Home Farm, Barrow Gurney, Bristol BS48 3RW, UK Fax: 01275 464887**

Thank you.

Bilingual booking form

À l'attention de:
To: _____

Date: _____

Madame, Monsieur
Veuillez faire la réservation suivante au nome de:
Please make the following booking for (name): _____

Pour	*nuit(s)*	*Arrivant le jour:*	*mois*	*année*
For	night(s)	Arriving:day	month	year
		Départ le jour:	*mois*	*année*
		Leaving: day	month	year

Si possible, nous aimerions   *chambres, disposées comme suit:*
We would like   rooms, arranged as follows:

À grand lit	*À lits jumeaux*	
Double bed	Twin beds	
Pour trois	*À un lit simple*	
Triple	Single	
Suite	*Appartment*	*ou autre*
Suite	Apartment	or other

Nous sommes accompagnés de _____ *enfant(s) âgé(s) de* _____ *ans.*
Avez-vous un/des lit(s) supplémentaire(s), un lit bébé; si oui, á quel prix?
Our child is/children are _____ years old. Please let us know if you
have an extra bed/extra beds/a cot and if so, at what price.

Notre chien/chat sera-t-il le bienvenu dans votre maison? Si oui, y a-t-il un
supplément à payer?
We are travelling with our dog/cat. Will it be welcome in your house?
If so, is there a supplement to pay?

Nous aimerions également réserver le dîner pour _____ *personnes.*
We would also like to book dinner for _____ people

Veuillez nous envoyer la confirmation à l'adresse ci-dessous:
Please send confirmation to the following address:

Nom: Name: _____

Adress: Address: _____

_____

_____

Tel No: _____ E-mail: _____

Fax No: _____

Index of Names

Index of Names

Index of Names

Index of Names

Index of Names

Index of Names

Index of Places

Index of Places

Index of Places

Index of Places

Index of Places

Index of Places

Exchange Rate Table

French FF	Euro	US $	£ Sterling
10	1.50	1.40	0.90
50	7.50	7.00	4.50
100	15.00	14.00	9.00
150	22.50	21.00	13.50
175	26.25	24.50	5.75
200	30.00	28.00	18.00
225	33.75	35.00	20.25
240	36.00	33.60	21.60
260	39.00	36.40	23.40
280	42.00	39.20	25.20
300	45.00	42.00	27.00
350	52.50	49.00	31.50
400	60.00	56.00	36.00
450	67.50	63.00	44.55
500	75.00	70.00	45.00
750	112.50	105.00	67.50
1,000	150.00	140.00	90.00

Rates correct at time of going to press August 2000

Spoofs

All our books have the odd spoof hidden away within their pages.
Sunken boats, telephone boxes and ruined castles have all featured.
Some of you have written in with your own ideas. So, we have
decided to hold a competition for spoof writing every year.
The rules are simple: send us your own spoofs, include the photos,
and let us know which book it is intended for. We will publish the
winning entries in the following edition of each book. We will also
send a complete set of our guides to each winner.
Please send your entries to:

Alastair Sawday Publishing, Spoofs competition,
The Home Farm, Barrow Gurney, Bristol, BS48 3RW.
Winners will be notified by post.

Symbols

Symbols

Treat each one as a guide rather than a statement of fact and check important points when booking:

 Working farm.

 Children of all ages are positively welcomed, with no age restrictions but cots, highchairs, etc are not necessarily available.

 Pets are welcome. There may be a supplement to pay or size restrictions.

 Vegetarians catered for with advance warning.

 Owners use certified organic produce.

 Most, but not necessarily all, ingredients are organic, organically grown, home-grown or locally grown.

 Indicates full and approved wheelchair facilities for at least one bedroom and access to all ground-floor common areas.

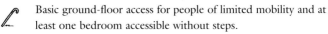 Basic ground-floor access for people of limited mobility and at least one bedroom accessible without steps.

 No-smoking anywhere in the house.

 Smoking restrictions exist, usually, but not always in the dining room and some bedrooms. For full restrictions, check when booking.

 This house has pets of its own in the house: dog, cat, parrot...

 Credit cards accepted; most commonly Visa and MasterCard.

 Your hosts speak English, whether perfect or not.

 You can either borrow or hire bikes here.

 Good hiking from house or village.

 Swimming pool on the premises.